EZRA POUND

The Solitary Volcano

EZRA POUND
The Solitary Volcano

JOHN TYTELL

Anchor Press
Doubleday
New York
1987

Grateful acknowledgment is made to New Directions Publishing Corporation for permission to quote from previously unpublished material, or to quote extensively from the following published sources:

WORKS OF EZRA POUND:

Personae. Copyright 1926 by Ezra Pound.

Collected Early Poems. Copyright © 1976 by the Trustees of the Ezra Pound Literary Property Trust.

The Cantos of Ezra Pound. Copyright © 1934, 1937, 1940, 1948, 1956, 1959, 1962, 1963, 1966, 1968 by Ezra Pound.

Selected Prose. Copyright © 1973 by the Estate of Ezra Pound.

The Literary Essays of Ezra Pound. Copyright 1935 by Ezra Pound.

Pavannes and Divigations. Copyright © 1958 by Ezra Pound.

Ezra Pound and Dorothy Shakespear: Letters 1909–1914. Copyright © 1976, 1984 by the Trustees of the Ezra Pound Literary Property Trust.

Selected Letters of Ezra Pound. Copyright 1950 by Ezra Pound.

Pound/James Joyce, *Letters and Essays.* Copyright © 1967 by Ezra Pound.

Gaudier-Brzeska. Copyright © 1970 by Ezra Pound. All Rights Reserved.

Jefferson and/or Mussolini. Copyright © 1963 by Ezra Pound. Used by permission of Liveright Publishing Corporation.

Guide to Kulchur. Copyright © 1970 by Ezra Pound. All Rights Reserved.

Excerpts from previously unpublished letters. Copyright © 1986 by the Trustees of the Ezra Pound Literary Property Trust.

H.D., *End to Torment.* Copyright © 1979 by New Directions Publishing Corporation.

Designed by Wilma Robin

Library of Congress Cataloging-in-Publication Data
Tytell, John.
Ezra Pound: the solitary volcano.
Includes index.
1. Pound, Ezra, 1885–1972—Biography. 2. Poets,
American—20th century—Biography. I. Title.
PS3531.082Z8687 1987   811'.52 [B]   86-25912
ISBN 0-385-19694-6

In memory of my parents, Lena and Charles

PREFACE

Ezra Pound detested the prospect of his own biography, resisting it as a sort of death announcement. Capable of intense adorations and great hatreds, Pound was the most controversial writer of our time. He was a man who did extreme things, a poet with enormous ambition, self-confidence, and pride, and a prophetic sense of message and mission. Some of his friends found him demented, others saw him as an actor playing a grand role for large stakes in the theater of history. In short, he was a man of complications with a compelling story.

Several years ago I visited James Laughlin, Pound's publisher, to inquire whether he thought there was room for another biography. Laughlin told me that none of the earlier attempts had successfully captured Pound, that there was a need for an interpretative biography that could explore the myths behind the man rather than merely debunking them. What he did not want to see was another behemoth biography, the nine-hundred-page loose and baggy monster in three volumes whose parade of facts would scatter like an army of ants in all directions.

Such an approach would contradict an essential part of Pound's own style, what he called his "luminous method"—the selection of crucially revealing details presented in a honed and chiseled manner. This book was conceived in such a spirit, and with it I hope to illuminate the tragic circumstances surrounding Pound's poems. My book is based on the reading of thousands of unpublished letters, psychiatric reports, FBI files, and dozens of published personal accounts, and on interviews with people who knew Pound. It was written in Venice, Pound's first and last European love, the place where he published his first poems and spent his last years.

ACKNOWLEDGMENTS

For their support and suggestions, and for their reading of my manuscript, I would like to thank Leon Edel, Joyce Johnson, James Laughlin, Mellon Tytell, and Barry Wallenstein. I owe a special debt to my agent, Berenice Hoffman, and to my editors, Marshall De Bruhl, Janet Byrne, and Kathy Antrim. In Italy I was helped by Olga Rudge, Mary de Rachewiltz, Danieli Fona, Serge Perosa, and Fernanda Pivano. For assistance with my research, I am indebted to Robert Bertholf of the University of Buffalo, Cathy Henderson of the Humanities Research Center in Austin, Texas, Madeline Korey and David King of the Free Library of Philadelphia, Frank Lorentz of Hamilton College, David Schoonover of the Beinecke Collection at Yale, Dan Traister of the Van Pelt Library at the University of Pennsylvania, Saundra Taylor of the Lilly Library in Bloomington, Indiana, and Dr. Harold Thomas, Public Information Director of St. Elizabeths in Washington, D.C. I was helped by my colleagues Morris Dickstein, Virginia Hlvasa, Eddie Epstein, Jack Reilly, and Michael Timko, and also by Richard Ardinger, William French, Wayne Lawson, John Morris, Herb Payton, William Phillips, and Ronald Sukenick. The manuscript was typed by Grace Romeo and Janice Di Giovanni of the Word Processing Center at Queens College.

CONTENTS

Life is terribly deficient in form. Its catastrophes happen in the wrong way and to the wrong people. There is a grotesque horror about its comedies, and its tragedies seem to culminate in farce.

Oscar Wilde
The Critic As Artist

What's madness but nobility of soul
At odds with circumstance.

Theodore Roethke
"In a Dark Time"

PART I

INTRODUCTION:
THE TRAGIC FRACTURE

Ezra Pound has been called the flaming Savonarola of modern poetry. James Joyce said he was an "unpredictable bundle of electricity." The poet H.D. wrote that he was a "whirlwind of forked lightning." T. S. Eliot acknowledged that Pound was more responsible for the twentieth-century revolution in poetry than any other individual. His friend Wyndham Lewis called Pound the Trotsky of literature—feared and suspected for his brilliance and unorthodoxy. On another occasion, Lewis wrote that Pound was a pedagogic volcano whose molten matter was language that seared through a "tragic fracture" in his personality, a broken seam of the sensibility, releasing an uncontainable energy or an anger that could persist for thirty years. Such comparisons are registers of Pound's galvanic impact on his generation, the modernist movement in the arts which he did so much to inspire and establish.

Another friend, the Irish poet William Butler Yeats, saw Pound as a solitary volcano. The image is grandly suggestive: we associate volcanic activity with great destructive change, cataclysms of steam, rivers of mud, and burning lava that will fertilize the land for centuries and leave deposits of diamonds, precious crystals, and gemstones. The ancients saw the volcano as a divine voice of displeasure and wrath and often worshipped the mountain from which it erupted as a god: exacting, impetuous, vengeful, and capable of drastic eliminations. In our nuclear age, we have made the volcano portable, to be dropped from an airplane or transported by a missile, manifesting itself as a nuclear cloud, an inverted catastrophe in the heavens.

In literary matters the volcanic action was perhaps less visible, more seething and subterranean, more the result of a fundamental insight, a surprising remark or poem, or as in Pound's case the aesthetic of "Make It New," which resulted in his development of Imagism as a new manner for poetry in his time, an entirely new technology of the imagination. Arriving in London in 1908 at the age of twenty-three with tremendous assurance, Pound had the conviction that he would be one of the great masters of the art of poetry. Poetry was the "dance of intelligence among words," but not all of it was commendable. He immediately upset the Edwardians by complaining about the "boiled oatmeal consistency" of their verse. British poetry was decorous, complacent, and dull, and Pound contemptuously dismissed most of the poetry he read as "poppycock and rhetorical din" crippled by "painted adjectives" and "emotional slither." He claimed that no one remembered that poetry was an art, that it had a conscious perfectible technique, that it needed a constant change of manner if it was to live. He spoke of art and beauty with an authority that no one had heard in England since Oscar Wilde, and Wilde had been made to pay for the insolence of his upsetting opinions with his life. "Good art can NOT be immoral," Pound declared in an early essay. "By good art I mean the art that bears true witness. I mean the art that is most precise." And beauty, he maintained in the same piece, "The Serious Artist," the title a token of his own moral imperative and the high value he put on what he was trying to do, "Beauty in art reminds one what is worth while":

> I am not now speaking of shams. I mean beauty, not slither, not
> sentimentalizing about beauty, not telling people that beauty is the
> proper and respectable thing. I mean beauty. You don't argue
> about an April wind, you feel bucked up when you meet it. You
> feel bucked up when you come on a swift moving thought in Plato
> or on a fine line in a statue.

Such views of beauty were the dangerous legacy of Wilde and the decadent poets of the 1890s. The notion that the beautiful implies a higher morality enables the creative artist to imagine his own moral superiority no matter how he disregards the courtesies and conventions of society. But it is a notion, as well, that always serves to separate the artist from his audience. Pound exaggerated what he felt was the innate worth of the artist to permit any license in the search for beauty or experience—the ultimate romantic, Faustian quest. The genteel Edwardians arched over their tea and complained of Pound's boots, his cowboy manners, Philadelphia accent, and American barbarisms.

Always self-conscious and nervously aware of others, high-strung, impatient, mercurial, and exuberant, Pound presented himself as the figure of the poet, much as Whistler had offended the staid decorum of an earlier London generation with his caustic wit and cutting appearance. "It is impossible to talk about perfection without getting yourself very much disliked," he declared. To established London, it was not only his talk that seemed bizarre; for to Pound, the very arrangement of his clothing was one way to signal the new. Pound used a silver-topped malacca cane on the London streets as part of his flourish; like *Ripostes,* the title he chose for one of his early books of poetry, the cane was part of his aggressive thrust into the center of things. Appearance was a way to clearly establish differences and demarcations. With green trousers made of billiard cloth, with his pink velvet coat and its blue glass buttons, a hand-painted tie, his mane of reddish blond hair tucked under a sombrero, his green eyes, a beard cut to a point to resemble a Spanish conquistador, and as a final touch a singular turquoise earring, Pound strode the London streets as operatically endowed as any character of Puccini's.

Living on two pounds a week in one room in Kensington, he met William Butler Yeats and Ford Madox Ford and a group who moved in the orbit of Yeats's Monday evenings at home and Ford's magazine, the *English Review.* Yeats and Ford were impressed by Pound's theatricality, but even more by the vehemence of his sweepingly absolute declarations: "Western ethics were a consummate filth in the middle of the last century," he wrote in *The New Age,* a gadfly publication in which Pound would publish dozens of journalistic forays. Yeats saw his intransigence as quintessential American rawness and admired Pound's vigor. There is "no man now living in America," Pound pontificated, "whose work is of the slightest interest to any serious artist." The characteristic overstatement was bravado self-justification, the expression of an impatient, headstrong drive, an exasperation with mediocrity, a recklessness about making enemies. But beneath the brash impetuosity there was the desire to be noticed, to be a cynosure. Once at a literary luncheon Pound deliberately and delicately munched a centerpiece of tulips when he felt neglected. Such ploys for attention made Pound seem the fool or the madman, a role he enjoyed but one that often served only to annoy or irritate the more phlegmatic British.

During the prewar years in London, a time of gaiety and social whirl, Pound lectured on medieval poetry and in 1909 offered a lecture series on medieval Provence at the London Polytechnic. He was using what he had once studied in graduate school to both support himself and establish a name as a young critic in London. He was meeting men of power like Edward Marsh (who heard Pound talk at Cambridge and whose friend was the young Winston Churchill) and C. F. Masterman, who was to become a member of the cabinet that declared war on Germany in 1914. There were the Fabian Socialists, Shaw and H. G. Wells and the suffragettes, vegetarian philosophers like Bertrand Russell, and underground artists like novelist and painter Wyndham Lewis. In Lewis's Rebel Art Centre Pound caused a considerable stir at an opening by draping a flag that proclaimed the "End of the Christian Era." The act was spontaneous, rambunctious, disreputable, a slap in the face of convention. For the British, Pound was clearly a spectacle, an American curiosity, a renegade who could never be fully trusted in polite society.

"A sound poetic training is nothing less than the science of being discontented," Pound asserted epigrammatically. Some of the other artists in London recognized a kindred spirit, another dissident imagination. Even the abstracted and dreamy Yeats, already an established literary figure, listened to Pound's criticism and advice. His poems were appearing in magazines and his books—*Personae, Canzoni, The Spirit of Romance*—were being published and getting noticed. Reviewers took strong stands on his poems, either finding them harsh, ungainly, and awkward, causing readers to dance with fury or quake with laughter, according to one of them; or appreciating his confident celebrations, the striking freshness of his rhythms, the vigor of a poet who seemed able to push past models like Browning to discover his own voice: brusque, defiant, yet exquisite and new.

The years before the outbreak of World War I were a period of brimming vitality for Pound. He was occupied with his poetry, with journalism, with his work as foreign editor of *Poetry,* a Chicago magazine that became a central organ for the new poets, and with the new writers like Eliot and James Joyce, whom he had sponsored, and an unknown sculptor named Henri Gaudier-Brzeska, whom he had found under a railway arch working in poverty and neglect.

Life was full of poetry and courtship, he met a young woman named Dorothy Shakespear, whom he later married, but suddenly everything was shattered by the international catastrophe of the First World War: Pound received frontline reports from his friends Gaudier-Brzeska, who was killed in 1915, Ford, who was shell-shocked, and Wyndham Lewis. Pound felt the best part of his generation had been ravaged by an absurdly wasteful war, and he expressed some of his bitterness in his most powerful poem of the period, "Hugh Selwyn Mauberley": "laughter out of dead bellies," he declared, "for an old bitch gone in the teeth," "a botched civilization." Pound had begun his career with a prolonged study of the love poetry of the French twelfth-century troubador poets, but later venom, antagonism, and invective were to become as important motivations for his own work. He loathed Western civilization because it had no room left for its artists, and because it seemed systematically bent on its own extinction through warfare.

Pound took as his models two masters of hatred, Dante and Villon. He hated the liberal modern state, where there seemed to be no strong leaders and where the idea of responsibility had become corrupted by bureaucratic labyrinth. He hated the influence of organized religion and the small comforts of the middle class. He began to release some of his scorn in *The Cantos,* a long epic poem of 120 sections that juxtaposed various historical moments—classical, Confucian, and sequences drawn from early American politics—with his own memories, reading, and awareness. *The Cantos* were to be a lifework, his supreme achievement, but they were also inaccessible, dense, and difficult to an extreme.

Dissatisfied with England after the war, Pound moved to Paris in 1921. At first he recaptured some of his former ebullience, writing to William Carlos Williams about all sorts of projects "artoliteresque in the Peaceconferentialbolshevikair." On Pound's thirty-fifth birthday, the day James Joyce completed his great novel *Ulysses*, Pound proclaimed that a new historical period had begun which with his typical irreverence he called the Pound Era. T. E. Lawrence characterized him at this time as all exclamation points. For E. E. Cummings, Pound was the "gymnastic personality" who "disengaged himself from a pillar and bowed" on their first meeting. Pound began composing an opera. He met a concert violinist who became his mistress. And he continued *The Cantos*.

His letters from Paris were jaunty and excessively cheerful. He adopted various dialects, the homespun backwoodsman's voice or one that resembled the punning pages of Joyce's *Finnegans Wake*. His friends were the Dadaists, Cocteau, the painters Picabia, Duchamp, and Léger, Ernest Hemingway, and a hard-drinking cynical Midwestern writer named Robert McAlmon. He had liver and digestive problems, partly because of the excitements of Paris, partly because of the continuing experiment of *The Cantos*, partly because of an insidious self-pity, a feeling that he had not received his due measure of acclaim.

After four years in Paris he moved south again, settling in Rapallo on the Italian Riviera. Pound believed artists were the antennae of the race, and he began to fear the imminence of another great war, a second instance of organized madness. He became obsessively interested in economics, railing against Western banking practices, the monopoly on credit, and interest rates, which he felt were usurious. He imagined a Jewish conspiracy to influence political systems, the banking business, and the munitions industries, which he asserted would begin the next war to create a huge debt and new profits. He began writing letters to American senators and congressmen advocating Major C. H. Douglas's Social Credit scheme, a plan to reduce taxes drastically and nationalize credit. In *The Cantos*, but to a greater extent in his voluminous correspondence, he started to release a stream of invective and abuse: President Wilson was a "verbal masturbator," Harding a "slob," Hoover a "sausage headed crook," French premier Léon Blum a "bank pimp," and the economist John Maynard Keynes an imbecile and a "pusillanimous louse." He wrote T. E. Lawrence that England was a "filthy country" where "every man in high office is a thief's accomplice." He campaigned against the passport system and the obscenity laws affecting literary works like Joyce's *Ulysses*. In 1927 he started a magazine called *The Exile*, whose title was one clear register of his own desperate disaffiliation. He seemed almost intent on outrage and scandal as a means of calling attention to himself and his work. But instead of insolently munching tulips, he was defaming men of power and their institutions, men who had the capacity to one day bring him to book for what he had said.

Some of his closest friends saw the warning indications, the intemperance, the hysterically bilious vilification, and began to protest. Eliot complained that his letters were becoming incomprehensible. Sir Herbert Read called Pound's ideas on Social Credit "amiable lunacy." H. L. Mencken told him he was describing an imaginary United States, that it had been a great mistake to "set up shop as a wizard." Archibald MacLeish wrote, "I think you are wrong as hell about America," and E. E. Cummings pungently advised him to "haul your catgut out of the petty pond of practical politics."

But Pound's invective only increased. During World War II he made the mistake of doing a series of broadcasts on Italian State Radio in which he defended fascism and continued his defamations. The radio broadcasts were an example of what might be called a negative susceptibility, a self-destructive capacity shared by a number of modern artists. Hostile and hysterical, the talks bordered on incoherence as Pound savaged America and its political leadership with venomous bitterness. Pound's own talk intoxicated him, although it made little sense to the outside world. However, his diatribes were monitored by the Federal Bureau of Investigation. Pound's friend the French writer Jean Cocteau had once told him, "The tact of audacity consists in knowing how far to go too far." Pound, crazed and off center because of the war, had gone far too far, and there was a serious price to be paid. The sixty-year-old man of letters was seized after the Allied invasion of Italy, incarcerated and isolated for three weeks in an exposed six-by-eight-foot wire cage, subject to broiling sun and searchlights all night, and underwent interrogation in a U.S. Army detention center in Pisa for American and Allied troops who had looted, raped civilians, or disobeyed their officers. No one was allowed to talk to him, not even his guards, and he saw from his "gorilla cage" several inmates machine-gunned in escape attempts. Finally, after his weeks of privation and fear, he believed something snapped in his head, and he suffered a nervous breakdown.

He was flown to Washington, where preparations were begun for a treason trial, a crime punishable by death. He asserted that no one had heard the broadcasts, that even if they had they probably would not have understood them. In a letter to Attorney General Biddle he defended his action as a "protest against a system which creates one war after another, in a series and in system." The examining psychiatrists found him paranoid and too unstable to stand trial. They prevented the embarrassment of having one of the world's leading democracies execute one of its leading writers, but the judgment was controversial and disputed. Pound had seen himself as Tiresias, a prophetic witness, and Ulysses, a wandering voyager, and became convinced of his own intellectual omnipotence and indestructibility.

In his actions and words as well as in his art, he was mixing fact and fiction in the borderline zone of creativity which many artists inhabit, moving from moments of clarity to moments of frenzy. Melville, a century earlier, had compared this state of ambiguous sanity to the lack of demarcation between the colors in the rainbow. But after the horror of the Second World War such sympathetic explanations seemed only a rationalization for treason. Why should an artist deserve special treatment, even if he had contributed more than most to the general cultural level of the times?

Ezra Pound had first challenged the poetry establishment in London, then the state with his political broadcasts during the Second World War, and finally, it seemed, fate itself. He refused to admit that he had been wrong—he had played the madman-poet so long that he could no longer distinguish between a role and reality. Pound was an overly sensitive man who in the midst of a maelstrom had shouted terrible words, absurdly defending some ideal of free speech from a stage while the theater was burning.

He was sent to what he called the "Hell-hole," a ward for lunatics in St. Elizabeths in Washington, D.C., an insane asylum where he was to be kept for the next twelve years of his life, from age sixty to seventy-two. His friend Cocteau had once remarked that the "artist is a kind of prison from which the works of art escape"; in St. Elizabeths the metaphor became brutal truth. His sentence was virtually indeterminate: he had to spend his time in the company of screaming men in straitjackets until the psychiatrists and politicians agreed that he could be freed. Despite his suffering and confinement, he continued writing his *Cantos,* adding some of its most powerful and personal sections. Released in 1958 after pressure from some of the writers he had helped as critic and editor—Eliot, Hemingway, and Frost —he returned to Italy, at first still insubordinate and unregenerate. During his last years, however, he recognized that he had made tragic choices which had been flawed by a certain pride in the infallibility of his judgment. He had been arrogant, what he had said was an expression of vanity. For the last ten years of his life he almost ceased writing and speaking, the poet and releaser of words then muted, caught in the prison of his own sensibility and contrition. The theatricality of Pound's silence was consonant with many of the flamboyant acts that in previous years he had used to gain attention; the silence may also have been a considerable convenience to Pound, since by refusing language he would not have to answer embarrassing questions about his wartime activities. With blasts of bardic energy, he had tried to transform the world in his own image; toward the end all images were hazy, unclear, confusing. His last years had the wordless terror and dignity of mythical atonement.

Pound's life presents the puzzle of a humanist who studied many languages ancient and modern, who read and translated in a vast expanse of the

world's literature, who changed the way poets used language in our time,
but who became our archetype of the literary pariah, a sort of King Lear of
modernism, lost in a storm on the heath but still declaiming insistently at the
top of his voice, the poet bawling and boiling in the abyss, full of denial and
bitterness, a fury of rage and disappointment which came close, at times, to
a terrifying barbarism. It is a singular story of the outcast artist, a Prome-
thean figure who chose exile, a volcanic antagonist reminding his world of
ancient ways. But it is a story with brilliantly illuminating cultural signals as
well: the artist who pushes the limits of conventional behavior, who violates
the accepted and derides authority, who makes of his life so exceptional a
case that more mundane exigencies are exposed, and who thus allows us to
examine the very virtue and nature of our common behavior and governance.

AN AMERICAN YOUTH

*With the real artist there is always a residue, there is always something in
the man which does not get into his work. There is always some reason why
the man is always more worth knowing than his books are. In the long run
nothing else counts.*

"Patria Mia"

1. ANCESTRAL ACTIONS

Ezra Pound once imagined the possibility of writing a social history of the
United States from his own family annals: "the disorderly trek of four or
five generations across the whole teeming continent." Though he was never
to fulfill so Balzacian an ambition, genealogy became a critical element in
his conception of himself. Like some of our earliest writers—Cooper, Hawthorne, Melville—Pound could trace his family back through the colonial
past to the adventure of the first settlers. It was a history rich enough to
impress a young boy, with disparate though exotic elements, a story of New
England Brahmins and whalers, of lawmakers and outlaws, of military officers and congressmen.

Much of the family legend was rehearsed for young Ezra by his maternal grandmother, Mary Weston. When he visited her in her rooming house
on East Forty-seventh Street in Manhattan, she would encourage him to
browse in one of her genealogical treatises: *Two Hundred and Fifty Years of
the Wadsworth Family in America.* Pound read about his predecessors, sturdy,
independent Puritans, who landed in New England twelve years after the
Mayflower on a ship called the *Lion.* One member of this line was Captain
Joseph Wadsworth, who had helped frame Connecticut's constitution. The
right to establish commonwealth governance had been granted in a charter
by Charles II in 1662. His successor, James II, sought to renege on these
rights and sent Sir Edmund Andros to seize the charter. The daring Wadsworth, with an élan that characterized the insubordinate spirit of some of

the colonials, secreted the charter in a huge spreading oak tree which had for generations served as a sacred Indian meeting place. The act was swift and sly; it was ripe for historians and legend and Mary Weston loved it. As a child, Pound was taken to see this tree; later in his life when he justified his radio talks for Mussolini as the last defense of free speech, in some manner he may have been acting out his version of Wadsworth's rebellion.

Mary Weston filled her grandson with family pride and a sense of possibility. She so impressed him with the magic of family legend and lore that she surely contributed to the storyteller in Pound at a formative stage. She read to him from Sir Walter Scott's novels and explained that his family line went back at least as far as the Battle of Crécy in the fourteenth century. But the most exciting and influential family figure for young Ezra was his paternal grandfather, Thaddeus C. Pound, a full-bearded model of enterprise and accomplishment. In his autobiographical fragment, *Indiscretions,* written with the coy veil of Jamesian periphrasis and tone, Pound pictures his grandfather as a picaresque hero, a man who could have figured in the pages of Fielding or Dickens. Born in a log cabin in Elk, Pennsylvania, in 1832, he earned and lost three fortunes during his lifetime. An engaging talker, interested in phrenology and spiritualism, he toured the West with a brother and a medicine show, demonstrating magnetic and spiritual healing. As Melville described it in *The Confidence Man,* such operations usually involved the sale of elixirs whose most effective ingredient was an opium tincture which worked wonders for pain. No one knows whether good Thaddeus earned his first stake in this manner, but he did marry Sarah Angevine Loomis (and his brother married her sister). Sarah Loomis was a woman from an upper New York State family of country justices and horse thieves. The young couple settled in the town of Chippewa Falls, Wisconsin, where Thaddeus first taught school, worked as a bookkeeper, then bought a general store. Most of his customers were Scandinavian immigrants who cut trees in the virgin forests, and before long the enterprising storekeeper had organized a group of them into the Union Lumber Company. He would buy their logs with his own scrip which they would then use to purchase his goods. Thaddeus was a pure capitalist: his natural resource was the timber, he had the labor to cut it, the river to provide cheap transport to his markets, and with his own scrip he could print and distribute what amounted to his own capital. In *Indiscretions* Pound associates his grandfather with the daring and danger of frontier life, the robust vigors that would serve to domesticate a wilderness. Pound relates how Thaddeus used to wrestle with his lumberjacks for sport and to maintain his prestige and how Sarah Loomis would prepare food for forty hungry men.

Pound was impressed by his grandfather's enthusiasm for the future: "He had the ability to regard possibilities rather than facts." It was the outlook of perennial American optimism, eagerly inventing a future no

matter what the obstacles. Thaddeus Pound had been a living example of
the American Dream—by hard work and imagination he had made his own
way up through the ruling class in the Horatio Alger tradition of the self-
made man. Thaddeus became a builder of railroads, but instead of joining
the buccaneers of American capitalism, he ran for state assembly, got
elected, and ended up as speaker and then acting governor of Wisconsin in
1870–71.

Thaddeus Pound was known as an orator. He was relied on by his
fellow Republicans in presidential campaigns, and his firebrand populist
economics clearly anticipated his grandson's: "The monstrous proposition,"
he declared in one of his speeches, is "to turn the mints of this republic over
to the owners of bullion," that is, the bankers. The fact that private bankers
through the Federal Reserve System had been given the power to print and
then rent money to the government Thaddeus considered a basic violation
of the Constitution and the intentions of the founding fathers. He ran for
Congress and served in three successive terms. Early in his congressional
career, his wife left him (with a hundred-thousand-dollar settlement, which
she then lost when a bank failed) and he began a liaison with a married
woman. President Garfield promised him a cabinet position, but J. G.
Blaine, politically more powerful, refused to serve with Pound because of
his marital irregularity. Thus ended Thaddeus Pound's political career.

Ezra Pound asserted that though his grandfather left Washington with
less money than he had had when he arrived, he had been a leader, close to
the center of political power. He had had the "ability to stand unabashed in
the face of the largest national luminaries," Pound wrote in *Indiscretions,* and
that familiarity in the face of power became a family legacy. In the 1930s, in
Italy, when he met Mussolini and began agitating for Social Credit, Pound
claimed that his grandfather had as early as 1878 been "urging his fellow
Congressmen the same essentials of monetary and statal economics that I am
writing about today."

"The actions of one's ancestors, especially if recited to one in childhood, tend to influence one's character," Pound confessed in *Indiscretions.* If
the paternal side of his lineage, the whalers and Thaddeus, signified fearless
industry, the maternal side was a reminder of history, gentility, and culture.
The Westons had towns named after them in Connecticut, Massachusetts,
and Vermont; the Wadsworth family had been connected in business and
friendship with John Quincy Adams. The ninth president of Harvard had
been a Wadsworth, as was the poet Longfellow. A great-aunt had danced
with General Grant when he was inaugurated and had appeared at subsequent inaugurals. It was a family with its own intriguing legends and strong
biblical names on both sides: Elijahs and Ezekiels, an Eliphalet and a Bath-
sheba.

Thaddeus named Pound's father Homer—a classical departure from

Old Testament thunder. Homer was a placid, quiet, persevering man, not a climber or a builder of fortunes but a civil servant. "Probably the first white male born in the northern part of Wisconsin," Pound speculates in *Indiscretions,* adding that his father had a male Indian as nurse. Homer, though, did have a stubborn streak as a boy. He left one school on his own and was then placed in a military academy. Thaddeus obtained a commission to West Point for him, but Homer decided, while on the train, that he would not attend. He returned to Chippewa Falls to work in a butcher shop, possibly some version of Thaddeus's old general store. While this shift in plans may seem to indicate a failure of nerve, the fact is that at this point Thaddeus suffered one of his financial reversals. West Point was still a gentleman's school, and a cadet (as Edgar Allan Poe had learned two generations earlier) needed a generous allowance to achieve respect.

Thaddeus's name was still sufficiently admired for his son to trade on when he met Isabel Weston in Washington and married her, a case of the country boy attracted to the city girl. There was also enough political influence left to have Homer appointed to establish a government land office in Hailey, Idaho. A frontier town of two thousand people, Hailey was an outpost for miners or men selling mining supplies out of wooden shacks. The one minister there collected his salary in bars and miners would carry sticks of dynamite in their boots. Born in Hailey on the night before Halloween, October 30, 1885, Pound characterized the town as having one dusty main street with planks for sidewalks, a hotel, and forty-seven bars. Homer remembered that "there were times when it seemed as if one might be mutilated by some angry seeker after lands." According to the law at that time, any prospector could claim land and effectively gain title to it by filing in the land office and working the land. Thaddeus had certain unused claims that Homer was unable to protect, but this was the Wild West, where disagreements were often settled with guns. Genial and kindly by nature, Homer was not the man for the job, and furthermore Isabel hated Hailey. Even though Homer had built for her the only plastered house there, she complained of the altitude, the extremes of weather, the lack of manners, of the Chinese manservant who removed the table crumbs one evening, at a dinner meant to impress visitors, with a hearth brush. Tall, stately, with perfect carriage and a sibylline poise, Isabel was the stiff Victorian Grand Lady who found herself in a dreadful colony. And when Isabel's mother, Mary Weston, came to visit, she was shocked by the lack of curtains and door locks in the hotel where the walls were so thin one could hear the moans of a drunken miner on a binge in the next room. Isabel, with all her affectations and her trained "society" voice, could never communicate with the more primitive accents of the mountain men of Hailey. She had been schooled in a more practiced diction, as Pound would recall in *The Cantos:*

and in my mother's time it was respectable,
it was social, apparently,
      to sit in the Senate gallery
or even in that of the House
      to hear the fire-works of the senators
(and possibly representatives)

Precipitately in a blizzard Isabel took her son on the train back to New York. Luckily, the train was equipped with the first rotary snowplow; unluckily, her eighteen-month-old son developed a severe cough, for which the inventor of the snowplow, who was on the train, gave her a mixture of sugar and kerosene. It was a story Pound loved to retell, a memory of the privations and heartiness of the frontier. Infant Ezra, "Gargantua," as he calls himself in *Indiscretions*, then spent the next six months in Grandmother Weston's rooming house in Manhattan, and another six months on Thaddeus's Wisconsin farm.

2. MISCARRIED GENTILITY

In June of 1889, the Pounds moved to Philadelphia. In Hailey, Homer had learned assaying and part of his duty there had been to determine the percentage of gold in a miner's ore. Since Isabel couldn't tolerate Hailey, again Thaddeus intervened on behalf of his son to obtain for him the position of assistant assayer at the United States Mint in Philadelphia, where he remained for the next four decades. Ezra had been uprooted from the rugged, exciting atmosphere Hemingway later captured in his early stories and was transported to a place that for him would represent miscarried gentility. In 1921, in a letter to Thomas Hardy, he complained that "I come from an American suburb—where I was not born—where both parents are really foreigners."

The exaggeration is typically Poundian. Isabel would have been happier in New York City, but even Philadelphia was a clear improvement over a backward mining town. The Pounds lived in a brick row house on the edge of the city for two years, then moved ten miles north to Jenkintown, and a year later purchased with Mary Weston's help a spacious seven-bedroom house, with a large yard, in nearby Wyncote. It was a comfortable beginning for a growing child. Homer planted peach and cherry trees and there was an old apple tree under which Ezra could build a hut with his friends. The house was furnished in the plush, cluttered Victorian style. There were the customary family portraits, a precious Ming vase, some Oriental drawings, India prints on the chairs, a few heirlooms, lots of books, a piano, and a small Hammond organ. Isabel had a maid and maintained pretensions of grandeur. Pound remembered her as always in rustling silks and satins and fancy lace. She read the classics to her son before his nap, or perhaps a bit of Longfellow to lull him to sleep. Poetry was not considered unusual in Pound's family, as he later told Donald Hall. Thaddeus Pound used to correspond with the president of the Chippewa Falls Bank in verse, and Mary Weston wrote verse letters to her brothers.

The Pounds were comfortable but not rich. Homer earned just enough to satisfy their needs, and Isabel would take in a boarder if she felt she needed more. Gentle, informal, remarkably approachable, Homer Pound was content in his circumstances. His work involved precise measurements, and he brought his son to the Mint at the intersection of Juniper and Chestnut streets and showed him the process of assaying gold, the weighing, the refining, the delicacy of the balances. Ezra was fascinated, claiming later that it affected his poems, teaching him the importance of precision. He described how his father could weigh a man's name, first by weighing his card, then by weighing the card with a signature. One day a worker pointed to a bag of gold coin and told the boy he could keep it if he could carry it away, but, of course, it was far too heavy, even for a grown man. Then there were the infamous "goldbricks," lead bricks covered with a layer of gold or even solid in some parts so that the seller could bore through to show it to be so. When Ezra was eight, there was a recount of the silver coinage and he watched the workers shovel coins into giant counting machines: "All the bags had rotted in these enormous vaults, and they were heaving it into the counting machines with shovels bigger than coal shovels. This spectacle of coin being shoveled around like it was litter—these fellows naked to the waist shoveling it around in the gas flares—things like that strike your imagination."

Homer was civic-minded: he was president of an association for amateur theatricals, president of the Christian Endeavor Society, a member of school boards and superintendent of the Sunday school in the Presbyterian Church in downtown Philadelphia. Wyncote was wealthy, respectable, and small, with a population of only sixteen hundred people. Even if the local streets were still unpaved, the neighbors were Cyrus Curtis of *The Saturday Evening Post* and, just two houses down, George Horace Lorimer, who owned the *Ladies' Home Journal.* There were also the country estates of eminent Philadelphians like the Wideners and the Wanamakers. When Ezra was ten, a popular Wyncote hotel announced that it was discontinuing boarding Jews, and the local paper declared, "Just no more Italians in Wyncote. Is our budding hope that this place will be entirely aristocratic squelched?"

Ezra, pampered and spoiled by his mother, an only child herself, remembered protesting because she made him wear his hair in curls at the age of four in an effort to make him "an object of beauty." His mother liked "pretty things" and he was to become one of them. At six, attending a Quaker school, he was known as the Professor because of his glasses and his use of complex polysyllabic words. There were signs of his temperamental precocity: he records that when he was six, fearing that his father might lose his civil service position at the Mint, he hurled his baby rocking chair across the room when he heard that Grover Cleveland was reelected. Nevertheless, he was allowed to play in the surrounding hills, he had a favorite cave, and he enjoyed the treat of a buggy ride from the local stable. He also had accidents and was up to the usual boyish pranks. Once during a flash flood, he and another boy were almost drowned rescuing a dog in a swelling creek. On another occasion he locked his elementary school teacher, Miss Ridpath, who was visiting the house, in a shed. At the age of seventy-two, Pound remembered Miss Ridpath, in "despair at being unable to control the uncontrollable," crying when she kept him after school. His earliest writing was letters to Santa Claus and rhymed letters to cousins: he was allowed to type these by placing a board on the arms of a square oak mission chair in the red wallpapered living room and setting the machine on top.

At twelve he entered Cheltenham, a military school only a two-mile walk from home. He wore a cadet's uniform, was introduced to Greek and Latin, and detested the routine of military drill. But the inconveniences of the school were made more palatable by the diversions of youth. He took up fencing and chess; and in winters there was sledding and ice skating on the Wanamakers' pond. And Pound showed some early signs of difference. One of his classmates, Hensel Eckman, thought that "Ray Pound was an odd dresser. He usually wore a hat. I thought he had a complex." Another neighbor, E. H. Perry, said, "I'll never forget the day he walked by on our street in his white flannel trousers to call on Katherine Proctor." A neighbor with the improbable name of Sue Nice recalled that people "made fun of him. He was all books."

To be sure, there were more serious pursuits for a boy. With his parents he attended the local Calvary Presbyterian Church, where his father was an elder. Its minister, the Reverend Carlos Tracy Chester, exerted considerable influence on young Pound. Chester had published a number of short stories and articles and helped edit several literary publications. He encouraged Pound's interests in writing and persuaded him to study the Bible as well. Pound dedicated *Exultations.* an early book of poems, to Chester. Chester's successor at Calvary, the Reverend William Barnes Lower, who boarded with the Pounds for a year when Ezra was sixteen, was also known as a poet in local Philadelphia circles.

Pound had written his first poem at the age of eleven, about William Jennings Bryan. It was in the year of William Jennings Bryan's populist "Free Silver" campaign, and his attempt to defeat the banking establishment and the gold standard left a formative impression on Pound if we consider his later economic theories. He heard discussions about Bryan at home and in New York, where he periodically visited his grandmother.

In the 1890s New York City was experiencing great changes: Edison's electric lights transformed the streets into a nocturnal fairyland, and the electric streetcar was replacing the horse-drawn cab. The Brooklyn Bridge had been completed and the Metropolitan Opera expressed a continuation of European civilizations. The center of the city was shifting to midtown, and in his grandmother's rooming house Pound heard discussions of current political issues. His grandmother attended St. Bartholomew's Presbyterian Church on Park Avenue, whose minister, the Reverend Charles Henry Parkhurst, may have been an early model for Pound. Parkhurst was a militant moral crusader who challenged the Tammany Hall politicians, using his parishioners and himself as private detectives to document instances of graft and corruption. His sermons sounded like a preview of what Pound would say a generation later. With heat and passion, Parkhurst condemned the municipal authorities as a "damnable pack of administrative bloodhounds, polluted harpies, and a lying, perjured, rum-soaked, and libidinous lot." In New York City, the suburban lad found much that was intriguing: once, he recalled in *Indiscretions,* he was bewildered by the fact that a man threw a jackknife at another fleeing man fifty feet away in a vegetable market and no one else seemed to notice it or care. An even greater lesson in the differences between a suburban setting and metropolitan mores was offered to him at the age of twelve when he accompanied his mother and his aunt to Europe.

His aunt by marriage whom he called Aunt Frank ran a rooming house in Manhattan which she parlayed into a small hotel, the New Weston. But she overextended herself and went bankrupt in 1909, losing all her money in the process. Since she had no children and adored Pound, he certainly would have inherited money from her when she died, a turn that might have made him less rebellious. Until her bankruptcy she was considered the wealthiest member of the family, and the most generous. In the summer of 1898 she took Pound and his mother on a three-month tour abroad. Of the trip Pound remembered his aunt's ninety-seven packets of green tea distributed through her many pieces of luggage and her "wide and white bodiced figure" perched on a narrow mule in Tangiers. Europe, particularly Venice, made a powerful impression on him. He was determined to return.

The European trip was like an opening door for Ezra, a push in the direction of history and culture. At the precocious age of fifteen, urged by his mother to start early, he was ready to begin university study. He already had defined a purpose in the poet's vocation:

I knew at fifteen pretty much what I wanted to do. I resolved that at thirty I would know more about poetry than any man living, that I would know the dynamic content from the shell, that I would know what was accounted poetry everywhere, what part of poetry was "indestructible," what part could not be lost by translation and—scarcely less important—what effects were obtainable in one language only.

His parents were encouraging, believing his grand declaration that "I want to write before I die the greatest poems that have ever been written." Later, when her son was in England, Isabel used to rise at evening parties with his latest compositions and declaim them to the Wyncote Ladies Club. She may have been the only member of that association who was not wealthy, but her son was a poet! Nancy McCormack, a sculptor who visited Isabel after World War I, reported on her worshipful attitude to her son's work, noting that she had "eyes that looked out as if she was a bit puzzled over some object on the distant horizon." Was her son that object? She had tried her best to form him, but there had been resistance to her stress on manners, convention, Victorian proprieties.

Just before his marriage, writing to his future wife, Pound said his mother was a prude if ever there was one, and it is possible to see much of his own rebelliousness as a reaction to her attempted control. On the other hand, she surely contributed to Pound's sense of himself as a dandy. An acquaintance had described her as walking "as if in ermine," a presence her young son would feel and admire. Ezra had always felt a deeper affinity with his father, who had "provided continuous sympathy" and a supportive texture of unusual harmony. In *Indiscretions* Pound admitted that Homer had been the "naivest man who ever possessed sound sense." His uncomplicated considerateness, his combination of tenderness and practicality, made him easy to idealize and easy to live with. In 1955, in a letter from St. Elizabeths, he remembered that Homer's support had been total and unqualified, while his mother had rarely agreed with him about anything.

3. COLLEGE DAYS

Pound described himself as a "lanky whey faced youth" when in 1901, at almost sixteen, he was admitted to the University of Pennsylvania. Lean and erect, he wore his auburn hair in a leonine mass. "I make five friends for my hair for one for myself," he told a friend. The untrammeled hair was a distinguishing feature; with its flecks of red and gold, it was something he flaunted as the sign of his nonconformist poet nature. And even at this time Pound accented his sense of difference with a gold-headed cane or a broad-brimmed hat with a swooping feather. He wanted notice.

As a student he performed rather unremarkably and was generally reserved and quiet. If he was bored in class, he would take out an old tin watch and wind it incessantly. His purpose was to learn as much as he could about poetry in as many languages as possible, but the structure at Penn did not facilitate this. Students were not supposed to know what they wanted; they were led down the proper paths of learning. As a result, Pound recalled, he "fought every regulation and every professor" who tried to make him conform to degree requirements. One of his freshmen instructors remembered him as being abrupt, wanting recognition, and disliked by "teachers and classmates for what seemed like unnecessary eccentricities." He could indeed be impetuous, irrepressible, and sometimes tactless—like the time he declared to one of his professors that Shaw, then seen as an untried radical in theater, was greater than Shakespeare. He played the smart aleck in class, but he could also be oversensitive and emotional: once he defended a poem under attack in class, read it aloud, and was overcome by his own tears.

Such release of feeling made Pound suspect among his classmates. He was reading the Latin poets and Browning and Rossetti, while they were pragmatically preparing for careers in law or medicine. One classmate, Professor Stanley Swartly, recalled that Pound seemed aloof from his peers, indifferent to their concerns. Another, Samuel Wanamaker Fales, saw him as a "lone wolf . . . a shy dreamer who didn't seem to have or want any friends." Still another, Walter Johnson, found him "a sort of screwball very easily duped and the basis of many practical jokes." F. Granville Munson confirmed this, pointing to Pound's lack of guile and his naïveté. Pound lived in the university dormitories only in his sophomore year, but that was time enough for his roommates to pour a pitcher of water on his cot as a trick, to send him out in freezing snow to fetch a doctor for a student feigning to be sick, and ultimately to duck him in a muddy lily pond. The ducking incident was caused by Pound's refusal to accept the conventional code established by his fellow students: the rule was that no freshman could wear loud clothing, especially socks, and Pound's were red.

Pound did meet one friend who shared his interests, a medical student named William Carlos Williams. Williams had gone to Horace Mann High School and had been admitted directly to medical school. The youngest student in his class, he had chosen to attend the University of Pennsylvania because his grandmother lived in West Philadelphia. Williams was fascinated by the extent and seriousness of Pound's literary commitment, his decision to devote his life to poetry. The two young men played chess, tennis, and billiards. Williams found Pound to be a "brilliant talker and thinker" who often seemed to disguise his lively intelligence with the mask of a "laughing boor" or some other unbearably artificial mood. Yet his new friend was the "essence of optimism" and had a "cast-iron faith." Writing to his mother, Williams added that Pound was too proud to try to please people, that he was full of "conceits and affectation." As a result "not one person in a thousand likes him and a great many people detest him."

Pound was importunate, demanding and persistent in his views: Williams wrote Burton Hessler, a mutual friend, that "he might as well agree with Ez because in the end you'll have to from sheer exhaustion." In his autobiography Williams remembered Pound's "painful self-consciousness," a trait that became pronounced whenever Pound attempted to read his poems to Williams. His voice trailed off and became inaudible, as if Pound was finally content with communing only with himself. Williams noted that he could tolerate Pound only on occasion, that he would get "fed to the gills with him after a few days." For Williams, Pound was often "brilliant but an ass," and even if Pound had an "inexhaustible patience" and an "infinite depth" of sympathy and imagination, he could also be neglectful, catty, vicious, and posturing.

In the spring of 1903 Pound played a role as part of the chorus in Euripides' *Iphigenia Among the Taurians,* performed in Greek at the Philadelphia Academy of Music. Williams remembered his friend dressed in a toga and blond wig, waving his arms and heaving "massive breasts in ecstasies of extreme emotion." That spring Pound also played with the college chess team and took fencing lessons from the university coach. Fencing, with its historic place in the courtly tradition Pound was to study, with its lunging, parrying, thrusting, and attack, was to become an important index of Pound's personal style: one of his first books is called *Ripostes,* the term for the quick retaliatory thrust in fencing. William Carlos Williams was on the University of Pennsylvania fencing team, and one day when he came to visit Pound in Wyncote was challenged to defend himself with one of Homer's walking sticks. Ezra attacked relentlessly, almost succeeding in dislocating Williams's eye, an event that made Williams wonder whether his friend could be trusted.

Pound's parents may have also distrusted certain of Pound's choices at this time, and some of his new Philadelphia friends. They encouraged him to transfer to Hamilton College in upstate New York, a small school that promised a more controlled environment. In his first two years at the University of Pennsylvania his grades had been only average. Basically shy and isolated, he was spending time at the Philadelphia home of William Brooke Smith, an art student and painter whose awareness of currents in contemporary art stimulated Pound. Tall, dark, graceful, and consumptive, Smith, who died very young in 1908, attracted a circle of artistic friends, a fast set who alarmed Pound's staid mother. It was Smith who introduced Pound to the London aestheticism of the 1890s, to Pater and Wilde's affectations on the self-sufficiency of art. While his parents were working charitably among the children and the poor in the Italian section of Philadelphia, their son was consorting with nascent bohemians. Smith and his circle clearly impressed Pound, and he dedicated his first book of poems, *A Lume Spento,* to Smith, as "Dreamer of Dreams."

Hamilton College afforded the advantage of country seclusion, an intimate setting with a small, closely supervised student population of "the right sort." Reverend Carlos Chester had gone to Hamilton and recommended it to Isabel Pound. The Loomises, Homer's mother's family, came from the area, but more important for Pound's parents was Chester's assurance that Hamilton provided a proper Christian atmosphere. The college president, Melancthon Woolsey Stryker, was a red-faced clergyman who preached to his two hundred undergraduates at Sunday services. Stryker could be insulting, disparaging President Theodore Roosevelt in one of his angry sermons, and his pugnaciously bluff, impatient, and cutting manner may have influenced Pound.

Admitted as a special student in the fall of 1903, Pound was immediately suspect to the other students because he arrived accompanied by his mother. He at once was considered wealthy and spoiled, a false impression fostered by the overbearing presence of Isabel as well as the accommodations she found—because of his late enrollment, only the most expensive suites in the dormitory were available. Actually, Pound was frequently short of funds and had to appeal to his father for assistance.

The Hamilton students were all fraternity members and on a first-name basis with one another. As a transfer student, Pound was an interloper, and he was denied admission into the one fraternity in which he evinced interest. Freshmen were routinely hazed at Hamilton; if unlucky enough, they could be cornered and painted green by upperclassmen. According to local legend, Pound's room was stripped and all his possessions were piled on his bed which was moved onto the college quadrangle. This, like the ducking in the lily pond, was a public reminder of Pound's difference, a humiliating denunciation of the outsider.

Pound's fellow students regarded him as a restless oddball; he was characterized as nervously rushing with a long stride while declaiming the poetic virtues of Dante. The only other nonfraternity member in his dormitory, Claudius Hand, stated that Pound would frequently wake him in the middle of the night to read him his poems which he would then shred into a wastebasket. It was the sign of a melodramatic intensity his classmates could hardly comprehend.

At Hamilton, Pound's professors became his peers, and he had many long talks after classes with them which continued on into the night. Concentrating on language, he took two thirds of his course work in French, Italian, Spanish, and German. William Pierce Shepherd, formal, reserved, cadaverous, squinting with suspicion but an able medieval scholar who generously responded when he met a willing student, introduced Pound to Dante and the Provençal troubadors, which became his basic interests for the next decade. Reverend Joseph Darling Ibbotson—known to the students as "Bib," as Pound became known as "Bib's pride"—professor of English and Hebrew, introduced Pound to Anglo-Saxon. It was during one of their long talks that Pound conceived the idea of a long epic poem about history that would become *The Cantos.*

At the beginning of his first year at Hamilton, Pound considered careers in law and on Wall Street (several of his Wadsworth cousins were prominent New York stockbrokers) and then the diplomatic service because of his love of foreign languages. Teachers like Shepherd and Ibbotson inspired him to pursue an advanced degree and teaching. He was writing some of the poems that would find their way into his first volumes, and although he was not sure that he had yet found an appropriate voice, he already considered himself a poet. Instead of drinking beer with fraternity brothers, he was reading omnivorously and forming his own taste. He wrote to his mother that he would continue to study Dante, that there was no "phenomenon of any importance in the lives of men and nations that you cannot measure with the rod of Dante's allegory."

Pushed on by Professor Shepherd, Pound devoted himself to his study of Provençal, and in his senior year translated "Belangal Alba," the oldest extant poem of the region. The poem appeared in the *Hamilton Literary Magazine,* and its stress on early rising and opening gates, as well as the dangers of voyaging and ambush, seemed an apt poetic beginning:

> Dawn light, o'er sea and height, riseth bright,
> Passeth vigil, clear shineth on the night.
>
> They be careless of the gates, delaying,
>   Whom the ambush glides to hinder
> Whom I warn and cry to, praying,
>
>   'Arise!'

Pound was to spend years deciphering, translating, and describing Provençal poetry, the songs and ballads performed by wandering minstrels in the courts of the South of France in the period between the end of the Middle Ages and the early Renaissance. He would see the troubadors, the first poets to write after the Dark Ages, as beginning the modern period while at the same time reaffirming the more pagan consciousness of the Greeks. Provençal poetry was important, Pound believed, because verse and music were still united and the connection to the classical world was still strong. It was "a radiant world" he wrote in his essay on Guido Cavalcanti, an Italian contemporary of Dante's, "where one thought cuts through another with clean edge." In the way that Robert Browning mined the Italian Renaissance, Pound used Provence as subject matter and code of values for his poetry. The world of twelfth- and thirteenth-century Provence suffused his

early poems, sometimes detrimentally subsuming his own voice. The Provençal troubadors (the old French word for poetical composition is *trobar*,
which literally meant "to find") wrote their poetry to deny medieval asceti-
cism of flesh and intelligence, and as the celebration of delight in beauty.
Troubador poetry was courtly, not only because it was addressed to an
aristocratic audience but because it often was an appeal to love through
grace and courtship. The relationship between the troubador and his lady
generated a special intensity, a psychic tension possibly leading to divine
vision or transcendental understanding of the world and of the lovers' place
in it. Pound connected the troubadors with late medieval heretics, men who
could still claim that religious impulse was connected to sensual experience
and not to be uniformly governed by a church based on bodily denial. He
made of the troubador legacy a ritual, practically a religion of itself though
much more pagan than Christian in outlook. As T. S. Eliot suggested later in
his 1928 introduction to Pound's *Selected Poems*, "if one can readily penetrate
the life of another age then one is really penetrating one's own." Pound, in
his absolute absorption of the poetry of Provence, as Eliot recognized, was
"giving the original through himself" and in turn was "finding himself
through the original."

4. YOUNG LOVES

At Hamilton his estrangement from the other students had freed him
for his own concerns, and he had seriously tried to master all there was to
know about the history and art of poetry. Still, he was not a hermit. He
wrote to William Carlos Williams that he had met a young woman, Viola
Baxter, with whom he had become infatuated and "who made hell home-
like for me during my exile in upper New York." He continued to write to
her for years.

A more significant instance of young love was his attachment to Hilda
Doolittle, a fifteen-year-old schoolgirl whom he met in his first year at the
University of Pennsylvania. The occasion was a Halloween night party
(Pound had just turned sixteen the night before) and he wore a green
Tunisian robe he had acquired on his first trip to Europe four years earlier.
Hilda could not help but notice the young man's bronze-gold hair, his green
eyes. Williams had remarked that meeting Pound was like the difference
between B.C. and A.D., but it was even more momentous for Hilda. The
friendship simmered with meetings in a tree house built by one of Hilda's
brothers, with the heat of furtive adolescent embraces and declarations, with
country walks where Hilda, ever careless in her dress, leaped over fences in
fields and ran in rain, invoking the gods as in some ancient ritual of purification. For Hilda it was first love, which, as she herself remarked, can never

be overestimated; their meetings were marked with the "significance of the first *demi-vierge* embraces."

The relationship was complicated by the friendly rivalry of Williams and the youthfulness of all three important poets discovering the world and the work that lay before them. Of the three, Pound was most certain of his direction and he was already forming ideas about the nature of poetry. Hilda and Williams were still inchoate poets, musing about the words they might someday release, prodded and instigated by Pound. Most of Pound's encouragement to Hilda was epistolary: when he transferred to Hamilton, the friendship naturally tempered and cooled, though it resumed when he registered for graduate study at the University of Pennsylvania. Pound spent the summer of 1905 employed by the town of Wyncote, working on tax records, a "profitable graft" he detested but one with certain private compensations like "strewing ink over everything," he confessed to Viola Baxter. In his free time he was translating Latin poetry, Martial's epigrams transformed into American slang. As he explained to Viola Baxter, he had "spent four years learning to be a college man and it seems to be the only thing I can do." Presently, he added, the choice seemed to be between graduate work and "an insane asylum although maybe that isn't so very different." He was to discover the difference forty years later.

Hilda had by then become a full disciple. Instead of concentrating on her own classes at Bryn Mawr, she began an informal tutorial with Pound in the Greek and Latin classics. Hilda's father was a professor of astronomy at the University of Pennsylvania and director of the observatory which was situated in Upper Darby, where the Doolittles lived. Upper Darby at that time was very rural, ideal for long country rambles with many open fields and lightly wooded areas. All breathless impatience, Hilda was provocatively indifferent to propriety. Williams saw her as a bizarre beauty, tall, willowy, angular, hair in bangs, with a peculiarly unaffected grace as if "walking on the tips of grass stems." Wistful, dreamy, detached from the immediate, according to her Bryn Mawr classmate Marianne Moore, she seemed to lean forward following her long strong jaw as if resisting a high wind, her body an expression of the same kind of eagerness that invigorated Pound.

Hilda revealed to Williams that she was attracted to the odd and lonely, to "people that feel themselves apart from the whole—that are somehow lost and torn and inclined to become embittered by that very loneliness." She commented in her memoir of Pound, *End to Torment,* that it was "his curious beauty that made people hate him." She saw him as "immensely sophisticated, immensely superior, immensely rough-and-ready," a man unlike her brothers or their friends. Nursing a buried sadness that would surface only in later years, struggling with a repression that she symbolically denied by splashing ink over her clothes to feel free when writing, she was galvanized by Pound's exuberance. "Haie! Haie! Io," he would call to her. He named her his dryad, his wood nymph, and encouraged her wildness. In *Hilda's Book*, a book of twenty-five poems he wrote for her and bound himself in vellum, poems of mostly unconvincing and inflated labor and tenuous passion, there are two lines that suggest what Pound wanted her to become, a mythological impossibility perhaps only imaginable by the very young.

> She hath some tree born spirit of the wood
> About her, and the wind is in her hair.

Hilda's Book was one visible reminder of Pound's love, but it also exists as a record of his apprentice efforts:

> I strove a little book to make for her,
> Quaint bound, as 'twere in parchment very old,
> That all my dearest words of her should hold,

Filled with the burden of an inexpressible and thwarted love, the twenty-five poems to Hilda are flushed with tentative and youthful passions set in the context of a medieval heroic heraldry showing the influences of William Morris and Dante Gabriel Rossetti. The circumstances Pound imagines for his lovers, however, are not significant enough to support the pomp of some of the language. The lovers' world is nebulous, their embraces less felt as a presence than the murmuring, whirring wind that accompanies them, or the spells of wood faeries, fluttering wings, or trembling hands. In a world of disembodied spirits seeking earthly incarnation, Pound seems trapped in the "Celtic twilight" mood of William Butler Yeats's poems of the 1890s, and indeed throughout Pound shows his imitation of the honeyed sentiments and rococo mannerisms of the 1890s. At times Pound does show signs of the kind of rich, orotund sweep of sound that one hears in Swinburne:

> As mown
> Grain of the gold brown harvest from seed sown
> Bountifully amid spring's emeralds fair
> So is our reaping now.

Although often the diction is florid, the language vague, strained, and sometimes inflated and clumsy, one poem, "The Tree," shows a promise of his later talent:

> I stood still and was a tree amid the wood
> Knowing the truth of things unseen before
> Of Daphne and the laurel bow
> And that god-feasting couple old

That grew elm-oak amid the wold
'Twas not until the gods had been
Kindly entreated and been brought within
Unto the hearth of their hearts' home
That they might do this wonder thing.
Nathless I have been a tree amid the wood
And many new things understood
That were rank folly to my head before.

The tree stands as an expression of Pound's developing paganism. His whole life became a challenge to contemporary Western systems, and he decried modern religion as the handmaiden of those systems. He based his values on more ancient sources, classical Chinese or pagan Greek. Actually, the notion that divinity could be reached or perceived through nature was central to the nineteenth-century romantic thought Pound rejected. Such a notion, also, is the continuation of perennial animist belief prevalent before churches and high priests, when man was still nomadically dependent on nature's rhythms. In his allusion to Daphne's metamorphosis into a laurel tree when pursued by Apollo, Pound draws on Ovid, and behind the controlling, quiet assertiveness of his poem is his fascination with the element of story (and thus history or "his" "story") that lies behind myth. In a note on the poem Pound commented on the formative embodiments of mythmaking that are basic to the imaginative process leading to the poem, and his comments seem to be a touchstone for much of his subsequent poetry:

The first myths arose when a man walked into "nonsense," that is to say, when some very vivid and undeniable adventure befell him, and he told someone else who called him a liar. Thereupon, after bitter experience, perceiving that no one could understand what he meant when he said that he "turned into a tree," he made a myth—a work of art, that is—an impersonal or objective story woven out of his own emotion, as the nearest equation that he was capable of putting into words. The story, perhaps, then gave rise to a weaker copy of his emotion in others, until there arose a cult, a company of people who could understand each other's nonsense about the gods.

Pound was "wonderfully in love," according to Williams, who felt Pound exaggerated Hilda's beauty ridiculously. But Hilda and Ezra were young lovers learning about love and, as is usually the case, both playful and dreadfully serious about the process. Hilda declared in a letter to Williams that she had decided to dedicate her life to Pound "who has been, beyond all others, torn and lonely—and ready to crucify himself yet more for the sake of helping all." The couple met at dances and parties and at musical

evenings at the Pound home in Wyncote. Pound was writing his daily sonnet while Hilda, with less facility, was chiseling out a few lines every few
days which she would timidly proffer for criticism. Though they had poetry
in common, their major impediment was Professor Doolittle. A tall, gaunt
man, his main interests in life were the precise measurements he made at the
observatory of the earth's oscillations. Seldom, even at dinner, Williams
recalled, did he ever focus "on anything nearer, physically, than the moon."
The good professor had once absentmindedly stepped off a moving trolley
car believing he had reached his destination, but he still had enough presence of mind to suspect that Pound was not the perfect suitor. In *End to
Torment,* strangely revealing title, Hilda remembers her father interrupting
an embrace:

> We were curled up together in an armchair when my father found
> us, I was "gone." I wasn't there. I disentangled myself. I stood up;
> Ezra stood beside me. It seems we must have swayed trembling.
> . . . My father said, "Mr. Pound, I don't say there was anything
> wrong this time. I will not forbid you the house, but I will ask you
> not to come so often."

She later learned that her father had disliked Pound from the start, that he
had burned some of Pound's letters. But Hilda herself knew that practically
the love was hopeless: when Pound suggested elopement, she asked how he
would support her. Isabel Pound liked Hilda and would have accepted her;
the opposition was from Hilda's parents. When the two families were finally
gathered for dinner at the Doolittle home, Pound baffled Professor and
Mrs. Doolittle by reciting his poems after dinner. He had appeared hatless
and without a tie, his shirt open at the neck like some young Byron on the
loose. He wore tortoiseshell eyeglasses and was determined to relieve the
suffocating atmosphere of Sunday dinner with the spectacle of himself. Unsympathetic earlier, Professor Doolittle was then even more apprehensive.
When Hilda raised the possibility of Ezra as a serious suitor, Professor
Doolittle contemptuously dismissed her with the rebuke that Pound was
"nothing but a nomad."

Pound remained embedded in Hilda's consciousness, and she followed
him to England a few years later. But he had never been quite as faithful as
she had. While seeing her, he was still writing to Viola Baxter and beginning to court Mary Moore, a young woman from Trenton, New Jersey,
whom he had met when working as a tutor on a farm in the summer of
1907. Mary Moore lived in a large stone town house opposite the New
Jersey State House and her father was president of the street railway system
of Trenton.

Mary Moore was carefree, frank, and healthy, a small-town innocent
without the tortured insecurities that afflicted Hilda Doolittle. Pound took

her canoeing on the Delaware River, on long walks and picnics in the woods. He claimed in a letter to her that he was the greatest poet of his age but that he would prefer to sit in her drawing room than be admitted to red-covered reference books. In another letter he declared that he had loved her passionately. There is little doubt that he loved her romantically, and that she found his style intriguing but suspect: he would visit her by coming over a balustrade and into her window like some medieval knight rescuing a damsel in distress. Mary Moore, however, was sensible enough to realize that a poet might not be able to give the daughter of the richest man in Trenton what she had been taught to expect. But like Viola Baxter, she was fascinated by Pound and continued to correspond with him.

5. THE WABASH FIASCO

During the period of his courtship of Hilda and Mary Moore, from 1905 to 1907, Pound was taking classes at the University of Pennsylvania. He was still serious as a graduate student, realizing that an academic position might allow him the freedom to continue with his poetry, but he was irreverent and even contentious in class. One of his professors felt that he was an idler and told him he was either a humbug or a genius. As part of the scatology of graduate school, Pound had written and circulated some verse that caricatured certain professors, a fact that when discovered hardly ingratiated him with the graduate faculty. Such acts showed that Pound was ready to disturb, violate, or simply laugh at the decorum that protects pretense in institutional settings. But with such attitudes he would never fit. He reminded Viola Baxter in a letter of his "ancient belief that the world was only a joke." He was full of impudence; "sassiety" was a word he coined for Viola Baxter. He had glimpsed the sources of his own creativity and doubted that they could be sustained in the dryness of academe. Later, in "How to Read," after he had embarked on a lifelong career of denouncing universities, he complained that as a student he had not met a professor "with a view of literature as a whole" and that "the system lacked sense and co-ordination."

Nevertheless, he had some good teachers. Professor Walton Brooks McDaniel introduced him to Catullus and a curt ironic style that had great appeal to the young poet. He studied the romantics with Felix Schelling and Cornelius Weygandt, a professor who had visited Yeats in England and who was responsible for inviting Yeats to the University of Pennsylvania for a reading when Pound was away at Hamilton. The young man worked hard. He wrote Viola Baxter in February that he was studying Spanish when he woke, and Provençal after breakfast. Latin was for midday, French in the late afternoon, Italian after dinner. To relax he played chess, went ice skat-

ing and sledding, and took ten-mile hikes. He received an M.A. after a year
of graduate study, in June of 1906, and was made a Harrison Fellow in
Romantics, a much desired appointment which granted him a five-hundred-
dollar stipend and tuition. He used his stipend to finance another trip to
Europe in the summer of 1906.

He described his adventures in Spain to his former minister, Carlos
Tracy Chester. Velázquez's paintings in Madrid, the blazing scarlet of pop-
pies, stretches of yellow and purple and chalk-white set in reddish brown
soil of irrigated hillsides where water catches the glow of sunset—the colors
of the countryside made him see why Spain was a country of painters. On
his own in Provence, he began to grow in ways that were impossible in
Hamilton or Philadelphia, and to record with a new sharpness in detail:

> I have lain in Rocafixada,
>   level with sunset,
> Have seen the copper come down
>   tingeing the mountains,
> I have seen the fields, pale, clear as an emerald.
> Sharp peaks, high spurs, distant castles.

He returned to study with Professor Hugo Rennert, who had written a
biography of the medieval Spanish playwright Lope de Vega. Pound later
characterized Rennert as an arch academic, a "plaintive falsetto" who pared
his fingernails during his seminar. Writing to Viola Baxter, he remarked that
it was perfectly appropriate that he should scientifically focus on the fool in
Lope de Vega's four hundred plays as a dissertation subject. He was rash
enough to conceive of getting a doctorate in two years, he wrote, and had
spent two hours researching the etymology of the word "genius" that afternoon. But Pound would do more than simply study the fool in Lope de
Vega or in literature generally. It became a role he would often adopt as a
definite strategy, as a means of calling for attention, or indirectly criticizing
convention through burlesque. The role of the fool permitted the release of
Pound's spontaneously rapid judgments; the unpredictability of the fool and
his defiance of acceptable manners and mores caused suspicion and disfavor.

The Harrison Fellowship was customarily awarded for a two-year period; after that, one could expect a part-time teaching appointment in the
university until all requirements for the doctorate were completed. But late
in the spring of 1907, Pound was informed that in his case the fellowship
was nonrenewable. His graduate record had not been brilliant, he had
"spatted with nearly everybody," he admitted to his friend Burton Hessler,
and he had managed to fail a course in the history of literary criticism taught
by the dean of faculty, a person of considerable power who decided fellowship awards. The exact circumstances of Pound's failure are unknown, but
he claimed that he had been the "only student who was making an attempt

to understand the subject" and the only student who was genuinely interested. He had also antagonized and bewildered other members of the graduate faculty and was gradually becoming aware that he might not fit into the university system well enough to get his Ph.D., much less establish a successful academic career.

He had, however, spent the summer of 1907 looking for an academic position and learned, through one of his former teachers at Hamilton, of a possibility at Wabash College. A small Presbyterian school in western Indiana, Wabash was trying to expand its curriculum, enlarging the department of modern languages by adding Spanish to existing French courses. The position was for an instructor, Pound was informed when he was interviewed by Dr. George Lewes Mackintosh, a dour Scotsman with a doctor of divinity degree who was president of the college. Mackintosh was impressed by Pound's three trips to Europe and the recent trip to Spain as a Harrison Fellow. But Mackintosh, who had a reputation for being a shrewd pragmatist, should have anticipated that Pound would have had difficulty accepting the blandness of Crawfordsville, Indiana. Instead, he tempted Pound with the lure of a full professorship in a few years and the duties of a department head in which there were no other members.

The possibility does exist, of course, that no other applicant as qualified as Pound would have chosen to settle in a small town with 8,500 residents and a college population of 150 students. Crawfordsville was a town of stately houses and tree-lined streets but even cigarettes were forbidden. At Wabash, attendance at morning chapel was compulsory and absences noted in the school newspaper. The school was known for its fraternities and its football spirit. The town was so tiny it did not even merit a postman. As far as the possibility of any literary sophistication, the townsfolk took great pride in General Lew Wallace, author of *Ben Hur*, who had lived there.

Something in the confining smallness of Crawfordsville—a matter not just of physical size but of mental scope as well—provoked Pound into flamboyance. He made social visits to fellow faculty with a rum flask in his pocket which he used to fortify his tea. He disdained the usually modest professorial demeanor of his colleagues, the formality of gray trousers, white shirts with stiff collars, and frock coats, and instead wore a soft-collared shirt, a black velvet coat, a floppy wide-brimmed hat after the manner of Whitman, and a malacca cane after that of Whistler. He smoked. For a time Mary Moore sent him cigarettes—Bonhommes Rouges—and when President Mackintosh, whose office was down the hall from Pound's, caught him smoking, he admonished Pound as one would a schoolboy.

To make sure his students were listening, he would say outrageous things in class—religion is useful only to the extent that it popularizes art—and address subjects like graphology, palmistry, and spiritualism at social gatherings. Professor Rollo Walter Brown, who left Wabash for Harvard, thought he saw the signs of the showman and the charlatan in Pound. Another colleague complained that he turned an elementary French class into a course on Dante—one of Pound's three classes had 57 students and he was bored by the prospect of drills and exercises, so he moved the course in the direction of his own pursuits. "I do not teach, I awake," Pound jotted in a manuscript note written on "Histrion," one of the poems he was working on. The comment is suggestive: all of his life, Pound was a firebrand, the man who energizes others, the galvanic spirit. There could be little room for such a man, given the stiff and stuffy decorum of academic life in 1907. Some of the students found him exhibitionistic and self-indulgent and they complained to the dean about his excesses of language.

He wrote Mary Moore that his classes were all over before noon, which left him time for his own poetry and reading, but he hated the prospect of correcting papers four times a week. His letters are in green ink, sometimes in purple, one sign of need for notice, to impress the world with his presence and power. He wrote frequently and she answered flirtatiously, creating the impression that she would be content to marry him and share his life in Crawfordsville. "It will take five years to get caught up with all the things we want to do together," he wrote, recommending that she read William Morris and Yeats, adding that they could live in one room if necessary—Morris's ideal—with a corner for cooking and another for sleeping and another for work. Such Spartan arrangements actually did form the circumstances of Pound's existence for years to come, but Mary Moore was hardly the type to share them.

Pound had met a local painter, a muralist named Fred Nelson Vance, who had studied in Paris and Rome. Vance warned Pound that he would have to marry to be able to stay in Crawfordsville. He sent Mary Moore as an engagement ring a ring given to him as a love token by another woman. Mary Moore responded that she didn't like geniuses and that she was getting engaged to one Oscar Macpherson, a man who was paralyzed and in a wheelchair. She instead married yet another man several years later, but she used the possibility to cool Pound's ardor, perhaps to dismiss him altogether. Pound was stung by this rejection and it made him wilder.

Pound then began to despise his surroundings and his teaching. He wrote that he felt "stranded in a most Godforsakenest area of the middle west," the sixth circle of Dante's desolation, that the college library was utterly useless to him in his work, that he would rather be descended from thieves than a president of Harvard. His name was consistently misspelled as Pounds in the college and town papers. He detested the compulsion of morning chapel and Mackintosh's pious sanctimonies.

He had his Dante and Provençal studies and his work on his own poems to buoy him up. One of them, "In Durance," sounds the plaintive note of his unhappiness:

> And I am homesick
> After mine own kind that know, and feel
> And have some breath for beauty and the arts.

He tried to invent his "own kind," using Fred Vance and some of the painter's friends along with a few interested students as the core of a circle where he could talk and develop ideas. He rented rooms with a private entrance in a curiously shaped house with sloping gables and elaborate Gothic windows. His landlady's sister, a Southern widow in her thirties named Mary Young, came to visit, stayed to work as a nurse, and Pound began to court her. She liked him but she was ten years older and was being courted by President Mackintosh, a widower. Pound used the parlor to entertain Mary Young, and his room for discussions with Vance and interested students and observers who wanted to experience the cosmopolite from the East. Seated on a chair, the others at his feet on the floor, Pound would discourse randomly, criticizing academic life, political institutions, the relation of sexual passion to art, what he saw as philistine values. When these sessions began to last till the early morning hours, his landlady had an excuse to ask him to leave.

In late October, Pound moved into a residence favored by itinerant actors and actresses. Crawfordsville had several theaters that offered live entertainment, often as accompaniment to or interlude for silent films. Here he met an English actress who worked as a male impersonator. The woman's name is unknown, but Pound enjoyed an intermittent relationship with her over the next few months.

His friendship with the male impersonator was to have dire consequences because as a bachelor Pound was violating local propriety. When he was discovered sharing a simple meal with her, tremors rippled through his residence. He described the incident in jocular terms to Burton Hessler, a college friend teaching rhetoric at the University of Michigan:

> Two stewdents found me sharing my meagre repast with the lady-gent impersonator in my privut apartments.
>
> keep it dark and find me a soft immoral place to light in when the she-faculty-wives git hold of that jewcy morsel. Don't write home to me folks. I can prove an alibi from 8 to 12 p.m. and am at present looking for rooms with a minister or some well established member of the facultate. For to this house come all the traveling show folk and I must hie me to a nunnery ere I disrupt the college. Already one delegation of about-to-flunks have awaited on the president to complain erbout me orful langwidge and the number of cigarillos I consume.

Pound was then forced to move again. Just before Thanksgiving he found
rooms in a boardinghouse run by the elder spinster sisters Hall. The previous occupant of his new quarters had been a studiously quiet professor of
Greek who had died in his church pew—no end could be considered more
respectable in Crawfordsville. The Halls were prim and nosy, and friendly
with President Mackintosh, so they allowed Wabash professors into their
house, but decidedly no performers.

Pound spent Thanksgiving alone frying oysters in a chafing dish in his
room and Christmas was equally lonely. He had written in one of the poems
he was composing, "For I am weird untamed/that eat of no man's meat." It
was a cry of the isolated, separate man whose alien nature is both his wound
and the source of his poetry. On a bitterly cold night late in January, he
ventured forth in a blizzard to mail a letter and ran into the English male
impersonator—later Pound claimed that she had no lodging, that she was
homeless, cold, hungry, and penniless—and invited her to spend the night
in his bed. In the morning, he left to conduct his eight o'clock class and the
suspicious Misses Halls, having heard disturbances in the night, found the
woman in his rooms. Pound was summoned by President Mackintosh. He
argued that he had acted out of charity, that he had remained on the floor in
his coat through the night. But Mackintosh had heard enough about Pound,
and there was the added factor of the rivalry for Mary Young, who was still
friendly with Pound.

Pound was paid till the end of the semester and dismissed in disgrace.
He wrote Hilda Doolittle, Mary Moore, and Viola Baxter that he had assisted a stranded young woman in a storm in the night. "I'm so damn
natural and trusting and innocent," he wrote Mary Moore, "that I create
scandal about my ways continually." The Wabash incident was Pound's final
rupture with respectability. Traumatized by the sudden termination of his
position, Pound immediately began to project a benevolent myth of courtly
action for the sake of the women he was still courting in letters. He had
begun to believe in and live such a myth, which was fostered by his studies
in Provençal. Now he was being rejected by a puritan world, and as a result
he would permanently distrust social convention and declare himself an
artist.

"They say I am bisexual and given to unnatural lust," he wrote to
Hilda Doolittle. In *End to Torment* she noted that Pound's reputation at
home had been ruined because of his dismissal: "Almost everyone I knew in
Philadelphia was against him after that Wabash debacle." Much of Pound's
subsequent bitterness over it and his earlier failure to convince his graduate
professors that he was worthy of an advanced degree was released in a
steady stream of denigration of universities which persisted for half a century. For Pound, universities existed to "perpetuate routine and stupidity."
All any American college would do for a man of letters, he declared, is to
"ask him to go away without breaking the silence."

LONDON:
ART FOR ITS OWN SAKE

Go, my songs, to the lonely and the unsatisfied,
Go also to the nerve-racked, go to the enslaved-by-convention,
Bear to them my contempt for their oppressors,
Go as a great wave of cool waters,
Bear my contempt of oppressors.
                              "Commission" (Lustra, *1916)*

1. WITH TAPERS QUENCHED

In February of 1908 Pound left for Europe, where he would "break the silence" for the next four decades with a voice more strident and contentious than would any American contemporary. With only his Wabash severance pay to support him, a matter of some eighty dollars (equivalent to about a thousand today), he took a cattle boat, the least expensive type of freighter because of the noise and smells. Disembarking in Gibraltar in April, he met a Jewish man who helped him find accommodations and work as a guide, and who took him to a synagogue, where Pound watched a rabbi pass around a snuffbox after a ceremony. The snuff was passed to Pound— the event itself curious only in the light of Pound's subsequent anti-Semitism, an ironic communion between a people who were forced to become international wanderers and the nomadic poet. From Gibraltar he sent poems to *Harper's Magazine* and began writing fiction which he hoped to be able to sell.

By summer he was in Venice, the place that had most impressed him on his trip to Europe with Aunt Frank. Venice was an inspirational choice for the young poet, a fantasy of Renaissance embroidery in architecture, the meeting of Byzantine grace and baroque intricacy. The labyrinth of canals, winding streets, bridges and alleys, the lapping presence of the sea and its salty tang in the air, the mysteriously curving and angled houses with their elongated windows and their blistered façades of orange, yellow, and red, the Tintorettos and Titians on church ceilings, the glittering reflections of the changing light off the water at sunset, the poise and balance and rhythm of the gondoliers—all were both stimulating and entrancing. Pound found himself on a stage setting more intriguing than anything he had ever imagined. It seemed as if time had forgotten to proceed after the Renaissance. Though the temporal world seemed blocked out to Pound, just to the northwest the Austrian Empire was about to annex Bosnia and Herzegovina, two Serbian provinces that would become one of the aggravating seeds of World War I, a major source of loss for Pound and most of the writers of his generation. Nearby in Milan, socialists were marching and farmers were striking in the countryside. In Forli, a young journalist named Benito Mussolini was writing blistering editorials for *Avanti,* a socialist newspaper. But Venice seemed insulated, protected from the world, an Atlantean fantasy surrounded by the lapping waters of the Adriatic. Pound had chosen it almost as an act of literary tribute to the writers who had preceded him there: Byron, Melville, Ruskin. He later recalled it in *The Cantos:*

> And the waters richer than glass
> Bronze gold, the blaze over the silver,
> Dye-pots in the torch-light,
> The flash of wave under prows,
> And the silver beaks rising and crossing.
>   Stone trees, white and rose-white in the darkness,
> Cypress there by the towers,
>   Drift under hulls in the night.

(Canto XVII)

Pound spent the summer obsessively exploring, observing, recording—the work of the poet. He lived over a bakery near the San Vio bridge in Dorsoduro, then nearby across from a gondolier repair shop in San Trovaso, a ten-minute walk over the Accademia bridge to the center at the Piazza San Marco. Life was frugal: morning bread and coffee, baked sweet potatoes at a corner stall for lunch, barley soup—*ministra d'orgo*—for dinner. From home, he heard that the poems he had submitted to *Harper's* had been rejected without explanation, discouraging news. Worried about his dwindling resources, he tried to get work as a gondolier but realized he could never learn to maneuver a thirty-six-foot craft in the narrow canals. He found no employment but worked on a novel and several short stories—soon to be discarded—and on his poems. One of them, "Alma Sol Veneziae," indicates the sustenance Venice was providing:

> Thou that has given me back
> Strength for the journey,

> Thou has given me
> Heart for the tourney,
> O sun venezian,
> Thou that through all my veins
> Hast bid the life-blood run . . .

Some of Pound's time was spent on the steps of the old customshouse at the edge of Dorsoduro, pensively gazing at the water, sensing the plenitude of the ocean in one direction and, in the other, San Marco and Venice, the monument to human ingenuity built by artisans into a living museum, a city reclaimed from the sea. More time was spent reworking the poems he had written at Wabash and writing new ones. He had come to Venice because he thought he could arrange to print a small book of these poems for very little money. But he was uncertain about the quality of his poems and wavering in his judgment. In *The Cantos* he remembered contemplating pitching his poems into the canal and choosing another life:

> by the soap-smooth stone posts where San Vio
> meets with il Canal Grande
> between Salviati and the house that was of Don Carlos
> shd/I chuck the lot into the tide-water?
>   le bozze A Lume Spento/
>   and by the column of Todero
> shd/I shift to the other side
>   or wait 24 hours . . .

(Canto LXXVI)

He admitted to Viola Baxter that his poems were not good enough for the best magazines, that they were full of raptures and childish enthusiasms. One of those enthusiasms, the accomplished concert pianist Katherine Ruth Heyman, whom he had originally met in Philadelphia in 1904, almost became the "other side," the route abandoning poetry for the world. Heyman was fifteen years older than Pound and she specialized in contemporary music, performing Scriabin and Charles Ives in later years. It is clear that "Her Ladyship," as Pound referred to her in a letter to Viola Baxter, held the upper hand in their relationship. Heyman had introduced Pound to Swedenborg, to Balzac's *Seraphita,* yoga, and Freud, and she also knew many people in London. He was attracted to her potential star status and believed he could become her manager. He may have fallen in love with her, especially because she took such an interest in him: "Why the devil do I love so many people so much?" he complained to Mary Moore. Katherine Heyman had already given Pound her mother's pearl wedding ring as a token of engagement when they first met in 1904, but no matter what sort of fling they might have enjoyed, she was to be married to her art and could never have maintained any sort of permanent relationship with Pound. Furthermore, his parents wrote that they disapproved of Miss Heyman, confusing Pound all the more as to what direction to take. In the middle of one night, dreaming of vanity, he shaved off one of his red muttonchop sideburns and was obligated then to remove the other before breakfast. All at once he was writing letters to concert halls, booking Heyman on a world tour. He sent his friend Burton Hessler notices for her appearances in Berlin and Wiesbaden, offering him a commission if he could arrange a concert at Ann Arbor, where he was teaching rhetoric. He added that Heyman was the "greatest livin' she pyanist" but warned Hessler not to tell his parents what he was doing lest they think that he had "gone clean crazy instead of partway." Pound sent a letter to the Paris edition of the *Herald Tribune,* held a press conference in Venice, and then suddenly his services were no longer required. Had the young man been too brash, too importunate, too demanding, perhaps?

His career as a concert impresario over, he was freed again for his poetry and his plans to publish a book. An old family friend, the Reverend Alex Robertson, was the minister in the Presbyterian church in Venice and he recommended an inexpensive printer to Pound and also cashed his final Wabash check. One hundred copies of the seventy-two-page *A Lume Spento* were printed for eight dollars on paper that had been left over from a supply used for a history of the church. Pound's title, translated as "With Tapers Quenched," was taken from Dante's *Purgatorio.* Dante's line refers to Manfred, son of the Holy Roman Emperor Frederick II, whose remains were transported from his place of death "with tapers quenched" because of his heretical views. Pound completed it by midsummer and sent copies to William Carlos Williams, Hilda Doolittle, and other friends and forty copies to his father to try to get reviews. "The American reprint," he wrote to his father over the signature "Modest Violet," "has got to be worked by kicking up such a hell of a row with genuine and faked reviews that Scribner or somebody can be brought to see the sense of making a reprint. I shall write a few myself and get someone to sign 'em."

When Whitman self-published *Leaves of Grass* in 1855, he wrote three of its five reviews, so Pound was following in the American tradition of the self-made man when he appraised his own book:

> Wild and haunting stuff, absolutely poetic, original, imaginative, passionate, and spiritual. Those who do not consider it crazy may well consider it inspired. Coming after the trite and decorous verse of most of our decorous poets, this poet seems like a minstrel of Provence at a suburban musical evening. . . . The unseizable magic of poetry is in the queer paper volume, and words are no good describing it.

The review appeared in the *Evening Standard* in London, and Pound followed it in person, realizing that London was where he would have to establish his reputation as a poet. He wanted to meet Yeats, whom he considered the leading figure writing in the English language, and he wanted to get to know as many other poets as possible. Pound had a mystical belief in the tradition of high letters: "The light moves as per apostolic succession," he wrote many years later. London was the center of literary life; Henry James had been *the* American expatriate in residence for forty years. The British were known for their insularity, but among artists, according to art critic Clive Bell, there was a receptivity to new ways of thinking and feeling in the early part of the twentieth century. His wife, Vanessa, Virginia Woolf's sister, impressed by the vitality of feminism and Fabian socialism, felt that "a great new freedom seemed about to come." Pound arrived in London as one of its avatars.

2. APOSTOLIC SUCCESSION

Pound struck hard for the new, especially as he tried to redefine what a poem could do and how it could appear on the page. At first the way was difficult. There was before anything the problem of finances and dwindling resources. Almost all of his money, not very much to begin with, had been spent in Venice on three months' food and lodging and *A Lume Spento*. He moved from one boardinghouse to the next; one had only cold water, another execrable food. His first few weeks in London were grim, and he wrote home for assistance. He raised a tiny amount in a pawnshop, sold some of his books, and borrowed another small sum from a contralto, a friend of Katherine Heyman. He sent poems to a group of American magazines—*Harper's* again, *Century, Scribner's*—but they were all rejected. His parents sent some money but pleaded with him to return to Philadelphia to find work.

At the end of September, tipped off by a family friend that there might be a lecturing position at the Regent Street Polytechnic, a vocational school which had recently expanded to offer cultural programs for the working classes, Pound proposed a series of talks on the development of the literature of southern Europe. His application was accepted and the series of six lectures were scheduled for January and February. He found inexpensive lodging near the Polytechnic at 48 Langham Street, only a penny bus ride from the British Museum, where he intended to prepare for his lectures.

He was still very much alone in London that fall, with virtually no friends or contacts. He received a letter from William Carlos Williams, who commented that *A Lume Spento* seemed flawed by bitterness and a spirit of vagabondage. Pound was by then assembling a new collection of poems from the best of what he had written in Venice and was very conscious of his own literary direction. His reply to Williams, written in late October, and the first of many letters to follow, offers a clear statement of his early aims:

> To me the short so-called dramatic lyric—at any rate the sort of thing I do—is the poetic part of a drama the rest of which (to me the prose part) is left to the reader's imagination or implied or set in a short note. I catch the character I happen to be interested in at the moment he interests me, usually a moment of song, self-analysis, or sudden understanding or revelation. And the rest of the play would bore me and presumably the reader. I paint the man as I *conceive* him. Et voilà tout!

He agreed that *A Lume Spento* did have its "gloomy and disagreeable" moments but argued that no collection of "mild pretty verses" would convince any publisher or critic that "I happen to be a genius and deserve audience." Finally, he added for Williams a list of four basic goals which would guide his vision:

1. To paint the thing as I see it.
2. Beauty.
3. Freedom from didacticism.
4. It is only good manners if you repeat a few other men to at least do it better or more briefly. Utter originality is of course out of the question.

Practically on his twenty-third birthday the *Evening Standard* printed his poem "Histrion," one of the poems he had written in Venice and kept in a notebook he called San Trovaso. "Histrion" offers an early version of Pound's notion of persona, the adoption of a mask through which the poet speaks to dramatize an historical, emotional, or ideological reality: "And yet I know, how that the souls of all men great/At times pass through us." It is an exaggerated sentiment, and Pound wrote Mary Moore that the poem caused people "to tremble for my 'mental balance' as well as my respectability." In "Histrion" Pound was extending Browning's device of dramatic monologue—letting a character speak directly without an intermediary or explanation. Persona, he wrote Mary Moore, was like the "first absolute surrender, the first utter overwhelming annihilation of self flowing in and existing thru and for another." Its charm and holiness, Pound added, were like love, and what interested him as a poet was the fusion of art and ecstasy —"the sensation of the soul in ascent," which could be expressed in a poem. Persona becomes a central element in Pound's early work, and "Histrion" presents it with a transcendental notion of the literary tradition:

> Thus am I Dante for a space and am
> One François Villon, ballad-lord and thief,

> Or am such holy ones I may not write
> Lest blasphemy be writ against my name;
> This for an instant and the flame is gone.

As a young man Pound frequently referred to himself as a genius and at this time saw himself as connected to a great chain of poets whose lessons he could master and who could speak through him in his poems. Much of Pound's most successful early work was imitative—he had the best ear among poets of his generation and could mimic to perfection. Of course, he had his own taste and his struggle during the early years of his apprenticeship, from 1908 through 1912, was to forge his own voice.

While part of this struggle had to do with how well he understood what had preceded him, another part required criticism. The major poet in his own country in the nineteenth century had been Walt Whitman—though this was hardly recognized at the time—and Pound set to work on an essay explaining his position regarding Whitman. Like Dante, Whitman wrote in the vernacular, and though it took Pound years to learn how to use a natural idiom with facility, he knew from the start that this was the right direction. Pound claimed that for the first time, because he was in Europe, he was able to perceive what Whitman was trying to do. He was able to read him, but not always with pleasure:

> He *is* America. His crudity is an exceeding great stench, but it *is* America. He is the hollow place in the rock that echoes with his time.
> He *does* "chaunt the crucial stage" and he is the "voice triumphant." He is disgusting. He is an exceedingly nauseating pill, but he accomplished his mission.

Pound's problem with Whitman was with his unabashed romanticism, his indulgence in Self without filters or persona, his rapturous release. From Whitman he would learn a great lesson; however, it took him years to fully master it. The braggadocio, the extravagant and often magnanimous air, the refreshing though sometimes insolent familiarity, the naturalness of Whitman's direct address to the reader all influenced Pound and helped him deflate the literary quality, the bookishness of his poems. Pound realized that the "vital part of my message, taken from the sap and fibre of America, is the same as his." Pound used the same image of wood and sap a few years later when he wrote "A Pact," a poem of reconciliation with Whitman. As he admitted in his essay, he was a Whitman who had learned how to wear a collar and a dress shirt.

Just before the end of 1908, he arranged for the printing of a hundred copies of fifteen of the Venice poems which he called *A Quinzaine for This Yule.* Two weeks later one of the publishers with whom Pound had left *A*

Lume Spento. Elkin Mathews, agreed to reprint *A Quinzaine* and to publish a larger collection to be called *Personae.* In January of 1909 Pound saw both *A Quinzaine* and his lecture series advertised in the London papers and felt that at least in some small sense he had arrived. Facetiously he wrote his friend Hessler that he was the author of two books of "unintelligible worse" and a lecturer on the "Devil upment of literachoor in Southern Yourup." He delivered the six lectures on Thursday afternoons and concentrated on Provençal song and Renaissance lyricists who used Latin. When the series was over late in February, Pound began to worry about whether the Polytechnic would allow him to begin a more elaborate series in the fall and how he would support himself until then.

3. LITERARY LONDON

In the meanwhile he intended to discover literary London. The leading figures were James, Conrad, and Hardy. H. G. Wells and Arnold Bennett were the stars of current fiction, and Shaw the theater. There was no dominant poet: Swinburne had done his best work years before and was soon to die in 1909. Alfred Austin, the poet laureate, characterized the lack of affect of Edwardian poetry. A cock sparrow of a man, formerly a journalist specializing in foreign affairs, it was said that when butlers announced his name, nothing entered the room. Elkin Mathews had a bookshop which was known as a writer's place, and he invited Pound to browse through his shelves to become more familiar with the poetry being written at that time. But unfortunately Pound had arrived during a lull. Through Mathews, he met Maurice Hewlett, a poet who had written several successful popular romances, one of which was set in medieval Provence and naturally interested Pound. Through Hewlett he met Henry Newbolt, a poetry critic then lecturing in the Royal Society of Literature, one of the "crusted lice," Pound later declared, an "advocate of corpse language." Pound was being a bit unfair to Newbolt, who had stressed to him the importance for future poets of expressing sensation rather than emotion, which would become a key modernist principle. He also met Laurence Binyon, another would-be poet, who was an expert on Oriental art and who worked in the British Museum. Binyon's cousin Stephen Phillips was then being touted as a great poet and dramatist, a reputation that soon fizzled. Both Binyon and Hewlett were translators of Dante, creating for Pound a commonality of interest, although their poetry was too old-fashioned for him to admire.

In January, Pound met a lover of Greek lyric poetry, a young Australian poet named Frederic Manning. Another mannered and stilted poet, Manning lived in the country with his former tutor, Arthur Galton, then a vicar. Manning encouraged Pound's troubador research and was willing to listen to him read his poems. "Are you never coming up to London again even if it is only to be filled with deep doubts about my sanity," Pound wrote in February. He had a most disquieting and bloody sestina for Manning to see, he added, warning that Manning would probably find him not only mad but dipsomaniac when he heard it. Pound's remark is revealing because something about the decorousness and the reserve of Englishmen like Manning and the stultifying proprieties of the upper classes continued to provoke him, causing him to release his own angry flamboyance, his potential to jar and outrage.

Manning brought Pound to a tea where he met Olivia Shakespear, "surely the most charming woman in London," he wrote his mother. An isolated man with affection for matrons and virgins, suave and distant, Manning had been courting Olivia's daughter, Dorothy, for three years. Since he was timid and exceedingly genteel, his method of courtship was epistolary: he sent Dorothy elegant poems like his "Canzone"—about an ideal woman, a "veiled bride of the night" who walks through a moaning forest, spectral and cursed like Poe's Ulalume. With love poems as macabre as "Canzone," no wonder Dorothy discouraged him. In fact, she was bored by him, but Manning thickly felt their union was destined.

London life in the Edwardian era was a time of transition between a stiff Victorian code governing conduct and the emerging modern spirit. It was characterized by King Edward VII, who had a passion for pomp and pageantry but who loved theater and music halls as well. There was a photograph of him in the *Illustrated London News* on Sunday, June 27, 1909, which Pound may have seen, at a garden party for eight thousand guests, the King himself portly, overdressed, smiling and sociable, representing a life-style of ostentatious luxury. Genial and indulgent, and disreputable as far as his secret liaisons with women were concerned, Edward had tremendous appeal for all classes in a society absolutely regulated by class distinctions. But even these hard social rules were affected by the new technologies: the wireless telegraph, the telephone, the cinema and the X ray, the incandescent lamp and electricity, the automobile and the airplane. In 1909 the English Channel had been crossed by airplane in thirty-seven minutes, affecting the British sense of insular security. On the streets, motorcars were replacing hansom cabs and covered carriages, although coachmen in top hats and boots and footmen in livery and long coats were still evident. Van Wyck Brooks, the American critic, then in London, remembered the pageantry as a perpetual ballet. One day outside his grimy Soho lodging, he confronted a footman in livery sent to him by an English cousin and seeming like a figure in "a Sheridan comedy or a Hogarth picture." Women were still wearing long skirts that brushed the ground, tightly laced corsets, and eighteen-button gloves in the evening; men wore black waistcoats with tailcoats and gloves. Ladies had "at home" days which gentlemen could attend if properly attired

in hats and gloves, with walking sticks. At dances a man would change his
stiff white collar three times in an evening and bring several ties and a spare
pair of white kid gloves. He would never address his partner by her first
name unless they were engaged. And although men no longer powdered
their noses or colored their cheeks, such practices were not long out of
fashion. The golden age of the Edwardians was symbolized by the weekend
house parties at country estates, with the formal lawns and rose gardens, the
banquets and attending servants, the endless conversations about the inane
which Henry James had caricatured in 1901 in *The Sacred Fount*.

Especially among artists and intellectuals, there was intensifying resistance to the Victorian hangover. The rich were still racing, riding, shooting,
sailing, and gambling and the Empire had extended itself to nearly thirteen
million square miles with 370 million subjects. Britain had tripled its military budget for the sake of a few South African mine owners in the imperial
adventure of the Boer War, the "white man's burden," as Kipling called it,
but there was still no decent plan for worker pensions or health or unemployment insurance. The national average income reached fifty-one pounds
a year just before the beginning of World War I, but the purchasing power
of the pound was rapidly shrinking, causing a real decline in workers'
wages. As a result, socialists, labor unions, and syndicalists who advocated
power through general strikes were gaining adherents. The time of turmoil
was at hand. When Pound arrived in London in 1908, a quarter of a million
women had assembled in Hyde Park to demand the vote; the King of
Portugal had just been assassinated with his son; two years earlier when
Pound had been in Madrid doing research on Lope de Vega there had been
an unsuccessful attempt on the King of Spain; and in 1913 King George of
Greece was to be assassinated at Salonika. In Germany the naval and military buildup had begun and Kaiser Wilhelm was proclaiming his "Divine
Right."

As an American in London, Pound could only observe and assimilate.
His primary interest was not social reform but penetrating the artistic community. Meeting men like Hewlett, Manning, and Binyon, then Ernest
Rhys, who edited Everyman's Library, and May Sinclair, a thin, dark-haired
distinguished-looking feminist novelist, and the actress Ellen Terry gave
him the sense that he was part of it. He wrote to Williams, urging him to
visit: "Am by the way of falling into the crowd that does things here, London, deah old Lundon, is the place for poesy."

Suddenly Pound was immersed in a series of teas and "evenings." He
was brought to literary societies and private clubs; he took the train to
country estates and met literary hostesses. Mathews invited him to the
Poet's Club, as it was informally called, where he met George Bernard
Shaw and Hilaire Belloc—he found the setting stodgy. Organized by a big,
burly Englishman named T. E. Hulme, the club spent evenings discussing

poetic theory. Hulme's arguments about the need for purity of expression would have a great impact on Pound. Pound also met one of Hulme's key followers, F. S. Flint, a critic who informed Pound about the latest developments in French poetry. He wrote home, "I seem to fit better here in London than anywhere else, if I can only guess wot's the answer to the problem of sustinence." The answer thus far had been paternal generosity, but still it had been a hard and lean winter: "I used to starve in London," he remembered years later, "not only for warmth but for light, eyes fatigued in the murk."

One source of genuine warmth was Olivia Shakespear, who continued to invite him for teas and lunches. Pound wrote Mary Moore that he had sat on the same hearth rug as Yeats had and talked of life and read his own poems. Mrs. Shakespear knew Yeats intimately—she had been the poet's lover in the nineties and is remembered by him in his diaries as Diana Vernon—and she was first cousin to Lionel Johnson, one of the nineties poets. As a novelist herself, she belonged to a living literary circle. Her husband, Henry Hope Shakespear, a possible but at any rate distant descendant of William Shakespeare, was a family solicitor, and the marriage had been a tolerated balancing of very different sensibilities: Henry pragmatic, scrupulous, and dull; Olivia lively with her artistic and psychic interests. In a later time they might have separated, but it was only in 1909 that King Edward appointed a royal commission to liberalize the divorce law. Their daughter, Dorothy, had completed her schooling and was living at home in the Victorian fashion, painting watercolors, reading, trying needlework, attending lectures and concerts with her mother. She was at home when Pound visited the first time and she was swept away. She recorded her initial impression in a notebook entry on February 16, 1909:

> Listen to it—Ezra! Ezra! And a third time—Ezra! He has a wonderful, beautiful face, a high forehead, prominent over the eyes; a long delicate nose, with little, red, nostrils; a strange mouth, never still, & quite elusive; a square chin, slightly cleft in the middle— the whole face pale; the eyes grey-blue; the hair golden-brown, and curling in soft wavy crinkles. Large hands, with long, well-shaped fingers and beautiful nails.

Dorothy marvels over everything Ezraic, his accent, the way he perched back in his chair and then dropped down, cross-legged, in front of the fire, talking all the while of his admiration for Yeats, reading a Yeats poem in a voice curiously similar to the Irish poet's. She surmises that he has lived most of his life in barren wastes and wonders whether he is a genius or "only an artist in Life?" Finally there is his face, "his mobile, moving, beautiful face." She does not think he knows how beautiful he is, and she does not know herself that she is already in love.

Only a year younger than Pound, and like him on certain levels a perennial innocent, Dorothy was very wrong about one matter. Pound knew very well he had the power to attract women, and he felt that his sexuality was profoundly related to his creativity. Two years earlier, just before the Wabash debacle, he denied Viola Baxter's request for a photograph: "I am not so beautiful in a picture as in real life. . . . The real drama about my face is its play of expression." With Viola, with Hilda Doolittle and Mary Moore, with the actress in Wabash and with Katherine Heyman, Pound had played the courtier and experienced differing degrees of passion. Given the mores of the Victorian age, the probability is that all of Pound's alliances, except perhaps for the one at Wabash, remained on the level of flirtatious courtship, with nothing more intimate than passionate embraces, lots of poetry reading, hand-holding, and long walks in nature. With Dorothy, however, he began a more prolonged courtship. In one moment of quiet communion, he whispered to Dorothy: "You are Triste, Little Brother?" and the words reverberated for her with meaning and connection. She announced to her notebook that she was ready for the "chivalry and trust and joy of a great love."

The period of courtship extended over six years, and there were impediments along the way, tests and rivals to overcome. Of more immediate interest to Pound was his conquest of social London, and he entered that contest with great cheer and vigor. He wrote Mary Moore that in one week in early spring of 1909 he had gone to a tea party with Rhys, had lunch with Laurence Binyon, who talked of Chinese art and "inflicted his latest effusion on me," had dinner with Maurice Hewlett to determine which of them had been most bored at the last Poet's Club meeting, had tea with May Sinclair, who, he believed, was using him as a type in the novel she was writing, and met Yeats's friend Lady Gregory, who told him he read his poems the way Yeats did. Pound had sent *A Lume Spento* to Yeats just before leaving Venice and Yeats had described the book to a friend as "charming." But there had been no opportunity for Pound to meet the Irish poet since he had been in Dublin working with the Abbey Theatre. In April, Olivia and Dorothy Shakespear were able to bring Pound to Woburn Buildings, where Yeats had regular gatherings for poets in his dimly lit rooms decorated with Pre-Raphaelite paintings. Word of Pound's admiration of Yeats had reached the older poet through Olivia Shakespear and Lady Gregory: no wonder he took to the visiting American, whom he regarded as a potential acolyte.

There was a second triumph for Pound that April, the publication of *Personae,* which he dedicated to Mary Moore of Trenton "if she wants it." The diffidence of the dedication was not intended only for Moore, who had already rejected him as an unfit suitor, but to a public at large that might not be able to sympathize with his intentions and experiments. Like the aestheticists of the nineties, Pound was pursuing his art for its own sake. He had told Williams when he sent *A Lume Spento* that "no art ever yet grew by looking into the eyes of the public." "Damn their eyes," he added, stating that he could not write for them, that he didn't have "that kind of intelligence."

Half of the thirty-three poems in *Personae* had already appeared in *A Lume Spento,* but most of the new ones were as remote and arcane, explorations of later medieval moods and characters like the troubador Arnaut of Marvoil or the Countess of Beziers. The chief influence still seemed to be a mixture of Browning's bravado and Yeatsian fog, the dominant mood still the languid melancholy of *A Lume Spento.* One of the better poems, "The White Stag," suggests that Pound may have soaked his sensibility in the early work of Yeats, poems of romantic complaint, pining lovers, and unfulfilled longings, poems that seemed to indulge in resonating sound values for their own connective and musical qualities. The last, italicized lines of the poem, sounding so much like one of Yeats's refrains, seem applicable to Pound's own situation as a young poet in London:

> I ha' seen them 'mid the clouds on the heather.
> Lo! they pause not for love nor for sorrow,
> Yet their eyes are as the eyes of a maid to her lover,
> When the white hart breaks his cover
> And the white wind breaks the morn.
>
> *" 'Tis the white stag, Fame, we're a-hunting,*
> *Bid the world's hounds come to horn!"*

In *A Quinzaine* Pound had declared in an epigraph, "Beauty should never be explained," a principle quite evidently controlling *Personae* as well, much as certain of his less trained readers might have longed for more assistance. The reviewers, however, were on the whole quite positive. The *Daily Chronicle* commended the book's "brusque intensity" and *The Bookman* claimed that "no new book of poems for years past has had such a freshness of inspiration, such a strongly individual note, or been more alive with indubitable promise." Even better was praise from two poets, Rupert Brooke, writing in the *Cambridge Review,* and Edward Thomas in the *English Review,* who stated that Pound was incomparable, full of personality, power, and passion.

Personae opens with "Praise of Ysolt," whose first lines may apply to Pound's own position among the London poets in 1909:

> In vain have I striven
>   to teach my heart to bow;
> In vain have I said to him
> "There be many singers greater than thou."

In one poem, "Revolt Against the Crepuscular Spirit in Modern Poetry,"
Pound suggests that his future intention is to be less fabulous and less nebulous in subject:

> I would shake off the lethargy of this our time,
>   and give,
> For shadows—shapes of power—
> For dreams—men.

But the poem does not fulfill its promise and its resolution seems bombastic,
like much of the collection:

> I bid thee grapple chaos and beget
> Some new titanic spawn to pile the hills and stir
> This earth again.

The most interesting poem, certainly in the light of Pound's later development, is a little one called "Piccadilly," where Pound seems able to combine
his Yeatsian lushness with clarity, ear joining eye to create a new kind of
power:

> *Beautiful, tragical faces,*
> *Ye that were whole, and are so sunken;*
> *And, O ye vile, ye that might have been loved,*
> *That are so sodden and drunken,*
> > *Who hath forgotten you?*
>
> *O wistful, fragile faces, few out of many!*
>
> *The gross, the coarse, the brazen,*
> *God knows I cannot pity them, perhaps, as I should do,*
> *But, oh, ye delicate, wistful faces,*
> > *Who hath forgotten you?*

4. LES JEUNES

The success of *Personae* launched Pound into another meeting which
would prove invaluable. May Sinclair introduced Pound to Ford Madox
Hueffer, who after the war changed his name to Ford Madox Ford because
of anti-German sentiment. Ford's grandfather was the renowned painter
Ford Madox Brown, a member of the Pre-Raphaelite Brotherhood. Led by
Dante Gabriel Rossetti and William Morris, the Pre-Raphaelites were an
influential school of poetry and painting that posed the challenge to Victorian conventions as early as the 1870s and 1880s. Both Rossetti and Morris
were medievalists, which endeared them to Pound, and he was tremen-

dously impressed by the fact that Ford used Rossetti's brown velvet coat as his dressing gown. Ford had grown up with Dante and Christina Rossetti, with Browning and Swinburne, and as a result had access to leading men of power in the British government—William Rossetti, for example, Dante's brother, was chief tax collector in England. Ford's father was a German historian who wrote a distinguished book on Provence and as music critic for *The Times* advocated the music of Wagner. Married to Ford Madox Brown's daughter, he died when his son was only fifteen, at which point Ford began to live in his famous grandfather's household surrounded by artists. Pound was drawn to Ford particularly because, like Yeats, he regarded writing as an almost priestly vocation. A brilliant talker who could weave vast monologues for hours and manage to keep them dramatic, Ford was a born storyteller, and with him Pound felt he was close to one of the sources of English literature.

Ford also happened to be the editor of the most important literary magazine in London. The *English Review* had been conceived in Conrad's home, H. G. Wells had been one of its instigators, and Ford ran it according to the highest standards of taste—he had once described himself as an Englishman "a little mad about letters." The magazine was so much his life that he lived in its offices, which were located above a combination poulterer and fishmonger but decorated with portraits of Christina Rossetti and Conrad and photographs of the Pre-Raphaelites. There were Chippendale chairs, an inlaid Spanish cabinet formerly owned by a queen for the magazine's manuscripts, and the desk Christina Rossetti used to write her poems on. Ford had many literary friends, among them Conrad and the popular novelist W. H. Hudson, and he fancied himself a friend of Henry James. Such a literary pedigree certainly impressed Pound, especially the connection to James, though Pound could not have known then that James and Yeats as well as a number of other writers distrusted and even disliked Ford. Nevertheless, the first issue of the *English Review* in December 1908 had included a poem by Hardy and fiction by Conrad, Hudson, James, Wells, and Arnold Bennett. It was practically a pantheon of the literary art of the moment, and Pound was delighted when Ford informed him that his work would appear in a subsequent issue. In June 1909, barely six weeks after he had been introduced to Ford, Pound's powerful poem about medieval warfare, "Sestina: Altaforte," appeared in the *English Review.*

Pound has explained that he was thinking about the troubador Bertran de Born, perplexed because he found him untranslatable, when he decided on the complicated rhyme scheme of the sestina:

> I wanted the curious involution and recurrence of the sestina. I
> wrote the first strophe and then went to the (British) Museum to
> make sure of the right order of permutations, for I was then living

in Langham Street and had hardly any books with me. I did the
rest of the poem at a sitting.

Pound knew that technically the poem was one of the best things he had
done, that its violent exuberance perfectly caught Browning's dramatic
form. Appearing in so distinguished a place as the *English Review,* the poem
was the announcement of Pound's growing power among the poets. The
opening lines strike like a clarion call the notes of that new power:

> Damn it all! all this our South stinks of peace.
> You whoreson dog, Papiols, come! Lets to music!
> I have no life save when the swords clash. . . .

Pound read his new poem at a poet's dinner organized by T. E. Hulme
at the Tour Eiffel, a restaurant owned by Rudolf Stulik, who had once been
chef to Emperor Franz Joseph and had a special fondness for artists. The
restaurant was decorated simply with small tables and pink-shaded lights.
Pound's reading was so forceful that the other diners were alarmed and
waiters hurried over with screens to seclude the poets. Hulme had reorganized his poet's group, purging some of the duller members and focusing
on essential questions of sound and meter. Pound was invited to join the
new group, which included Flint, the Irish poet Joseph Campbell, Yeats's
friend the actress Florence Farr, Padraic Colum, and Ernest Rhys. Their
common purpose was the renewal of English poetry. As part of the attempt
to fashion new forms suitable for the age, they were experimenting with
"free verse," discussing imagery and trying to separate it from mere decoration, searching for instructive models in other languages, and generally
preparing to free themselves from stale patterns of rhyme and iambic pen-
tameter.

The center of the group was still Hulme, a considerable intellectual
with training in philosophy at Cambridge, who had studied Bergson and
was developing fresh perspectives of his own. Pound compared Hulme to
the "Pickwickian Englishman who starts a club." Hulme was a genial
though blunt man with a sharp, acerbic style. "Throughout all the ages," he
noted, "the conversation of ten men sitting together is what holds the world
together." Hulme needed a forum for his ideas, which would help to revo-
lutionize the poetic word. Pound absorbed these ideas, let them simmer for
a few years, and then turned them to his own purposes when he was ready.
Hulme's position was that romanticism had died, that Victorianism had prolonged its existence long past its time, and that the Pre-Raphaelites and the
poets of the nineties had perpetuated the romantic mood out of habit. The
new century, he asserted, would be a time of dry, hard, classical poetry. He
formulated some of the ideas he had discussed with his friends in a piece he

published in *The New Age*, a magazine to which Pound soon began to contribute on a regular basis:

> In prose as in algebra concrete things are embodied in signs or counters, which are moved about according to rules, without being visualized at all in the process. There are in prose certain type situations and arrangements of words, which move as automatically into certain other arrangements as do functions in algebra. Only one changes the x's and y's back into physical things at the end of the process. Poetry, in one aspect at any rate, may be considered as an effort to avoid this characteristic of prose. It is not a counter language, but a concrete visual one. It is a compromise for a language of intuition which would hand over sensations bodily. It always endeavors to arrest you, and to make you see a physical thing, to prevent you from gliding through an abstract process.

Pound's life at this time was crowded with social incident and he felt his poems were being read by the right people. Elkin Mathews agreed to bring out another collection which Pound began preparing. He wrote Williams in a crowing flush of overconfidence that he had been praised by Yeats, "the greatest living poet. I am, after eight years hammering against impenetrable adamant, become suddenly somewhat of a success." Some of his financial uncertainty was ameliorated when the Polytechnic agreed to let him resume his lectures in the fall. Ernest Rhys encouraged him to work his lectures into a book on Provence and told him that he had found an interested publisher.

"I made my life in London," Pound remembered, "by going to see Ford in the afternoons and Yeats in the evenings." Douglas Goldring, one of Ford's acolytes and assistant on the *English Review*, noted the way Pound began to assume a more central role in Yeats's Monday evening gatherings: "He dominated the room, distributed Yeats' cigarettes and Chianti, and laid down the law about poetry." Pound was becoming giddy with stimulation. Williams remembered that Pound always walked a few steps ahead of him no matter what the pace and that his insistence on moving ahead first was a source of real annoyance. Ford has described the way he used his malacca cane on the streets, characteristically approaching "with the steps of a dancer, making passes with his cane at an imaginary opponent." The flourishing cane, the quickened pace of his walk were reflections of a heightened intensity, the desire to get on with his work, to quicken the process of building a poetic reputation. The result was a mood that shifted from ebullience to impatience, one that could be easily misinterpreted by the British. Pound was usually oblivious to how others would see him: the early London years, he later told the poet Charles Olson, were "the high period of my life."

But there are signs that the success was bubbling in his system like untempered champagne. He met Wyndham Lewis, another young poet and painter who became a close ally. Lewis discerned that Pound was uncomfortable among the British, "tensed, nervously straining, jerky." He was, Lewis observed, "like a drop of oil in a glass of water; the trouble was, I believe, that he had no wish to *mix:* he just wanted to *impress.*" When the young and then-unknown D. H. Lawrence visited Ford with his friend Jessie Chambers, she was startled when Pound sprang to his feet, "bowing from the waist with the stiff precision of a mechanical toy." Pound interrupted other guests in mid-sentence and spoke in mysterious aphorisms, trying, perhaps, to sound like an Oscar Wilde. At first Lawrence was impressed by Pound but discerningly noted that "his god is beauty, mine life." He spent a night in Pound's rooms when he missed a train and felt that Pound was full of pretense and pose, an irascible version of the strolling minstrel, a "sort of latest edition of jongleur," and thus not to be taken seriously. A number of other Englishmen began to regard Pound with suspicion, finding him presumptuous because of his inclination to declare himself an expert on matters that he may not have mastered. If the conversation turned to classical poetry, Pound offered his theories with absolute conviction, if the conversation turned in other directions, Pound still always had his opinion. Douglas Goldring, who was one of the group that Ford called "les jeunes," used the word "charlatan" when recording his initial impression; he was put off by Pound's pince-nez and the showy blue glass buttons on his coat. A more conservatively indignant reaction was voiced by Edmund Gosse, an establishment writer, a dapper man full of easy urbanity, who called Pound "that preposterous American filibuster and charlatan."

Lawrence was correct in seeing the extent to which Pound could strike a theatrical pose. His model was Whistler, who Pound at this time felt was supremely significant: "I count him as our only great artist." Whistler epitomized to Pound the artist as outsider and exile. Born in Massachusetts, spending his childhood in Russia, then expelled from West Point, Whistler went to France where he began to study art. He received some recognition as part of the Pre-Raphaelite circle in London, but he had a penchant for publicity and outrage. Whistler, often attired with a wide-brimmed dark hat and a three-foot walking stick, loved the bon mot; he published his letters under the title *The Gentle Art of Making Enemies,* a book that Pound read with relish. No wonder Oscar Wilde chose as his first journalistic assignment to review a Whistler show at the Grosvenor Gallery in 1877. The American painter William Merritt Chase did a portrait of Whistler in 1885, the year of Pound's birth. From his portrait, one cannot really tell that Whistler is an artist. There are no brushes or canvases as there are in the self-portrait of the period of Chase in smock and studio. The Whistler is all poised gentleman, one foot forward, the high thin cane reaching almost to his shoulders, an elongated swagger of a man, a dandy with a monocle, his face expressing an impudent smirk of complete disdain. As a man Whistler was arrogant and bellicose, a compulsive quarreler. He went bankrupt after suing John Ruskin for libel when Ruskin criticized his work, asserting that Whistler's paintings were "only flinging a pot of paint in the public's face." At the time of his death in 1903, no public gallery in England owned one of his paintings and he was considered disreputable.

At the same moment that Pound chose to play the reborn dandy, he could shift gears to believe in himself as a sort of populist messianic missionary of the new poetry. Shortly after the publication of *Personae,* he had conceived of a poem in which one of Christ's apostles explains Jesus' capacity for masculine camaraderie, certainly an unusual view of Christ. He set down the even more unusual circumstances of composition in an essay called "How I Began":

> In the case of the "Goodly Fere" I was not excited until some hours after I had written it. I had been the evening before in the "Turkish Coffee" café in Soho. I had been made very angry by a certain sort of cheap irreverence which was new to me. I had lain awake most of the night. I got up rather late in the morning and started for the Museum with the first four lines in my head. I wrote the rest of the poem at a sitting, on the left side of the reading-room, with scarcely any erasures. I lunched at the Vienna Café, and later in the afternoon, being unable to study, I peddled the poem about Fleet Street, for I began to realize that for the first time in my life I had written something that "everyone could understand," and I wanted it to go to the people.

"The Ballad of the Goodly Fere" was turned down by every magazine and newspaper to which Pound offered it because of its very unconventional view of Christ, but eventually Ford ran it in the *English Review.* When *Exultations* was ready for the printer, Elkin Mathews balked at printing "The Ballad of the Goodly Fere," afraid of adverse repercussions from religious circles. Pound insisted on including the poem, so Mathews inserted a note of disclaimer. The book appeared a few days before Pound's twenty-fourth birthday. Half of its twenty-seven poems had been written during 1909. The strongest were "Sestina: Altaforte" and "Francesca," a quiet lyric written with firm control and grace, but nothing else in the little book was as inspired as its title. The rest of the book, medieval in origin and interest, still moaned with the unfulfilled longings and sorrows of the nineties, the torpid and plaintive mood of the *fin de siècle* period, which Pound had not yet learned to escape.

Again, however, the reviewers were generally impressed. F. S. Flint, writing in the *English Review,* by then certainly a friendly organ, described Pound with a slight note of irony "hammering, as it were, word into word" and spoke for his vitality and "determination to burst his way into Parnassus." But the reviewer in *The Spectator* shrewdly pointed to a central problem of sensibility which would later be echoed by others:

> Mr. Ezra Pound is that rare thing among modern poets, a scholar. He is not only cultivated, but learned. . . . We feel that this writer has in him the capacity for remarkable poetic achievement, but we also feel that at present he is somewhat weighted by his learning. His virility and passion are immense, but somehow we seem to know their origins. He strikes us as a little too bookish and literary, even when he is most untrammelled by metrical conventions.

The conservative *Fortnightly Review* paid Pound for a poem—money he needed as he had virtually no income.

Pound's father was still sending money, but his mother repeated her request that Ezra return to Philadelphia. He placated her with the news that he had received his contract from Dent for *The Spirit of Romance* and had already begun lecturing at the Polytechnic. Just before his first lecture, Pound moved into new quarters at 10 Church Walk in Kensington, a clean three-story brick building with flower boxes, near St. Mary Abbots Church. Restored in 1872 with the then highest spire in London, St. Mary's had been the site of a church since the twelfth century. Church Walk was an area with its own rich history, Pound learned; the shoe repair shop had been there for fifty years, and the newsstand had been owned by the same family for several generations. The new location was close to the *English Review* and the Shakespears. His room, with its two windows looking out on a courtyard, was cheap at eight shillings a week and furnished with an iron bed over a tub that slid out, a few cane chairs and a long oak worktable, a fireplace and a tall wardrobe—altogether a picture of genteel shabbiness.

The series of twenty-one weekly lectures on medieval literature began in October and continued into the spring. Olivia and Dorothy Shakespear enrolled for the course, which Dorothy remembered as "dismal." Pound could not have succeeded in communicating with his audience because of his habit of addressing his talks to the highest possible level of listener. His audience consisted of a group of workingmen, disillusioned, as Dorothy put it, who had no idea of what to expect—"the whole passell lacking the vaguest notion what it was all about or why," Pound later recalled. The problem may have been more with Pound than with his auditors and related to the observation on arcane knowledge made by the *Spectator* reviewer considering *Exultations.* The same need to distance himself from his audience with an intricate network of allusion and history determines the difficulty of *The Cantos.*

During the winter of 1909–10, Pound was busy preparing his lectures and writing *The Spirit of Romance* and a series of poems inspired by his

Provençal studies and Dante, which appeared in *Canzoni* in the following year. By concentrating on the poets of Provence, Pound had made a crucially intelligent choice affecting his own development as a poet. The troubadors were the first poets to shift from Latin to their own language and local dialect. Pound was shifting as well from the formality of classical English style to a more idiomatic American.

All that winter there were the weekly dinners with the Poet's Club, where Hulme and Flint and the others would listen to recent work after a chop and ale and offer criticism in terms of their new stance. Pound lectured to the club on Arnaut Daniel in December. He visited Frederic Manning and Arthur Galton in Lincolnshire and sent Manning's poem "Kore" to the *English Review.* This was the first of Pound's acts as advisory editor, a role for which he became justly famous in the future. He replied to Manning's poem with "Canzon: The Yearly Slain," which also appeared in the *English Review.* His name was beginning to appear in prominent places: *Punch* did a parody where he was called Ezekiel Ton; his poems were praised in the *Mercure de France; The Literary Digest* published a piece on him; and R. B. Cunningham-Graham, in a letter to the *Saturday Review,* observed that "Conrad, Galsworthy, George Moore, Henry James, and Ezra Pound—are devoting themselves more and more to short pieces, and in them doing some of their best work." In America there were pieces in the Boston *Herald* and in a number of Philadelphia papers. His mother wrote again, sending New Year's greetings and asking when he was planning to return. Pound was then thinking seriously of returning temporarily and applied to the University of Pennsylvania for fellowship assistance: "Continued residence in America is of course most revolting to think of. But I might survive one winter and it might be useful perhaps," he told his mother. He regarded the conditions for poetry in America as miserable and declared that poet Bliss Carman was the only living American poet who "would not be improved by drowning."

Pound was buoyed by a week's visit in March from William Carlos Williams, who was on his way back to the States after taking a postgraduate course in Leipzig. He took it upon himself to show Williams his London, taking him to museums to see Turners, the Elgin marbles, the work of Bellini and other Renaissance painters, and bringing him to dinner at the Shakespears'. Once that week Pound and Williams were walking near St. Mary Abbots, which he said irritated him because of its incessant bells. They passed a bunch of faded violets on the pavement and Pound placed them on the high wrought-iron churchyard fence, "all with a swagger not to be overlooked," Williams remembered. On another evening they went to a cheap local restaurant, and when Williams tried to help Pound on with his fur-lined coat after the meal, Pound turned on Williams, "laying me out in no uncertain way for my presumption, jerked the coat out of my hands and, presenting it to the waiter, made him hold it, as he continued scolding me, saying that one didn't do things that way in London." Undoubtedly, Pound believed he was educating his old college chum in the more sophisticated ways of the Europeans. He continued to lecture Williams for years, always regarding him as a sort of provincial turtle. Actually, Pound was acting as imperiously with Williams as he acted with the English, many of whom found his manners to be deplorable.

He also took Williams to one of Yeats's Monday night evenings, which Williams describes in his *Autobiography:*

> It was a studio atmosphere, very hushed. We tiptoed in. Yeats in a darkened room, was reading by candlelight to a small, very small gathering of his proteges, maybe five or six young men and women, members of the Abbey Theatre group. He paid no attention whatever to us as we entered and seated ourselves, but went on reading; reading, of all things, Ernest Dowson's "Cynara"—in a beautiful voice, I must say, but it was not my dish.

Williams's point of view is always that of common sense, practical and honestly tuned to the world's necessities. While poetry was a necessity for him, it was a private need, not one that the world shared. So he was amused by the courtly gallantry and seriousness with which Pound and some of the London writers treated their art. On another night they went to hear Yeats lecture at the Adelphi Club, and Yeats tried to rationalize the decadence of some of the nineties poets, Lionel Johnson in particular, and to explain that their self-destructiveness resulted from their having been denied an audience. The affair was fashionable, presided over by Edmund Gosse, who interrupted Yeats's appeal for sympathy by banging a bell in front of him. Yeats tried to resume, and Gosse again banged the bell. Yeats tried once again, and Gosse retaliated with his bell, ending the lecture. It was all too much intensity for Williams and he could not understand how his friend could tolerate it: "it would have killed me in a month. It seemed completely foreign to anything I desired. I was glad to get away."

Pound was still seeing Yeats and Ford, separately because the Irish poet would have nothing to do with Ford. Yeats wrote to his friend Lady Gregory:

> This queer creature Ezra Pound, who has become a really great authority on the troubadors has, I think, got closer to the right sort of music for poetry than Mrs. Emory [Florence Farr]—it is more definitely music with strongly marked time and yet it is effective speech. However, he cannot sing, as he has no voice. It is like something on a very bad phonograph.

Another interest Pound would come to share with Yeats was mysticism. For years Yeats had been studying hermetic lore, the cabala, Indian philosophy, the tarot, astrology, telepathy, and alchemy. Yeats had consulted Olivia Shakespear in her capacity as a psychic in 1895 and seven years earlier had heard voices from the dead at a séance which had frightened him. At the time Yeats met Pound, he had decided that to know himself fully he had to confront those voices and come to terms with his other self, what he called his mask. In 1911 at the home of an American medium, he heard a voice that identified itself as Leo Africanus and claimed to be that other self. Another spirit Yeats believed he had reached was Dante's. A few years later Yeats married Olivia Shakespear's cousin Georgie Hyde-Lees, who was a medium also; Leo Africanus then spoke to Yeats through his wife to give him metaphors for poetry. Yeats and Olivia were involved with theosophy, a term that for centuries had been applied to the study of secret doctrines that united and illuminated all religious seeking and cosmic quest. A Russian woman, Helena Blavatsky, had formed the Theosophical Society, an esoteric group that used occult practices like mesmerism and séances to explore the bases and bonds of Eastern and Western religions. One of Olivia's friends was G. R. S. Mead, who became a sort of mentor to Pound during his early years in London, telling him of the "rising psychic tide." At the time of Pound's birth, Mead had been Blavatsky's personal secretary during the last years of her life when she was completing *The Secret Doctrine* and with her edited *Lucifer,* a scholarly journal published by the Theosophists. Olivia and Florence Farr had coauthored *The Beloved of Hathor,* a play drawn from Egyptian mystical sources, and Olivia's friend Dion Fortune reorganized Blavatsky's Society of the Golden Dawn; both Olivia and Georgie Hyde-Lees were members. Dorothy Shakespear and Pound were reading Ramacharaka's *Advanced Course in Yogi and Oriental Occultism* in 1910 and were interested in astrology. Dorothy asked Pound for the exact moment of his birth and had his astrological aspects charted. She summarized her findings in a notebook entry:

> You are very broad-minded—too much so. Very artistic. All for colour. Very sensitive—over-sensitive. At a very great turning point in life . . . . you will marry twice & have two children. You will live abroad. Travel is connected with you.

Contact with Yeats, Mead, and Olivia Shakespear and the world of psychic phenomena nourished Pound's own paganism, his literal acceptance of the powers of ancient Greek deities, an anticlericism which Dorothy shared, and the position that monotheism had been invented as a form of social control, a dissenting attitude that was confirmed in the troubador poetry he was studying. Through their songs the troubadors had maintained an enthusiastic non-Christian and inextinguishable source of beauty which Pound connected to the Albigensian heresy in the South of France. The Albigensians had been ruthlessly persecuted at the end of the Middle Ages as

Manicheans, secret devotees of devil worship, but Pound felt that what had actually inspired them were the early Greek pagan remnants of a secret cult of Eleusis. The Eleusinian mysteries were centered on the underworld myth of the rape of Persephone by Pluto, and the cult expressed a religious reverence for sexuality.

5. AMERICAN RISORGIMENTO

At the end of March, when proofs for *The Spirit of Romance* were ready and his course at the Polytechnic completed, Pound left for Italy, going first to Verona, where Dante had written much of the *Commedia,* and then to Sirmione, a town on Lake Garda in the north that had been frequented by poets from Catullus to Tennyson. There he began to extend his interest in the twelfth-century Italian poet Guido Cavalcanti, an interest that became a lifelong preoccupation. Loafing "to invite his soul," as Whitman had once put it, he heard that Small, Maynard in Boston was willing to publish an American edition of his poems. In April, Olivia and Dorothy Shakespear joined him and they took the train together to Venice. Pound returned alone and remained in Sirmione till mid-May, preparing himself emotionally for the trip back to America. In February he had written his father to place the following advertisement:

POET
Out of a Job

Specialities: incisive speech, sarcasm, meditation, irony (at special rates), ze grande manair (to order). Will do to travel, or stand unhitched while being fed. Price 1£ per hour. Special rate for steady customers.

The tone of the advertisement suggests a certain crisis of confidence, the youthful sarcasm merely the mask of Pound's own natural uncertainty and fear. Despite his accomplishments, Pound was dissatisfied with his own progress as a poet, and he knew that his parents, especially his mother, wanted him to find some regular employment near Philadelphia. The solitude and study and sun at Sirmione had calmed and steadied him, but he still had great apprehensions. He wrote to Katherine Heyman: "America presents itself to my mind as rather a horrible nightmare, a jaw of Tartarus effect ready to devour me if I loose my grip on things present. A distortion? Perhaps, Ibsen says all life is contact with phantoms of the brain." There is no way of knowing whether Pound's fear of living in America was a distortion, as he put it, or the result of deep antipathies to a culture that seemed too disparate, that lacked the homogeneity and settled qualities of European nations. What is clear is that his nomadic impulse, as Professor Doolittle had once impugned, was a factor, and that his self-imposed exile had become an absolute necessity, especially after what had happened at Wabash.

He was already on his ship when *The Spirit of Romance* was published near the end of June. The book had tried him—"I'd rather eat nails than write prose," he told a friend. His style shows signs of a cocksure bravado, perhaps appropriate for a man of twenty-five but a quality that always remained as a part of his voice. It shows, too, his attempt to escape the conventions of the politely organized paragraph. Like Emerson, he did not concern himself particularly with consistency. His sentences are full of intuitive leaps, conflicting ideas and digressions, spurting, illogical, boats lost in a storm. The history of art, he asserted in a preface that reads like some Carlylean decree, is a record of masterwork, not failures or mediocrity, and the study of literature is a form of hero worship. In a book of much paraphrase and summary of troubador legend and poetry, Pound insists on his own central beliefs almost as a way of attacking the academy that had rejected him, and for which the book was intended: "Great art is made to call forth, or to create an ecstasy. The finer the quality of this ecstasy, the finer the art." The dullness of some of the analysis is enlived by Poundian buckshot in definition: "Poetry is a sort of inspired mathematics which gives us equations not for abstract figures, triangles, spheres and the like, but equations for human emotions." The most interesting praise in the book is for the vagabond poet Villon, for his "unvarnished intimate speech" and his outspokenness: "what he sees, he writes." Without literary ambitions or pretensions and without illusions, Villon presented a gaunt version of the medieval gutter, certainly unlike the graceful chivalry of the other troubadors. By championing Villon, Pound was trying to deemphasize his own debts to Whitman and preparing to reject a crucial part of his poetic heritage before returning to the United States. In the essay on Villon, he chastised Whitman for what he called his self-complacency, the rectitude with which Whitman enjoyed being Whitman. Only three years later Pound began to realize his literary debt to Whitman by praising him in his long essay on New York, "Patria Mia," for his generosity, his carelessness, his looseness, his largeness of spirit, his willingness to stand exposed. But the directness and outspoken naturalness were qualities Pound would have to adopt whether the signal flag came from Whitman or Villon. It was as if Pound had to write *The Spirit of Romance* to purge the medievalism out of his soul so that he could become a modern poet.

Pound spent the summer in Philadelphia recuperating from jaundice. The illness may have had an emotional dimension, the result of an insidious self-pity and the shock of returning to what Pound considered an unstimulating and hostile environment, to the proximity of his parents, particularly his mother, who implicitly evaluated his accomplishments and found them lacking. He visited Hilda Doolittle, other college friends, and relatives and wondered whether it would be possible to continue living in what by then seemed to him a cultural backwater. He worked on his Cavalcanti translations and did a review for the *Book News Monthly*, a Philadelphia publication that had accepted his work when he was still at the university. His application for fellowship assistance had been denied and his dim plan to resume graduate studies faded. In the fall, he found rooms on Park Avenue South in Manhattan. There he met Yeats's father, the painter, who had moved to New York as a testament that artists could survive there. He described Pound in a letter to his son:

> Have you met Ezra Pound? Carlton Glidden, an artist of talent who has a lot to learn, but who is a very nice fellow indeed, told me today that Ezra Pound was at his studio a few days ago and talked a lot about you, quoting quantities of your verse, which he had by heart, placing you very high, and as the best poet for the last century and more. I tell you this as he is going in a few days to Europe to stay in Paris, etc. Quinn met him and liked him very much. The Americans, young literary men, whom I know found him surly, supercilious and grumpy. I liked him myself very much, that is, I liked his look and air, and the few things he said, for though I was a good while in his company he said very little.

He introduced Pound to John Quinn, an attorney and art collector who later became a patron for Pound and his friends. The three men went to Coney Island, and Pound recalled in a letter to Quinn, "Yeats pere on an elephant, smiling like Elijah in the beatific vision, and you plugging away in a shooting gallery."

By November Pound had completed his work on Cavalcanti and sent the manuscript to Small, Maynard; a week later it released *Provença*. The American reviews were mixed. The Boston *Evening Transcript* advised him to read Longfellow, a nasty cut considering his lineage, but one that may have encouraged the editor of the Harvard *Advocate* to read Pound and to pass the book around to his fellow editors, Conrad Aiken and T. S. Eliot. There was one important review in the Chicago *Evening Post*. Floyd Dell, a poet himself, compared the book to the Postimpressionist exhibition which had opened in the Grafton Galleries in London and had caused violent controversy:

> Mr. Pound is a very new kind of poet. Thinking of the art exhibition just held in London, one might, for want of a better figure, call him a Neo-Impressionist poet. Like the Neo-Impressionist painters, like the Impressionists in their day, Mr. Pound is open to misunderstanding, and even to ridicule. . . . But though these

poems have often an unconventional form, bizarre phraseology, catalectic or involved sentence structure and recondite meanings, yet it is always apparent that the poet knows what he is doing. . . . Ezra Pound is a true poet; his singing has distinctive spiritual and stylistic qualities which command the most respectful attention; and to those who approach his work in some humility of spirit it is capable of giving a deep aesthetic satisfaction.

In London, Elkin Mathews also brought Pound's works to the attention of another American poet, Harriet Monroe. Set to embark on a journey to Russia and Siberia, she visited Mathews's bookshop after having lunched with Mr. and Mrs. Herbert Hoover, recently returned from China, where Hoover had been working as a railroad engineer. (She had almost missed getting to the bookshop because of a two-mile-long suffragette procession blocking many streets.) Mathews recommended Pound's books to her and she purchased them. The books were not selling well, and Mathews later discontinued publishing Pound, but with this one recommendation, he may have done more than anything else for Pound.

Pound spent Thanksgiving with William Carlos Williams and his family in New Jersey. Both poets chose to read poems after they finished the turkey, but Williams's father was unimpressed. He asked Pound what he meant when he used the word "jewel" in a poem and was dissatisfied with Pound's explanation, asking why Pound didn't say exactly what he meant. Pound's diction was still indirect and elusive, draped in romantic mists. Much later, in his *Cantos,* the indirection would become a function of obscure references, allusions too arcane for the ordinary reader. Williams, a more pragmatic man, always demonstrated a greater capacity for directness. The two poets quarreled over their differences for fifty years, Williams insisting that he stood for bread in poetry, a nourishing elemental quality, while Pound stood for caviar, something suitable for only the most elite of audiences. In his *Autobiography,* Williams remembers another matter raised by Pound and negated by his father:

It was at this time that Ezra made the proposal, which, when I asked my father about it, caused him only to shake his head. It was as follows: That we get a big supply of "606," the new antisyphilitic arsenical which Ehrlich had just announced to the world, and go at once with it to the north coast of Africa and there set up shop. Between us, I with my medical certificate and experience, he with his social proclivities, we might, he thought, clean up a million treating all the wealthy old nabobs there—presumably rotten with the disease—and retire to our literary enjoyments within, at most, a year. Maybe there was something in it, I don't know.

Williams noted that practical details never mattered to Pound, the conception was enough, and then the language to convey that conception. And Pound was all language and rejoinder. Once when Williams and Pound were walking, remembering their long hikes in Upper Darby, Williams pointed to the winter wheat rising to greet Pound, as he put it. "It's the first intelligent wheat I've ever seen," Pound replied.

In New York City there were visits to Katherine Heyman, who was championing Prokofiev, and visits from Hilda Doolittle. Pound was gathering observations for "Patria Mia." He admired the mammoth Pennsylvania Railroad Station and the glistening power of the Metropolitan Life Insurance building, and disliked the fact that the Public Library was shrouded by surrounding buildings. In a characteristic and quixotic act of Poundian pique, he went to the firm that had designed the library to complain. He wrote this essay in London a year later, where it appeared in *The New Age*. In it, while he admires the vigor and immediacy of New York City, he demeans both the working and bourgeois classes there because they have no interest in art: electricity has "made the seeings of visions superfluous." He complains that practically any American with enough mental energy to make him interesting was engaged in business, not the arts, and that Americans were nomadic anyway, with no time to develop the roots or stability that sustain real culture. He also, in a forecast of some of his own political perversions of the thirties, deplores the racial characteristics of the city, its horde of new Slavic and Jewish immigrants, who were producing, he asserted, a mongrel nation.

Pound's antipathy for the Eastern Europeans was not without a legacy. Theodore Roosevelt, for one, felt that such immigrants would dilute the native American stock, which was primarily English. Similar views were voiced by some leading intellectuals of Roosevelt's era, a formative period for the young Ezra Pound. Henry and Brooks Adams both believed that the modern age was a time of disintegration and disorder. Brooks Adams, in his *Law of Civilization and Decay,* a book Pound constantly recommended, stated the fear that "the old native American blood is hardly reproducing itself" and warned that it would be sapped by the peasant and usurer. Another book Pound recommended was Owen Wister's *Philosophy Four,* a novel that contrasts healthy and superior Anglo-Saxon characters to a plodding Jewish student at Harvard. In a sense Pound was echoing the Jamesian snobbishness he admired. Olivia Shakespear, asking about Americans, queried, "Are they ladies and gentlemen like we are?"

When Pound first came to New York he had argued that it was like London without its two hundred most distinguished inhabitants. After a while he was not so sure and he felt threatened by the teeming animal energies of the newcomers. Despite the immigrants, Pound predicted a general reawakening led by artists, "an American Risorgimento." To facilitate such a renaissance, he conceived of a college of one hundred artists supported by government subsidy. Actually, such an awakening was already in process without government or institutional assistance. But the situation for poetry was much more scattered and random. Carl Sandburg was working as secretary to the Socialist mayor of Milwaukee, Marianne Moore was teaching stenography at the Carlisle Indian School in Pennsylvania, Vachel Lindsay was traveling the back roads as a sort of American minstrel, Williams was beginning his humble pediatric practice in Rutherford, New Jersey, T. S. Eliot was at Harvard studying philosophy and Sanskrit, Wallace Stevens was practicing law in New York—they all were writing but without any mutual support system and without any shared recognition. That was soon created by two women, Harriet Monroe, who was raising money for *Poetry: A Magazine of Verse,* and Margaret Anderson, a book reviewer for the *Evening Post* in New York who was planning to begin *The Little Review.* Another center was begun in 1910 when the Poetry Society of America held its preliminary meetings in New York. Pound attended an early meeting, heckling and joking from the sidelines, amused by the excess decorum and stuffiness of the occasion. He was still very much the jaunty youth of poetry. For example, on a visit to Witter Bynner—who had recommended him to Small, Maynard—he wore purple trousers, a mauve jacket, a wide-brimmed straw hat with large pink polka dots on its white band, a black shoe on his left foot, a blue one on the other.

A year after Pound returned to London, Mabel Dodge Luhan moved from Florence, Italy, to lower Fifth Avenue in the Village, where she decorated her apartment all in white and began a regular series of evenings, a salon that became a center for ideas on art, bohemianism, and revolution. Here Pound, had he chosen to remain in New York, could have conversed with men like Max Eastman, John Reed, Alfred Stieglitz, or his friend William Carlos Williams, or with women like Margaret Sanger and Emma Goldman.

6. 1910

Away for merely half a year, Pound came back to an England that was subtly different. Virginia Woolf made the now-famous observation that "on or about December 1910, human nature changed." The date, of course, is gratuitous: the process was not quite as swift as the laying of an egg, she conceded. The change had been gradual, related to the accumulation of a series of developments in technology that affected values. As the French critic Charles Péguy stated in 1913: "The world has changed less since the time of Jesus Christ than it has in the last thirty years." That period was practically equivalent to Pound's lifetime: Edison had developed the phonograph in 1877 and two years later the first incandescent filament light bulb; in 1882 there was the recoil-operated machine gun, the first synthetic fiber in 1883, the Parsons steam turbine in 1884, the Kodak box camera and Dunlop pneumatic tires in 1888, the Ford car in 1893, the cinematograph and the gramophone disc in 1894, the Diesel engine in 1895. By the year 1895 the speed at which culture was reinventing itself through technology was staggering: Roentgen discovered the X ray, Marconi invented radio telegraphy and the Lumière brothers the movie camera, the Russian Konstantin Tsiolkovsky first articulated the principle of rocket drive, and Freud published his studies on hysteria. And on it went till the Wright brothers took their first powered flight in 1903 and Albert Einstein formulated his Special Theory of Relativity in 1905, amounting to the greatest alteration in man's view of the universe since Isaac Newton.

In London in 1910 there seemed to be a growing sense of public drama. King Edward died in May. His successor, George V, stood for responsibility and respectability; his court was much more exclusive, without Edward's Jewish financiers. Two men, inventors of modern journalism, also helped undermine the old order. In 1908 Northcliffe bought *The Times* and the *Daily Mail* and introduced sensation to the staid and the settled. Moreover he was forever changing his mind on issues and confusing the public with each shift. Prime Minister Lloyd George once said that talking with Northcliffe was like "taking a walk with a grasshopper." The result was greater public bewilderment. Max Aitken, later Lord Beaverbrook, came to England in 1908, the year Pound first arrived. Nine years later he assumed control of the *Daily Express.* Both men felt the day of serious journalism was over: the formal essay was going to be replaced by the blurb or headline, and if they didn't like the news, they could create it.

The death of Edward seemed like an opportunity for reformers and revolutionists. Many intellectuals had been persuaded by the Fabians of the invidious economic injustices of the class structure. They were then determined to redress them. The Fabians offered a view of a world governed by experts. Not a political party but more a pressure group for a change in consciousness, their aim was a rational socialist state. Shaw and for a time H. G. Wells were spokesmen. But Wells, a red-faced man with a shrill, asthmatic, half-cockney squeak of a voice, who looked as if he were always on the verge of a stroke of apoplexy, betrayed the Fabians with his satire *The New Machiavelli* in the *English Review* in 1910. Earnest, bleakly moralistic, and utilitarian, Beatrice and Sidney Webb led the Fabians and succeeded in creating a climate of opinion that wanted change.

While the Fabians were gradualists, more-militant elements of the labor movement exhorted workers to act. In 1910 shipyard managers locked out the boilermakers, and clothing manufacturers prevented a hundred thousand garment workers from going to their jobs. At this time dockworkers earned about a pound a week; Yeats was earning half that from his poetry. By the time of Pound's return, miners, dockworkers, and railway men were striking, and the possibility of a general strike, at least in London, seemed imminent. No coal was available and food lay rotting on the docks for weeks. The strikes persisted, were settled with concessions, and flared up again. One offshoot of the labor trouble was that in a large confectionary factory in London women went on strike, demanding parity with male salaries. This strike activated the women's movement on a national scale with the demand for the vote, a demand satisfied only after the war. There were violent protests, mass rallies. A steel spike was thrown through the window of Prime Minister Lloyd George's cab, missing his eye but piercing his cheek. A bomb was exploded in his house, wrecking four rooms. Flaming rags were dropped in mailboxes, racetrack grandstands were burned, shop windows were smashed, and women were pushed down and arrested.

The turmoil of 1910 was abetted by backlash. On the one hand were those like Pound who brashly denounced Victorian rationalism, evangelicism, and prudery. The signs of their success were immediately evident. Many women no longer would wear their starched collars or their stiff straw hats, they removed corsets and padding from hips and buttocks, hemlines rose from the dust, daring ladies slashed their evening skirts up to the knee and wore plumed headdresses and clashing colors. Such women faced condemnation, public insult, and an arthritic resistance. Reverend James Marchant organized his Crusade for Social Purity and advised young men to take cold baths, avoid modern fiction, and practice abstinence. The writings of Havelock Ellis on sex and of Freud were castigated from pulpits. Books by Balzac and Dickens were regarded as unfit for London schoolchildren, and a series of public morals conferences in London, Dublin, and Edinburgh were organized to exert pressure against "sex-novels" and contraception. There was a feeling that religion and the family were endangered by indecency, and that the social stability of the country was being adversely affected. The result for the arts was that whatever artists created was considered suspicious by the middle classes, and artists were generally classed as dangerous dissidents.

A clear example of this attitude was expressed in the press treatment of the first Postimpressionist show, held in the Grafton Gallery in London in the winter of 1910. The art critic Roger Fry brought from France eight paintings by Manet, twenty-one by Cézanne, twenty-two by van Gogh, and thirty-six by Gauguin. Desmond MacCarthy, who assisted Fry with the show, commented on the press reaction:

> Soon after ten the Press began to arrive. Now anything new in art
> is apt to provoke the same kind of indignation as immoral conduct,
> and vice is detected in perfectly innocent pictures. Perhaps any

mental shock is apt to remind people of moral shocks they have received, and the sensations being similar, they attribute this to the same cause. Anyhow, as I walked about among the tittering newspaper critics busily taking notes (they saw at once that the whole thing was splendid copy) I kept overhearing such remarks as "Pure pornography," "Admirably indecent."

The critics denounced the show as a scandalous disgrace. *The Times* called it a childish rejection of civilization, declaring that "to gain simplicity it throws away all that the long-developed skill of past artists had acquired and perpetuated." Of course at this time the press had no movie stars to canonize, so painters and poets could still be treated as celebrities. One of the most publicized attacks on the show was written by Robert Ross, who had been a friend of Oscar Wilde's and perhaps should have known better. Ross believed that the artists being shown were mad, and he argued in the *Morning Post* that their emotions "are of no interest except to the student of pathology and the specialist in abnormality." He described van Gogh as a lunatic degenerate and Matisse as a madman, and the show seemed to him to be an example of charlatanism and chicanery. A number of artists wrote letters in support of Ross's view. Philip Burne-Jones called it a huge French practical joke, and Sir William Richmond warned that English youth could be contaminated by the "unmanly show." As a result the public came to see what the fuss was about, and remained to mock. According to Virginia Woolf, the show caused public "paroxysms of rage and laughter." Ladies strolled through the galleries tittering, even Henry James was aghast, and one man laughed so hard at Cézanne's portrait of his wife that he had to be led outside. E. M. Forster confessed that the Gauguin and van Gogh were too much for him, and the poet and diplomat W. S. Blunt wrote the following account in his diary:

> To the Grafton Gallery to look at what are called the Post-Impressionist pictures sent over from Paris. The exhibition is either an extremely bad joke or a swindle. I am inclined to think the latter, for there is no trace of humour in it. Still less is there a trace of sense or skill or taste, good or bad, or art or cleverness. Nothing but that gross puerility which scrawls indecencies on the walls of a privy. The drawing is on the level of that of an untaught child of seven or eight years old, the sense of colour that of a tea-tray painter, the method that of a schoolboy who wipes his fingers on a slate after spitting on them. There is nothing at all more humorous than that, at all more clever. In all the 300 or 400 pictures there was not one worthy of attention even by its singularity, or appealing to any feeling but of disgust. . . . Apart from the frames, the whole collection should not be worth £5, and then only for the

pleasure of making a bonfire of them. Yet two or three of our art
critics have pronounced in their favour. . . . These are not works
of art at all, unless throwing a handful of mud against a wall may
be called one. They are the works of idleness and impotent stupidity, a pornographic show.

The hostile reaction to the show reveals the conditions with which Pound
and other artists of his generation had to contend. This reaction is all the
more interesting when one remembers Floyd Dell comparing Pound's poetry to the exhibition because of "its unconventional form, bizarre phraseology, catalectic or involved sentence structure and recondite meanings."

7. THE NEW AGE GROUP

Everyone in London was still talking about the Grafton show when
Pound returned from America and he quickly went to see it. For Pound, the
show was the confirmation of the new spirit in the arts which he saw himself
as leading, at least as far as the art of poetry was concerned. Just as promptly
he left for Paris, staying in a pension, meeting with Arnold Bennett and
frequently with Yeats, and tried to find out what was happening with current French poetry. Pound went to the art galleries, looking for more of
Matisse and Cézanne. At this time in Paris a group of painters, most of
whom were still experimenting with early Cubism, were using predomi-
nantly blacks and browns: Duchamp was painting *Each Young Man on a
Train* in ominously dark browns and blacks; Picasso was doing *The Poet* in
similar tones; Braque's *The Clarinet* was only a bit lighter in hue; Juan Gris
was painting in brown and black; even Mondrian, known for his yellows
and reds, was doing his strange grids in browns. These were colors presaging war and the sadness that follows.

By early spring Pound was living with Walter Morse Rummel, a musician he had met through Katherine Heyman. Rummel set several of his
poems to music and introduced him to a friend named Margaret Cravens.
He received page proofs for *Canzoni* from Elkin Mathews in May, corrected
them, and returned to Sirmione. In Italy he met William Carlos Williams's
brother Edward, who was studying architecture, and together they in-
spected some handmade stone columns signed by their maker at San Zeno
Church in Verona—Pound later referred to these columns as an example of
ancient craftsmanship replaced by the modern anonymity of steel beams. He
then set out for Giessen, a small university town north of Frankfurt, to visit
Ford.

Ford was in Germany with his mistress, Violet Hunt. He had been
married at the age of nineteen, fathered two children, and passively watched
his marriage deteriorate while he struggled to earn a living as a writer. He

and his wife had been separated for some time, she being a Roman Catholic who objected to divorce. Ford had met Violet Hunt in 1908 when she came to see him about publishing some of her stories in the *English Review*. She was eleven years older than he was and he had known her as a child: her father was Holman Hunt, the Pre-Raphaelite painter and a close friend of Ford's grandfather. A successful novelist, Violet had a reputation for being a malicious wit with a caustic cleverness, but she was very kind to Ford, nurturing him and practically mothering him. He ran his magazine, she felt, with a pathetic inefficiency, "an infant in charge of a motor car," she wrote. Pound later revealed to Richard Cassell, who was preparing a dissertation on Ford, that he told Ford "that if he were placed naked in a room without furnishings, I could come back in an hour and find total confusion." Violet Hunt tried to advise him. Ford telephoned frequently in his "languid, plangent tenor," as H. G. Wells characterized his voice in *Boon*, calling for consolation, full of insinuations of his misery.

Ford had gone to Germany with the foolish notion that just because he had been born there, he could get a divorce there. When Pound visited, he brought an advance copy of *Canzoni*, a very literary and affected collection. Ford's reaction stunned Pound:

> And he felt the errors of contemporary style to the point of rolling (physically, and if you look at it as a mere superficial snob, ridiculously) on the floor of his contemporary quarters at Giessen when my third volume displayed me trapped, fly papered (possibly hyphen), gummed and strapped down in a jejune *[sic]* provincial effort to learn, mehercule, the stilted language that then passed for "Good English" in the arthritic milieu that held control of the respected British critical circles, Newbolt, the backwash of Lionel Johnson, Fred Manning, the Quarterlies and the rest of 'em.

The event was incongruous, the heavy older writer in hysterical convulsions because of the inflated rhetoric of Pound's poems. Ford had been advising Pound to write more naturally, to listen for the sounds of actual, contemporary speech. His message, Pound recalled, was that a poet could say "nothing, nothing, that you couldn't in some circumstances, in the stress of some emotion, *actually* say." But Pound had still been responding to the influence of his Provençal studies and was still imbrued with the romantic ambience of Yeats's poems, miasmic mysteries that served only to cloud the poems and prevent the poet from breaking through to clear insight. For Pound, the incident was a gestalt, a sudden recognition that he would have to revise his entire concept of what made for effective language in poetry.

He received a very different reaction to *Canzoni* from Dorothy Shakespear writing from London, thanking him for the dedication to Olivia and herself, full of longing, loneliness, and a wistful sadness. In her notebook she confessed life could be enjoyable but never really happy; her place, she felt, was to serve beauty rather than make it herself, and she could best do this through Ezra Pound. The days spent with her lover a year earlier at Sirmione were remembered and cherished. The occasion had proven a sort of opening for her, and for the next twenty years the subject of her water-colors would be the lake at Sirmione.

At the end of the summer Pound returned to London, living first in a boardinghouse, then sharing quarters with Rummel until his room on Church Walk was again free. Hulme was holding an open house on Tuesday evenings in the home of one of his many female admirers, Mrs. Kibblewhite, who lived in what had been the Venetian Embassy in the eighteenth century and was still furnished with First Empire mirrors and chandeliers of that era. An enormously sociable man, capable of a disarming honesty that endeared him to many artists, Hulme knew people from all quarters and admitted everyone to his evenings except women, on the grounds that the "sex element interfered with intellectual talk." There Pound met A. R. Orage, editor of *The New Age.* Orage had heard of Pound, for Flint had reviewed *Personae* in his pages, and he agreed to let Pound write articles on a regular basis. This was an important step for Pound. When he left America it was with the knowledge that his father was not willing to help him as much as he had for the past three years, that he would have to find a way to support himself as a writer.

The New Age, a weekly review of politics, literature, and art, was a potpourri of controversy, a forum for artists and intellectuals, for Fabian socialists, pacifists, suffragettes, and apostles of sexual liberation. Its offices were reached through a dank alley, up a narrow stone staircase, where Orage could be found behind a battered rolltop desk in a cubicle smelling of printer's ink. Orage had written two books on Nietzsche and was suspicious of organized religion, but a follower of theosophy and, later, Gurdjieff. He supported young and unknown writers like Middleton Murray, Katherine Mansfield, and Herbert Read, but a number of already established writers were affiliated: Shaw, who had started *The New Age* with a five-hundred-pound loan, Wells, Arnold Bennett, Havelock Ellis, John Galsworthy. Often Orage was unable to pay his contributors, but on Pound he settled a regular salary of a pound a week—a laborer's family lived on that in 1911. Orage's system was to gather his contributors for conversation at the A.B.C. coffeehouse on Chancery Lane in the late afternoons, or at Bellotti's, an inexpensive Italian restaurant, on Monday nights. Genial but capable of sarcasm, with an argumentative nature, he would prod his writers into an awareness of political trends and what he wanted in *The New Age.* The result was often cantankerous, sometimes scathing, almost always controversial and consequently not taken seriously by the British public. Pound had found his milieu, and in the next few years wrote nearly three hundred articles for Orage.

One of the men Pound met in the Orage circle was Allen Upward. Upward was a friend of G. R. S. Mead, editor of *The Quest*, a journal of gnosticism and theosophy, so Upward heard Pound lecture to Mead's group on troubador paganism in the fall of 1911. A lawyer by profession, Upward preferred writing poems and plays and books like *The Divine Mystery*, a comparative study of religion which Pound reviewed, noting Upward's belief that the fate of genius is to be crucified. Upward began telling Pound about Oriental art. He had also collected and printed himself a little collection of Confucian sayings. At the same time, Pound was reading his friend Laurence Binyon's *The Flight of the Dragon*, a book about Chinese art and poetry published in 1911. Binyon worked in the Department of Oriental Prints and Drawings at the British Museum and told Pound that "slowness is beauty," a Confucian precept Pound would cherish in contradiction to the accelerating tempo of his time and his own racing inner needs. These two sources, Upward and Binyon, coalesced to engender Pound's fascination with Chinese and Japanese poetry.

Pound's first contribution to *The New Age* was the result of earlier inclinations, a free translation from Anglo-Saxon, a poem he called "The Seafarer," which starkly and powerfully presented the hardship, harshness, and loneliness of the "wretched outcast" who chose the ice-cold sea for his life. "The Seafarer" had the dramatic impact of "Sestina: Altaforte," but Pound's talent was maturing and a brooding presence controls the poem, giving it a weight and dimension not present in his earlier work. In "Patria Mia" Pound speculated that music and art came to England from the south, from Spain, Italy, and Provence, but a certain toughness in the English national character added a fiber and temper that he sought in his own work. He sent the poem to Frederic Manning, who was jealous of Pound's courtship of Dorothy. Manning replied that Pound's attempt at translation showed he was only a fool. Actually, a number of Pound's translations over the next few years were misunderstood, challenged, and condemned, especially by scholarly types like Manning who could not see that Pound was not content with the literal and thus lifeless translations of the past. In the preface to his Cavalcanti book, Pound conceived that "poetry of a far-off time or place requires a translation not only of word and of spirit, but of 'accompaniment,' that is, that the modern audience must in some measure be made aware of the mental content of the older audience, and of what these others drew from certain fashions of thought and speech."

F. S. Flint, in the piece he had done on Pound for *The New Age*, had argued, perhaps a bit prematurely, that Pound seemed to prefer translations to making his own poetry, and that even when he succeeded in writing independently, his work still had the flavor of translation. Up until the time of *Personae* this was true, but Pound was at this time preparing a major shift in diction and image that governed his future as a poet. What may have irritated the British, especially other writers like Manning and Flint, was Pound's manner of announcing to the world as discovery through translation—whether it was the architectural beauty of Venice, the troubador material, or later the Chinese poets or Propertius—what was actually well known in his time and studied by specialists who quarreled over commas like biblical exegetes convinced of their holy calling. At the same time, translation was related to the idea of personae, the masks through which Pound could most effectively speak, and it was the emotional result of his own reverent pilgrimage to the past, an impulse that made him admire old stone columns and take walking tours through Provence.

The New Age next ran a serial presentation of what Pound called the "new scholarship," an intuitive Emersonian lurch through his own ideas on poetry, its rhythm, pitch, and music. Pound defined his method as that of luminous detail, the investigation of certain facts giving one "a sudden insight into circumjacent conditions, into their causes, their effects, into sequence, and law." Essentially, this was to be his method as a prose writer, never methodically arranging an argument but hyperbolically exploding a recognition that had become for him a gestalt that established a pattern. Later he would use the German anthropologist Frobenius's term for this method, calling it *paideuma,* a revealing tangle or complex of inrooted ideas and the "gristly roots" of those ideas in action. The study of such a tangle would expose, Pound believed, the germinal and active principles of an era. The extravagant title of his first series in *The New Age* was "I Gather the Limbs of Osiris," a sign of his own poetic license and the importance he gave to the subject. King Osiris's mission had been to civilize the Egyptians, who kill him. His wife, Isis, recovers his remains and accords him divine honors. Pound's title expresses his view of the primal function and risk of the artist and points to his own rescue of neglected poets. Arguing that his purpose as a poet is to disintegrate cliché with a simplicity and directness of utterance that is still dignified, he first conceives of his notion of the vortex, the poem as a hollow steel cone charged with a force like electricity, sucking in and radiating that force.

8. PUPPIES WITH TIN CANS

Devising the bases of his own aesthetics in *The New Age,* where he wrote art criticism under the pseudonym of B. H. Dias and music criticism as William Atheling, Pound was pondering how to push English poetry into the twentieth century. His own work, as Ford had demonstrated on the floor in Germany, was still crippled by mannerisms, archaisms, involutions of the past, formalities which Pound realized could no longer speak to an age of such rapid change. The British poets had formed themselves under the banner of Edward Marsh, who anthologized them as the Georgians; Pound saw they were simply continuing the pallid and unimaginative conventions of their Edwardian predecessors, who, in turn, had continued the saccharine melodies of the nineties poets. Marsh liked poetry that he could learn by heart, poetry that was organized according to an easy narrative, and most of all intelligibility. As one critic said, the poetry he gathered tended to be "facile, sentimental, socially and morally non-significant." John Masefield, Walter de la Mare, Edmund Blunden, and Lascelles Abercrombie, and the other Georgians who gathered in Harold Monro's Soho bookshop, wrote gracefully though inconsequentially.

Pound had been in the process of building a tradition he could respect and use, one that valued Dante and Cavalcanti and the troubadors. At this point he began to concern himself with what he considered dangerous influences for the poet, leading to corrupt practice. His head full of rejection and criticism, he began to spend more and more time with T. E. Hulme and his group. The Hulme evenings were becoming occasions for intellectuals: journalists, Fabians, and politicians were apt to visit, the economist W. L. George came, and so did Orage and Mrs. Hastings, the sculptor Jacob Epstein, even representatives of the Georgians like Edward Marsh, Harold Monro, and Rupert Brooke. With Hulme, Pound agreed that the romantic mood in most of its manifestations was the real hazard for modern poetry. He attacked Tennyson and the genteel Victorians for perpetuating that mood with their sentimental effusions. His angriest criticism was reserved for Tennyson, whose "pretty embroideries" and "ladylike attitude" were an expression of his notion that the poet could write for the middle classes and his ability to dilute his poetry so that they could absorb it. He even belittled Browning for his "jejune remarks about God" and blamed the poets of the nineties for their "decayed lily verbiage" and "riot of decayed fruit." For the poetry that Pound had read while in England he had nothing but contempt: "The common verse of Britain from 1890 was a horrible agglomerate compost, not minted, most of it not even baked, all legato, a doughty mess of third-hand Keats, Wordsworth, heaven knows what, fourth-hand Elizabethan sonority blunted, half-melted, lumpy." He predicted a change for the poetry of his generation in a piece he wrote around Christmas of 1911 which was printed as "Prologomena" in Harold Monro's *Poetry Review:*

As to twentieth-century poetry, and the poetry I expect to see written during the next decade or so, it will, I think, move against poppy-cock, it will be harder and saner, it will be what Mr. Hewlett calls "nearer the bone." It will be as much like granite as it can be, its force will lie in its truth, its interpretative power (or course, poetic force does always rest there); I mean it will not try to seem forcible by rhetorical din, and luxurious riot. We will have fewer painted adjectives impeding the shock and stroke of it. At least for myself, I want it so, austere, direct, free from emotional slither.

Hulme, with his massive presence—standing well over six feet, broad-shouldered with legs like a racing cyclist, and a florid countenance—was the sort of man who could lead others. Hulme was also an admirer of French authoritarian thinkers like Georges Sorel, whose *Reflections on Violence* he had translated. Sorel was antidemocratic and felt men could be renewed and energized through violent conflict. His book was a harbinger of rule by fascist mob. Another French authoritarian who influenced Hulme and his group was Charles Maurras, who thought that liberty led only to chaos and anarchy and that a hereditary elite should manipulate the masses for the sake of the social order. Maurras argued that society needed fixed rules, stratification, hierarchy, and a strong leader for the masses to admire. Hulme was eccentric and outspoken, and he had wit: his chief pleasure in life, he once declared, was in reading Kant's *Critique of Pure Reason* while lying supine in a warm bathtub. He spoke with forceful arrogance in a harsh, North Country accent, and with a booming, assertive conviction: "All a man ever thought," he told Pound, "would fit onto a half a sheet of notepaper. The rest is application and elaboration." Pound himself began applying what he was learning from Hulme in the spring of 1911 when he took a brief trip to Paris. Emerging from the metro at La Concorde, he "suddenly saw a beautiful face, and then another and another, and then a beautiful child's face, and then another beautiful woman, and I tried all that day to find words for what they had meant to me, and I could not find any words that seemed to me worthy, or as lovely as that sudden emotion." Instead, he radically abbreviated his response and revised it over a year until he had a short poem modeled on Japanese haiku which he called "In a Station of the Metro." It became one of the first soundings for a new poetry:

> The apparition of these faces in the crowd;
> Petals on a wet, black bough.

Hulme had heard Henri Bergson discuss the image as a locus between intuition and concept, and he realized that in poetry the image could become a new lever suggesting feeling. Pound attended a series of Hulme's lectures on Bergson and then described to Hulme the difference between what Pound called Petrarchan "fustian and ornament" and Guido Cavalcanti's more "precise interpretative metaphor." Pound argued that Cavalcanti thought in more accurate terms, that his "phrases corresponded to definite sensations." In a later essay on Cavalcanti, Pound recalled that Hulme found Pound's observations "more interesting than anything I ever read in a book." But Pound may have been much more indebted to Hulme, whose ideas he appropriated when devising Imagism. Hulme's evenings were becoming more and more successful, there was not enough room for two leaders, and soon there was some resentment between Hulme and Pound.

Another source of difficulty was Dorothy, or more properly speaking, her parents. Olivia regretted having taken Dorothy to meet the young poet at Sirmione because she could see that in the lush surroundings of Lake Garda her daughter had fallen completely in love. She then began a series of strategic visits to Dorset and Southampton with her daughter, intended to separate the pair so that ardor could cool. But Pound's attraction to Dorothy only increased when he sensed parental resistance; it was in his nature to develop desire and energy in the face of opposition. He wanted Dorothy because she was beautiful, but also because she represented a living link in the literary tradition. She was a Shakespeare, even without the final "e," and her mother had been Yeats's lover. And finally, Pound knew she was a woman he could completely dominate, who would serve him faithfully. Dorothy continued to correspond during the summer of 1911 and by late summer was encouraging Pound to formally request her hand. When he in fact did approach Henry Hope Shakespear, allegedly flourishing a handful of bank notes he had received that day for a translation of some French songs by Villon and others, he was told to prepare an exact statement of his financial position and prospects. Pound had said that his income was then two hundred pounds a year and asked his father to write to H. H. Shakespear confirming it, but Dorothy's father was suspicious about the permanence of any literary income and decided that it was "obvious that he is not in a position to marry."

Pound's income had increased considerably since his return from America. He was doing free-lance translation, and the publisher Steven Swift had agreed to guarantee him a hundred pounds a year for ten years in exchange for a book of his own work or a translation each year. Swift specialized in "unorthodox writers, free-thinkers and mystics" so Pound's good standing in *The New Age* group would have been a helpful credential. The firm was directed by Charles Granville, whose friend Dora Marsden founded *The Freewoman*, a magazine Pound later influenced.

During the winter and early spring of 1912, Pound was working on new poems which Swift would publish as *Ripostes*, the first collection in which Pound showed evidence of his authentic voice. One of the poems, "A Virginal," may reflect the frustration he felt in his pursuit of Dorothy. The poem was written with the dramatically charged intensity of John Donne's best love poems. However, the woman in "A Virginal" had been idealized as in much of the troubador poetry Pound had studied:

No, no! Go from me. I have left her lately.
I will not spoil my sheath with lesser brightness,
For my surrounding air hath a new lightness;
Slight are her arms, yet they have bound me straitly
And left me cloaked as with a gauze of aether;
As with sweet leaves; as with subtle clearness.
Oh, I have picked up magic in her nearness
To sheathe me half in half the things that sheathe
      her.
No, no! Go from me. I have still the flavour,
Soft as spring wind that's come from birchen
      bowers.
Green come the shoots, aye April in the branches,
As winter's wound with her sleight hand she
      staunches,
Hath of the trees a likeness of the savour:
As white their bark, so white this lady's hours.

Pound's virgin had her transcendental qualities: the "gauze of aether," the "magic in her nearness," her associations in the poem with the pagan, regenerative powers of the dryad or wood nymph. The virgin in Pound's poem becomes much more than Dorothy, a blend of a number of women including Hilda Doolittle and Dante's Beatrice. She is courted by a troubador singer in the spring wood. Intoxicated at having just left her presence, he lyrically weaves the spell of his song of remembrance. It was a favored persona for Pound, the poet as suitor, praising grace and beauty and connecting such qualities to nature. The poem begins noisily, a reminder of Donne ordering the "unruly" sun to depart because daybreak interrupts his lovers; it ends with an image of miraculous healing, the woman with the power to summon spring, a wood goddess who throughout the poem is identified with natural forces, sweet leaves, spring wind, the smell of the birch trees. The rich and subtle half rhymes, the archaically flavored words, the sonnet form with its traditional notions of constraint and courtly appeal, all make "A Virginal" seem a successful imitation of the seventeenth-century mood.

But while the poem is clearly an example of a young poet honoring the masters of his tradition, in it Pound had begun to develop a technique of projection through dramatic situation that remained a permanent part of his poetic manner. The act of dramatization represented an active commitment to his subject that made the creation of poems a real expression of felt experience, not merely fictive or imagined but believed, an act of passion. The perfection of elaborately convincing dramatic masks became Pound's purpose as a poet, and the kaleidoscopic presentation of a discontinuous series of such masks became the structure for *The Cantos*. Pound later explained in a memoir written during the war how the artistic value of this dramatic method had a personal importance and a formative effect on his imagination:

> In the "search for ones-self," in the search for "sincere self-expression," one gropes, one finds some seeming verity. One says "I am" this, that, or the other, and with the words scarcely uttered one ceases to be that thing. I began this search for the real in a book called *Personae,* casting off, as it were, complete masks of the self in each poem. I continued in long series of translations, which were but more elaborate masks.

The spring of 1912 was a time flushed with new stimulation. His friend F. S. Flint introduced him to the writing of Remy de Gourmont and Pound became intrigued with de Gourmont's account of the sexual origin of poetic vision. After the war he translated de Gourmont's *The Natural Philosophy of Love.* He was also seeing Henry Slominski, whom he had originally met in graduate school. Slominski had finished a doctorate in Germany and published his thesis. He spoke passionately about Greece in the pre-Classical era with a brilliance and authority that impressed Pound, although his eloquence was superior to his prose style. Pound brought Slominski to one of Hulme's evenings and was even more impressed by the way the young philosopher was able to stand up to Hulme.

He took Dorothy to see Pavlova and Nijinsky and the Russian Ballet at the Royal Opera House at Covent Garden. The dancing seemed miraculous because of its primitive wildness. The Russian dancers were spontaneous enough to become absolutely absorbed by their art and they danced in a spirit of Dionysian intoxication instead of stressing technique and artificiality. Diaghilev's flair and the set designs and costumes by Bakst had helped make the Russians the entertainment spectacle of the moment. The music by Stravinsky and Debussy signaled a modern note to Pound: Edward Marsh, writing to Rupert Brooke, called it a "Post-Impressionist picture put into motion."

Pound was still attending Hulme's evenings and Yeats's, still seeing Ford and Violet Hunt, spending more time with G. R. S. Mead and attending a lecture series at the Quest Society with Dorothy. Pound gave one of the lectures, and a short series on Cavalcanti, Arnaut Daniel, and Anglo-Saxon poetry at Lord Glenconner's private gallery. As a result of his lectures he met Lady Low, who lived in De Vere Gardens, near Hyde Park, the same building that Henry James lived in before moving to Rye. Pound then met James but told his parents he only "glared" at "the Master" across the same carpet. He saw him twice more in March, once at a small luncheon where James, in a checkered waistcoat, flourished his conversation like an art form in itself and told Pound his ideas were too heretical. Pound set down his memory of James's periphrastic excesses in a memorial essay written six years later:

> The massive, the slow uplift of the hand, gli occhi onesti e tardi, the long sentences piling themselves up in elaborate phrase after phrase, the lightning incision, the pauses, the slightly shaking admonitory gesture with its "wu-a-wait a little, wait a little, something will come"; blague and benignity and the weight of so many years' careful, incessant labour of minute observation always there to enrich the talk. I had heard it but seldom yet it is all unforgettable.

James was important to Pound for two reasons. First, he was an older writer, the major American novelist of the time and a great stylist. He represented the exact artistic tradition that Pound so admired. Second, James was an expatriate, an American who had chosen to live abroad and to dramatize the differences between his countrymen and the Europeans.

When Pound had been in New York he had convinced Hilda Doolittle that London was the place to be if she wanted to become a poet. When she arrived there, about a half a year after he had returned, Pound had helped her to find a place to live and settle in. Now he was taking an almost proprietary interest in her, introducing her to Yeats, the Shakespears, Harold Monro, and Ernest Rhys. Hilda seemed the perfect satellite, a poet with no reputation but an appearance that seemed Grecian and very much in vogue. The popular interest in the Greek look—dresses cut from the shoulder in an unimpeded flow, loosely knotted hair held with a band cutting across the forehead—accompanied a renewed interest in the classics. Hilda, long and lean, looked like one of those maidens on a Greek vase, and Pound's friend Brigit Patmore described her in such terms:

> But no goddess ever showed such extreme vulnerability in her face, nor so wild and wincing a look in her deep-set eyes. She had soft brownish hair, a pallid complexion and a pouting sensitive mouth, but a magnificent line of jaw and chin gave a reassuring strength. Her voice was high, light and musical, with even less trans-Atlantic intonation than that of Ezra's.

But Brigit also found her frail and stooping, and perhaps she became too dependent on Pound. There were passionate, secret kisses in May Sinclair's Kensington studio, with Hilda, perhaps, still hoping to renew Pound's interest in a more permanent attachment, knowing also that this was impossible, that the old objections of her family would still prevail. But she seems to have been quite in Pound's power. Unexpectedly and unpredictably—the words are Hilda's—Pound appeared as she was preparing to leave for

Belgium to accompany her friend Frances Gregg on her honeymoon. In *End to Torment* Hilda describes how Pound thwarted the escapade by pushing her into a taxi, pounding his stick, and insisting she could not go. They all met later at Victoria Station, where "glowering and savage" Pound made sure the honeymoon couple left alone.

Pound's domination abated only when, at a party, Brigit Patmore introduced Hilda to Richard Aldington, a bluff, powerful, downright man, as Virginia Woolf later described him, but "not our kind." No two people could have been less suited to each other: Hilda, tall, slim, lithe, with a pale oval face set off by masses of brown hair and a nervous shyness of manner that signaled fragility, tuned to the slightest vibration, demanding and impetuous, emotionally and sexually ambivalent and volatile; and Aldington, hearty, square-shouldered with an athlete's body, bluff and beefy, a coarse man used to taking what he saw in front of him without apology or evasion even though he was only twenty. No wonder Virginia Woolf cringed and characterized his eyes as greasy. But clearly Hilda needed to be rescued from Pound even as Pound was about to make her into a poet.

But before that the three became friends, going to Paris in May together, frequently seeing Slominski who, on a bench in the Jardin du Luxembourg, discoursed an ancient Greek culture. In one of the bookstalls on the quays of the Seine, Pound bought a Latin version of the *Odyssey* and two translations of *The Iliad,* all three of which became sources for *The Cantos.* Pound left Hilda and Aldington at the end of May and set out for a walking tour in Provence with the intention of writing a prose book on the physical and intellectual factors shaping troubador poetry. He did not write the book —after all, he had already done *The Spirit of Romance* and perhaps he felt he had not learned enough to surpass what he had said there—but he did write an essay for G. W. Prothero's *Quarterly Review,* a magazine for which Pound confessed a "naïve respect."

In June, Pound returned to Paris for Walter Rummel's marriage to a French musician and was shocked by the resultant suicide of Margaret Cravens, Rummel's friend who had been Ravel's student. Margaret Cravens's father had committed suicide a year earlier and it was first conjectured that the surprise of Rummel's marriage was too much for her. However, she, like so many other women before her, had been taken by the cavalier presumptions of Pound's style and had developed a crush on him. Rummel claimed that he had told Margaret that Ezra and Dorothy Shakespear were engaged, and that his news had precipitated her suicide. In Paris, Pound tried to work on the troubadors in the Bibliothèque Nationale and corrected the proofs of *Ripostes,* but he was affected by Cravens's death. He wrote Dorothy that he found it "hard to exercise so wooden a Thing as my profession, that is, words—even to you." Hilda and Aldington, worried about his reaction to Margaret's death, tried to spend time with Pound.

Hilda identified with Margaret because she too had been "dropped" by Pound. One evening when Hilda and Pound had walked for hours in the city, on a bridge crossing the Seine near the Île St.-Louis, Pound despondently waved his ebony walking stick at the river and turned to Hilda, whispering, "And the morning stars sang together." The conception was so lyrical; for Pound, it seemed to be a benediction of sorts.

While he was there, dismayed and disoriented by Margaret Cravens's suicide, one of the first sure signs of his new voice, a poem called "The Return," appeared in the *English Review:*

> See, they return; ah, see the tentative
> Movements, and the slow feet,
> The trouble in the pace and the uncertain
> Wavering!
>
> See, they return, one, and by one,
> With fear, as half-awakened;
> As if the snow should hesitate
> And murmur in the wind,
>   and half turn back;
> These were the "Wing'd-with-Awe,"
>   Inviolable.
>
> Gods of the wingèd shoe!
> With them the silver hounds,
>   sniffing the trace of air!
>
> Haie! Haie!
>   These were the swift to harry;
> These the keen-scented;
> These were the souls of blood.
>
> Slow on the leash,
>   pallid the leash-men!

Written Pound claimed in merely a quarter of an hour, the poem was evidence of new control and mastery. Yeats praised it as "almost perfect": "The most beautiful poem that has been written in the free form, one of the few in which I find real organic rhythm." As an illustration of the principle Pound had used as the epigraph for his second book—Beauty must never be explained—the poem's enigmatic grace is haunting, mysteriously evoking some primal sense of wonder. Depicting the return of the gods to earth, moving like hunters exhausted by a chase, but also unconcerned and unrelenting, the poem is less a narrative than it is the *presentation* of a mythical mood or psychology. "The Return" is a de-romanticized version of Keats's "Ode on a Grecian Urn," a poem in frieze without a real resolution, presenting beauty outside time. Keats's poem is more painted, voluptuous in comparison, and Keats is more self-consciously neoclassical. Pound is harder, nearer to the bone, to use his own phrases. But behind the steel façade of his poem is his evident struggle with the romanticism his generation found it necessary to deny. Pound argued for an absolute rhythm in his "Prolegomena," which Monro had printed a year earlier, and "The Return" was an example of what he meant. Like the chiseled matter of Hilda Doolittle's poems set in the pre-Doric past of ancient Greece, Pound managed in "The Return" an intense vitality, the sharpest of visual senses, and combined this with an exceptional ease of movement, balance, and a very melodic line. Pound had insisted in "Prolegomena" that he believed in "technique as a test of a man's sincerity," which was a moral as well as an aesthetic position, and "The Return" was an important instance of his own faith in his art.

By July, Pound was back in Provence, walking for ten to fifteen miles each day and making notes on what he saw, some of which were later reflected in *The Cantos*, like the incident in which a stray gypsy asked him whether he had seen a party with apes or bears:

> The wind came, and the rain,
> And mist clotted about the trees in the valley,
> And I'd the long ways behind me,
>   gray Arles and Biaucaire,
> And he said, "Have you seen any of our lot?"
> I'd seen a lot of his lot . . .
>   ever since Rhodez,
> Coming down from the fair
>   of St. John
> With caravans, but never an ape or a bear.

By traveling on foot Pound was participating in an old tradition for poets. The troubadors, of course, had been perpetual walkers; in a later era, Wordsworth and Coleridge walked through the Lake District of England. Going on foot was an expression of the Confucian adage that "slowness is beauty" that Binyon had communicated to Pound, but it was also a way to refute progress and the emphasis on speed that determined the culture.

By August, Pound was back in his room on Church Walk in Kensington. He was restless because of what he considered the stagnant condition of poetry. He remembered later that "Nineteen twelve was a bad year, we all ran about like puppies with ten tin cans tied to our tails. The tin cans of Swinburnian rhyming, of Browningisms, even in Mr. Ford's case of Kiplingisms, a resonant pendant, magniloquent, Milton, sonorous." He was stimulated by a long essay Flint had published in *Poetry Review* on the various schools in contemporary French poetry and their relation to *symbolisme,* the movement of Verlaine and Baudelaire, which had determined the character of French poetry at the end of the nineteenth century. It had been a remarkable summer for art in Paris in 1912: Duchamp had completed his *Nude Descending a Staircase* and Apollinaire had published *Les Peintres cubistes*. Flint's piece may have given Pound the idea of beginning a movement in London to be organized around the radically condensed impact of poems like "In a Station of the Metro" and "The Return." He was pondering over the French poet Remy de Gourmont's remark that "idea is only an imperfect induction from fact." When Harriet Monroe wrote from Chicago—the letter came as he was reading Flint's article—asking Pound to contribute to her new magazine, *Poetry*. Pound realized he might find a forum for himself, Hilda Doolittle, and a few other friends.

9. THE ARCHIMANDRITE OF IMAGISM

Harriet Monroe, a direct descendant of President James Monroe, was a member of a distinguished American family. Her sister's husband was minister to China and she had extensive connections in the business community which she used to raise capital for *Poetry*. Pound agreed to submit poems and proposed himself as the European editor, but he warned her that he regarded poetry as an art of some complexity which ought not to be confused with the metrically arranged "sociologic dogma" that appeared in most magazines. He sent two poems, "Middle Aged," which he warned was an Imagist piece without bothering to define his new term, and "To Whistler American." The second poem, inspired by a retrospective Pound saw at the Tate Gallery, caused considerable controversy and a flurry of angry letters because of its tribute to the painter:

> You and Abe Lincoln from that mass of dolts
> Show us there's chance at least of winning through.

Pound was Ezekiel, Harriet Monroe answered the magazine's critics, accusing Americans of their stolid indifference to things artistic. The "mass of dolts" phrase was impolitic, another one of Pound's characteristic exaggerations. But it also proclaimed his scorn for most of humanity, the attitude that they were like sheep to be herded. He often abused the public in his letters, but soon he began to attack and then defile them in his poems. At first he was almost playful about it; later, he seemed convinced that the public was responsible for the success of mediocre art and muddled mores.

With energy and dispatch, Pound began collecting poetry for the new magazine. Through Yeats he had met the Indian poet Rabindranath Tagore and convinced him to contribute. He got poems from Yeats, suggested some editorial changes to him, and next began a long discussion with the older poet on diction based on his new Imagist attitudes, which Yeats first found presumptuous. He then asked Hilda Doolittle to show him some poems in the tearoom of the British Museum, in the "rather prissy milieu of some infernal bun shop full of English spinsters," as Aldington put it. Pound read Hilda's new poems with admiration. According to Aldington, Pound popped his pince-nez, an affectation he had learned from Yeats, when he read her "Hermes of the Ways," a poem he immediately cut and changed to make its pristine clarity even more penetrating, and signed the poem "H.D., Imagiste." In the space of a few moments Pound had created a literary movement and its first acolytes. He sent five of H.D.'s poems, and a few of Aldington's as well, to Harriet Monroe with instructions that they be printed before any more of his own work. H.D.'s poems, Pound wrote, were modern even though the subjects were classical. Her poems were "the sort of American stuff I can show here and in Paris without its being ridiculed. Objectivity—no slither; direct—no excessive use of adjectives, no metaphors that won't permit examination. It's straight talk, straight as the Greek!" In his letter he also described the intentions of the group he was now calling the Imagists:

> Objectivity and again objectivity, and no expression, no hind-side-beforeness, no Tennysonianness of speech—nothing, nothing, that you couldn't in some circumstance, in the stress of some emotion, actually say. Every literaryism, every book word, fritters away a scrap of the reader's patience, a scrap of his sense of your sincerity. When one really feels and thinks, one stammers with a simple speech. It is only in the flurry, the shallow frothy excitement of writing, or the inebriety of a metre, that one falls into the easy, easy—oh, how easy!—speech of books and poems that one has read.

In October, Pound's *Ripostes* was published in London by Stephen Swift. *Ripostes* included three important poems, "The Seafarer," "The Return," and "Portrait d'une Femme." In these poems Pound demonstrated his turn to a more natural, direct phrasing, free of the stilted mannerism and stuffiness of mood that had come with the territory of Provence. "The Seafarer" was an example of Pound's new free-form translation, "The Return" one of the poems that Flint had charged looked like a translation but was not, but "Portrait d'une Femme" was a new sound, a concentrated suavity in definition, the exploration of a sort of soiled muse, a woman who was extremely literate herself but who only serviced other writers with her knowledge and affection:

> Great minds have sought you—lacking someone else.
> You have been second always. Tragical?

> No. You preferred it to the usual thing:
> One dull man, dulling and uxorious,
> One average mind—with one thought less, each year.

Dedicated to Williams, the book also had an appendix called "The Complete Poetic Works of T. E. Hulme," a group of five brief Imagist poems. The act seemed a rare occasion of literary generosity. It was also a tacit acknowledgment of the place Hulmes's ideas on the image had taken in Pound's mind. *Ripostes* was the beginning of Pound's breakthrough as a poet, but it did not become the success he wanted. Within weeks of its publication, Stephen Swift and Company foundered.

Pound spent the Christmas holidays with Ford, Violet Hunt, and novelist Compton Mackenzie and his wife in a cottage at Farnham Common in the north of England that had once belonged to Milton. On the day before Christmas, Pound talked nonstop about literature and good writing, releasing a torrent of language. Ford, feeling badly about his separation from his daughter, retired early for the night; when he emerged again the next morning, Pound was still talking. Pound's marathon monologue was an early warning sign of an uncontainable manic and feverish energy. Pound was at this time full of his new Imagist ideas, his new objectivist principles that would replace the nineteenth-century statement of emotion with concrete sensations and tactile, observable realities. But his new ideas welled inside him and poured forth as a crusade, an attack on the element of polite euphemism in poets like Tennyson.

Pound began to receive visitors at home on Tuesday evenings in the winter of 1913. Poets came with poems that he revised according to his new precepts, cutting out archaisms, "painted" adjectives, unnecessary words, trite decorative images, and the holy terror, abstraction. "I've got a right to be severe," he wrote to Alice Henderson. "For one man I strike there are ten to strike back at me. I stand exposed. It hits me in my dinner invitations, in my week ends, in reviews of my own work. Nevertheless, it's a good fight." He was reading Henry James and "Patria Mia" was appearing in weekly installments in *The New Age*. He lectured on the new poetry at Cambridge. Hulme attended and brought Edward Marsh, who was about to issue the first of his popular anthologies of Georgian verse. Pound then set out to define Imagism, realizing that he could use it as a banner to advance himself and his causes, and to challenge the placid and genteel Georgians and their "interminable effusions." The Imagists, he reported for the January issue of *Poetry*, the issue containing H.D.'s poems, had come together out of shared taste:

> The youngest school here that has the nerve to call itself a school is
> that of the Imagistes. To belong to a school does not in the least
> mean that one writes poetry to a theory. One writes poetry when,

where, because, and as one feels like writing it. A school exists when two or three young men agree, more or less, to call certain things good; when they prefer such of their verses as have certain qualities to such of their verses as do not have them.

In the March issue of *Poetry* he made his definition more categorical. In "A Few Don'ts by an Imagiste" he listed certain cardinal features: "Use no superfluous word, no adjective, which does not reveal something"; "Go in fear of abstractions. Don't retell in mediocre verse what has already been done in good prose"; "Use either no ornament or good ornament." His summary of the Imagist position was accompanied by a brief article by Flint which included three rules for the new movement:

1. Direct treatment of the "thing," whether subjective or objective
2. To use absolutely no word that did not contribute to the presentation
3. As regarding rhythm: to compose in sequence of the musical phrase, not in sequence of a metronome

The first rule meant that poets could use no explanations, that the poem had to rely exclusively on images that could be seen or heard or smelled. The point was impact, and that the Imagists believed could be best achieved by a ruthless concentration on the senses. The second rule was merely a corollary to the first, but according to Pound it was the most important principle and the most difficult to attain. The third rule was a call for free verse, for the end of metrical arrangement that depended on using a certain number of stressed and unstressed syllables in a line, with a rhyme tacked on at the end for prettiness. The point for the Imagists was that such confining restrictions only forced a poet to corset his meaning into a preconceived pattern, and this they saw as tantamount to a sort of lie. A case in point was a poem Pound had just written about the new painting, called "L'Art 1910":

Green arsenic smeared on an egg-white cloth,
Crushed strawberries. Come let us feast our eyes!

The key words in Pound's compact and contracted little poem are "smeared" and "crushed." As a feast of colors, the poem plays with our sense of the beautiful in the way that the new painters were beginning to redefine conventional notions of how beauty could be portrayed. Pound's poem was a singular response to a new sense of color and design, a poem that could smear and crush as the borders of representative objects had been extended since Cézanne's *Rocks at Garonne* series. Pound may have been motivated by the art critics who had denounced Matisse's painting *The Open Window* with the accusation that Matisse knew nothing about color theory, since the red and green he used were opposites creating conflicting intensities. For the nineteenth-century critic, beauty meant harmony; for Pound, it meant the discovery of some powerfully new illuminating pattern. Arsenic and strawberries form an illogical association which just might liberate the reader to the point where the new could be apprehended. The Imagist poem intended to focus on a finite moment of experience, free of the elements of vague complaint and anguished statement that Pound deplored in much Romantic poetry. "L'Art 1910" did not try to *argue* for the new as much as it *presented* the new itself, concretely, dramatically.

The gist of the matter, Pound advised, had already been understood by Sappho, Catullus, and Villon. Actually Pound was trying to accomplish for poetry what was already occurring as a matter of general style. The Victorian idea had been to fill space, whether the literary page or the living room, with knickknacks, objects, curlicues and cornices, gilded pictures and heavy furniture. Art Nouveau in the nineties had influenced designers to eliminate excessive ornament and men like the Dutch architect Hendrik Berlage, the American Frank Lloyd Wright, and the Austrian Adolf Loos were using simple materials—wood, stone, brick, and glass—and stripping away ornamental façades. And the new look in building, as in poetry, was not immediately understood or accepted.

In early spring of 1913, Flint introduced Pound to another young American poet then living in London but detached from literary circles. This was Robert Frost, whose first book, *A Boy's Will,* was soon to be published. Frost had experienced the same disdain for the arts that Pound felt prevailed in America, "I have lived for the most part in villages where it were better that a millstone were hanged about your neck than that you should own yourself a minor poet," he admitted in a letter to Flint. Pound read an advance copy of his book and immediately saw that Frost spoke directly in his own voice with the "seeds of grace," he wrote to Alice Corbin Henderson, the assistant editor at *Poetry.* Pound wrote a praising review, sent it to *Poetry,* and began to pressure Harriet Monroe to print both Frost and William Carlos Williams. However, he soon revised his opinion of Frost because of Frost's insistence on formal regularity. Pound wrote Alice Henderson after Frost's poems appeared in *Poetry* that Frost was "honest, homespun, dull and virtuous" but "pig headed as any New Hampshire hick that ever put pumpkin seed into a granite field with a shotgun." To Pound, Frost was no modernist and therefore lacked true power. Ironically, forty years later Frost became the unofficial poet laureate of America and personally interceded in the highest political levels on Pound's behalf, helping to gain his release from St. Elizabeths.

Pound had been working with Yeats, going over the earlier volumes written in the 1890s, poems about Irish faeries and impossible loves that were suffused with redolent atmosphere and rhetoric. He wanted Yeats to

write more naturally, according to the new Imagist taste for which he was
proselytizing. Yeats himself had defined rhetoric as "the will trying to do
the work of the imagination" and he understood the advantage of Pound's
propositions, but it did not come to him without struggle, as he confessed to
his friend Lady Gregory:

> My digestion has got rather queer again, as a result I think of
> sitting up late with Ezra and Sturge Moore and some light wine
> while the talk ran. However, the criticism I got from them has
> given me new life and I have made that Tara poem a new thing
> and am writing with new confidence having got Milton off my
> back. Ezra is the best critic of the two. He is full of the middle ages
> and helps me to get back to the definite and concrete away from
> modern abstractions. To talk over a poem with him is like getting
> you to put a sentence into dialect. All becomes clear and natural.
> Yet in his own work he is very uncertain, often very bad though
> very interesting sometimes. He spoils himself by too many experi-
> ments and has more sound principles than taste.

Yeats's letter suggests the immediate bond forming between the two poets.
An aloof and self-conscious man, extremely deliberate in statement and
appearance, Yeats was often seen as affected, living through a pose. He had
once infuriated Dublin in the way Pound was antagonizing the English, with
aplomb and lots of self-assurance. For his part, though, Yeats detested reverence or adulation and his best friends were, like Pound, younger men who
treated him as an equal. At the same time, Yeats made everyone aware that
he was a poet and that this was a very special role. Like Pound, he used an
air of arrogant superiority as a means of imposing his own tastes. Yeats
could be chilling and severe, his wit like a rapier, and he would speak in a
sonorous chant in sentences that seemed written, formalized, and controlled. He could be forbidding and even pompous, full of a ridiculous
straining solemnity, a seriousness about artistic questions that Pound shared.

Hilda Doolittle introduced Pound to John Cournos, a reporter for *The
Philadelphia Record.* A Russian Jew four years older than Pound, Cournos
had been raised in the black section of Philadelphia, sleeping on a mattress
on the floor and selling newspapers. While Pound's father was working at
the Mint and had a house in the suburbs, Cournos's father was vainly trying
to fabricate synthetic gold and living in a grimy street of deserted ware-
houses, coal yards, and freight trains. Cournos was certainly from the other
side of Pound's hometown tracks, but Pound generously responded to him.
Cournos interviewed Pound, sent back a story "Native Poet Stirs London,"
and the two men became friends. Realizing that Cournos was lonely, Pound
introduced him to Yeats, Ford, and Hulme, took him to a poet's dinner
attended by Edward Marsh and Henry Newbolt, encouraged him to write a

book on American painting. For Cournos, Pound was all "frank eagerness" and "exuberant kindliness," an ideal missionary for culture.

The spring of 1913 was crucial for Pound's career as a poet because *Poetry* published his "Contemporania," a series of poems in Pound's new conversational manner. Certain of the poems that Pound had submitted had a sort of brazen freshness and natural directness that made Harriet Monroe balk at printing them. The beginning of "Salutation the Second" had a positively Whitmanesque ring:

> You were praised, my books,
>   because I had just come from the country;
> I was twenty years behind the times
>   so you found an audience ready.
> I do not disown you,
>   do not disown your progeny.
> Here they stand without quaint devices,
> Here they are with nothing archaic about them.
> Observe the irritation in general.

Ruffle the skirts of prudes, dance the phallus dance and make people blush, salute the grave and stodgy with "thumbs at your noses," Pound urges in the poem. He is also ready to make a pact with Walt Whitman: "I am old enough now to make friends," he declares. "It was you that broke the new wood."

Pound could make his peace with Whitman because his own style had matured and his voice was at last his own. There was no longer any reason to be jealous of Whitman's facility. He had organized the Imagists as the first phalanx in his private campaign to make a modern literature and in the next few years he recruited Yeats, Eliot, and Joyce to his modernist standards. All of these writers were affected by the technological and social changes they saw about them, the ways men and women related to one another and the world. The years from 1908 to the First World War, the exact period of Pound's European initiation, were a time when each of the arts evolved the use of a new idiom. For Pound these were the ebullient years, but also a time of militance, of attack on entrenched values in literature or culture that made him stand closer and closer to the edge of things. Pound was gradually alienated by the extremity of his own positions, and his sensitivity to counterreaction in the arts or criticism increased. He adopted Whitman's familiar tone, but not out of "adhesiveness," as Whitman called it, not out of love for humanity but from scorn and ironic distance. Only a few years earlier it had been predicted that pregnant women looking at Impressionist paintings would lose their babies; at this point the Cubists were preparing for the dissolution of perspective, and Pound pushed his Imagist friends even beyond their fringe.

Pound realized from the start that Imagism was a finite means to improve the line as a unit in poetry, to curtail the element of discourse in the poem as James had revised the old-fashioned omniscient narrative control in the novel. Poetry should not be the "packmule of philosophy," Pound declared, perhaps thinking of Tennyson's "Locksley Hall." Another source for this stance may have been Théophile Gautier, a French writer who in his essay "L'Art" in 1858 had maintained that "only an art purified of irrelevant intrusions of morality and socio-political ideas could resist time." Almost as soon as it had begun, the Imagist assault had accomplished its ends, according to Pound, and he was already preparing an anthology, *Des Imagistes.*

In April 1913 Pound took a trip to Paris to meet a group of French poets. He described the meeting in his 1915 obituary notice of de Gourmont as the occasion of a concerted prank to elect a retired railroad inspector—a crackpot author of a book trying to prove human descent through the frog—as the prince of thinkers, an attempt to satirize recent literary elections by critics and journalists in Paris. The *blague* was to instruct Pound on tactics to use in London in the following years, tactics that would not endear him to the British:

> When I was in Paris some years ago I happened by merest accident to be plunged into a vortex of twenty men, and among them five or six of the most intelligent young men in Paris. . . . These men were plotting a gigantic blague. A "blague" when it is a fine blague is a satire upon stupidity, an attack. It is the weapon of intelligence at bay; of intelligence fighting against an alignment of odds. These men were thorough. They had exposed a great deal of ignorance and stupidity in places where there should have been the reverse. They were serious and they were "keeping it up." And the one man they mentioned with sympathy, the one older man to whom they could look for comprehension, and even for discreet assistance, was Remy de Gourmont. Remy would send them a brief telegram to be read at their public meeting.

The French poets Jules Romains, Charles Vildrac, and Georges Chennevière brought him to a party where Pound met Natalie Barney, heiress of the Barney Railroad Car Foundry, a flamboyant American who had arrived in Paris at the turn of the century. Young, pretty, witty, wealthy, and notorious, she surrounded herself with women lovers and became, as Mauriac claimed, "le pape de Lesbos." De Gourmont had fallen in love with her and his letters to her, *Lettres à l'amazone,* were then appearing in the *Mercure de France.* Pound was beginning to venerate de Gourmont and hoped Natalie Barney would be able to introduce him. He was also impressed by the fact that Natalie's mother, a portrait painter, had studied with Whistler.

Pound also met two American poets, a Philadelphian named Skipwith Cannell and John Gould Fletcher, a man of independent means who had already published five of his own little books of poetry. Fletcher, with his queer white skull-like face, seemed to have been born old and there was something dejected about his big stooped frame and his sloping shoulders. Fletcher had been to Harvard, where he had begun writing poetry, and left to study the French Symbolists at firsthand in France. Pound borrowed from Fletcher's library of French verse and wrote an account of what was happening among French poets, "The Approach to Paris," which would be serialized in *The New Age* the following fall. From Paris he traveled to Sirmione, where he resumed reading Catullus and Propertius, and then went back to Venice, where he met Aldington and Hilda Doolittle and her parents. It was clear to Pound that Hilda and Aldington would soon marry and that the good Professor Doolittle had approved of Aldington because he seemed more sober than Pound.

By summer Pound was back in London and beginning an involvement with a new magazine. He had already experienced difficulty with Harriet Monroe; her taste had to reflect that of her backers, who were mostly wealthy businessmen or their wives who preferred inconsequential light verse to what Pound regarded as real poetry, so each issue was a balancing of the inane and the more serious. Pound objected strenuously to what he called the "rot" in *Poetry* and wanted a magazine in which he would have more control. He was put in touch with Harriet Shaw Weaver and Dora Marsden, two feminists who had just started a magazine, *The New Freewoman: An Individualist Review.* Published out of the Blavatsky Institute, the magazine had developed out of the new consciousness of women, beginning as a small discussion group that featured guests who, like Mrs. Havelock Ellis, would speak on eugenics, celibacy, or prostitution. Dora Marsden, the small, handsome, grimly intellectual woman who backed the magazine, was primarily interested in linguistic philosophy and grand theories about the emancipation of women. She agreed to permit Pound to begin a literary section in her magazine after Pound had convinced John Gould Fletcher to help with financing. Soon, there was an article by the young Rebecca West on Imagism, and a continuing representation by Imagist poets. Pound printed his "Contemporania" again and poems by Flint, Williams, H.D., and Aldington. He also published his essay "The Serious Artist," which argued for a moral perspective, the function of art being to "bear witness and define for us the inner nature and condition of man, and to remind us of what is worthwhile." Given this responsibility, he argued, accuracy is honesty: "the touchstone of an art is in its precision." He seems in his essay to be caught between the polarities of the Imagism he has just invented—"Good writing is perfectly controlled, the writer says just what he means . . . with complete clarity and simplicity"—and a more energetic, leaping conception which emerged only a year later as Vorticism: art is a force like "electricity or radioactivity, a force transfusing, welding, unifying."

One visitor to London in that summer of 1913 and an American "freewoman," to be sure, was Amy Lowell, a member of the prominent Boston Lowell family. One of her brothers was president of Harvard, she was a cousin of James Russell Lowell, and her nephew's wife, who accompanied her, was one of the Roosevelts. With an "imperious ambition for a literary career" and a "ponderous regal air," as Harriet Monroe put it, she had come to London to meet the new poets. Amy Lowell brought with her a book which had been published in America, *A Dome of Many-Colored Glass,* a muffled and timid collection of poems which Aldington called "fruity and facile." She invited Pound to meet her at her suite at the Berkeley Hotel with its sweeping view of Piccadilly and read him some poems. Pound, realizing that Amy Lowell was wealthy enough to patronize some of his own aesthetic projects, criticized the verse as saccharine but was exceedingly diplomatic, determined to convert her quickly to free verse and Imagism. He introduced her to Yeats and to Ford, accompanied her to Oxford, and brought over John Gould Fletcher to meet her at her hotel. While Pound read "The Seafarer" and "Sestina: Altaforte" as a demonstration of the new poetry, two waiters began serving the intimate party a six-course dinner. That Pound chose two poems that were so clearly antique in origin and sensibility, poems using old forms and diction, shows that he himself was not yet clear about what direction the new could take. Both, however, were poems that he could read powerfully and this must have been his prime consideration. Afterward, Miss Lowell lit one of her long cigars which she claimed were good for her nerves. All in all, Pound had impressed her very favorably, as she wrote to Harriet Monroe:

> Figure to yourself a young man, arrayed as "poet" and yet making the costume agreeable by his personal charm; a sweep of conversation and youthful enthusiasm which keeps him talking delightfully as many hours as you please; the violence of his writings giving way to show a very thin-skinned and sensitive personality opening out like a flower in a sympathetic circle, and I should imagine shutting up like a clam in an alien atmosphere; in personal conversation not in the least didactic, rather dreading the attitude, in fact. That he will outgrow some of his theories, I feel sure. His taste is too fine to confine itself within the walls of any school, even his own. He is so young that all sorts of developments may be expected. I think the chip-on-the-shoulder attitude will disappear in time.

Amy Lowell was right on one point: Pound did quickly outgrow Imagism, at least as she conceived of it, and there developed a rift between them. The "chip-on-the-shoulder," however, would slowly develop into a boulder.

10. THE HIGH PERIOD

Pound spent most of the summer at Violet Hunt's semidetached villa in Kensington. Called South Lodge, it became a gathering place for the *English Review* crowd. The magazine had steadily lost money during Ford's term as editor and he had been pushed out of control, but his circle remained loyal. Pound told an interviewer that he would rather talk about poetry with Ford than with any man in London and that "Fordie knew more about writing than any of 'them' or of 'us.' " "Them" were what Pound called the "gargoyles," the would-be poets like the Georgian group who could not imagine a fresh voice for the age. Ford was a man with a passion for good writing, he objected to vagueness and bookishness, and he told Pound it was better to situate his poetry in the life he felt around him than in derivative medieval emotion. It was even better to be vulgar than to be affected, he insisted.

At South Lodge, Violet Hunt threw large and frequent parties with quail and champagne and Viennese waltzes. The house from the outside was unpretentious, with a small garden and a yard with trees. Inside it was full of Pre-Raphaelite memorabilia, the drawing room wallpaper was by William Morris, cream with self-effacing pink flowers, the chairs were covered with chintz with blue flowers and delicate foliage, the woodwork was painted white, and the walls were covered with William Hunt's landscapes, which had been admired by Ruskin. In this setting the young writers—Ford called them "les jeunes"—would mix with older members of the Pre-Raphaelite group like Rossetti's daughters, with suffragettes like Christabel Pankhurst, and with some of the more radical aristocrats like Lady Barlow and Lady Low.

At this same time many people were ready to shun Ford because of his scandalous relationship with Violet Hunt, his wife's divorce suit, and also because of certain flaws in his own personality. Ford was forty and discouraged. A tall, portly man with smooth blond hair, cold blue eyes, and a huge mustache that seemed sometimes to swallow his words, Ford spoke with a melodious voice. Wyndham Lewis, a frequent visitor to South Lodge, described Ford with his usually incisive malice:

A flabby lemon and pink giant, who hung his mouth open as though he were an animal at the Zoo inviting buns—especially when ladies were present. Over the gaping mouth damply depended the ragged ends of a pale lemon moustache. This ex-collaborator with Joseph Conrad was himself, it always occurred to me, a typical figure out of a Conrad book—a caterer, or cornfactor, coming on board—blowing like a porpoise with the exertion—at some Eastern port.

Ford had written sixteen novels and seven books of nonfiction without fame or fortune. His German aunt had just disinherited him because he refused to break off with Violet Hunt, and he felt neglected and abused. He felt that artists were usually despised and seen by the middle class as useless. He repeated to Pound what Hilaire Belloc had said in the House of Commons in 1910: "There is perhaps nothing an educated man or woman can do which requires less intelligence than the writing of books." Ford had written that a "man of letters is regarded as something less than a man" but he was also capable of a vain, almost pontifical benevolence, a pompous condescension. His own lack of self-confidence sometimes made him lie or stretch the truth in the way a novelist might. Aldington, in his autobiography, *Life for Life's Sake,* relates that he brought Ford to his parents' house for dinner, during which Ford eloquently told story after story about Ruskin, the Rossettis, Conrad, James, and Swinburne, but then told his father how he had met Byron—an impossibility given Ford's age and the date of Byron's death. Perhaps because of the lurid way in which his love for Violet Hunt had been picked up by the new sensation-seeking press, Ford began to disguise the truth with fables. H. G. Wells wrote that Ford had become "a great system of assumed personas and dramatized selfs." His old friend Conrad—they had once even collaborated on a novel together—now gouty and playing croquet, called Ford a man with a fierce and exasperating vanity, a "megalomaniac who imagines that he is managing the universe and that everybody treats him with the blackest ingratitude."

Even Pound admitted that Ford had been a *halluciné,* but he began to be influenced by Ford's mannerisms: the recklessly sweeping statements, the dogmatic pronouncements and laws. Ford was a master of shifting and intersecting personae in his novels as well as in his inventions at dinner. It was a key modernist technique, and Pound knew he needed to study it in life as well as in art. Ford was the perfect model, and though he could be an affected literary walrus, at the same time he could be brilliant. Ford was writing his study of Henry James that summer, so Pound again began reading James, recognizing in James's evolved sensibility and his willingness to sacrifice for his art a source as important to him as Whitman, though quite different. He also took over at South Lodge as he had earlier at Yeats's soirées, sallying "forth in his sombrero," Douglas Goldring recalled, "with all the arrogance of a young, revolutionary poet who had complete confidence in his own genius." Ford himself was completely subjugated by this American exuberant:

> His Philadelphian accent was comprehensible if disconcerting; his beard and flowing locks were auburn and luxuriant; he was astonishingly meagre and agile. He threw himself alarmingly into frail chairs, devoured enormous quantities of your pastry, fixed his pince-nez firmly on his nose, drew out a manuscript from his pocket, threw his head back, closed his eyes to the point of invisibility and looking down his nose would chuckle like Mephistopheles and read you a translation from Arnaut Daniel.

Opposite South Lodge was a communal garden with a grass tennis court, and Pound began to organize matches. He had a good reach, was lithe, wiry, and fast on his feet. Violet Hunt describes Pound's game in her autobiographical account of her time with Ford, *I Have This to Say:*

> The young American poet played like a demon or a trick pony, sitting down composedly in his square and jumping up in time to receive his adversary's ball, which he competently returned, the flaps of his polychrome shirt flying out like the petals of some flower and his red head like a flaming pistil in the middle of it.

She subtitled her book "The Flurried Years," partly because of the social pressure she felt from the notoriety of her union with Ford—her friend Henry James refused to visit but wrote letters praising her valor— and partly because of the confusion in her household of writers who "sat up all night and every night choosing words, drinking strong coffee," writing, she continues, "in every room of the house, completely dressed or not, as they pleased, or as the fury of composition permitted." If someone happened to consider the bathroom a more appropriate study than the parlor, too bad for her other guests. And in the midst of all this confusion of poets Violet Hunt had her own writing to continue. Her novels show a marvelous ear for dialogue, some of which may have been her own. Iris Barry, a young protégée of Pound's, described Violet as "chattering with sublime regard for practically everything, dishevelled hair, obviously a beauty of the Edwardian age." Pound was less impressed, especially by Violet's attempts at poetry, which he condemned as "paste jewels in molasses."

Pound was an uncomfortable young man. His friend Phyllis Bottome remembered him at this time as being like an electric eel. Nevertheless, in such chaotically bohemian surroundings, Pound could feel creative and self-possessed. Brigit Patmore, who noted that, like Ford, Pound was at ease in masquerade because it helped him keep his poet-nature inviolable, first met him in Violet Hunt's drawing room:

I saw a long slim young man leaning back in a low armchair, withdrawn as an animal from creatures it does not know. His head was unavoidably noticeable, not only because of the reddish spring hair, but for the Florentine delicacy of the pale face. His eyes were a little wrinkled in closure, whether in humour or observation, I didn't know. His mouth, sensitive and undoubtedly sweet, covered small, very white teeth, but he revealed them seldom, neither speaking nor smiling often. Not that he was confused or shy, no, he was as self-possessed as Violet's superb grey Persian cat sitting on the window-sill, though fortunately he did not give out the cold, feline resentment of that beautiful animal. Once or twice he smiled at me as if I were a friend, and the very un-Englishness of this pleased me, for the poker faces of Englishmen are intimidating.

At South Lodge Pound was able to solicit material for H. L. Mencken's *The Smart Set, Poetry,* or *The New Freewoman,* whose name he convinced Dora Marsden to change to *The Egoist* because the name was embarrassing— Henry James, for one, had refused to contribute, teasing Pound with the warning not to become a "bondsman." But clearly the most important feature of South Lodge for Pound was the friendship and stimulation of Ford. Ford had written an essay on literary Impressionism that appeared in *Poetry* and his ideas would become important for Pound. In his piece Ford argued that the poet's work was not the search for fine sentiments "so much as the putting of certain realities in certain aspects" using a method of juxtaposition that could suggest emotions. Essentially, this was to lead to Pound's Ideogrammatic method of *The Cantos,* where images are set against one another as part of an effort to deny the possibility of romantic complaint or declaration in poetry, to render or present rather than state.

The Ideogrammatic method is an extension of Imagism that depends on a central misconception, Pound's belief that the Chinese written character was a "verbal medium consisting largely of semi-pictorial appeals to the eye," that this written character was based less on sound than it was the picture of an object—in the way the Chinese ideograph for "to speak" is a mouth with emerging fire. Pound had been introduced to Chinese by the widow of the leading Western scholar of Japanese and Chinese art, Professor Ernest Fenollosa. A Harvard graduate interested in philosophy, Fenollosa had gone to Japan in 1878 to teach the most brilliant sons of the feudal nobility. He was astonished by the beauty of Japan, as Lafcadio Hearn had been before him, amazed at a culture whose newspapers reported on the opening of buds, where families traveled long distances to see the blossoms before dawn. Fenollosa had arrived at the moment when the old culture was being pillaged and destroyed in a lust for modernization. He began to study

Japanese painting but was dismayed by the complete absence of books or museums. So he started collecting and what he bought later became the basis of collections in Boston, Tokyo, and Kyoto. He developed an interest in Chinese and Japanese poetry, and particularly in the fifteenth-century theater form known as Noh, a nonmimetic, operatic fusion of dance and Shinto legend. For twenty years Fenollosa studied posture, chanting, and the Noh form of dance and translated some fifty plays. He died in London in 1908, almost exactly at the time of Pound's arrival there, where he had been working on his *Epochs of Chinese and Japanese Art,* a fifteen-year effort he did not live to finish.

His second wife, Mary McNeil, a woman who had married an American diplomat posted to Japan, had been Fenollosa's faithful assistant and collaborator, and she saw the book through to publication. She had also written several novels under the name Sidney McCall. When she met Pound at an evening arranged by a Hindu nationalist poetess in London, she felt burdened by the masses of manuscript material that remained—hundreds of pages on Japanese and Chinese poetry, eight large notebooks of material on Taoist poems which Fenollosa had translated, and literary history. Then there were the volumes of notes on Noh. In October of 1913, having read Pound's "Contemporania" series in *Poetry,* she gave her husband's material to Pound. It was like the discovery of "a new Greece in China," Pound said.

Also in October, Pound attended the wedding of Richard Aldington and Hilda, accompanied by her parents. He heard from John Cournos that a new American magazine, *The Globe,* was looking for material. He offered the anthology he was preparing, which it accepted. That fall Pound also met a young French sculptor while attending an art show at the Albert Hall with Olivia Shakespear. Most of what they saw seemed mediocre until they came before the work of a man with what Pound took to be an unpronounceable name. As he was joking about the name, Gaudier-Brzeska, the sculptor emerged from behind a pedestal. Gaudier (the Brzeska was not his but belonged to an older Polish writer of short stories who posed as his sister and with whom he lived) was charged with life, extremely energetic and robust. Full of gaiety, with little self-consciousness, he was the sort of man who could enter into a friendship without preliminaries, speak to strangers, or dance and sing in the street. Pound recognized a kindred spirit and promised to visit the sculptor in his studio.

When he accompanied Yeats in November to Stone Cottage in the Ashdown Forest in Sussex, Pound realized that Yeats was ready to accept his new ideas on the image and convert to a harsher, leaner presentation. He had written Alice Corbin Henderson that Yeats "now sees that his manner is played out and he himself setting about to get rid of it. . . . His work has been to cut away and cut away and cut away from the bash and blarn of English sloppiness." Yeats had heard his friend Synge, the Irish playwright, declare that for poetry to become human it would first have to become brutal, and he knew the dissidence in Ireland could not be contained by sentimental verse any longer. Pound had the capacity to provoke Yeats, but also to compliment him. Full of eager goodwill, unintimiditable and persistent, Pound began reading Yeats's early work aloud to him, pointing to the soft spots, the moments of excessively lush luxuriance in sound at the sacrifice of sense. It must have been a delicate process; the older poet could easily have become enraged. He had written to his friend, the painter Sir William Rothenstein, that Pound was "a man with a rugged and headstrong nature" who had the "capacity to hurt people's feelings." But the two men, cared for by the sisters Wellfare, proved compatible and content over a period of three months. Pound tried to teach Yeats what he knew about fencing. At forty-five, the older poet "thrashed about like a whale," Pound later remembered; Yeats offered instruction on spiritualism and astrology. Yeats worked on his friend Lady Gregory's researches into Irish folklore and read Doughty's Icelandic sagas and Wordsworth. Pound worked on the Fenollosa material which he had brought with him, particularly on the Noh plays, which appealed to Yeats because he wanted poets "to write as all poets once did, not for the printed page but to be sung." The element of legend and the presence of ghosts all reminded Yeats of Irish myth. Even the bare staging and symbolic scenery—a willow branch representing a ship, four posts for a house—were suggestive for Yeats, indicating to him a way out of the naturalistic theater of Ibsen to a more mythically stylized presentation involving mask and gesture.

Pound spent parts of three winters with Yeats at Stone Cottage, an experience he later nostalgically remembered in "Canto LXXXIII":

> There is fatigue deep as the grave.
> The Kakemono grows in flat land out of mist
>   sun rises lop-sided over the mountain
>   so that I recalled the noise in the chimney
> as it were the wind in the chimney
>   but was in reality Uncle William
> downstairs composing
> that had made a great Peeeeacock
>   in the proide of his oiye
>   had made a great peeeeeeecock in the . . .
> made a great peacock
>   in the proide of his oyyee
>
> proide ov his oy-ee
> as indeed he had, and perdurable

a great peacock aere perennius
   or as in the advice to the young man to
breed and get married (or not)
   as you choose to regard it

at Stone Cottage in Sussex by the waste moor
(or whatever) and the holly bush
   who would not eat ham for dinner
because peasants eat ham for dinner
   despite the excellent quality
and the pleasure of having it hot
well those days are gone forever
   and the travelling rug with the coon-skin tabs
and his hearing nearly all Wordsworth
   for the sake of his conscience but
preferring Ennemoser on Witches

did we ever get to the end of Doughty:
   The Dawn in Britain?
   perhaps not

At Stone Cottage Yeats learned that Harriet Monroe wanted to award him a prize of fifty pounds. He wrote to her, recommending that forty of them go to Pound:

> I suggest him to you because, although I do not really like with my whole soul the metrical experiments he has made for you, I think those experiments show a vigorous imaginative mind. He is certainly a creative personality of some sort, though it is too soon yet to say of what sort. His experiments are perhaps errors, I am not certain; but I would always sooner give the laurel to vigorous errors than to any orthodoxy not inspired.

Pound, always on the lookout for new contributors to the magazines he represented, asked Yeats whether he knew of any worthwhile unknowns. Yeats told Pound about an Irish writer named James Joyce who was living in Trieste, and several weeks later he found a copy of Joyce's poem "I Hear an Army Charging," a poem originally inspired by Yeats's own "He Bid His Beloved Be at Peace," a tribute to Olivia Shakespear. Pound immediately wrote, asking Joyce's permission to include the poem in *Des Imagistes*, the anthology he was preparing, initiating a literary association that would become central for him and modernism.

In January 1913, just before returning to London from Stone Cottage, Yeats and Pound joined a delegation of other poets—Aldington, Flint, Victor Plarr, Sturge Moore, and Frederic Manning—who traveled to Newbuildings in Sussex to honor the poet Wilfred Scawen Blunt on his

seventieth birthday. Blunt had been the friend of leading British statesmen
like Lloyd George, Asquith, and the young Winston Churchill, but he had
staunchly opposed British imperialism. Working as a diplomat, a scholar of
Arabic, he gained deep knowledge of India, Egypt, and Persia and he frequently advised those in power on Eastern affairs. At the same time, he
could contribute money to anarchist bombers seeking to end Czarist oppres-
sion. Actually, Blunt's politics often contradicted his class origin. He was
very much a country squire, with a vast estate on which he raised peacocks
and lambs, but he had gone to prison in Ireland as a protest against English
rule. The poets were there to honor him for his resistance. Pound saw in
Blunt a quality he very much wanted for himself as a poet, the ability to
persuade those in power on matters of public policy. This was, after all, the
heritage of Thaddeus Pound, his grandfather. Pound brought him a reli-
quary carved in marble by his new friend Gaudier-Brzeska, and after a
luncheon of roasted peacock he read a poem for Blunt:

> Because you have gone your individual gait,
> Written fine verses, made mock of the world,
> Swung the grand style, not made a trade of art,
> Upheld Mazzini and detested institutions,
> We who are little given to respect,
> Respect you, and having no better way to show it,
> Bring you this stone to be some record of it.

Blunt had not made a "trade of art" for money, prestige, or power but had
remained pure in his intentions, and defiant of the state. Yeats's remarks
were more to the point, praising Blunt as a poet in terms Pound had first
suggested, the war on abstraction and generalization, the effort to use natural speech instead of inflated diction. Yeats's remarks reveal the extent of
Pound's influence upon him:

> When you published your first work, it was at the very height of
> the Victorian period. The abstract poet was in a state of glory. One
> no longer wrote as a human being, with an address, living in a
> London street, having a definite income, and a definite tradition,
> but one wrote as an abstract personality. One was expected to be
> very much wiser than other people. The only objection to such a
> conception of the poet was that it was impossible to believe he
> existed. Now instead of abstract poetry, you wrote verses which
> were good poetry because they were, first of all, fine things to
> have thought or to have said in some real situation in life. We are
> now at the end of Victorian romance—completely at the end. One
> may admire Tennyson, but one can not read him. If I take up today
> some of the things that interested me in the past I can no longer

use them. They bore me. Every year some part of my poetical machinery suddenly becomes of no use.

One of the first things Pound wanted to do when he returned to London was to visit Gaudier-Brzeska's studio. Gaudier lived much closer to the edge of penury than did Pound, a testimonial to his dedication, Pound felt, and Pound used some of his *Poetry* prize money to purchase two small statues. The studio was under a railway arch leading to the Putney Bridge and every ten minutes a train would roar by. The floor of the studio was dirt, the roof a poor overhead protection, so when it rained Gaudier would have to work in three inches of mud. Like Pound, Gaudier wanted to be considered avant-garde and shocking: he told the sculptor Jacob Epstein that he was homosexual with this end in mind. Gaudier was clearly an exotic: he spoke of his ambition to live in the jungles of India so he could carve elephants and tigers and wanted to put a four-inch piece of wood through his nostrils. Actually he was the descendant of a family of stone and wood carvers who had helped to build Chartres. In his blue workman's shirt, missing a few teeth, looking like something between a faun and Christ, Gaudier would work indefatigably though he could afford only irregular pieces of poor-quality stone. Pound was impressed with his work because, like the Imagists, Gaudier had stripped away artificial decoration and ornament; there were no more "cupids riding mermaids, garlands, or curtains stuck anywhere," Pound remarked. As an artist, Gaudier searched for the purification of essential form, but he was aware of classical Greek sculpture, Egyptian, African, Polynesian, Incan, and Chinese art.

Pound bought Gaudier a piece of rectangular marble and began to sit for a portrait called *Hieratic Head.* Horace Brodsky, another artist who knew Gaudier, claimed that the sculptor was essentially a prankster, and he carved his nervous and shy subject into a giant phallus as a joke. Gaudier told Pound the head would not resemble him, that he wanted to represent only the poet's emotions. Pound had just published a poem called "Coitus" in Harold Monro's magazine, *Poetry and Drama,* which had caused a stir. Gaudier may have been aware of Pound's reputation with women, and his artistic instincts may have led him to portray Pound as a seminal fount for poetry. Pound admired the head and always tried to keep it near him, first placing it in Violet Hunt's garden at South Lodge.

Gaudier brought Pound to visit Jacob Epstein, who had constructed what he called the Rock-Drill, an assemblage of a machinelike robot with a menacing visor carrying its progeny, armored, within itself, all mounted on an actual drill. Pound immediately praised Epstein's work in *The Egoist,* even though it might be expected to "infuriate the denizens of this superficial world," and years later he called a section of his *Cantos* "Rock-Drill." Pound was beginning to see matters in a more experimental light. For exam-

ple, at the Regents Park zoo with Dorothy on a Sunday afternoon, shortly
after the visit to Epstein's studio, he noticed a Japanese man prancing about
near the birds of prey, imitating their movements in a strange dance. He
told Yeats about this man, whose name was Michio Itò, and introduced
them. Yeats began to watch Itò and the result was *At the Hawk's Well,* the
first of his plays that showed the Noh influence.

11. AN UNCOMFORTABLE MAN OF GENIUS

Pound saw Gaudier frequently in the early spring of 1914, perhaps
because the sculptor encouraged a recklessness Pound needed to release.
Another artist and writer that Pound spent much more time with was Wyndham Lewis, who involved him in an entirely new milieu. One reason that
Pound plunged into circles that seemed to have a slightly disreputable flavor
was that his long courtship of Dorothy was approaching an end. A year and
a half earlier, the engagement had seemed at an impasse with Olivia and
Henry Hope Shakespear still strongly against it. Olivia wrote Pound begging him to break off with her daughter, "as she obviously can't marry you"
and "must be made to realize that she can't go on as though you were her
accepted lover—it's hardly *decent.*" Olivia then urged Pound to leave England because "Englishmen don't understand your American ways." Even
as recently as the summer before the lovers had quarreled. Walter Rummel
had given a private recital at the Shakespears' house and Pound had tried to
dictate the guest list. "I think you fortify yourself too much against other
people," Dorothy wrote, without realizing "how much you hurt them by
doing that kind of thing. I think it is a great interference on your part. . . .
You affect not to care about other people—but you try to interfere a good
deal with their doings when they affect yourself." Dorothy had written
Pound a short note exclaiming that she could not marry him, to which
Pound replied:

> You can not
> You can not
> You can not

He was twenty-eight and Dorothy twenty-seven, and Olivia was losing hope
that her daughter would ever marry, especially since her relation to Pound
was becoming known and would be an impossible hurdle for most potential
suitors. By winter Olivia's defenses had been broken and she was ready to
try to persuade her husband of the inevitability of the union. However,
when Henry Hope Shakespear suggested a church marriage, another final
problem emerged. Pound, in a letter to his future father-in-law, objected,
preferring the simple dignified service at the registry in Kensington that he

had seen when Hilda married Aldington. "Spiritual powers," he wrote Mr. Shakespear, who must have found the letter most curious, "are affronted when a person who takes his religion seriously complies with a ceremony which has fallen into decay." The result, Pound claimed, was superficial conformity and an outrageous lie. In the same letter he stated that the bishop of London himself would not be suitable as an officiating priest because he was only another "cad." Henry Hope Shakespear was appalled. He was a man who valued appearance and convention. As a lawyer, he had served to buttress social institutions. His prospective son-in-law had revealed that everything and anything was open to question: it was not only in the worst of taste, it was subversive in the deepest sense. Pound, for his part, despised the trappings of organized religion and loathed the restrictions and general narrowness of perspective caused by the moral strictures of Christianity. But on this matter he knew he would have to bend.

The marriage did occur in a church, St. Mary Abbots whose bells had for some three years so plagued Pound. It was April 20, 1914, a Monday morning, usually a serious time. London was budding with lilac and laburnum and purple willowweed. Dorothy wore a coat and skirt. The six guests were members of her family, one being Frederic Manning, a distant cousin of Olivia's. Manning had quarreled with Pound, ostensibly over poetry, but actually because of his own love for Dorothy. "Perhaps some day," he had written Pound, "we shall be able to talk to each other without getting our hackles up." In 1915 Manning's father died, leaving him the independent income the Shakespears wanted their daughter to have. In the end they had provided it themselves, settling £150 a year on Dorothy, a sum that basically supported the couple along with the uncertain amounts Pound earned. A perceptive commentary on the match was provided by John Butler Yeats. Writing to his son from New York, he observed that Dorothy was beautiful with the "most charming manners." He saw the marriage as a reaction to her upbringing: "When rich and fashionable people bring up a daughter to be intellectual, naturally she will turn away from the 'curled darlings' of her own class and fall in love with intellect which is mostly wed to poverty as well. I hope it will turn out that Ezra Pound is not an *uncomfortable* man of genius." Hilda Doolittle Aldington saw her after the wedding. As usual Dorothy looked picturesque—delicate and exquisite were Pound's terms—she was poised and tall, light-haired with grayish blue eyes. Hilda said she looked as if she belonged in a painting by Gainsborough. Everything had an aesthetic connotation for H.D., but by her remark she undoubtedly meant that Dorothy looked stiff, posed, artificial. Of course Hilda may have been speaking with the voice of envy, as she had never really recovered from her love for Pound and regarded her own husband as a temporary bulwark. At any rate, she would have numerous opportunities to see Pound after his marriage because he took rooms in Holland Park Chambers, across the courtyard from the Aldingtons.

For their honeymoon the couple went to Stone Cottage, where Pound continued his work on the Noh dramas. Dorothy was occupied with sketching and doing watercolors and the study of Chinese, which she had begun when Pound received the Fenollosa material. In a sense, they had spent the romance of their relationship early in their period of courtship. They had waited five years to be together, and there are signs that Pound had become brittle on the subject of marriage. He had written in *The Egoist* in 1913 that modern marriage was "derived from the laws of slave concubinage." In the same year, quite prophetically, Dorothy had copied for him in a letter Bacon's adage that wives are young men's mistresses, companions in middle age, and old men's nurses.

12. THE ART UNDERWORLD

Wyndham Lewis had been one of the men Pound had seen frequently at South Lodge in the period just before his marriage. The two men had first met at the Vienna Café, a coffeehouse with red plush chairs which was a known gathering place for European émigrés. Pound, who had only recently arrived in London, had been brought there by his friend Laurence Binyon. Lewis was seated at a table with Sturge Moore and a few other Englishmen. According to him, Pound approached him as one might a panther, "tense and wary, without speaking or smiling: showing one is not afraid of it, [but] inwardly awaiting hostile action." Pound and Lewis, both similarly hypersensitive, were silent, suspicious of each other, and surly. Lewis's impression was that Pound was a "cowboy songster." He suspected Pound might be a disguised Jew.

It took several meetings and a few years for the two men to trust each other, but when they did they realized they had much in common. Lewis had been educated at good English schools, though he had been asked to leave Rugby when it was discovered that he had transformed his study into a painter's studio. "All English training is a system of deadening feeling," Lewis asserted in his novel, *Tarr.* He went to Paris, where he heard Bergson lecture on the proposition that intuition was the only way to express reality, he met the anarchist Kropotkin, he painted and wrote. Painfully shy, secretive and mysterious, Lewis was also temperamental: "Being misunderstood was one of his pleasures," his friend the painter C. R. W. Nevinson wrote. Lewis saw himself as a solitary outsider and by his dress created an aura of villainy, wearing steeple-black hats and a huge black cape. Lewis resembled the protagonist of *Tarr,* an isolated figure with a persecution mania and "no social machinery"—"when he had to be amiable he usually only succeeded in being pretentious." He was capable of infuriating his acquaintances and reveled in grotesqueries, managing to offend the impeccable manners of the English as often as Pound did. He had written stories and published some of them in the *English Review:* the tale, perhaps apocryphal, is that he found Ford in his bathtub—his bathroom door was always unlocked—and read him his story "The Pole," which Ford immediately accepted. He was capable of brutal caricature and in drawing and painting had developed a hard, energetic style.

Lewis had shown a particularly compelling series of drawings based on Shakespeare's *Timon of Athens* at the second Postimpressionist show, held in 1912 at the Grafton Galleries and organized by Roger Fry. The six drawings drew considerable attention. They were of highly stylized figures, looking like truncated Renaissance warriors in helmeted masks, all in black and white, and fragmented by overlapping and intersecting planes. The effect was ominous, an abstraction with glimpses of representational detail. Pound commented that the series showed what the play exposed: the "fury of intelligence baffled and shut in by a circumjacent stupidity. It is an emotional motif." Pound wrote about the series in *The Egoist* with a spirit of unrepentant antagonism, a hatred for the philistine British, who could not or more probably would not understand or accept the new art he was championing:

It is no easy matter to express the Zeitgeist nor even immediately to comprehend it when we find it laid forth before us in word or in diagram. The "man in the street" cannot be expected to understand the "Timon" at first sight. Damn the man in the street, once and for all, damn the man in the street who is only in the street because he hasn't intelligence enough to be let in to anywhere else, and who does not in the least respect himself for being in the street, any more than an artist would respect himself for being hung in the Royal Academy. But the man whose profoundest needs cannot be satisfied by Collier or by Mr. Sargent's society pretties, the man who has some sort of hunger for life, some restlessness for a meaning, is willing to spend six months, any six months, in a wilderness of doubt if he may thereby come to some deeper understanding; to some emotion more intense than his own; to some handling of life more competent than his own fumbling about the surface. So it is amply worth while taking half a year to get at the "Timon," fumbling about, looking at Matisse and Cézanne and Picasso, and Gauguin and Kandinsky, and spoiling sheet after sheet of paper in learning just how difficult it is to bring forth a new unit of design.

With his defense of Lewis, Pound began a withdrawal into the under-world of art. The artists would meet in a nightclub situated below the ground. Its owner was the notorious Madame Frida Strindberg, whose excesses are supposed to have motivated her more famous husband's tirades against married women. Always theatrical herself, but with an iron emotional constitution, she had taken Veronal after an unsuccessful love affair and recovered after nothing worse than a stomachache. Pound remembered watching her wave a customer away from her table, saying as she did so that "sleep with him she would, but talk to him never—'One must draw a line *somewhere.'* " She had decided to decorate her new club, grandiosely called the Cave of the Golden Calf, with the work of the new artists, and she persuaded Jacob Epstein to do some decidedly nonclassical columns. Lewis did two paintings, two screens, decoration for several walls, and an abstract backcloth for the stage containing figures in a frieze. Osbert Sitwell remembered the walls to be "hideously but relevantly frescoed" with lunging and wheeling primitive figures. Violet Hunt was reminded of "raw meat" when she saw the "Bismarckian images, severings, disembowellings mixed pell-mell with the iron shards that did it, splashed with the pale blood of exhausted heroes." In the early morning hours the club was apt to be a garden of gesticulating figures, dancing, drinking, twisting, talking to the new ragtime music. Feverish, uninhibited, and gay, the Cave of the Golden Calf was a place of defiant unconventional expression.

The new artists were meeting with their friends at the Café Royal earlier in the evening, at the Tour Eiffel for dinners, later on at South Lodge or Hulme's salon. Some of them were about to follow Lewis in a break with Roger Fry's Omega Workshop, an artists' cooperative based on William Morris's idea that artists should be responsible for interior design and fabrication of furniture and all household accessories. Lewis felt he had been exploited by Fry's "curtain and pincushion factory"—certainly he did not like the anonymity Fry insisted on—and he formed the Rebel Art Centre on Great Ormond Street. This slap at Fry, which Pound applauded, was tacitly an attack on the Bloomsbury circle led by Virginia Woolf and E. M. Forster, since Fry was Woolf's close friend and her sister's secret suitor. For Lewis, the Bloomsbury circle represented art as the province of the socially established, dilettantism of the effete. One member of the Bloomsbury circle, Herbert Read, met and admired Pound at this time, remembering him in his book *The Tenth Muse* as "an agile lynx, beautiful in features, aggressively dressed, who sprang from conversational point to point very much in the manner that the animal he reminded me of might spring from branch to branch." Pound felt the Bloomsbury writers were clogged with their own stuffy English notions of class. He called them Bloomsbuggers and he knew that, like Aldington, he would be judged not their kind. He chose to ally himself with Lewis's group, painters like Nevinson, David Bomberg, Edward Wadsworth, and Frederick Etchells, whom he later called the Vorticists.

As with Imagism, however, the theoretician of the new movement was Hulme. Hulme had met the German art historian Wilhelm Worringer, who in 1908 had published *Abstraction and Empathy*. Worringer claimed that there was a connection between restlessness, political fear, despair, and the tendency to abstraction. The breakdown of representational forms was apocalyptic foreshadowing, a warning of broader social disintegration. For Worringer abstraction was both the expression of transcendental urges as well as the artist's denial of a terrifying imminence. Partly inspired by Worringer's idea that the art of any period develops as a cumulative spiritual response to the inner needs of the era, Hulme predicted the end of representational naturalism and the rebirth of an angular, geometric art. Hulme argued this thesis at a lecture sponsored by the Quest Society at Kensington Town Hall which Pound attended early in 1914. "The new 'tendency towards abstraction' will culminate," Hulme concluded, "not so much in the single geometric forms found in archaic art, but in the more complicated ones associated in our minds with the idea of machinery." Pound immediately recalled Epstein's Rock-Drill sculpture and Lewis's paintings when he heard this.

Another sound in the art world had been the fulminations of the Italian Futurist F. T. Marinetti, whose concerted polemical onslaught on traditional art certainly impressed Pound and Lewis. The first of Marinetti's thunder in England had been heard in a magazine edited by Douglas Goldring, an open letter called "Futurist Venice," which appeared in August of 1910: "Burn the gondolas, those swings for fools," declaimed the Futurist leader, "and erect up to the sky the rigid geometry of large metallic bridges and manufactories with waving hair of smoke, abolish everywhere the languishing curves of the old architecture." In March 1912 the Sackville Gallery organized a Futurist exhibition—"Nightmare Exhibition" was one headline and there were over 350 newspaper articles about it. Even the catalogue to the show was calculated to outrage the sensibilities of the usually genteel English art world: "We shall sing the love of danger, the habit of energy and boldness," it began, with a tone much more challenging than anything Fry had attempted at the Grafton. Marinetti's *Initial Manifesto of Futurism* was quoted: "Set fire to the shelves of the libraries. Deviate the course of canals to flood the cellars of museums! Oh, may the glorious canvasses drift helplessly! Seize pickaxes and hammers! Sap the foundations of venerable cities!" The sensational revel of the Futurists included the ugly apocalyptic fever of an embryonic fascism: "We wish to glorify War—the only health giver of the world—militarism, patriotism, the destructive arm of the Anarchist, the beautiful ideas that kill, the contempt for women." The Futurists insisted on the importance of the present, praised the joys of motion and

speed, and advocated violent action as the swiftest way to destroy the old
bankrupt culture that still relied on dead values and decorative forms. The
new art, they asserted, would grow out of the mechanized environment of
the new century.

Much of the Futurist program seemed simply hilarious to the English,
but what impressed Pound was Marinetti's technique of art propaganda, the
brash statement and aggressive public stance. Pound saw Marinetti lecture
in Bechstein Hall at the time of the Sackville Gallery show and heard him
attack the English as snobs and sycophants "enslaved by worm eaten traditions, social conventions and romanticism." Marinetti himself was as much a
spectacle as what he had to say. He wore spats and tailored suits, wing
collars and bow ties, and a turned up mustache that Dali later imitated. He
spoke frequently in London from 1912 to 1914, once at a Soho dinner
organized by Lewis, at the Dore Gallery, and in several lecture halls. He
would mix his crashing onomatopoetic poem "The Siege of Adrianople"
with a torrent of Italian. Jacob Epstein remembered that as a performer
Marinetti used an astonishing amount of energy, and his veins would swell
in his head. He would imitate machine-gun fire, the whirr of airplane en-
gines, and the boom of cannon, but the poems were of "a commonplace and
banality that was appalling." Douglas Goldring described him as "adorned
with diamond rings, gold chains, and hundreds of flashing white teeth."
Lewis claimed he got his money from his father's chain of Egyptian brothels.
In America, Theodore Roosevelt saw examples of Futurism at the Armory
Show in New York in February of 1913 and characterized it as "only a
smirking pose of retrogression," the work of a lunatic fringe with the
"power to make folly lucrative." In France, the young André Gide, irritated
by Marinetti's posturing, was more severe in his judgment: "He paws the
ground and sends up clouds of dust; he curses and swears and massacres.
. . . [He is] animated in the Italian fashion, which often takes verbosity for
eloquence, ostentation for wealth, agitation for movement, freshness for
divine rapture."

At his Rebel Art Centre in the spring of 1914, Lewis vainly tried to
create the same sort of frenzied excitement that Marinetti had succeeded in
manufacturing, but Lewis was a poor organizer and poisoned by his own
paranoia—Fry felt that his vanity touched on insanity. Lewis had persuaded
Kate Lechmere, another painter influenced by Cubist ideas, a woman who
had a little money of her own, to back his venture. The place was decorated
in the new manner: doors in scarlet, luminous gold curtains, and pale lemon
walls. One room was to be deliberately left empty for the latest form of
artistic expression. The Rebel Art Centre was to be an artists' commune
flexible enough to allow members to express themselves without feeling
they had to adhere to the formal outlines of any particular school. Lewis was
so fearful of imitation that he kept most of his own work locked away, only

permitting his friend Pound to view it. Once when a young woman was contemplating the purchase of a painting, Lewis paranoically locked her in the room with the paintings. To raise money Marinetti was asked to lecture. Kate Lechmere remembered him "making loud puffing noises, pretending he was a train." "Caruso tenor-instincts of inflation, of tiptoe tirade," Lewis exclaimed disparagingly. Ford delivered a lecture, appearing absentmindedly in a tailcoat, and was stunned when one of Lewis's large paintings fell on him from the wall. The episode was characteristic of the improvised and disorganized events that occurred at the Rebel Art Centre. The entire enterprise collapsed when T. E. Hulme and Kate Lechmere became lovers. Lewis's anger over this development was related to the fact that Hulme thought much more of Epstein's work than of his own. At one point, in a frenzy, Lewis ran to Hulme's Frith Street salon declaring that he was going to kill the philosopher. Kate Lechmere followed him, screaming. Lewis marched in and seized Hulme by the throat, but the bigger man dragged Lewis out to Soho Square, where he hung him ignominiously upside down from his trousers on the iron railings and calmly returned to his soirée.

In *Tarr*, Lewis's Nietzschean antihero proclaims, "I am the panurgic-pessimist, drunken with the laughing gas of the Abyss," a remark that seems to reflect some of the flavor of Lewis's capacity for absurd irresponsibility. Ford remembered walking down Holland Street near his house with Pound, the "incomprehensible Philadelphian" arguing in one ear while Lewis, in the other, was conspiratorially and vitriolically murmuring,

> *"Tu sais, tu es foûtu! Foûtu!* Finished! Exploded! Done for! . . . .
> What people want is me, not you. They want to see me. A Vortex.
> To liven them up . . . I . . . I . . . I . . ." He struck his chest
> dramatically and repeated: "I . . . I . . . I . . . The Vortex.
> Blast all the rest."

But the Lewis-Pound axis had gone askew. "Artists are the antennae of the race," Pound had exclaimed, and it is understandable that their own belligerence and mounting mania were related to the political tension presaging World War I. Lewis later spoke of Pound's "obstreperous intractableness" at this time, which Pound demonstrated in a shrill diatribe in *The Egoist.* "The artist has been at peace with his oppressor long enough," Pound wrote, sounding a bit like Marinetti and D. H. Lawrence. The time for humanism was long gone, the artist could not hope to arouse an "unbearably stupid" public through art. The artist "has dabbled in democracy, and now he is done with that folly. We turn back, we artists, to the powers of the air, to the djinns who were our allies aforetime, to the spirits of our ancestors." The aristocracy of title is dead, that of commerce decaying, and it was the time for the aristocracy of arts: "We who are the heirs of the witch-doctor and the voodoo, we artists who have been so long the despised are about to take over control." Pound's aggressiveness was practically out of control; he had become Shakespeare's Timon railing against the mob. At this time, Pound offered a pathetic demonstration of his new aristocracy. When the Georgian poet Lascelles Abercrombie published an essay urging a return to Wordsworth in a search for true values, Pound retorted with a letter challenging Abercrombie to a duel: "Stupidity carried beyond a certain point becomes a public menace." The phrase had a brave clarion ring, but it was far out of proportion. Wordsworth was hardly worth a war. Abercrombie was perturbed when he heard of Pound's skill as a fencer, but as the challenged party, he had the right to choose weapons, and he proposed that they bombard each other with the unsold copies of their books. The "duel" did not occur: doubtless Pound himself realized it would have had too much of the flavor of Don Quixote.

Shortly after the opening of the Rebel Art Centre in the spring of 1914, Pound had offered a lecture to Lewis's group on the principles of Imagism. He had already realized that Imagism was a limited though useful tool, good for short poems and as a control for making each individual line taut and lean, but too finite for any more sustained effort. Influenced by the new art movements he saw around him, by French Cubism, by Lewis and Gaudier, by Kandinsky's *Concerning the Spiritual in Art,* he sought a more embracing definition for the new art scene that would help him as a poet. Only a year earlier he had mentioned the word "vortex" in a letter to Williams describing the cross-conflicts of art and ideology in London, and also in a letter to Dorothy: "Energy depends on one's ability to make a vortex-genius même." He had used it earlier still in the poem "Plotinus" in *A Lume Spento;* he had heard it used by Yeats, who had read it in Blake and Swedenborg. Hulme had told him Bergson defined the atom as an ever whirling vortex ring. He saw the word in Henry Adams's autobiography published just before he left America: Adams had described his own thought as "caught and whirled in a vortex of infinite forces."

In his Rebel Art Centre talk, Pound proposed a new term to describe what the new artists were doing—Vorticism. The Vorticists drew on the harsh urgency of Expressionism, on the new perspective suggested by Cubism with its emphasis on static, monumental forms, and on Marinetti and Italian Futurism. The Vorticists would rely on what was intrinsic in art:

EVERY CONCEPT, EVERY EMOTION PRESENTS ITSELF TO THE VIVID CONSCIOUSNESS IN SOME PRIMARY FORM.

Pound made his declaration on primary form in capital letters in an essay that formulated the principles he had first offered in his talk. Published the following fall in *The Fortnightly Review,* it announced that the image was not an idea:

It is a radiant node or cluster; it is what I can, and must perforce, call a VORTEX, from which, and through which, and into which, ideas are constantly rushing. In decency one can only call it a VORTEX. And from this necessity came the name "vorticism." *Nomina sunt consequentia rerum,* and never was that statement of Aquinas more true than in the case of the vorticist movement.

Pound needed a definition large enough to accommodate innovative elements in painting, sculpture, poetry, and music. For him the vortex whirlpool was a metaphor for that creative sector of the imagination that conceives the new through a kind of seething fermentative process. He saw it as a catapulting spring, coiled tightly so that the vital creative intuition was both vibrantly pulsing in its center and ready to leap out to an audience.

But Imagism had presented a much more coherent program: it was fixed, precise, concerned with an exact and vivid depiction and therefore measurable. At its best, the Imagist poem as Pound had conceived it was capable of an implacable clarity, a reassurance of order in a disordered universe. Such calm certainty was evident in a poem like "Alba":

> As cool as the pale wet leaves
> of lily-of-the-valley
> She lay beside me in the dawn.

"Alba" was especially deft, and it was sensuously tactile, but Pound was beginning to realize that the radical condensations and the sharp focus of Imagism would force poets to contract their scope to the point where no broad social comment would be possible.

With Vorticism Pound was able to imagine a contrary direction. He used Vorticist principles to expand the poetic field, the scope or range containing movement in a poem. From its inceptions, Vorticism had been about movement. It had been inspired in part by the propulsive gestures of Marinetti and Italian Futurist painters like Umberto Boccioni, analysts of movement who attempted to scan the component parts of a realistic sequence, tried to present simultaneously all the multiple phases of an activity. Boccioni, for example, had painted a running horse with twenty legs. The Vorticist painters had set out to discover and use as a trigger the concentration of energy needed to begin an action in the first place. The basis of the Vorticist approach was dissidence and disruption, an artistic anarchy in which new forces might be released, forces about which the artist was not always sure and of which he was not always in control. Such principles could certainly stimulate poets, but also lead them down dangerous paths. The Vorticists were interested in abstraction. On the other hand, Imagism had been designed to purge the abstract, the general, all rhetorical language; its purpose was purification and control of the poetic line, not release. Vorticism was impure, it was a hybrid of painting, sculpture, and writing, an amalgamation that would advance no single art form, a new sort of mongrel born in the chaotic anxiety of the prewar years with a mania for recognition and a circus sensibility but with no clear program and less real innovative value.

Though Vorticism now seems like a transient phase in the history of art, the attempt by a splinter group of British painters like Lewis and Nevinson to assimilate the Futurist fury of Marinetti and the greater Continental lessons of Cubism, it gave Pound the space he needed to abandon the short format of a poem like "Alba" and to conceive of a structure for *The Cantos*, where he could allow disparate realities and moods to conflict chaotically without transition or explanation. While such a perspective was more modernist in character, it also reflected a sacrifice of control and certainly coherence, a change of direction that would come to affect Pound's ideology as well as his aesthetic.

The first literary expression of Vorticism was conceived by Lewis and Pound as an oversized folio almost a foot long in puce wrappers with the single word "BLAST" inscribed on a diagonal across front and back. It appeared at the end of June in 1914, only one week before the Archduke Franz Ferdinand, heir to the throne of the Austro-Hungarian Empire, was assassinated in Sarajevo, beginning the chain of events that culminated in war. The magazine began with a comic indictment, the list of the blasted— Galsworthy, the bishop of London, the Strachey family (which included Virginia Woolf), the conductor Thomas Beecham—and then the blessed— the socialist W. L. George, James Joyce, Frank Harris, Madame Strindberg. Included also was a Vorticist manifesto by Pound and Lewis; Ford's "The Saddest Story," which was part of his best novel, *The Good Soldier;* a story by Rebecca West, "Indissoluble Matrimony," which had been rejected by Austin Harrison, Ford's successor at the *English Review;* comments by Kandinsky; writing and paintings by Lewis; drawings by Gaudier-Brzeska and Epstein; and a group of poems by Pound. Lewis had been forced to censor part of a poem by Pound because of the line, "The twitching of two abdominal muscles cannot be a lasting Nirvana." John Lane, the publisher of *Blast* and of the famous *Yellow Book* magazine, which had been the voice of the Art for Art's Sake movement in the nineties, insisted that the line be blacked out, but the bars laid on the line by the printer were transparent and the words were visible after all. Aldington felt Pound had been carried away by Lewis's rage in his *Blast* contributions: "Mr. Pound is one of the gentlest, most modest, bashful, kind creatures who ever walked the earth; so I cannot help thinking that all this enormous arrogance and petulance and fierceness are a pose." But Pound's poems in *Blast* did have a raucous edge; the spirit behind them was no longer Whitman but a rancid Villon: "You funghus," Pound called his audience, "you continuous gangrene." In "Salutation the

Third" Pound addresses the "gagged reviewers," and "slut-bellied obstructionists" who oppose the new art and drive the artists to madness or suicide. He offers them only the taste of his boot, proposing that they "lick off the blacking."

The psychology of *Blast* was that art is primitive and the modern artist is savage. Its form had been partly inspired by Marinetti's book *Zang Tumb Tuuum* and Apollinaire's manifesto *Futurist Anti-Tradition*. Intelligence would be electrified by naïveté and humor, the magazine promised. Actually its tone was very similar to a remark Hulme made in regard to Epstein's sculpture: "In the present condition of things we have nothing to say but 'merde' and this wild new sculpture says it." More bombastic than explosive, *Blast* was barely noticed by Londoners. G. W. Prothero, editor of *The Quarterly Review*. spoke for the established press when he wrote Pound to say he was going to be virtually blacklisted: "I am afraid that I must say frankly that I do not think I can open the columns of the Q.R.—at any rate at present—to anyone associated so publicly with such a publication as *Blast*. It stamps a man too disadvantageously." Critics and the few members of the public who actually saw the magazine were put off by the anarchic presentation, the bewildering variety of typesetting, the abstract illustrations. Konody, the critic in *The Observer*. recommended that a reader would need ice packs because it was so obscure and unintelligible, a "production of naughty boys who are impelled by the love of mischief." For the *Morning Post*. it was a collection of "irrepressible imbecility." Instead of launching the new art movement with Lewis and Pound at its head, *Blast* only affected fashion as some women began wearing garish color combinations. "The common homo canis snarls violently at the thought of there being ideas which he doesn't know," Pound rationalized. But the fact was that most of London was much too busy enjoying itself. It was a generation desperate for gaiety, trying to spend an entire youth before the catastrophe that would begin that August. It was a moment of festivity and infectiously high spirits. Millionaires were still cantering along Rotten Row in Hyde Park with their pureblooded horses; the Derby and Ascot were not just horse races but grand social functions. The Russian ballet was still performing, at music halls like the Tivoli or the Palace one could hear Marie Lloyd or Victoria Monks, at Covent Garden Caruso sang nightly, the fancy balls at the Ritz had never been as resplendent and shining, there was dancing at Prince's, Ciro's, or the Savoy. At the Cave of the Golden Calf, Vorticism had already degenerated into the dances it inspired—the turkey trot and the bunny hop.

13. THE DEMON PANTECHNICON DRIVER

In the midst of the inebriation of new ideas and friends was Dorothy, always a stabilizing presence in Pound's life. At this point they were studying Chinese together. Violet Hunt had given them some of her father's paintings for their new flat, and they bought a clavichord from Arnold Dolmetsch, who specialized in making instruments as they had been made in the sixteenth and seventeenth centuries and organized his large family in concerts of that music. They installed the sculpture by Gaudier-Brzeska that Pound had purchased. Early in the summer of 1914 they encountered a portly Henry James promenading with his niece in Chelsea. For Pound, James represented a crucial figure in the modern tradition, a man who had mastered Victorian form in a novel like *Portrait of a Lady,* but who then had gone far beyond the confines of old-fashioned fiction in his experiments of the 1890s: *The Turn of the Screw, What Maisie Knew,* and *The Sacred Fount.* Pound had attempted to transfer James's idiom to some of his own work—"Portrait d'une Femme" is a case in point—and he continued to try. He had great respect for a novelist like James. Pound knew about the concentration of energies required to write novels and also knew that he did not have such qualities, that his inspirations came more in flashes than in sustained work. Writing prose was difficult, and he had already written lots of it, much of it hacked out because of the exigencies of income. James was the consummate stylist, the Flaubert of his time, and Pound had admonished that poetry must be at least as good as the best prose. In his curiously elaborate speech of hesitation and pause in midword, James congratulated the couple and then chatted with Pound as the women walked ahead. For Pound it was a visualization of the great tradition of letters being passed from one generation to the next. For one calm moment he was able to forget *Blast* and the Vorticist group.

During the debacle that became *Blast,* Amy Lowell steamed back to London complete with her retinue of maids, her liveried chauffeur, and her maroon limousine—like a good American, she went nowhere without her own automobile. She had returned to England determined to save the world with poetry, and she felt she had some credentials. Actually she had very little of a self-critical faculty. Arguing with her, Carl Sandburg observed, was like struggling with a "great blue wave." But one of the early students of Japanese Shintoism, and Fenollosa's friend, had been her uncle Percival Lowell, who had written letters to her describing Japanese art and customs, perhaps preparing her sensibility for Imagism. She had heard about the assassination of the archduke and her preparation for a possible war was to order ten thousand long cigars, an uninterrupted supply good for at least two lives. Lewis had organized a *Blast* celebration dinner at the Dieudonné restaurant and Amy Lowell had arrived just in time to join the festivities. The rotund Miss Lowell (Pound later called her the "hippo-poetess"), seated between a paunchy Ford Madox Ford and the lithe Gaudier, bragged to Ford that her family had descended from William the Conqueror. Gaudier marveled at Lowell's girth, imagining her as the subject of a Cubist drawing. Gaudier could not afford to pay for his meal but brought a faun carving instead, which he laid on Pound's plate. The artists were paying tribute to Pound—Lewis had just completed a sketch of him with a solid rectangle in place of the forehead, signifying what he felt was fanatical willpower.

Lowell, not to be outdone, decided to give her own dinner two nights later in the same restaurant. The twelve-course meal was attended by Pound and his wife, H.D. and Aldington, Flint, Allen Upward, John Gould Fletcher, and John Cournos. The dinner had already begun when D. H. Lawrence entered with the news that Edward Marsh had told him that England was going to declare war, but the poets were too full of their immediate concerns to appreciate it. John Cournos felt an undercurrent of hostility and condescension toward Lowell, but the real tension occurred when Allen Upward, in a sarcastic after-dinner speech, used as his text a poem by Lowell that Pound had printed in *Des Imagistes,* picturing her bathing in a moonlit garden in "a way to perturb and vex her puritanic soul," according to Cournos. Just then Pound entered with a circular tub he had found in an adjoining room and he placed it in front of Amy Lowell, announcing that *Les Imagistes* were about to be succeeded by *Les Nagistes.* Upward and Pound had conspired to embarrass Amy Lowell; it was a crude baptism in the politics of poetry.

She had come with a singular purpose. She wanted to assemble a second Imagist anthology, one that would be much more comprehensive than Pound's and issued by a major American publisher. She wanted its contents to be selected by the poets themselves rather than by an editor like Pound. With some reason Pound was afraid of Amy Lowell's taste. He thought, too, that the "democratic committee" of selection might sacrifice the standards he had applied and substitute values that would be "splay footed and sentimental." Aldington said that Amy Lowell's visit was Pound's Boston Tea Party, the dethroning of the Imagist Duce and the ending of his "capricious censorship."

The Imagists had seen that Pound was moving in new directions. Pound had complained in a letter to the *Daily News and Leader* that the newspaper referred to him as the Imagist leader "as if I were in some magisterial masonic manner the archimandrite of this order." The other Imagists did not quite see how they could fit in the Vorticist program. Five of them, H.D. and Aldington, Flint, D. H. Lawrence, and John Gould

Fletcher, agreed to participate in Amy Lowell's venture. She produced three Imagist anthologies which, though they helped popularize Imagism in America and certainly helped H.D.'s reputation, provoked lots of negative comment. In England, May Sinclair noted that while the Victorians had specialized in "hair-tearing," the Imagists seemed to lack strong human passions. In America, in the *New Republic,* a young writer named Conrad Aiken charged that they had become a "little mutual admiration society," a group of absurdly artificial "tea-tasters." "Miss Lowell was a delightful acquaintance," Pound wrote to Alice Henderson at *Poetry,* "if one were a civil engineer." He contemptuously called her movement "Amygisme" and to an extent his fears had been justified—the movement had been watered down and compromised. Pound explained his position to Harriet Monroe. He had resolved the possibility of overproduction in free verse by the most "rigorous suppression of what I considered faults." Lowell wanted a "democratic beer-garden" with Imagism coming to mean any kind of vers libre, and with all discrimination suspended. "My problem," Pound concluded gravely, "is to keep alive a certain group of advancing poets, to set the arts in their rightful place as the acknowledged guide and lamp of civilization." Pound's letter is high-handed and lofty, just as his initial direction of the Imagists had been. F. S. Flint told him, answering one of his "bolts from Olympus," that he had failed with personal relationships, "spoiled everything by some native incapacity for walking square with your fellows." "You have not been a good comrade," Flint added, and the reason for the success of Imagism in America was not due to Pound's propaganda but to the fact that Americans "seem ready to accept anything." For her part, Lowell wrote a history of American poetry and did her best not to refer to Pound except to charge that he had derived all his poetry from books and that he was a stylist who so warred against moralizing in poetry that he had excluded meaning itself. Lowell was not being quite fair, but her feelings had been hurt. "It was more due to Ezra Pound," Harriet Monroe wrote, "than to any other person that 'the revolution' or 'the renaissance' or whatever one chooses to call the freer modern impulse in poetry, was on."

One consequence of Pound's concern with Imagism was a deeper involvement with new writers. Joyce's poem "I Hear an Army Charging" had appeared in *Des Imagistes* and he had sent Pound a copy of *Dubliners,* a book of early stories, honed and chiseled to a quiet elegance, which had been rejected by forty publishers. Joyce later described the harrowing difficulties of publishing *Dubliners,* and his brief comment stands as a sign of the modernists' commitment to their art:

> Ten years of my life have been consumed in correspondence and
> litigation about my book Dubliners. It was rejected by 40 publish
> ers; three times set up, and once burnt. It cost me about 3,000

francs in postage, fees, train and boat fare, for I was in correspondence with 110 newspapers, 7 solicitors, 3 societies, 40 publishers
and several men of letters about it. All refused to aid me, except
Mr. Ezra Pound. In the end it was published, in 1914, word for
word as I wrote it in 1905.

He sent as well the first chapter of a novel, *Portrait of the Artist As a Young
Man,* then in its third revision, and Pound was immediately impressed with
what he felt was the presence of a new and vital voice for fiction. Pound
reviewed *Dubliners* in *The Egoist,* noting that it represented a return of style
in English literature. He described Joyce in *Drama* as one of the best of his
contemporaries: "He has written a novel, and I am quite ready to stake
anything I have in this world that the novel is permanent." Pound persuaded Harriet Shaw Weaver to serialize *Portrait* in *The Egoist,* and over the
next few years launched a one-man campaign on Joyce's behalf, writing to
Harriet Monroe, H. L. Mencken, and Margaret Anderson at *The Little Review,* who serialized *Ulysses* in America.

Pound's readiness to drop his own work to help Joyce or Yeats, or later
Eliot and Hemingway and others, is an important characteristic. Most of his
friends commented on his generosity, his efforts on their behalf. As a sort of
midwife of modernism, Pound not only would read what they wrote but
helped to get it published, and he tried to do the same for painters, sculp-
tors, and musicians. In one sense, of course, his generosity was a subtle form
of self-aggrandizement; Pound could feel that he was shaping his time by
formulating its artists. By extending himself, he could exert great influence
and perhaps even perpetuate his own taste.

Another new connection was Conrad Aiken, the young Harvard graduate who came to London in 1914, in part to see whether he could place
some poems for his friend, Thomas Stearns Eliot. Aiken, who called Pound
Rabbi Ben Ezra after a poem by Browning, liked Pound but saw that
Pound's attempt to form the Imagists into a cohesive group had damaging
results: Pound, "if a good teacher, was also something of a tyrant." Aiken
left several of Eliot's poems with Pound; no one else in England had shown
any interest. Pound was astonished, especially by "The Love Song of
J. Alfred Prufrock," and again felt the presence of a major voice.

A tall, sleek, sibylline figure, impeccably dressed, with a sort of Gio-
conda smile and the mournful air of a consumptive, Eliot arrived himself to
visit late in September of 1914. He had been in Marburg, Germany, on a
traveling fellowship from Harvard, pursuing a graduate degree in episte-
mology, but had to leave because of the outbreak of the war. An anxious
young man, thwarted by life, nervous and worried, Eliot was at the same
time capable of great poise and elegance. Prim and fastidious in his speech,
careful about details, he could also be self-depreciating, ironic, or mocking

in his comments. The two young men had tea among the stacks of books and papers in Pound's triangular study. Outside, wartime crisis suffusing the air, damp, gloomy, oppressive; inside, embers in the fireplace, candied apricots, and talk of poetry. "Beauty is a brief gasp between clichés," Pound might have declared between sips of his Earl Grey to his sedate visitor who was quietly examining the William Hunt paintings, the sculpture by Gaudier, the Dolmetsch clavichord. Pound was restless and fidgety and perhaps more than a bit overbearing—"I believe in technique as a test of sincerity," he might have admonished, or "Bad art is inaccurate art." He showed Eliot Lewis's Timon of Athens drawings and tried to expatiate on the Vorticist milieu. Eliot remained diffident, tactful but completely noncommittal. However, he was encouraged by Pound's enthusiasm for his work. Aiken had shown "The Love Song of J. Alfred Prufrock" to Harold Monro at the Poetry Bookshop; Monro had dismissed it as "absolutely insane," a remark which characterized the Georgian attitude toward any verse that did not resemble Wordsworth's. Pound, however, immediately wrote to Harriet Monroe informing her that Eliot had given him "the best poem I have yet had or seen from an American." Pound was amazed because Eliot as a poet seemed to have grasped certain essentials without the ardors of apprenticeship: "He has actually trained himself and modernized himself *on his own.*"

Pound introduced Eliot to Wyndham Lewis, but Eliot was studiously reserved and quiet. To relieve the tension Pound began to speak in a hillbilly accent, promising Lewis that Eliot was livelier than he seemed. Lewis, in his petulant and acrid style, also recalled the meeting:

> This very small room, in which Mr. Eliot had alighted, and in which he sat placidly smiling, was, allowance made for the comic side of Ezra's manic herding of talent, a considerable place. Dorothy Shakespear had become Dorothy Pound and of course was in this dwarf room too, nodding, with a quick jerk of the head, unquestioning approval of Ezra's sallies, or hieratically rigid as she moved delicately to observe the Kensingtonian Tea ritual. (Long habit in the paternal mansion responsible, she was a good turncoat *bourgeoise,* who wore her red cockade with a grim pleasant gaucherie.) In any event, all social transactions were necessarily *intime.* One at a time was their rule for genius.

Lewis was busy preparing a second number of *Blast,* and he included in it Eliot's "Preludes" and "Rhapsody on a Windy Night," which would be Eliot's first real publication anywhere. He also considered printing examples of Eliot's undergraduate ribaldry, "Bullshit" and "The Ballad of Big Louise," but remembering the difficulty he had with John Lane over a line by Pound in the first issue of *Blast,* he decided not to try.

The second number of *Blast* was less literary than the first issue, less dynamic and less venomous. The dissonance and asymmetry of Vorticism had not been appreciated by an English audience and Lewis was now trying to clarify the Vorticist position. Lewis took the trouble to list the major American artists who had seen, understood, and transcribed the social situation: Poe, Whistler, Whitman, and James. He ended his list with Pound, the "demon pantechnicon driver, busy with removal of the old world into new quarters."

Pound, in the poems he contributed, seemed even more defensive, outraged, and ready to attack:

> I cling to the spar,
> Washed with the cold salt ice
> I cling to the spar—
> Insidious modern waves, civilization,
>   civilized hidden snares.
> Cowardly editors threaten: "If I dare"
>
> Say this or that, or speak my open mind,
> Say that I hate my hates,
>   Say that I love my friends,
> Say I believe in Lewis, spit out the later Rodin,
> Say that Epstein can carve in stone,
> That Brzeska can use the chisel,
> Or Wadsworth paint;
>   Then they will have my guts;
> They will cut down my wage, force me to sing their
>   cant,
> Uphold the press, and be before all a model of
>   literary decorum.
>   Merde!

The cover of *Blast* was Lewis's painting *Before Antwerp*, three stark soldiers with rifles surrounded by jagged and ominous forms. The balance in *Blast* had shifted from the literal to the pictorial. One new contributor was Pound's wife using her maiden name, Dorothy Shakespear. Lewis observed that her visits to the Rebel Art Centre had given her a "shove out of the Victorian" and opened her art to new influences. Lewis had told her, watching her draw one day at the center, that what she was doing was "too tight—do something more free." Her first attempt in her new manner was the fierce red, blue, and gray *War Scare, 1914*, painted on the day the Stock Exchange closed just before the official declaration of war. On the back of her painting, she had scrawled, "Not to be shown to anybody," the sign of a reticence that kept her work in her poet-husband's shadow.

Ever since England had declared war in August, Pound had been at-

tempting to organize the Vorticists into an organized teaching body, a way
to formalize the work of the Rebel Art Centre with a university structure
catering to American students who were then unable to study in continental
Europe. Pound aimed at an intellectual level "no lower than that attained by
the courts of the Italian Renaissance," an ambition that itself would probably have frightened more potential students than it could attract. Pound's
idea depended on a faculty of established creative artists who would bring
the active sensibility of the workshop rather than the studiousness of the
scholar. Using an interdisciplinary approach, they would develop student
expression in painting, music, and words. The idea was only fifty years
ahead of its time. Its faculty was projected as Gaudier, Lewis, the painter
Wadsworth, Pound himself, the photographer Alvin Langdon Coburn, John
Cournos, and Katherine Heyman and Arnold Dolmetsch, who would teach
modern and ancient music. Pound's school would have had a remarkably
experimental and eccentric nature—Lewis, for example, would have taught
his students abstraction and the "repudiation of nature"—but the war pre-
cluded its possibility. Like the proposals for an ideal academy in "Patria
Mia," the project was impractical and destined to live only on paper.

14. AN ABYSS OF BLOOD AND DARKNESS

Most of the Vorticists were joining the war effort. Gaudier-Brzeska,
subject for service as a Frenchman, went to see the French consul who
advised him to return to France immediately. In a bureaucratic mix-up, he
was arrested as a deserter, threatened with ten years' imprisonment, and put
under guard. Gaudier escaped and returned once again to England to visit
the consul, who issued a safe-conduct pass. Lewis and Hulme, who soon
followed, accompanied Gaudier to the boat train, where he departed for
France a second time. Lewis remembered his excited eyes:

> We left the platform a depressed, almost guilty group. It is easy to
> laugh at the exaggerated estimate "the artist" puts on his precious
> life. But when it is really an artist—and there are very few—it is at
> the death of something terribly alive that you are assisting. And
> this little figure was so preternaturally alive.

Pound, steeped in his own projects, his Fenollosa manuscripts, the work
with Eliot and Joyce, had managed to postpone a full realization of the fact
of the war despite the billboard recruitment posters covering every available space in London. But Gaudier's letters began to suggest to him the
terrible reality. Gaudier had been part of a group of twelve men defending
a roadway and seven of them had fallen. He wrote that he slept on frozen or
sodden ground, that he would stand in the trenches for days in the mud,

that he had spent twenty-five straight days without finding a dry place or washing, that he was used to being surrounded by the stench of dead bodies. He sent Lewis a manifesto for the second number of *Blast,* dramatically entitled VORTEX GAUDIER-BRZESKA (Written from the Trenches). The piece asserted that the war had not changed the formal values underlying his craft: "MY VIEWS ON SCULPTURE REMAIN ABSOLUTELY THE SAME. IT IS THE VORTEX OF WILL, OF DECISION, THAT BEGINS." He presented a curiously aesthetic view of the circumstances of war: "I SHALL DERIVE MY EMOTIONS SOLELY FROM THE ARRANGEMENT OF SURFACES." Emotion tied to the topography of war and resulting in an imagination that would create the manifesto was a visible demonstration of Vorticist resonance:

> Just as this hill where the Germans are solidly entrenched gives me
> a nasty feeling, solely because its gentle slopes are broken up by
> earth-works, which throw long shadows at sunset, just so shall I get
> feeling, of whatsoever definition, from a statue ACCORDING TO
> ITS SLOPES, varied to infinity.

The manifesto included a bewildering note of ironic elitism, and a shocking recapitulation of the eugenic theory that was prevalent at the time. Winston Churchill was a believer in eugenics and the idea that the earlier stages of the industrial system had created work for an enormous mass of inferior Europeans who were less and less required as the system evolved. War, Gaudier's manifesto suggested, seemed to offer a temporary solution:

> This war is a great remedy.
> In the individual it kills arrogance, self esteem, pride. It takes
> away from the masses numbers upon numbers of unimportant
> units, whose economic activities become noxious as the recent
> trade crisis has shown us.

To the end Gaudier was writing Pound letters full of his evolving aesthetic theory. In one of his last acts he found a Mauser rifle and began carving its handle trying to counteract its brutality with gentler feeling. On the front lines and scouting at night between them, Gaudier had shown remarkable contempt for personal danger and had been promoted to the rank of sergeant. But his military career was brief; he was killed in battle at Neuville-Saint-Vaast on June 5, 1915. He had "gone out through a little hole in the high forehead," Ford wrote in an obituary note.

News of Gaudier's death shocked Pound into an awareness of the closeness of war. Gaudier had become for Pound a personal totem of the artist, a symbolic figure who had been sacrificed in a conflict that would prove nothing. For Pound, it was "so far, the worst calamity of the war. There was a loss to art with a vengeance." The poet Charles Olson wrote later, "It was as though Pound had never got over it, that Gaudier's death is the source of his hate for contemporary England and America." Pound compared Gaudier's death with that of the young poet Rupert Brooke, who had died at the same time of blood poisoning. Henry James had called Brooke's death "horrible and heart-breaking, a stupid and hideous disfigurement of life and an outrage to beauty," but Pound was less charitable, seeing his death as less a loss for art and more the loss of a "charming young man" who had "flocked with the stupidest set of Blockheads to be found in any country"—that is, the Georgians. Pound quoted Charles Ricketts, a friend of Yeats, who said, "What depresses me most is the horrible fact that they can't *all* be beaten." Writing to Harriet Monroe, he suggested that the war was a contention between two equally detestable forces and that it was only a "symptom of the disease." The real trouble with the war was "that it gives no one the chance to kill the right people." Such remarks were the beginning of a vitriolic intemperance that only festered and increased as the years passed.

Though the official declarations of war were on August 4, 1914, diplomats, journalists, and soldiers had all expected it for at least a year. Hilaire Belloc had predicted the obvious in an article in the *London Magazine:* that the Germans would attack France by coming through Belgium at Liège as the railway system demanded. On August 6 eleven thousand trains transported over three million German soldiers and the French sent some two million young men to meet them on the same day.

Amy Lowell had spent the weekend before August 4 in Bath and was surprised to find the market filled with cannons and the "town echoing with soldiers." She was told they were on maneuvers. When war was declared, she motored in her maroon limousine back to London to see "a great crowd of people with flags march down Piccadilly, shouting: 'We want war! We want war!' They sang the Marseillaise, and it sounded savage, abominable." She had her automobile shipped back to America the next day so that it would not be commandeered, and worked for a month helping stranded Americans before she returned home herself. On the day war was declared, Wilfred Blount, the anti-imperialist, buried a box of gold under a sycamore tree on his estate in Newbuildings, and H.D. learned she was pregnant. She told Pound a few days later; he regretted that the child had not been his.

On August 5 Henry James wrote to a friend in a mood of profound despair:

> The plunge of civilization into this abyss of blood and darkness by the wanton feat of those two infamous autocrats is a thing that so gives away the whole long age during which we have supposed the world to be, with whatever abatement, gradually bettering, that to have to take it all now for what the treacherous years were all the while really making for and meaning is too tragic for any words.

James knew that the war signaled the end of liberalism, that it proved that progress was an illusion. He would make the startling gesture of renouncing his citizenship and becoming a British subject before he died, all a result for him of the shock of the war. His friend Joseph Conrad returned from a visit to his Polish homeland ill and depressed over what the war had devastated. Virginia Woolf had the first of her nervous breakdowns. For Leonard Woolf the decade preceding the war had been one of political and social change and "it seemed as though human beings might really be on the brink of becoming civilized." Now, it was the "end of hope."

The war had an immediate effect on writers, as Richard Aldington observed: "Literary papers disappeared, literary articles were not wanted, poems had to be patriotic." Pound's income plummeted to forty-two pounds for the first year of the war; he had earned five times that the year before. Young writers were no longer content with simple prewar pleasures; they wanted more violent, hectic, and expensive amusements. The mood in London had shifted drastically. Streetlamps were blackened to dim the light or they were painted deep orange, creating a lurid, phantasmagoric effect. On air-raid nights, even the lighting of a match was forbidden. Suddenly there was a host of new rules and new enforcers everywhere.

Pound's Vortex had been converted from an aesthetic concept to a military operation as millions of German young men were propelled toward millions of French and then British, all to collide in the trenches. During the war years, Leonard Woolf claimed in *Beginning Again,* one felt as if one were behind bars. But at first no one believed the war would last more than a few weeks. Lord Kitchener advised that it would be a matter of four months at the most. The new technologies had facilitated the seizure of huge empires and territorial space was seen as a sign of national greatness, but the great armies were still mired in mud. Long-range artillery, machine guns, barbed wire, and gas immobilized men for long periods of time in cramped areas under circumstances of great stress. The poet Edmund Blunden remembered the "prevailing sense of the endlessness of the war." The war that was being ostensibly fought to preserve honor and integrity, country and justice, was the reality of rat-infested trenches and incessant shelling. And brutal casualties—nineteen thousand British in the first hour of the Battle of the Somme in July of 1915. Hemingway later called the war the "most colossal, murderous, mismanaged butchery that has ever taken place on earth." And the British, French, and German presses were told not to show any photographs of the corpses.

D. H. Lawrence, spending the war in Cornwall in a little sea-town cottage with its primroses and foxgloves, its magpies and hawks, was writing *Kangaroo* and measuring the war's early effects:

In 1915, autumn, Hampstead Heath, leaves burning in heaps in
the blue air, London still almost pre-war London: but by the pond
on the Spaniards Road blue soldiers, wounded soldiers in their
bright hospital blue and red, always there: and earth-coloured re-
cruits with pale faces drilling near Parliament Hill. The pre-war
world still lingering, and some vivid strangeness, glamour thrown
in. At night all the great beams of the searchlights, in great straight
bars, feeling across the London sky, feeling the clouds, feeling the
body of the dark overhead. It was 1915 the old world ended. In
winter 1915–1916 the spirit of the old London collapses; the city,
in some way perished, perished from being a heart of the world,
and became a vortex of broken passions. The integrity of London
collapses, and the genuine debasement began. . . .

Nietzsche had predicted that modern leaders would philosophize with
hammers. Virginia Woolf heard their noises all round, axes smashing,
"breaking and falling, crashing and destruction." For Richard Aldington, it
was twenty-two men in an eight-man tent, dirty blankets, lumpy mattresses.
Ford Madox Ford, an officer during the war, under fire for ten days during
the Battle of the Somme, suffered a nervous collapse from shell shock and
lung difficulties later because of the gas he had inhaled. Wadsworth had
enlisted in the navy, Bomberg in the Royal Engineers, and Wyndham Lewis
in the artillery, where he served in France as Gunner Lewis. (While Lewis
was in the army, Pound acted as his agent in London, selling his writing to
The Egoist and The Little Review, and his paintings to the collector John
Quinn.) In Tarr Lewis had popularized some of the views of Georges Sorel,
whose 1908 book Reflections on Violence had been widely discussed in London, in particular by Hulme and his group. Lewis had been attracted by
Sorel's belief that man's potential for real liberation was connected to his
capacity for violence. It was a view that had underlined the formation of the
Rebel Art Centre. Lewis wrote to Pound, describing the guns that blazed
away day and night. He contracted trench fever, convalesced near Dieppe,
and then returned to the front, near Dunkirk, in August of 1917:

> My dear Pound. I am back now with my old Battery. I have come
> to a tedious spot. It is really extremely bad. The parapet of one of
> our guns was smashed last night. We were shelled and gassed all
> night. I had my respirator on for two solid hours. There is only
> one bright side to the picture: a good concrete dugout.

Two weeks later, in a tiny scrawl, Lewis wrote that he had been under
shell fire all day, "as all days and all nights," and there had been a direct hit
in his dugout, killing a man five feet away. Less than a quarter of a mile
away, the critic T. E. Hulme was too absorbed in thoughts of his own to

listen to the whine of an approaching shell. At Cambridge years earlier, he had been dismissed as a student because of some irreverence and had arranged a mock-funeral for himself, riding a hearse on top of his own coffin with his schoolmates grieving beside him. This time there was no funeral, not even a grave: the shell was a large one and the hit was direct, an ironical fate for a philosopher who had doubted the reality of phenomena, Aldington wryly observed.

On the home front Pound tried to enlist in the British Army but was turned down. The reason is unknown, but it could have been his nationality. There was tremendous pressure on all able-bodied men to enlist; aliens were registered. There were also food panics in London, a scarcity of sugar and no wheat, hoarding, government control of almost every facet of ordinary life and the suspension of civil liberties. Museums and picture galleries were closed, but Soho nightclubs and American jazz proliferated for the soldiers on leave and their new flapper girlfriends. The great Vortex war was total and depleting. T. S. Eliot wrote to his father that "everyone's individual lives are so swallowed up in the one great tragedy that one almost ceases to have personal experiences or emotion and such as one has seem so unimportant."

"Into everyone's breast, suddenly no longer one's own," wrote the German poet Rilke, "leapt a heart like a meteor, an iron heart from an iron universe." As Edmund Blunden wrote in his memoir of the disastrous Battle of the Somme, where four hundred thousand of his countrymen fell, "Neither side had won, nor could win, this war. The war had won and would go on winning." The victor claimed ten million souls or more and there had been thirty million maimed. F. Scott Fitzgerald, an American at Princeton who had not fought, remarked, "My lovely, safe world blew itself up."

"The war is eating everybody's subconscious energy," Pound wrote to Harriet Monroe, but his own pace was unflagging. At the start of the war he had been steeped in Fenollosa's versions of poems by Li Po, the eighth-century master of classical Chinese poetry. Pound was trying to render these poems more figuratively. Hugh Kenner has observed that the poems that emerged in April of 1915 as *Cathay* were Pound's expression of the poet's plight in wartime, a system of correspondence to the European horror, the poems of exiled bowmen, abandoned women, isolated frontier guardsmen and destroyed dynasties, remote privations and journeys to far places were all parallels to the dislocations of modern war.

"I keep the book in my pocket," Gaudier had written from the Marne, "to put courage in my fellows." The stark tone of *Cathay* is suggested by the compact "The Jewel Stairs' Grievance":

> The jewelled steps are already quite white with dew,
> It is so late that the dew soaks my gauze
>   stockings,
> And I let down the crystal curtain
> And watch the moon through the clear autumn.

Followed by a brief note, the poem exists almost as an explanation of Imagism and the centrality of the image in Pound's poetry: the jeweled steps signify a palace, the gauze stockings imply a lady of the court who has arrived for an early meeting or an assignation because the dew has soaked her stockings. "The poem is especially prized," Pound added, because the lady utters no direct reproach." Her disappointment, as Pound translates it, becomes a matter of high piercing sounds ("quite white") and broad open vowels which suggest pain and sorrow. Animating the poem also is an iridescent light of many sources, reflected in the jewels, the dew, the crystal curtain, and the moon.

The *Cathay* poems were stark, but at the same time capable of a kind of great lyrical resonance that had rarely been captured in Western poetry. *Cathay* was an important step for Pound because it allowed him to integrate Imagist technique into a narrative structure, and this combining of precise objectively rendered detail and an exotic story was exactly what he later tried to sustain in *The Cantos*.

One of the strongest poems in *Cathay*, "The River Merchant's Wife: A Letter," exists almost as a miniature model of Pound's intentions:

> While my hair was still cut straight across my forehead
> I played about the front gate, pulling flowers.
> You came by on bamboo stilts, playing horse,
> You walked about my seat, playing with blue plums.
> And we went on living in the village of Chōkan:
> Two small people, without dislike or suspicion.
>
> At fourteen I married My Lord you.
> I never laughed, being bashful.
> Lowering my head, I looked at the wall.
> Called to, a thousand times, I never looked back.
>
> At fifteen I stopped scowling,
> I desired my dust to be mingled with yours
> Forever and forever and forever.
> Why should I climb the look out?
>
> At sixteen you departed,
> You went into far Ku-tō-en, by the river of swirling eddies,

And you have been gone five months.
The monkeys make sorrowful noise overhead.

You dragged your feet when you went out.
By the gate now, the moss is grown, the different mosses,
Too deep to clear them away!
The leaves fall early this autumn, in wind.
The paired butterflies are already yellow with August
Over the grass in the West garden;
They hurt me. I grow older.
If you are coming down through the narrows of the river Kiang,
Please let me know beforehand,
And I will come out to meet you
              As far as Chō-fū-Sa.

Any poem about separated lovers risks false notes and sentimentality, but Pound superbly avoids such problems. The poem is full of an innocent sweetness which is due partly to its inversions and partly to the understatement and humility of its speaker. As in a Browning monologue, she defines her situation in terms of a series of clear images: her bangs, the bamboo stilts, her desire to mix the dust of her body with the dust of her husband's, the danger suggested by the river of swirling eddies, the moss that has grown in his absence, the falling leaves, the fragile butterflies that act as a reminder of their former togetherness. In "The River Merchant's Wife" Pound showed how poetry could give a dimension to speech that transcended discourse, and this was to become a major possibility for modernism.

The *Cathay* poems, which become much more than translations in Pound's hands, are poems of marvelous control and balance, prolonged rhythmic maneuvers releasing a new strain in Pound's sensibility, an easy natural voice without Whitman's cheering or Villon's scornfulness, more affirming and life-sustaining, a counter in melody to the clash and discord of the war. Such qualities are reflected in the last lines of "Exile's Letter," one of the strongest poems in *Cathay:*

    And if you ask how I regret that parting:
    It is like the flowers falling at Spring's end
        Confused, whirled in a tangle.
    What is the use of talking, and there is no end of
        talking,
    There is no end of things in the heart.

15. A UNIVERSAL COMMITTEE FOR THE ARTS

Pound and Dorothy spent the winter of 1914–15 at Stone Cottage with Yeats. Pound was reading Confucius, working on a series for *Poetry* on the possibilities for an American Renaissance, and writing for *The New Age* a series called "Affirmations." One of *The New Age* pieces had included a savage attack on art collectors who had neglected Epstein:

> One looks out upon American collectors buying autograph MSS. of William Morris, faked Rembrandts and faked Van-dykes. One looks out on a plutocracy and upon the remains of an aristocracy who ought to know by this time that keeping up the arts means keeping up living artists; that no age can be a great age which does not find its own genius.

In New York, John Quinn, who had met Pound with Yeats's father in 1910, felt that Pound was referring to him. Quinn owned a Cézanne, a van Gogh, a Gauguin, a Duchamp, and several Matisses. A lawyer, he had written the legislation allowing works of art to be imported without duty. Quinn wrote to Pound in the spring of 1915, reminding him that he had bought six of Epstein's pieces. He had helped organize the New York Armory Show and was committed to avant-garde art, and he inquired about purchasing Gaudier's work. Pound, detecting a potential patron, agreed to supply photographs of Gaudier's sculpture and suggested a program for the ideal collector, the patron as co-creator:

> My whole drive is that if a patron buys from an artist who needs money (needs money to buy tools, time and food), the patron then makes himself equal to the artist: he is building art into the world; he creates. . . .
>
> A great age of painting, a renaissance in the arts, comes when there are a few patrons who back their own flair and who buy from unrecognized men. In every artist's life there is, if he be poor, and they mostly are, a period when £10 is a fortune and when £100 means a year's leisure to work or to travel. . . .
>
> Besides, if a man has any sense, the sport and even the commercial advantage is so infinitely greater. If you can hammer this into a few more collectors you will bring on another cinquecento.

When Quinn heard that Gaudier had been shot through the head in a charge, he commissioned Pound to buy anything available, promising as well to underwrite the costs of a New York show for the Vorticists. Pound began negotiations with Roger Fry and Sophie Brzeska, who was reluctant to part with her husband's work, suspicious that she was not being offered enough for it, and perhaps a bit resentful that Pound had never liked her fiction or offered to help her. Pound was working on his elegiac memoir of Gaudier, in which he hoped as well to describe the Vorticists. He had also heard of a weekly paper that was for sale, *The Academy,* and tried to persuade Quinn to back it so that he could edit it. Quinn liked the idea, but the paper was sold to an Englishman, which enraged Pound: "Je m'emmerde du public, they want shit and they get it and they smack their dung smeared lips and holler for more, and when a good thing comes they hate it."

Joyce's *Portrait of the Artist As a Young Man* had completed its run in *The Egoist* and Pound had been trying to help find a publisher. He had also tried to place Joyce's play *Exiles* with a theatrical company. In the summer of 1915, B. W. Huebsch, a Jew, but "a fairly decent sort," Quinn informed Pound, published the book in New York and Harriet Shaw Weaver of *The Egoist* took 750 copies for England. Joyce had left Trieste because of the war and moved to neutral Zurich, where he was looking for work, facing medical costs because of his failing eyes, and, with two children, struggling to make ends meet. Pound had heard from Yeats about the Royal Literary Fund, which made grants to deserving writers. He got Yeats to approach Edmund Gosse on Joyce's behalf, and his mother-in-law, Olivia Shakespear, to intercede with her friend Henry Newbolt, while Pound lobbied with H. G. Wells. The fund awarded Joyce seventy-five pounds, allowing him to begin work on *Ulysses.*

Pound had been less successful in his efforts to assist Eliot. Harriet Monroe had been stalling with "Prufrock" for six months, feeling still that the poem might upset some of her readers. Pound wrote reminders and the poem finally appeared in June of 1915, printed with some reluctance and perhaps trepidation by Monroe and situated at the very back of the issue. In the next month Eliot married Vivien Haigh-Wood, an extremely anxious, deracinated English woman who suffered from acute nervous strain. To support himself he taught in a grammar school and then in a junior high school, delivering extension courses on literature at Oxford and the University of London at night. Pound conceived of a new poetry project to be called *Catholic Anthology*—a title that offended a number of Roman Catholics —which he was assembling in the hope of getting more Eliot into print and also as a rejoinder to Amy Lowell's Imagist anthologies. He had begun work on a new poem of his own, a long sequence to be called *The Cantos* which he described in a letter as a "cryselephantine poem of immeasurable length which will occupy me for the next four decades unless it becomes a bore."

In January of 1916, Pound was back at Stone Cottage with Yeats for the third winter in a row. The area was "prohibited" and Pound discovered that he was supposed to have registered as an alien. Yeats told Quinn that after the third visit by the police, Pound had left the house so precipitately that he had torn the coat hook from the wall. It was a sign of a dangerous irritability in the face of authority that only increased with time. The matter was resolved only when Ford's friend Masterman, a member of Asquith's cabinet, sent a telegram to the police. Pound was editing his version of the Noh plays and helping Yeats with an edition of his father's letters, and the two men took turns reading Walter Savage Landor's *Imaginary Conversations* aloud to each other. The Landor letters were important to Pound as another possible way to dramatize imagined voices—a central concern in *The Cantos.*

At Stone Cottage Yeats had been working on *At the Hawk's Well,* his neo-Noh play whose final version he was dictating to Pound. Later, back in London, Yeats introduced Pound to Lady Cunard, at whose home the play was first staged. Married to a much older man who was heir to the Cunard ship lines, she had left him and settled with her daughter, Nancy, renting a house on Cavendish Square in London from Herbert H. Asquith, Prime Minister of England. Lady Cunard had taken up with Thomas Beecham, the conductor who had worked for Diaghilev in the first London performances of the Russian Ballet. Nancy later opened a famous salon in Paris and came to Pound for help with her own poems. Pound, always intent on helping his friends, was still concerned about Joyce's ability to sustain his family. He knew that Yeats had received a government pension and asked whether another one could not be obtained for Joyce. Yeats told him the money would have to come through a parliamentary bill, but that the Prime Minister could make such a grant on his own discretion. Pound began visiting Lady Cunard's drawing room with its lapis lazuli table and its arsenic green lamé walls, encouraging her to read Joyce and then to lend Joyce's books to her friend Edward Marsh, who was Asquith's secretary. Marsh liked what he read, the fact that it came from Lady Cunard was important to him, and in the summer of 1916 Joyce was granted a hundred pounds. Joyce wrote to thank the "wonder worker" Pound who had raised another twenty-five from an anonymous donor and instigated a grant of two pounds a week for a six-month period from the Society of Authors.

Pound had devoted himself to the causes of the group Lewis termed "the Men of 1914": Joyce, Eliot, Lewis, and Pound. "I have never been so rushed," Pound wrote Quinn, "I seem to be a universal committee for the arts." With Joyce protected for the time being, Pound tried to interest Quinn in Lewis's paintings. Lewis had joined the Army and had no money; what little he had earned through his art had been dissipated in the Rebel Art Centre and *Blast.* "My God," Pound wrote to Quinn, describing the fullness and vitality of Lewis's work, "the stuff lies in a pile of dirt on the man's floor. Nobody has seen it. Nobody has any conception of the volume and energy and the variety." Quinn, then in the role of helping unknown indigent artists, a role that appealed to his vanity, immediately cabled Lewis thirty pounds. Pound collected work by Lewis and six other Vorticists for the New York show. He had particular praise for Lewis's paintings, describing them as showing "every kind of geyser, from jism bursting up white as ivory, to a storm at sea. Spermatozoan, enough to repopulate the island with active and vigorous animals." There were problems in transporting the artwork—at one point Pound tried to convince Eliot to take all of it on his ship to New York on his way back to Harvard for his Ph.D. exams—and then there was little interest on the part of the New York galleries. The matter ended with Quinn purchasing all of the Vorticist work, much more than he wanted, and setting up a show that received very little notice. For his part, Pound was happy that Lewis had been helped. He felt that Lewis was a prime force in English art, "crashing and opposing and breaking." He was not a commentator but a protagonist, Pound argued, a man who may have been frequently wrong about everything "except the superiority of live mind to dead mind." Lewis, rarely generous when writing about others, felt Pound needed the "disturbance" of defending unpopular artists: "He is never happy if he is not sniffing the dust and glitter of action kicked up by other, more natively 'active' men."

Pound pursued Quinn with the idea of a new literary magazine on the model of the *Mercure de France,* which Remy de Gourmont had edited, pointing out that Harriet Monroe had funded *Poetry* with a hundred guarantors who each had pledged $50 for five years. All he wanted was the chance to discuss life and letters in a literate manner without a frock coat or a mouth full of black gloves. Quinn said he would try to find backers and Pound announced that he was willing to return to America to edit such a magazine, but it never materialized. Instead, Quinn offered to subsidize Pound in an editorial capacity on *The Egoist* with £150 a year for two years, an offer Pound accepted, though much of the money went to the writers whose work he solicited.

In the early spring of 1916, Pound was reading in the Italian Renaissance as part of his preparation for the first *Cantos*—a "really LONG leviathanic" poem, he told Quinn—books like Browning's *Sordello* and William Roscoe's biography of Pope Leo X for its section on the Borgias. He had also begun rereading all of Henry James, since James had died in February and Pound wanted to write an essay. *The Catholic Anthology* had appeared as well as the little book on Gaudier—favorably reviewed by Roger Fry in the *Birmingham Magazine.* Pound had sent a manuscript of essays called *This Generation* to a young publisher in New York, John Marshall, who lost it. There were other difficulties. Harriet Monroe returned an eighty-four-line poem, "To a Friend Writing on Cabaret Dancers," because Pound had used the word "whore" instead of "prostitute." After a long and exasperating campaign to get Lewis's novel *Tarr* published, Harriet Shaw Weaver agreed to do it, largely because of Pound's tireless advocacy. He wrote a piece in

The Egoist on the hazards faced by such artists as Joyce and Lewis, who needed the same immunities as scientists in reaching for truth.

In April of 1916, Pound wrote to Iris Barry, some of whose poems he had seen (and liked) in Harold Monro's *Poetry and Drama*. A young woman of seventeen working in the post office in Birmingham, Barry had a bizarre background—her mother had been the first woman in England to sue for divorce because she had contracted gonorrhea from her husband. Barry sent Pound a manuscript, and he began advising her on revisions and sent some of the work to *Poetry*. A pretty, slim, tiny woman with closely cropped black hair, Barry was an amusing though sometimes tactless, truculent, and mocking conversationalist. She visited London and claimed that when she met Pound for a walk in Wimbledon Common he gave her little opportunity to talk, carrying on himself for an entire afternoon in a speech figured with his own peculiar intonations and rhythms:

> Pound talks like no one else. His is almost a wholly original accent, the base of American mingled with a dozen assorted "English society" and Cockney accents inserted in mockery, French, Spanish, and Greek exclamations, strange cries and catcalls, the whole very oddly inflected, with dramatic pauses and *diminuendos*. It takes time to get used to it, especially as the lively and audacious mind of Pound packs his speech—as well as his writing—with undertones and allusions.

Pound then began to write regularly advising Barry on how to write and what to read: one should always find a few things to read that no other living person has read, they become a "great defense against fools and against the half-educated and against dons of all sorts." He told her as well to read the Romans because the "Roman poets are the only ones we know of who had approximately the same problems we have—the metropolis, the imperial posts in all corners of the world." (He reflected his own reading of the Romans in "Homage to Sextus Propertius.") Barry eventually moved to London, where Pound told her she could manage on less than two pounds per week, as he had, and helped find her suitable lodgings. He began introducing her to his friends, including Lewis, back from the front. Barry later became Lewis's mistress and had two children with him. She described Pound in an American magazine, *The Bookman,* as she knew him in London toward the end of the war, when he attended a weekly literary gathering at a Chinese restaurant on Regent Street:

> Into the restaurant with his clothes always seeming to fly round him, letting his ebony stick clatter to the floor, came Pound himself with his exuberant hair, pale cat-like face with the greenish cat-eyes, clearing his throat, making strange sounds and cries in his

talking, but otherwise always quite formal and extremely polite. With him came Mrs. Pound, carrying herself delicately with the air, always, of a young Victorian lady out skating, and a profile as clear and lovely as that of a porcelain Kuan-yin.

Pound's efforts during the war years on the behalf of others were the expression of a private war, an unequal contest between the forces of art clamoring for recognition and the bourgeois community that wanted only security and bread. His friend Ford saw Pound at this time as "beautifully and immensely heroic" because Pound had assumed the leadership of battles Ford had begun with the *English Review.* "No one was ever busier, gayer," Iris Barry said, "seeing everything, meeting everybody, full of the latest gossip." Barry noted that by 1916 Pound's name in England stood for the "dangerously different," "the horridly new." It was heard in America as well, as Carl Sandburg observed: "All talk of modern poetry, by people who know, ends with dragging in Ezra Pound somewhere." The name, however, was not heard with universal admiration. "It is wonderful," John Butler Yeats wrote to John Quinn early in 1917, "how people hate him. But hatred is the harvest he wants to gather." Yeats compared him to a hair shirt. Lewis's remark on Pound's need to cause disturbances, Barry's phrase describing Pound's talk as full of strange sounds and cries, and Yeats's father's comment on the hatred Pound inspired in the smothering politeness of London create the picture of an antagonist for the arts flailing the philistines and finally reviling them. Pound's friend Alvin Langdon Coburn, an American photographer living in London who became interested in Vorticism and tried to carry its energies into his work, photographed Pound prismatically, his face doubled, inverted, placed sideways, with all these images floating freely between a harsh complex of rigid bars. Lewis painted him with his hair in long tongues of fire, his expression quizzical, his coat billowing and flowing, making him look oversized, larger than life, and emphasizing his force and dangerousness. "He had no luck with the English," Lewis remembered, "and was always in this country a perfect fish out of water." For Aldington, Pound had been a "small but persistent volcano in the dim levels of London literary society." London may have been amused, but it was not really about to take him seriously. After all, Pound was an American, and the British still saw Americans as provincial colonials without a real culture. When Aldington visited Pound near the end of the war, Pound kept tapping his Adam's apple, assuring Aldington that the English "stopped short there" and were without brains. In *Who's Who* he had listed his chief recreation as "searching *The Times* for evidences of almost incredible stupidity." The result was an impatience, an irritability, a nervous restlessness which T. S. Eliot understood:

He seemed always to be a temporary squatter. The appearance was due not only to his restless energy—in which it was difficult to distinguish the energy from the restlessness and the fidgets, so that every room, even a big one, seemed too small for him—but to a kind of resistance against growing into any environment. In America he would no doubt have always seemed on the point of going abroad; in London, he always seemed on the point of crossing the Channel.

Pound's growing anger and intemperance, the hatred that John Butler Yeats had noticed, was reflected in the poems he was writing that Elkin Mathews had agreed to issue as *Lustra*. But when Mathews read the page proofs, he was reminded of the scandal over D. H. Lawrence's *The Rainbow* in 1915. Certain of Pound's poems seemed blasphemous, others excessively risqué, and others exemplified a mocking savagery and condescension that Mathews, as a publisher, felt would alienate any possible audience. In a poem called "Meditatio," inspired perhaps by Catullus's rancor, Pound wrote:

> When I carefully consider the curious habits of dogs
> I am compelled to conclude
> That man is the superior animal.
> When I consider the curious habits of man
> I confess, my friend, I am puzzled.

The brief poem demonstrates Pound's new conversational ease, but also a bitterness endemic to the collection and contagious. A note on the title page of the volume offered the following definition for Pound's title which is as well an explanation of its tone: "Lustrum—an offering for the sins of the whole people made by the censors at the expiration of their five years of office." In the first poem of the collection, "Tenzone," Pound humorously pictures his readers fleeing from his poems, "Howling in terror." The poem is an early sign of Pound's turning away from a potential audience; their "virgin stupidity" is no attraction for him, and he will write for the sake of those other poets who are able to derive pleasure from his work. The poem ends on a note of lonely vigilance which might be interpreted as sentimental, were it not for the essentially comic tone and framework:

> I mate with my free kind upon the crags;
>   the hidden recesses
> Have heard the echo of my heels,
>   in the cool light,
>   in the darkness.

Throughout *Lustra,* there are poems that announce the poet's freedom to defy convention, to praise grace or beauty whether or not that corresponds to Victorian expectations. His poems, like fish in a lake, swim without clothing; they honestly proclaim the naked truth whether or not there is an audience ready to receive such truth. Existing without the "quaint devices" of the past, his poems, he writes in "Salutation the Second," will be greeted only with irritation:

> "Is this," they say, "the nonsense
> that we expect of poets?"
> "Where is the Picturesque?"
> "Where is the vertigo of emotion?"
> "No! his first work was the best."
> "Poor Dear! he has lost his illusions."

In "Further Instructions" he exhorts his songs to "express our baser passions," "our envy of the man with a steady job and no worry about the future." Contemptuous and severe, poems like "Commission" militantly disparage the social order of the "thoroughly smug":

> Speak against unconscious oppression,
> Speak against the tyranny of the unimaginative,
> Speak against bonds.
> Go to the bourgeoise who is dying of her ennuis.

Actually, Pound has declared war on his audience, urging his poems in "Salvationists" to "take arms against this sea of stupidities." A tone that might seem humorous in a single poem becomes in many more like a sustained argument, a breaching and a condescending dismissal of any who are unable to appreciate his poems. "Come, my songs," he declares, "let us speak of perfection—"; and he adds, with a wry British inflection in his "rather," "We shall get ourselves rather disliked." The conflict that Pound expects and almost seems to seek is neatly expressed in a little poem called "Ité" (which simply means "go"):

> Go, my songs, seek your praise from the young
> and from the intolerant,
> Move among the lovers of perfection alone.
> Seek ever to stand in the hard Sophoclean light
> And take your wounds from it gladly.

Implicit in *Lustra* is Pound's belief that the sins of the nation are reflected in the rejection of beauty and its poets. It is a dangerously romantic notion, especially if it is believed in too seriously, an idea that serves only to widen the gulf between writer and audience. In a poem like "Les Millwin" Pound presents a scene at the Russian ballet where a bourgeois family en-

joys art for what Pound considers the wrong ends, as diversion rather than a
moral source, as an event attended more to be seen than to see: the "mauve
and greenish souls" of the family are presented imagistically, lying on the
upper rims of their seats like "unused boas." The image exists in place of
more overt judgments, but it exists nevertheless as a kind of slur. Throughout his book Pound emphasizes the differences between those with money
and the leisure to appreciate art and the bohemian sensibility that makes art
and sacrifices comfort in the process. In "The Garret" he contrasts the rich
who have "butlers and no friends" to the beauty of lovers waking, enjoying
their moment of "clear coolness" together. But the argument seems unfair,
the connection between the rich and the lovers who have nothing but their
love, gratuitous. Pound is so exaggerating his desire to join with the unknown behemian artists that he risks the danger of sentimentalizing through
his distortion.

What saves *Lustra* from such damaging sentimentalities is Pound's own
Imagist legacy, his bare concentration on the visible. He succeeds in making
something new to the extent that his own eye remains sharp and penetrating, as in the marvelous opening lines of "The Garden," where the image
becomes central to the argument of the poem:

> Like a skein of loose silk blown against a wall
>> She walks by the railing of a path in Kensington Garden
> And she is dying piece-meal
>> of a sort of emotional anemia.

This same graphic intensity is present in "Gentildonna" and in "April," and
in the dry, understated drama of "The Encounter":

>> All the while they were talking the new morality
>>> Her eyes explored me.
>> And when I arose to go
>> Her fingers were like the tissue
>> Of a Japanese paper napkin.

"The Encounter" presents the best possibilities of Imagism, the poem that
moves from discourse or statement to exist on the level of primary sensation
and the observable, the image standing in the place of the commentary that
might have occurred in an earlier poetry and operating with greater dimension. That imagistic brilliance, added to the conversational ease of poems
like "The Lake Isle" or the playfulness of poems like "Epitaphs," demonstrated the presence of a potent new force in poetry.

Mathews, however, felt that what he called the nastiness in *Lustra* out-
weighed such delicacies, the evident new mastery of mood and rhythm.
Pound wrote to Iris Barry that most of the poems Mathews wanted deleted
had already appeared in magazines without scandal. "The scrape is both

serious and ludicrous," Pound exclaimed, and most of the "objections are too stupid for words." The Mathews affair, Pound told Quinn, who would be instrumental in getting *Lustra* published in America, could one day be included in a projected autobiography he ribaldly called "Reveries over Asshood and Imbecility." Pound at this point was aligning himself with the suppressed artists like Joyce, and on the one hand he seemed to be almost longing for battle on the grounds of censorship. On the other hand, he knew he had to be pragmatic—he did not hear legions of publishers clamoring for his work. To assuage Mathews, he agreed to a private edition of two hundred copies and a public, censored edition with nine poems omitted.

Quinn sent a letter of praise for *Lustra* and bought copies for his friends. He sent one to Alfred A. Knopf, a young publisher with high standards whom Quinn hoped would take on the American edition without Mathews's cuts. Knopf expressed interest but felt Pound's work was not well known enough in America. Quinn then proposed a brochure on Pound's work as a means of extending his audience, a project of which Knopf approved, provided that Quinn agree to pay for most of it. Pound asked Eliot to write it but advised that it be done anonymously: "I want to boom Eliot, and one can't have too obvious a ping pong match at that sort of thing."

Pound had been trying to persuade Elkin Mathews to publish Eliot's poems, but Mathews balked and demanded an advance guarantee, should the edition fail to sell. Disillusioned because of the experience with *Lustra* anyway, Pound convinced Harriet Shaw Weaver to lend him the printing facilities of *The Egoist* and Dorothy Pound subsidized the publication, thus opening the way for *Prufrock and Other Observations,* which appeared early in the summer of 1917 as one of the first major announcements of literary modernism. The book had been instigated and organized by Pound. Eliot later said of Pound at this time that "he would cajole and almost coerce other men into writing well so that he often presented the appearance of a man trying to convey to a very deaf person the fact that the house is on fire." Eliot himself had been typically diffident and afraid. He was also mired in emotional problems: his parents wanted him to return to Harvard and become a professor there. Pound wrote Eliot's father, predicting a brilliant future for Eliot as a poet if he stayed in London. Eliot's wife detested the idea of living in America and was beginning to suffer bouts of anxiety and depression; Eliot felt he had no time to write and that he could not even earn a sufficient income to live. Four months after the publication of *Prufrock* his wife's family helped obtain for him a position in the international finance section of Lloyd's Bank.

Pound reviewed Eliot's poems in *Poetry* and in the June issue of *The Egoist,* answering a piece by Arthur Waugh, who had compared Pound and Eliot to the drunken slaves of the Greeks who were exhibited before the

sons of nobility as a warning against "ignominious folly." His praise for
Eliot was unqualified: "Confound it, the fellow can write." He wrote to
Margaret Anderson of *The Little Review* of Eliot's "unusual intelligence":
"Eliot has thought of things I had not thought of and I'm damned if many of
the others have done so." After the publication of *Prufrock*, Eliot began to
attract attention because of bizarre behavior, putting greenish powder on
his face, for example, to suggest his discomfort with his wife's suffering.
Pound advised Eliot, according to Mary Barnard, that he was playing the
"wild man" and recommended that Eliot take the role of the ultrarespect-
able, polite, and precise young man. Pound also felt responsible for the
conservative tone of Eliot's later criticism: "I pointed out to him at the
beginning that there was no use of two of us butting a stone wall; that he
would never be as hefty a battering ram as I was, nor as explosive as Lewis,
and that he had better try a more oceanic and fluid method of sapping the
foundations."

16. A MANDARIN OF LETTERS

It took some five years for Dorothy Pound's investment in *Prufrock* to
be repaid, and Pound's own income was still precarious in 1917. Thomas
Beecham, whom he had met at Lady Cunard's, had generously commis-
sioned Pound to translate the libretto of Massenet's *Cinderella;* Pound had
done a piece on art and war for *Vogue,* and there was a book review for the
Times Literary Supplement and a few articles for *The Egoist* and *The New Age.*
Early that year Macmillan had published *Noh or Accomplishment: A Study of
Classical Theatre in Japan,* and Pound had been trying without success to get
published Fenollosa's essay on the Chinese language, "The Chinese Written
Character as a Medium for Poetry," which Pound felt contained an aesthetic
for the new poetry. Pound was committed to Fenollosa's essay, but no
longer to the *Noh* plays which he had assembled and translated more out of
a debt to Fenollosa than from conviction. "I don't really believe in *Noh,"*
Pound wrote Iris Barry. "It is too fuzzy and celtic, even too '90s.' " He told
Quinn that *Noh* was too soft, but the book was generously received by the
critics, so Pound approached Macmillan with an idea for a ten-volume international anthology beginning with the Greeks and early Chinese. The proposal, written hastily in an agent's office, was a list of over three hundred
possibilities with commentary. It included an unfortunate but characteristically Poundian remark—"It is time we had something to replace that dod-
dard Palgrave." Macmillan rejected Pound's proposal immediately; its success as a publishing company had been based in large part on Sir Francis
Turner Palgrave's famous *Golden Treasury of English Songs and Lyrics.* The
new patrons of literary art were the publishers, and it may be that Pound

could not or would not understand this: the world of commerce was not
similar to the courts of troubador memory, and rather than some forgotten
ideal of aristocratic taste, sales ruled the marketplace.

During the winter of 1916–17 Pound had been trying to shape the
material that would become the first three sections of *The Cantos*. He sent
them to Harriet Monroe in February and by April she agreed to print them,
but in separate issues, not together as Pound preferred, and not with the
essay on his work by the French critic Jean de Bosschère that was appearing
in *The Egoist*. By the time they did appear in the three summer numbers of
Poetry, Pound had changed them again, considerably reducing them for the
American edition of *Lustra* which Knopf published.

Quinn had helped with *Lustra* and then offered to assist with a magazine. What Pound wanted was a "place where I and T. S. Eliot can appear
once a month (or once an issue) and where Joyce can appear when he likes,
and where Wyndham Lewis can appear if he comes back from the war."
Quinn agreed to help *The Little Review*, an experimental magazine which was
much more adventurous than *Poetry*, for two years. He paid Pound $750 a
year, of which $450 was to go to the contributors he found. The magazine
was run by Margaret Anderson and Jane Heap, two women of independent
judgment, and Pound began his duties as foreign editor in March of 1917.
Quinn felt the editors would not be sentimental or maudlin. Pound believed Anderson had nerve; she had once printed half of an issue with blank
pages because she had not found satisfactory material.

The arrangement allowed Pound to print five thousand words a month
of his own choice. By May the magazine had published a sharp editorial by
Pound attacking *Poetry* for its record of "unflagging courtesy to a lot of old
fools and fogies whom I should have told to go to hell." He complained
that patrons could create artists only if they imposed the highest standards:
"H. Monroe seems to think that if her Chicago widows and spinsters will
only shell out she can turn her gang of free-versers into geniuses all of a
onceness." He had fought with Harriet Monroe over publishing his own
poems as well as those of the writers he most respected. Now he had an
organ where he might publish them with less resistance and exercise his
critical judgment. It was part of the process of shaping modernism and
Pound was its organizational intelligence. As Eliot observed, he regarded
his favorites, Joyce, Lewis, Eliot, as protégés to be treated "almost imper-
sonally, as art or literature machines to be carefully tended and oiled for the
sake of the potential output."

The Little Review printed a group of new poems by Yeats, poems by
Eliot, a play by Lady Gregory, prose by William Carlos Williams, and
Wyndham Lewis's story "Cantleman's Spring Mate," which was suppressed
when a suit was brought in the courts because of the sexual liberties it
suggested. The matter enraged Pound: "I can not have literature stopped

merely because Mr. Comstock suffered from a psychic disease, now accurately diagnosed by psychic-physicians; or because others follow in his arse-marks." Quinn, who had to defend Anderson and Heap, thought the suit had been prompted as much by political beliefs which he did not share, the editors' general pacificist slant and defense of Emma Goldman, and he began to change his view of Anderson and Heap.

Pound contributed to *The Little Review* a series of "Imaginary Letters" after the conversations of Walter Savage Landor that he had read at Stone Cottage with Yeats. In the June number of *The Egoist* he presented a group of extracts of reviews he had collected of Joyce's *Portrait of the Artist As a Young Man* as a means of keeping Joyce's name before the British public. Joyce needed the support, as he was ailing with glaucoma, which struck with such force that he needed an iridectomy on his right eye late that summer. To raise money to help pay for the operation, Pound asked his father to auction off two letters he owned written by King Ferdinand and Queen Isabella of Spain in 1492. Pound, who had poor eyesight himself, began to proffer medical advice to Joyce and to recommend doctors. The medical advice was an expression of Pound's extreme self-confidence, the feeling that he could master any subject he studied.

Spending the summer of 1917 in London, Pound worked in the British Museum on an essay on Elizabethan literature which he published in five installments in *The Egoist* in the fall. During the summer Yeats, then fifty-two years old, had proposed to his old sweetheart Maud Gonne, an Irish revolutionary. When she refused, he tried her daughter Iseult, who also refused. Undaunted, Yeats then proposed to Dorothy Shakespear's step-cousin and friend, Georgie Hyde-Lees. In a civil ceremony in London in October, Pound stood as Yeats's best man. As Yeats and his bride were departing, Yeats asked Pound to send a telegram to Lady Gregory, but cautioned, "NOT one that will be talked about in Coole for the next generation."

Pound at this time was collecting newspaper clippings illustrating what he believed was idiocy and running them in a long serial in *The New Age* under the heading "Contemporary Mentality." The series was an early sign of a shift in his sensibility from the wars of art to those of politics. He also assembled a collection of prose pieces, which he sent to Knopf, who would publish it as *Pavannes and Divisions.* In the fall Knopf released the American version of *Lustra,* with only one of Pound's original poems omitted, and the Eliot essay *Ezra Pound: His Metric and Poetry.* When copies reached Pound, he wrote to Quinn to thank him for having inspired the publications and helping with the negotiations with Knopf. There had been a problem with using a drawing by Gaudier which Knopf did not want, and Quinn had assiduously made many corrections. Pound was delighted with the presentation of both books and wrote to Quinn, "If America ever decides to pay my rent, it will be your doing."

Quinn also pleased Pound with the report of a recent visit made by Homer and Isabel Pound to his New York apartment. He had shown them his Vorticist collection, which excited them, even though John Butler Yeats, who was present, had been critical. "I never saw two persons who have a keener delight in things," Quinn wrote. Noting their genuine enthusiasm and youthfulness and their admiration of their son's efforts, Quinn congratulated Pound on his parents: "It is not so often that a man like you, or even me, has the approval of his parents." Quinn was putting his relations with Pound on familial terms, and it is true that there were great similarities between the two men.

Both men were racially elitist, believing that the English and Scottish-Irish were superior to other Europeans, particularly Eastern Europeans. Pound had expressed this quite clearly in "Patria Mia" and although his anti-Semitic observations became infamously public only in the 1930s, he heard similar remarks from Yeats, Lewis, and Quinn, who once wrote him that Justice Felix Frankfurter was a "Jew-prig" more suited to selling hot dogs in Coney Island than to sitting on the Supreme Court. All four—Quinn, Pound, Yeats, and Lewis—had accepted a prime tenet of nineteenth-century extreme conservatism, a belief in the enlightened firm hand of a noble despot and a rigidly controlled economy. They all shared the fear that democracy would gradually erode all cultural standards. T. S. Eliot in "Coriolan" and D. H. Lawrence in his letters revealed similar beliefs, while Lewis in his later book on Hitler or his *Art of Being Ruled* and Yeats in the marching songs he composed for O'Duffy's Irish Blueshirts expressed blatantly fascist sympathies.

In terms of prestige and power, of course, there were evident differences in status. Quinn was a successful lawyer who did frequent consulting for the United States government and earned a substantial income, most of which he invested in art. He also owned an estate in Westport, because no Jews had yet been permitted to settle there, he told Pound, and he was a close friend of Theodore Roosevelt.

Quinn realized that in backing Pound he was backing a controversialist and he was worried at the possible damage and cost to his own time this could incur. In Dublin the poet George Russell, (AE) had written to Quinn that Pound seemed a "preposterous literary creature . . . a mandarin of letters" and that Pound's editing of a volume of correspondence between Yeats and his father was an example of literary incest. For AE, Pound was the "keeper of a literary museum" and in his poems intelligence interfered with the imagination and music was blocked by learning. Quinn had sent *Lustra* to Joseph Conrad, who responded with a note of genial condescension but one that reflects a typical view in English literary circles:

E.P. is certainly a poet but I am afraid I am too old and too wooden-headed to appreciate him as perhaps he deserves. The critics here consider him harmless; but as he has, I believe, a very good opinion of himself I don't suppose he worries his head about the critics very much. Besides, he has many women at his feet which must be immensely comforting.

Just before the end of 1917, Pound received from Joyce a copy of the initial sections of *Ulysses,* his new novel. For Pound, it was the most astonishing thing he had read by a member of the modernist circle since "Prufrock," and it completely validated his faith in Joyce's art. He wrote in acknowledgment in a peculiar frontier backwoodsman's dialect:

Wall, Mr. Joice, I recon' your a damn fine writer, that's what I recon'. An' I recon' this here work o' yourn is some concarn'd litershure. You can take it from me, an' I'm a jedge.

Margaret Anderson was equally impressed and wrote to Pound: "This is the most beautiful thing we will ever have. We'll print it if it's the last effort of our lives." The first installment appeared in *The Little Review* in March and it was serialized over the next two years until the United States Post Office intervened with obscenity charges. Quinn warned Pound of impending prosecution and Pound tried to temper Joyce's excessiveness, his sometimes cloacal delineation of sexual and excremental functions, what Pound termed Joyce's "arsthetic" obsessions. Harriet Shaw Weaver wanted to serialize the work in London but had difficulty finding a printer who would set type. Finally a few episodes were included in *The Egoist.* Weaver had become Joyce's patron, sending him a regular living allowance so that he could continue writing. She proposed to Virginia and Leonard Woolf, who had established their own press, that they publish the book when it was ready. Virginia Woolf refused, sensing in Joyce a rival writer who could dominate the fiction of the age. She noted in her diary that the book was "underbred" and that it "reeked with indecency." Her comments may have been more snobbish and jealous than literary. In 1922, in a talk given to the Memoir Club, she remembered Lytton Strachey coming into a room where she and her sister Vanessa were sitting and pointing to a stain on Vanessa's dress, asking jocularly if it was semen: "Sex permeated our conversation. . . . We discussed copulation with the same excitement and openness that we had discussed the nature of the good." But the sections of *Ulysses* that did appear in *The Egoist* aroused great controversy in England. J. B. Priestley remembered that Hugh Walpole defended Joyce's work at the home of Alfred Noyes, who promptly asked Walpole to leave. John Quinn had been similarly disturbed by the language of the early episodes, but Pound understood that much of Joyce's language was the correlative for a civilization that had

gone awry because of the war. He told Quinn the international situation
had been in part caused by the American and English habit of keeping
"their ostrich heads carefully down their silk-lined sand-holes." In April he
wrote Quinn:

> I can't agree with you about Joyce's first chapter. I don't think the
> passages about his mother's death and the sea would come with
> such force if they weren't imbedded in squalor and disgust. I may
> say that I rec'd the fourth chapter some days ago, and deleted
> about twenty lines before sending it off to N.Y.; and also wrote
> Joyce my reasons for thinking the said lines excessive. He does not
> disgust me as Wells does.

In February, Pound published a piece on French writing in *Poetry* and
he took almost the entire issue of *The Little Review* for a piece on French
poetry in which he discussed Laforgue, Corbière, Rimbaud, de Gourmont
and de Régnier. Intellectual life demanded familiarity with French language
and culture, he insisted, and French writers were less puritanical than their
British counterparts. Pound was working on his own free translations,
which were written in the same spirit of honesty about sex that Joyce had
managed in the opening sections of *Ulysses,* and he sent these to Harriet
Monroe, who rejected them for their frankness. Pound placed the poems in
The Little Review and *The New Age,* full of plans to revive troubador music
and the art of setting words to music. He had met a singer, Raymonde
Collignon, who had agreed to help him and at the Aeolian Hall in April
sang some of the songs that Pound had done with Rummel in 1911.

By May, Pound had completed a long tribute to Henry James, which
he included in a special James issue he organized for *The Little Review.* Rereading James and then writing about him was a preparation for writing *The
Cantos.* James had the most complicated of sensibilities, one that had been
able to argue with itself, to circle around an object with a relentless intelligence, his weaving sentences mirroring the maneuvers and nuances and
carefully observed tremors.

Pound was contributing articles and book reviews to a magazine called
The Future, edited by Charles Granville, who had headed Swift and Company before its bankruptcy. Granville also reprinted Pound's first three cantos, currently in a different form, showing Pound's uncertainty about his
new form and his struggle to contain his material. Pound contributed a
three-part series to *The Egoist* on early translators of Homer and then another on translations of Aeschylus. One of the pieces on Andreas Divus,
which appeared in September, included Pound's translation of Divus's Latin
version of Book 11 of *The Odyssey,* which, when altered, would become the
final version of "Canto I."

The Cantos had been started during the war, and much of Pound's

reading and thought had been devoted to finding an appropriate way of
telling his story. He realized that to be considered a great poet he would
have to write an outstanding work, a long poem that would be not merely
encyclopedic but epic in character. As early as 1909, in a letter to his
mother, he had defined epic as the "speech of a nation through the mouth
of one man." At the same time, writing in *The Spirit of Romance*, he had
noted that the writer of epic must be able to "voice the general heart." A
few years later in his memoir of Gaudier-Brzeska, he offered the corollary
that "the man who tries to express his age, instead of expressing himself, is
doomed to destruction."

Pound knew that at the core of his long poem would be his own intellectual concerns, particularly his beliefs about the ritual value of archaic
worship of divine forces, a subject he felt might have universal dimension.
This subject had been a central interest during the London years, developed
in discussions with Yeats, with Allen Upward, and with Gaudier-Brzeska.
An interest in man's archaic beginnings was, of course, hardly original.
Nietzsche in *The Birth of Tragedy* had speculated on how early drama grew
out of primitive worship. Jane Harrison and Sir James Frazer and the school
of Cambridge anthropologists were at that time studying the reflection of
early Mesopotamian, Egyptian, and Greek religious practice in ancient literary texts. More dramatically, the cave paintings which so influenced early
Cubism had recently been discovered in southern France. Even the Fenollosa manuscripts had helped to push Pound along in the search for archaic
explanations for the human condition. Fenollosa had tried to demonstrate
how the pictorial dimension of Oriental languages was derived directly
from nature (a concept that he, in turn, got from Emerson's first major
essay, "Nature") and how all language ultimately reflected natural fact.
Pound, for example, read in Fenollosa's manuscripts that the word "exist"
was derived from the Aryan roots for breathing and growing. Pound's problem as a poet was to find a dramatic means to present such knowledge in a
poem that would imagine the old gods, the divine principles that existed
before the Judeo-Christian myth.

He realized that the epic structure depended on a questing hero, in this
case searching for the archaic gods who could possibly offer guidance in a
time of trouble and despair—these were the war years, after all. Homer,
Virgil, Dante had all employed the journey-to-the-underworld motif, a journey mixing demonic and divine elements, and Pound's first attempts presented a series of floundering figures confused by hellish circumstances.
Pound also saw that his technique would be to use a kaleidoscope of inci-
dents rather than to rely on one central story. The kaleidoscopic approach
was consonant with modernism, with its attempt to capture as many points
of view as possible in order to best suggest the flux of reality. Shifting point
of view had been used as a device by Browning and Henry James at the end

of the nineteenth century, but Pound chose to push the limitations of the device much further. Since he would have no central narrator or single story, the fragmenting effect of each kaleidoscopic shift of action or place or persona ran the risk of losing the reader. The range of what he wanted to include was large enough to require such a possibly confusing device, but he had to begin somewhere. He chose, originally, to begin with Robert Browning, particularly with a long, obscure poem called "Sordello," the fragmented history of a twelfth-century troubador told by an obtrusive and sometimes obnoxious narrator. Pound had felt closer to Browning than to any other of the Victorian poets—he had done the most to develop the technique of persona that was so central to Pound's early work—but Pound had systematically tried to disguise his dependence on Browning. In the early versions of his *Cantos* he imitated the rhetorical mannerisms of "Sordello," but he became quickly disenchanted with the dated quality that resulted and sought to control his poem with a more reflectively Jamesian manner which would be more suitable to his purpose—the dramatization of a sensibility in the process of understanding itself and history. Such a shift was not easy or mechanical. It required a certain maturation in Pound that was beyond his present age and circumstance. The result was that he was unhappy about what he had begun without quite being able to make it better, and it took another five years' trial until he found the right way to begin.

17. A MUSIC OF LOST DYNASTIES

In the summer of 1918, Britain and the European powers were struck by the "Spanish influenza" epidemic, which in a few months killed more people than had died because of the war. In London, schools, offices, and cinemas were closed, all services were disorganized and people wore masks in the streets. Pound received a letter from Aldington, who said he was in France searching for Gaudier's grave. "The war is just a commercial enterprise like any other," Aldington remarked with the cynicism that became a generational keynote after the war. Aldington was browsing through libraries stored in bombed-out attics, looking for Homer in villages erased by shell fire among frightened, half-starved civilians who had no fuel, no alcohol even, just swampy fields with bodies and the rusting implements of war. "It had been revealed that men's dwellings were thin shells that could be crushed as walnuts are crushed," Ford remembered in his memoir of the war, *It Was the Nightingale.* For Ford, the social system had crumbled as well, and Europe was drifting, and everyone who had participated in the war was abnormal, even mad.

The war ended on November 11. In London's streets a surging mass of people paraded for hours. Nearly a million young Englishmen had died and more than another million were disabled and disfigured. D. H. Lawrence snapped while watching a group of celebrants: "It makes me sick to see you rejoicing like a butterfly in the last rays of the sun before the winter. . . . Europe is done for, England most of all." Joseph Conrad, whose son had been shell-shocked in France, reflected, "I cannot confess to an easy mind. . . . Great and blind forces are set catastrophically all over the world." Pound spent Armistice Day with Stella Bowen, a young woman who had come to London to study painting. He later introduced her to Ford Madox Ford, who became her lover. Bowen described her day with Pound "with his hair on end, smacking the bus front with his stick and shouting to the other people packed on the tops of other buses jammed alongside ours." He was impressed when, walking later in the drizzle, he stood a few feet away from King George in an open carriage unprotected except for two policemen. "Poor devil was looking happy," Pound wrote Quinn, "I should think for the first time in his life."

Pound had not been as physically uprooted by the war as Aldington, Lewis, or Ford, but the emotional impact was profound and permanent. After the Armistice he was still steeped in the literary journalism that had previously supported him, reviewing numerous books for *Future,* appearing weekly as the art or music critic in *The New Age,* and visiting galleries and attending concerts regularly. He had published 71 times in periodicals in 1917, 117 times in 1918, and 189 times in 1919: "One buys leisure time to work by selling one's stuff for what one can," he advised Marianne Moore, the young American poet who had known H.D. at Bryn Mawr, and who was at this point sending Pound poems. Moore had written that she was attracted to the "saucy parts" of Pound's poems. Pound replied in a verse letter, expansive and revealing, in which he points to "the debacle of his temper," his failure to have received credit for what he had done. He added that he liked her poems but imagined how difficult it would have been for him to respond to them had she not described herself as red-headed, but had instead been a "dark, wooled Ethiopian." Pound recommended to Harriet Shaw Weaver that she print Moore's poems instead of collecting his own pieces on the early translators of Homer and Aeschylus. So yet another American poet got in print because of Ezra Pound, still determined to effect his American Risorgimento.

Pound began to spend more time with *The New Age* circle. Orage had assembled a group of intellectuals who were beginning to discuss the aftermath of the war and the political future. In Germany inflation was rampant: a worker needed five years' income to buy a new shirt. There had been a major revolution in Russia, and France was prostrate. Italy was paralyzed by general strikes and the strife caused by black-shirted vigilante groups formed to combat leftists. In England there would soon be a million unemployed men, and there were signs of an ugly nationalism. An Englishman named Henry Beamish had fought in the Boer War and afterward claimed all the industries in South Africa were controlled by Jews. Returning to England, he formed a party called the Britons, whose purpose was to eliminate aliens and Jews. Beamish accused a Jew, Sir Alfred Mond, of treason; Mond was the chief backer of the *English Review* who had forced Ford out and whom Pound loathed. Later, in 1939, Pound remembered Mond as "a poison to the Jews themselves, a leprosy," and the dismissal of Ford as a turning point preparing for the "subsequent triumph of hog journalism." Mond brought Beamish to court on libel charges and won five thousand pounds in damages, at which point Beamish fled England and went around the world preaching the existence of a Jewish conspiracy to control the world. He settled in Rhodesia but the Britons continued, eventually forming the basis for British fascism and publishing Victor Marsden's translation of the *Protocols of the Learned Elders of Zion,* a famous forgery fabricated by the czar's secret police accounting for supposed meetings of Jewish leaders around 1897 to formulate a plan for world domination through control of gold and the press.

Pound, who had already demonstrated his break with the English in his alliance with the Vorticists and in *Lustra,* had a predilection for conspiracy theories and eccentric attitudes. In the future he attended to men like Beamish and books like *The Protocols,* recommending them to others.

In the meantime, one of the intellectual mainstays of Pound's existence, *The New Age,* was about to change its character from iconoclastic challenger of the system to house organ for a self-made economist. Orage had lost faith in the cohering power of trade unions and socialism and soon he was to abandon *The New Age* to join Gurdjieff's monastery in Fontainebleau, selling the paper to one of his contributors, a Major Clifford Hugh Douglas, who was predicting the collapse of capitalism.

Douglas had been chief construction engineer for the British Westinghouse Corporation in India and had devised a new economic system called Social Credit. Essentially, Douglas's idea was that the power of government depended on taxation and credit, the invention and manipulation of money systems. Currency was the ostensible bedrock of such a system, but its value could be inflated or deflated according to the determination of bankers, who nearly always controlled government. The weaknesses of the economic system were those of distribution and a lack of purchasing power among the working class. Purchasing power would be extended through the issuance of dividends or credit to producers and workers, and Douglas believed this system would end distribution difficulties. Douglas began publishing his views in *The New Age* on how governments could pay dividends and issue general certificates of credit to workers instead of collecting taxes, but his prose was dense and often obscure. Pound, however, was sure that Douglas had discerned the truth behind international economic manipulations. Douglas asserted that a nation's real wealth lay in the people's capacity to produce needed goods and provide necessary services, but the banks with the aid of government had the power to print paper money regardless of production. Financial credit was controlled by the big banks, who were dictating usurious rates, Douglas charged, and dominated by an influential group of moneylenders, mostly Jewish, who conspired to assist the powerful and had the ability to create depression or finance war. Douglas warned of "the existence of great secret organizations bent on the acquisition of world empire." What appealed to Pound, who was anyway sympathetic to medieval traditions, was Douglas's guild socialism—the notion that a worker receive a proper return for his work. He also believed Douglas was concerned about the plight of the artist in an industrial context. Douglas, Pound wrote later, was the first economist "to include creative art and writing in an economic scheme, and the first to give the painter or sculptor or poet a definite reason for being interested in economics; namely, that a better economic system would release more energy for invention and design."

Pound's head was soon filled with Douglas's propositions. He met Arthur Griffith, the founder of Sinn Fein, the most militant branch of the Irish revolution, and spent "one of the most illuminating hours of my life in conversation." Pound had been informed of the Irish struggle for self-government by Yeats, whose own cultural nationalism had been expressed through his artistic direction of the Abbey Theatre in Dublin. The Irish had long considered themselves England's first colony—Swift had even dramatized England's imperial ambitions in Ireland in Book 3 of *Gulliver's Travels.* Pound sympathized with the Irish because he felt the First World War had been caused in large part by the British buccaneering lust for imperial spoils in Africa and Asia. Griffith was in London on a guarantee of immunity. He chose to meet with Pound in his hotel room "to avoid the detectives who infested the inn." Pound proposed Douglas's ideas as a program for free Ireland and Griffith answered Pound with a realistic observation: "All you say is true. But I can't move them with a cold thing like economics." Griffith's point was that political systems are far more complex than the economic principles inherent in them, that any economic arrangement is symptomatic of much deeper and more meaningful power relationships. While Pound admired Griffith's general insubordination, his ability to stand up to British strength, he was unable to hear the full truth of Griffith's remark and would dissipate enormous quantities of his own energy on a "cold thing like economics."

"In 1918 I began an investigation of causes of war, to oppose same," Pound wrote, and this was the beginning of his disastrous turn from art to the sociology of power and propaganda. His inquiries began with Douglas's

Social Credit schemes, in which credit would be nationalized and distributed to the populace. But instead of Douglas's ideas, the West had already accepted the economic theories of Maynard Keynes, which called for the centralizing of debt and credit as levers which could be plied to stimulate or slow economic growth. Douglas continued to broadcast his views for the next twenty years, and Pound became his most obsessive convert.

Homer Pound had worked in the U.S. Mint all his life, and his son had grown up with talk about devalued currency and government issuance of valueless scrip. Ezra's own family fortunes, as his maternal grandmother explained to him countless times, had been on the decline for a half century. His grandfather, Thaddeus Pound, had been able to reach the centers of power and wield influence beyond the limitations of his own political base —Wisconsin had been a new, remote, and unpopulated state. Now it was Ezra's time to influence those in power, but he had proven not to be a politician, he was as capable of irritating people as pleasing them. He had already displayed signs of a messianic propheticism, a capacity to denounce in jeremiad, and an absolute conviction in his ways. Major Douglas was the beginning of what would become a dangerous and delusional journey.

The period from 1919 to 1920 marked Pound's last two years in London. With his usual enthusiasm he had naïvely hoped for a renewal of the prewar ferment in the arts which had led to Imagism and then Vorticism and had stimulated the beginning of *The Cantos*. But London had become a vast apathy; the exhausted and desiccated feeling Eliot dramatized in "The Waste Land" was pervasive. It just could not be a serious time because there was the war to recover from, and the years following were a prolonged orgy of sex and gin, as Douglas Goldring put it in his memoir, *Odd Man Out*, the "strangest decade" paced by former officers scarred by the horrors they had experienced. Lewis and the other Vorticist painters had returned from the front and were meeting again at the Tour Eiffel, but suits and closely shaven chins had replaced the sombreros and beards. Pound organized a memorial to Gaudier at the Leicester Galleries and in his preface to the catalogue reiterated that Gaudier's death was the "gravest individual loss which the arts have sustained during the war." Lewis unsuccessfully tried to resuscitate *Blast*. When he had a one-man show called "Guns," Pound reviewed it and admitted a loss of vitality and earlier savagery, and he blamed this diminution on the new postwar mood: "The war was no joking matter, and satire has no place in the treatment of tragic situations; the point of satire is for smugness and hypocrisy and stupidity, not for grave unavoidable horror." Pound himself was working on a long poetic sequence, "Hugh Selwyn Mauberley," and in it he too had to struggle with the tonal conflict of satire and tragic loss.

For the February 1919 issue of *The Little Review*, Pound had edited a special tribute to Remy de Gourmont, who, like Henry James, had had

special influence for Pound. James's influence had been one of general sensibility, a matter of tone and style, a spaciousness and generosity of perspective and an elegance in phrasing that Pound sought to emulate and accepted
as an ideal. With de Gourmont the influence was more practical and direct.
Pound often quoted de Gourmont's remark that the singular pleasure for
the writer was "to put down one's thoughts frankly," and he subscribed
with conviction to de Gourmont's position that "the capital crime for a
writer is conformity, imitation and submission to rules of teaching." Writing
for the best magazine in Paris, *Mercure de France,* a facially disfigured man
suffering from lupus and wearing Trappist robes, de Gourmont was isolated
from his audience, independent, and autonomous. He wrote in "absolute
single-mindedness," Pound explained in his *Little Review* essay, without "regard for existing belief, with no afterthought or beside thought either to
conform or to avoid conforming. That is the sainthood of literature."

In the midst of such intellectual and artistic concerns, Pound still found
time for his old friends. He visited Ford Madox Ford, too nervous after his
military ordeals to tolerate London any longer, living far out in the country
in Sussex, painting, plastering, papering, and bricklaying in an old farm he
was renting. Pound hated country life, according to Ford, but came to see
his old friend out of duty, looking like "a bewildered Stewart pretender
visiting a repellent portion of his realms." Pound felt sorry for Ford, who
had been ravaged by his experience with shell shock. He described him in
one of the little vignettes that make up "Hugh Selwyn Mauberley":

> Beneath the sagging roof
> The stylist has taken shelter,
> Unpaid, uncelebrated,
> At last from the world's welter
> Nature receives him.

He also visited H.D., in confinement in a nursing home in Ealing, a suburb
outside London, at the end of March. He "hurtled" himself into her room,
she remembered in *End to Torment,* perhaps allowing a bit of melodrama to
color her recollections:

> Beard, black soft hat, ebony stick—something unbelievably oper-
> atic—directoire overcoat, Verdi. He stalked and stamped the
> length of the room. He coughed, choked or laughed. . . . He
> seemed to beat with the ebony stick like a baton.

As usual, Ezra was dominating his old girlfriend and she compared this visit
to the time when he had prevented her from joining her friend Frances
Gregg on a honeymoon trip. This occasion, however, was the day before
she gave birth to her daughter, and what she remembered was a sense of
her former mentor's "pounding, pounding *(Pounding)* with the stick against

the wall." Was this Pound's way of regretting not having fathered the child himself? Or was it just island fever—the behavior of a man who had become extremely nervous, impatient, and restless, unable to tolerate his marginal position in the world of letters, feeling trapped in a literary situation in which he could not make a real impression?

In the United States, Pound's prose was attracting notice, not all of it favorable. Several critics attacked *Pavannes and Divisions.* Conrad Aiken called it dull and without value: "It is difficult to imagine anything much worse than the prose of Mr. Pound. It is ugliness and awkwardness incarnate. Did he always write so badly?" In *The New Republic,* Louis Untermeyer found it an example of "criticism smothered in a mixture of snobbery and bad temper," and he categorized the writing as sterile, pedantic, and bizarre. Even Pound's friend H. L. Mencken found the book an example of mere bellowing—Pound trying to frighten the puritans.

Four sections of Pound's free translation of Propertius appeared in *Poetry* in the spring of 1919, followed by three more in *The New Age* destined to arouse a storm of condemnation from classical scholars who refused to understand that Pound had not intended a literal translation. Professor William Gardner Hale of the University of Chicago wrote, "Mr. Pound is incredibly ignorant of Latin." Of course, Pound's translation, as Aldington observed, was not without its "ludicrous difficulties," but even Aldington was full of admiration for Pound's attempt to recapture the Propertian flavor of an empire in decline. But the poem did suffer from obscurity. Thomas Hardy put it very tactfully in a letter to Pound, thanking him for having sent it, stating dryly that while lucidity was a virtue in poetry, "I gather that at least you do not care whether the many understand you or not."

The poem had been intended, Pound wrote years later, to present a Propertian perspective: the emotions in it were those of someone who had "faced the infinite and ineffable imbecility of the British Empire" just as Propertius had witnessed mistakes of the Roman Empire. Pound added that he used every method of definition available to him, including radical abbreviation, crosscutting, drawing on implications in Propertius's other writings. "My job," Pound told Orage, "was to bring a dead man to life, to present a living figure." With the Propertius poem Pound was developing yet another skill he needed for *The Cantos,* a mode of dramatic presentation that was conversational and natural in diction but at the same time capable of being both cuttingly satiric and poignantly sad. In one sense the poem was Pound's last homage to the poetic tradition, the end of an apprenticeship in which he had successfully imitated the voices of his masters: Greek, Roman, medieval, troubador, Renaissance lyricists of Italy and England, John Donne, and Robert Browning. By the time of "Propertius" Pound had mastered these voices and assimilated them in his own.

Pound was still acting as an editor and intermediary for Joyce as *Ulysses* was being serialized in *The Little Review*. Quinn was still warning both Joyce and Pound that *Ulysses* would be suppressed when it was published as a book unless it was "cleaned up." Pound tried to make some changes on his own, especially in the "Nausikaa" episode where Leopold Bloom has an involuntary orgasm at the sight of Gerty MacDowell's fringed drawers exposed in a swing. Pound reported to Quinn that for his efforts he got from Joyce a "thoroughly insulting and abusive letter," but he added that the excuse for the objectionable parts of *Ulysses* was the achievement as an entity. Quinn, however, was right about the legal action he had anticipated, and late that summer John Sumner, secretary of the New York Society for the Prevention of Vice, swore out a warrant against the owners of the Washington Square Bookshop for selling copies of the July issue of *The Little Review* featuring the Gerty MacDowell section. Pound wrote to Joyce, " 'Nausikaa' has been pinched by the po-lice."

Later that spring, Pound and Dorothy went to Paris on a honeymoon trip that had been postponed for five years because of the war. From Paris they journeyed to Toulouse, where Pound corrected the proofs of *Quia Pauper Amavi*, a new collection of poems containing his recent Provençal translations, and the entire "Homage to Sextus Propertius," which the Egoist Press published that fall. The Pounds then went to Provence, carrying their belongings in rucksacks, exploring on foot, sometimes sleeping in fields. At Foix, after several days of steady walking, they arrived to learn the peace had been finally signed at Versailles. Pound was working on a series of loose pastiches on his travels and the problems he envisaged for artists in the modern world which appeared all that summer and into the fall in *The New Age* in eighteen installments. T. S. Eliot met the Pounds in Provence and spent three weeks alone with Pound while Dorothy sketched. Eliot was depressed, burdened by his wife and her emotional demands, fatigued by long hours in the bank with book reviews to write afterward to pay the bills, leaving him insufficient time or inspiration for poetry. On their walking tour of the Dordogne, Pound tried on Eliot a strenuous cure with sulfur baths, sun and air and hiking. Eliot returned bearded and rejuvenated.

Back in Paris on his way to England, Pound had difficulties with the authorities because of the new passport requirements, a bureaucratic postwar change he could not accept or tolerate. The difficulty sounds merely comic in Pound's description, but a similar problem and Pound's impatience before the Second World War may have prevented him from returning to his country before the war:

There the vice-assistant-second-sub categorically forbade me to return to my home in London. I said: "I live there," and suggested that he ask the assistant-first-vice or some one higher up concerning the regulations. He disappeared behind a partition, and returned with a request that I "get a letter" from my employer, evidently knowing no strata of life save one where everyone has an employer. It was next suggested that I find some sort of "reference" for myself. Every American I had known in Paris before the war had left. I knew no one save the ambassador whom I had met two days before. . . . I stepped into a taxi and drove round to the embassy. The embassy dealt with the consulate, and I proceeded about my lawful occasions.

In the fall *The Little Review* published the essay by Fenollosa that Pound had edited and regarded as a fundamental study of aesthetics, "The Chinese Written Character as a Medium for Poetry." Pound was briefly appointed drama critic of a magazine called *The Outlook,* a remunerative and respectable position, but he told Quinn he had been fired in two weeks "in the most caddish possible manner." It was another sign of Pound's incompatibility with the conventional world. *The New Age* was running his series on "The Revolt of Intelligence," in which Pound declared that he was finished with faddish liberal experiments of the prewar years, with "suffrage, vegetarianism and eugenics" and "fabian crankist unhumanizing kulturbunds" which insisted that the committee system was ideal for getting things done. He pushed his scorn of the committee consensus system to larger organizations like nations, structures he now called loathsome and declared were barriers to civilization. He extended the argument to the newly proposed League of Nations, which he felt would only increase the possibilities for war. Such suspicion of institutional responses to political problems soon became prevalent among artists of the twenties.

He wrote his father that he was still struggling with his *Cantos.* He was working on numbers V, VI, and VII but worried about coherence and the fact that each new section seemed "more incomprehensible than the one preceding it; I don't know what's to be done about it." He wrote Quinn before Christmas that his *Cantos* were getting "too too too abstruse and obscure for human consumption." His mother-in-law told him that Arthur Galton, the vicar friend of Frederic Manning, had declared that Pound's work was a riddle, that the verse seemed without construction, the vocabulary eccentric, and the prose detestable. The reviews of *Quia Pauper Amavi* were unfavorable. Except for Ford and Eliot in *The Athanaeum*—"granite wreaths and leaden laurels," Pound thought—the critics were hostile, even contemptuous. Ben Hecht, an American critic, in *The Little Review* in a piece called "Pounding Ezra," wrote a rankling piece that called Pound's work suave and fastidious but made him seem more the mimic than the originator, less the master of his own style than an "exquisite showman minus a show." Hecht had been influenced by the American critic Van Wyck

Brooks, who in his book *The Wine of the Puritans* had echoed Emerson's warnings on the dangers of the European influence for American poets. Brooks had asserted that foreign training and the vitalizing beauty of older civilizations reached a point of diminishing returns, leading to an "overmastering" where the artist cannot go beyond the techniques he has imitated. Such a position was becoming dominant in American criticism and continued to be raised against Pound.

Hecht's piece was a sign to Pound that he would no longer have free way with *The Little Review.* Pound was bored with editing, he told Margaret Anderson, and he wanted only to continue with work on *The Cantos,* "to hear the music of a lost dynasty." Jane Heap of *The Little Review* had already commented in the magazine that the foreign editor has been "foreign to taste, foreign to courtesy, foreign to our standards of Art." Actually, as Ford observed, Pound's influence and ideas had made *The Little Review* vital, the "trying over ground for all sorts of badnesses, outrages, tastelessness and experimentalisms that a literature must get out of its system before it can begin to live." But Pound's editorial remonstrances had pushed even the patience of the zealous editors of *The Little Review:*

> What the ensanguined 1111111111111111 is the matter with this BLOODYgoddamndamnblastedbastardbitchbornsonofaputridsea-horse of a foetid and stinkerous printer ???????
> Is his serbo-croatian optic utterly impervious to the twelfth letter of the alphabet????
> JHEEZUSMARIAJOSE!!! Madre de dios y de dios del perro. Sacrobosco di Satanas.
> OF COURSE IF IF IF bloodywell IF this blasted numero appears with anything like one twohundredandfiftieth part of these errors we are DONE, and I shall never be able to cross the channel or look a French ecrivain in the face.

In March 1920 Quinn proposed to his friend Scofield Thayer, who had bought *The Dial,* a magazine originally started by Emerson and the transcendentalists before the Civil War, that Pound be appointed foreign correspondent at $750 a year. Pound agreed, sending Thayer a six-page letter, a lecture on his literary creed and biases, suggesting writers he might be able to recruit and offering to provide two cantos a year. He was now writing drama criticism for *The Athanaeum* and in the spring of 1920 published eighteen theater and ballet reviews and a piece on Major Douglas's *Economic Democracy.* He was, however, discharged when he too harshly criticized a production of Gogol's *The Government Inspector.* The dismissal was clearly unjust, but London was not quite prepared for the extent of Pound's ex cathedra vitriol. He was still the uncompromising perfectionist, and honesty was more important than tact.

18. FAREWELL TO LONDON

By May, Pound and his wife had left London for a trip to the Continent, a trial run for what might be a longer stay, as Pound realized that he had been in London for almost twelve years. In Paris he again met with Natalie Barney, who showed him a manuscript of poems and was willing to pay him for his advice. In Toulouse on his way to Italy, he detailed his objections to her rhythms, inversions, archaisms, and dead language. He told Quinn his itinerary was Paris, Milan, Venice, and then Trieste to meet Joyce, but in early June he was writing him about taking the hot sulfur springs of Sirmione "to keep off apoplexy." Dorothy had become ill in Venice, so they had gone straight to Sirmione. Pound was working on *Indiscretions*, his experimental autobiographical sketch which *The New Age* ran all that summer in twelve installments. He thanked Quinn for his help with *The Dial* and expressed his continuing concern for Eliot:

> I am momentarily at least & thanks largely to you, lapped in prospects of luxury.
>
> It is easier to lap me than Eliot.
>
> No use blinking the fact that it is a crime against literature to let him waste eight hours vitality per diem in that bank.
>
> Nor on the other hand that it will take £400 per year, with 3 or 5 years guarantee to get him out of it.
>
> (His wife hasn't a cent and is an invalid always cracking up, & needing doctors, & incapable of earning anything—though she has tried—poor little brute.)

Pound proposed that Quinn find four or five subscribers to secretly patronize Eliot so that he could be free of the bank. Actually, the idea may have been more a reflection of Pound's priorities than Eliot's needs. Pound considered the idea of regular employment a form of bondage and took great pride near the end of his life in the fact that except for the abortive experience at Wabash, he had never held a full-time job. Eliot needed the regularity and security of the bank; he never could have spent all his time with his distraught wife. Quinn offered the sum of fifty pounds for three years but was reluctant to try to get others to donate because of the difficulties he had experienced in fund-raising for *The Little Review*.

Pound had also written to Joyce, trying to persuade him to visit in Sirmione. Despite all that Pound had tried to do for the Irish writer, the two men had not yet met in person, and because of the war they had enjoyed only an epistolary relationship. Joyce agreed that a personal meeting was important but complained of difficulties: his hatred of traveling, the problems of finishing *Ulysses* in a flat shared by eleven people, with Joyce writing all day "sprawled across two beds surrounded by mountains of notes." Despite a fear of thunderstorms, Joyce promised to come, bringing his son to "act as a lightning conductor." Joyce and Giorgio appeared in early June. Joyce found Pound to be a "miracle of ebulliency, gusto, and help," a "large unpredictable bundle of electricity." Pound's impressions were sent to Quinn in a letter from Paris near the end of the month: beneath the "shell of the cantankerous Irishman" was the sensitive genius, the delicate temperament, and a "concentration and absorption" beyond Yeats's, but also the mulish stubbornness that had its positive aspect too—"Thank God, he has been stubborn enough to know his job and stick to it."

In June *The Little Review* published Pound's essay on the novelist W. H. Hudson, which was indicative of the ferocity of his hatred for the social order:

> A bloated usury, a cowardly and snivelling politics, a disgusting financial system, the sadistic curse of Christianity work together, not only that a hundred species of wild fowl and beast shall give way before the advance of industry, i.e. that the plains be covered with uniform and verminous sheep, bleating in perfect social monotony; but in our alleged "society" the same tendencies and the same urge that the bright plumed and fine voiced species of the genus anthropos, the favoured of the gods, the only part of humanity worth saving is attacked. The milkable human cows, the shearable human sheep are invited by the exploiters, and all others regarded as caput lupinum, dangerous: lest the truth *should* shine out in art, which ceases to be art and degenerates into religion and cant and superstition as soon as it has tax-gathering priests: lest works comparable to the Cretan vases and Assyrian lions should be reproduced or superseded.

In his book *Pavannes and Divisions,* Pound had imagined a dialogue between Rabelais and a student representing Pound's position on the conservatism of publishing. At the end of the dialogue Rabelais concludes that the student would have been burned alive in his century. Much of Pound's writing vindicated this observation.

Pound's fullest attack on the social order that had allowed the war as a step toward the destruction of civilization was a long poetic sequence published by John Rodker in London, "Hugh Selwyn Mauberley." In it Pound returned to a more formal arrangement of rhyme and regular strophe as if to try to contain the vindictive rage in the poem but also as a reaction, Pound admitted, on his part and Eliot's, to the dilution and "general floppiness" of vers libre and Amygism. "Mauberley" was, a prefatory note explained, "distinctly a farewell to London" but also an autobiographical rendering through the filters of various personae of what Pound had seen of the literary life in London. But it is not a confessional poem. The experience it projects is generalized, the failure of the modern poet to make any real difference in the world, the inability of sensibility to cope with the tawdry and cheap, to alter or improve it, and the retreat in aesthetic posturing available to the poet as part of a self-destructive and frustrating strategy. Written with sparse immediacy and a taut epigrammatic style, the sequence of poems contrasts sublime expectations and the attempt "to resuscitate the dead art of poetry" with the more mundane realities of an age of literary journalism in a numbing, sterile environment:

> The age demanded an image
>> Of its accelerated grimace,
>> Something for the modern stage,
> Not, at any rate, an Attic grace;

> Not, not certainly, the obscure reveries
> Of the inward gaze;
> Better mendacities
> Than the classics in paraphrase!

> The "age demanded" chiefly a mould in plaster,
> Made with no loss of time,
> A prose kinema, not, not assuredly, alabaster
> Or the "sculpture" of rhyme.

In the time of Martial or Catullus—two Roman poets whose moral seriousness are important influences for the poem—an epigram was meant to be engraved in stone, an intensity present in the fourth section of the sequence, with its account of the war horrors that had devastated Pound's generation:

> These fought in any case,
>> and some believing,
>>> pro domo, in any case . . .

> Some quick to arm,
> some for adventure,
> some from fear of weakness,
> some from fear of censure,
> some for love of slaughter, in imagination,
> learning later . . .
> some in fear, learning love of slaughter;

> Died some, pro patria,
>   non "dulce" non "et decor" . . .
> walked eye-deep in hell
> believing in old men's lies, then unbelieving
> came home, home to a lie,
> home to many deceits,
> home to old lies and new infamy;
> usury age-old and age-thick
> and liars in public places.
>
> Daring as never before, wastage as never before.
> Young blood and high blood,
> fair cheeks, and fine bodies;
>
> fortitude as never before
>
> frankness as never before,
> disillusions as never told in the old days,
> hysterias, trench confessions,
> laughter out of dead bellies.

In the center of the "Mauberley" sequence Pound inserted his evocation of Edmund Waller's "Go, Lovely Rose," a sixteenth-century lyric renowned for its sweetness and musicality. In Pound's hands his "Envoi" becomes a testament to how he was able to absorb the spirit of an ancient text and make it his own:

> Tell her that goes
> With song upon her lips
> But sings not out the song, nor knows
> The maker of it, some other mouth,
> May be as fair as hers,
> Might, in new ages, gain her worshippers,
> When our two dusts with Waller's shall be laid,
> Siftings on siftings in oblivion,
> Till change hath broken down
> All things save Beauty alone.

The delicacy and sweetness seem jarring, out of place in a poem of such recrimination and uncomfortable irony, a poem that tried with a Jamesian circularity to suggest Mauberley's deficiencies in sensibility—his preciousness and aestheticism—while picturing the forces that crush him. The entire "Envoi" acts as requiem, a connective tissue holding together the splintering pains of the poem, and as a reminder or a reaffirmation of one of the pursuits of romanticism that no poet could safely discard, the Keatsian quest for truth in beauty. The poem proceeds to eulogize and satirize Pound's predecessors in the search for art in London, the Pre-Raphaelites, the aestheticists of the "90s," Ford Madox Ford, all "out of step" unappreciated, unnoticed, unwanted. "Mauberley" is a study in defeat by gross necessity and the demands of the marketplace of the literary tradition that is dedicated to beauty. In a vignette in the poem, a "Mr. Nixon," based on the novelist Arnold Bennett, advises Mauberley to "butter reviewers" and "give up verse, my boy" because there was no money in it; Lady Valentine, a prototype of the literary patron, uses poetry as one would a precious vase in a drawing room, "a hook to catch the Lady Jane's attention." All Mauberley's efforts to persuade the world of the significance of beauty are in vain. But he is seen ironically: like Eliot's Prufrock, he will not dare to eat the peach, nor will the mermaids sing to him. Mauberley lacks a heroic capacity to challenge his world; he lacks the social and historical vision that inspired Pound to embark on his *Cantos.*

Some of Pound's antipathy for the English was experienced by another young American writer, Robert McAlmon. The youngest of ten children of a Midwestern Presbyterian minister, McAlmon had come to New York, where he had worked as a salesman, a reporter, and a copywriter in an advertisement agency. When he met William Carlos Williams he was a coldly intense young man posing in the nude for a dollar an hour for up to nine hours at a time for art students at Cooper Union, and living in a fisherman's scow in the harbor south of the Brooklyn Bridge. The two men became friends and started *Contact,* a poetry magazine. At a cocktail party he met the small, dark, illegitimate daughter of one of the richest men in England, a lover of H.D.'s who used the name Bryher. Also a writer, and needing the disguise of marriage to shield her homosexuality from her family, Bryher proposed a marriage of convenience to McAlmon. Before accepting, he came to London to meet Sir John Ellerman, her father, a shipping magnate. McAlmon found the smoky heaviness of the city "muffling as a dull illness driving one with its despairing delerium." In the first pages of his autobiographical account, *Being Geniuses Together,* McAlmon remembered the stuffiness of Sir John's parlor, its dull unknown French paintings a tacit support of Pound's charges on the careless philistinism of the rich. The fact that McAlmon was American caused Ellerman to regard him as "alien, strange, one whose reaches he could not judge." McAlmon met Pound, Eliot, Wyndham Lewis, and H.D., who explained to him that the war had "cleaned out all the best young people of the generation." He was impressed but a bit put off by all the talk of literary cliques, the intrigue, distrust, and dislikes among writers.

With "Mauberley" published, Pound began to think of leaving England permanently. He wrote Quinn, considering a move to New York, perhaps to work on *The Dial.* Quinn discouraged him, warning that he would hate the city with its Jews, its vulgarity, and "no art that would interest you except imported art." James could not have lived in the city,

Quinn wrote, and those who did were "a million Jews who are mere walk-ing appetites, seven or eight hundred thousand dagos, a couple of hundred thousand Slovaks, fifty or sixty thousand Croats, and seven or eight hundred thousand Germans." The United States in general seemed like the worst spot in the universe,

> the most backward economically, the most provincial socially, the most reactionary, the most capitalistically controlled, the most in-fluenced by money, has less freedom of the press, less of the sense of freedom, less real democracy than any civilized country in the world, with the possible exception of Germany.

Quinn was again showing his intemperance and his shortsightedness, and he had failed to account for an intellectual and artistic revival, of little theaters and of magazines like *The Dial, The Masses, The Freeman, The Seven Arts,* and *The New Republic,* which were all intent on extending press freedoms and defining democracy.

Pound was then ready to face the fact that he had failed, despite an abundance of genius, energy, and bravado, to dominate literary London. In September of 1920 he wrote William Carlos Williams that "there is no longer any intellectual *life* in England save what centres in this eight by ten octagonal room." A month later he wrote the American critic and editor H. S. Canby that the tendency in England was to want the "lyric boy," the "simple poet whom they can pity and patronize and who will never inconve-niently SEE anything he wasn't intended to." Osbert Sitwell, in his memoir, *Laughter in the Next Room,* offers a picture of the estrangement of Pound and members of his circle at that time. He stated that on Thursday evenings he would dine with his brother and several other writers, Lewis, Herbert Read, and Pound, in a restaurant in Piccadilly Circus. Each writer sat at a separate table, the "distance helping to make conversation self-conscious or desul-tory. Ezra Pound was inclined to mumble into his red beard, a habit perhaps brought on by his defensiveness, the result in turn, of attacks delivered on himself during the years of his domicile in England. He was particularly a type the English do not understand or appreciate."

Aldington, back from the war, noted that the old bohemian society seemed riddled with affectation and that he could no longer be satisfied by the "attractive but sophomoric exultation in the latest thing which for so long satisfied my friend Ezra." Pound always "wanted to be the center of the party," his friend William Carlos Williams remembered, consciously acting the role of "the 'poetic' hero doing crazy things, eccentric things, for attention." Starting with the Vorticist Rebel Art Centre and *Blast,* Pound had embraced the causes of the extreme fringes of radical art. Besides this ideological choice, Pound's manners were purely American. His casualness and frankness in speech made the English cringe. For example, he would lean back in his chair, wear his hat in a room, cross his legs, raise his voice in enthusiasm—these things were just not done. Hugh Kenner has observed that Pound had become a "Beerbohm cartoon of the salon artist." Pound was now declaiming that England was only a corpse. In the fourteenth and fifteenth cantos, written with a savage Swiftian loathing, he imagined England as sinking in a slough, its politicians addressing the multitude in the mire, its war profiteers drinking blood, the betrayer of language and the lying press in the bog with sows eating their litter, all sinking in the horrible stench. The postwar English were interested in revivals of former glory; the theaters were staging late Elizabethan drama and Restoration comedy, and there was an attempt to revive Victorianism.

Disgusted, Pound and his wife left for Paris at the end of 1920. Orage, who was soon to follow, wrote a sort of obituary notice for the London period in *The New Age:*

> Mr. Pound has been an exhilarating influence for culture in England; he has left his mark upon more than one of the arts, upon literature, music, poetry, and sculpture; and quite a number of men and movements owe their initiation to his self-sacrificing stimulus; among them being relatively popular successes as well as failures. With all this, however, Mr. Pound, like so many others who have striven for the advancement of intelligence and culture in England, has made more enemies than friends, and far more powerful enemies than friends. Much of the Press has been deliberately closed by cabal to him; his books have for some time been ignored or written down, and he himself has been compelled to live on much less than would support a navvy. His fate, as I have said, is not unusual. . . . Taken by and large, England hates men of culture until they are dead.

Orage's comment was, of course, subjective, the biased words of a friend who was himself a perennial outsider. Pound had chosen a similar path, he had been the provocative antagonist, he had imagined and invented enemies even before they were prepared to oppose him. He had organized the Imagists with a firm hand, and some of them felt his hand was too self-serving, too throttling, so they moved from his orbit to the more supple and ample nurturing provided by Amy Lowell. Vorticism had been a desperate plea for attention, a combination of literary high jinks and aesthetic mumbo jumbo that left the stolid British unimpressed. The establishment, through the voice of G. W. Prothero and *The Quarterly Review,* had sent Pound a clear message: because of his involvement with the Vorticists, he would no longer be considered respectable or taken seriously in England. Even sympathetic men like Douglas Goldring had seen Pound as a sort of charlatan. Critics had found his earlier poems promising but suffocated by a shoddy and affected learning. For his part, Pound had denounced all schools of poetry since the British Romantics. In *Lustra* he had rejected the middle classes. In "Mauberley" he had eulogized the Art for Art's Sake movement of the 1890s poets and clearly identified with them. With Yeats and Ford, with Eliot and Joyce, he had composed a view of the writer as besieged minority, oppressed, victimized, thwarted by a false morality. His own early uncertainty about the first three cantos is the sign of a crucial insecurity, the difficulty in accepting the full consequences of a choice to repudiate his audience with a poem of unsurpassed density and difficulty, bordering at times on incomprehensibility. In England he had created for himself an untenable paradox: emotionally he needed the admiration every poet seems to want; intellectually he was making with his poems an insurmountable barrier. Clearly, it was the time to move on.

PARIS:
THE HERESY OF ART

It is after all a grrrreat littttttterary period.

Pound to Eliot

1. THE LABORATORY OF PARIS

Pound had frequently gone to Paris before the war and knew it as a lively center for innovative art. In Paris, much more so than in London, there was an atmosphere of engaged concern about artistic questions. De Gourmont's *Mercure de France* and Gide's *Nouvelle revue française* provided a cultural forum, and the organ for the avant-garde painters and poets had been Apollinaire's *Les Soirées de Paris*. In his own poetry Apollinaire had departed from the lofty seriousness of the Symbolist poets, stressing instead levity and surprise in new formal arrangements, the use of ordinary conversation and unorthodox syntax. Popularizing the Cubists, Apollinaire told the world about de Chirico and Delaunay, generally forming a bridge between poets, painters, and other artists who were unafraid to challenge or flout public taste and the expectations of what art should be. In prewar Paris, even more than in prewar London, there had been a surge of artistic fermentation as the Cubists used exotic sources like African primitivism and Oceanic folklore as well as the doodles of children and the insane. Paris, less homogeneous than London, depended more on an international mixture and a number of the most exciting new artists were foreigners: Picasso, Stravinsky, Miró, Arp, de Chirico, Brancusi, Man Ray, and Max Ernst, among others.

Unlike in London, the prewar fervor continued through the war. One of its highlights was *Parade*, a ballet extravaganza commissioned by Diaghilev for his Russian Ballet and written by Jean Cocteau. An exquisitely epicene poet with a high-pitched nasal voice, Cocteau's elfin face was set off by hair brushed so high up on his head it seemed to be standing on end. "Astonish me!" Diaghilev demanded of Cocteau, and *Parade* was his shocking reply. Cocteau persuaded Picasso to do the stage sets, great Cubist sculptures that looked like costumes. The music was by Erik Satie, "so simple, so raw, so naively intricate," the composer Poulenc said, that the audience was shocked by its breeziness. Satie's score incorporated the sounds of a typewriter, a ship siren, machine guns, and the cries of a circus barker. It sounded like the parenting of a new music, and *Parade* itself seemed like the fulfillment of Nietzsche's prediction that the arts would come to depend on spectacle—his word was *Gesamtkunstwerk,* the total art work. The program note for *Parade* was written by Apollinaire, who introduced the word "surrealism" to describe the effect of such a union of the various arts. It was this sort of collaborative spirit that characterized Pound's Paris years, and Cocteau became one of his closest friends.

Another force to which Pound responded was Dada. Conceived in Zurich during the war by a Romanian poet, Tristan Tzara, Dada had been named arbitrarily with a word Tzara had found in his dictionary, a nursery term for a rocking horse, which would accommodate some of the rage, anguish, and absurdity a group of dissident painters and poets felt because of the war. Dada stood for a totally eclectic freedom to experiment; it regarded play as the ideal human activity, and its main tool was chance. In a very real sense Dada was the artistic legacy of the war years, an aesthetic nihilism that was caused by a vacuum of values. The war had destroyed belief in the sanctity of property, in the patriarchal family, the dogma of sin, the principle of obedience to authority. The sharp borderlines of the old morality were currently blurred. Revolting against society and morality, the Dadaists used public demonstration to disseminate their ideas. Dada was "nothing," they exclaimed with paradoxical glee, as they used it to try to reshape middle-class expectations of art. They staged exhibitions, wore strange clothing—on one occasion, long funnels on their heads suggested that they were trying to reach their audience with their minds—and indeed Dada was a more conceptual art process than the French had ever seen. Their audiences, however, were usually outraged and often hurled vegetables, eggs, and tomatoes. For Pound the Dadaists were a case of *blague,* a French term which he explained as a "satire upon stupidity, an attack. It is the weapon of intelligence at bay; of intelligence fighting against an alignment of odds." Tzara called this group "circus directors whistling amid the winds of carnivals convents bawdy houses theatres realities sentiments restaurants Hi Hi Ho Ho Bang." Dada tried to invert accepted values, even artistic ones. In Dada the *Mona Lisa* received a mustache, a painting called *The Blessed Virgin* was an ink spot on a bare canvas. Tzara advertised that the new way of creating poetry was to take a newspaper article, cut out each word, then put them in a bag and shake it. The "writer" would then take out the words and the order of their reappearance would form the order of the poem. As a result there was lots of gibberish and nonsense in Dada art, but the Dadaists thought art was taken much too seriously anyway and tried to create humor in art on every possible occasion. The playfulness of the Dadaists was extended to dress codes, and one of the members of the Dadaist circle, the Baroness Elsa von Freytag-Loringhoven, once wore a plum cake on her head, and pots, pans, items of hardware, and a brassiere of milk tins as part of her costume.

Tzara, who had been publishing manifestos and declarations and a magazine that included Pound's work, came to Paris in the beginning of 1920 and joined forces with a painter, Francis Picabia, who was also interested in writing, and their ideas soon reached a group of other young writers, Louis Aragon, Philippe Soupault, and André Breton. Several new little magazines were started—Pierre Reverdy's *Nord-Sud, Dada,* and Breton's *Littérature*— and a network of poets, painters, and musicians was formed. Pound had been following the group closely since its origin in Zurich, intrigued by its subversive capacities. He realized it could be a source of artistic excitement like the Vorticists. In England, he claimed, the water was beginning to creep up over the islanders, who would probably soon develop webbed feet. Paris offered more solid ground, though the Dadaists seemed to prefer earthquakes. Pound was drawn to the Dadaists because of the international character of the movement, and their belief in the reciprocity of all the arts, the mixing of forms and disciplines. In Paris, Pound began composing music, he wrote an opera, he continued his interest in painting and developed a new one in film, and he tried sculpture. He had carried over his *New Age* criticism of music and art to the point where he was then making more than merely criticizing. He described the "young and very ferocious" new group in *The Dial* as a poetic serum to save English and American letters:

> The young began in Zurich about two years ago, they have published papers which are very, very erratic in appearance, and which contain various grains of good sense.
>
> They have satirized the holy church of our century (journalism), they have satirized the sanctimonious attitude toward "the arts" (toward the arts irrespective of whether the given work of art contains a communication of intelligence). They have given up the pretense of impartiality. They have expressed a desire to live and to die, preferring death to a sort of moribund permanence.
>
> They are so young and healthy that they still consider suicide as a possible remedy for certain troubles. . . .
>
> They have as yet no capital sunk in works and they indulge in the pious hope that their remains will not be used to bore others. . . .
>
> Louis Aragon, Philippe Soupault, André Breton, Drieu la Rochelle contribute to *Littérature* and are published Au Sans

Pareil. They are, I think officially, on good terms with Tristan
Tzara, Picasso, Picabia.

One wonders, a little vaguely, how to introduce them to a
society where one is considered decadent for reproducing pictures
by Cézanne.

By Christmas of 1920, Pound had found a ground floor flat at 70 bis
rue Notre Dame des Champs which faced onto a garden and a courtyard. It
was a street that Whistler had lived on as a young man. Books, sculptures,
and paintings were transported from London to Paris. The walls were decorated with drawings by Dorothy, Gaudier, and Lewis. *The New Age* had
informed Pound that it could no longer afford to pay for his music or art
commentary, its interests at this time almost exclusively in Douglas's ideas,
and Pound realized he might have to rely even more on his wife's income.
The exchange value of British sterling, like that of the dollar, was very high
in postwar France, and Pound found living cheaper in Paris than it had been
in London. From the beginning, Dorothy had refused to cook, so preparing
meals on a shaky alcohol stove became one of Pound's duties, but Paris also
had innumerable cheap eating places. To save money, and as a demonstration of his own independence, Pound decided to fabricate his own furniture: a low coffee table built out of packing crates and painted scarlet, a long
narrow worktable, and two large armchairs made of white pine board and
canvas.

The cafés of Paris were as much a medium for intellectual life as were
the literary magazines or the art galleries: they were the place to meet, to
debate, to write or draw and to ponder, the natural living room of exiles
and the sign of their metropolitanism. As Pound observed in one of his
"Paris Letters" to *The Dial*, Paris was the place for the defiant and new in
art, for those who had "cast off the sanctified stupidities and timidities."
Ford was thinking of moving to Paris and Joyce was already living there.
Pound, the eternal helper, had found him an apartment.

The Pounds spent the first three months of 1921 in the South of
France, at St.-Raphaël on the Côte d'Azur, waiting until their apartment was
ready, but before leaving they saw Francis Picabia's exhibit at the Galerie
Povolozky. Pound was impressed by the machinelike forms that were reminiscent of Lewis and Vorticism. When he returned to Paris in the spring, he
asked Picabia to become foreign editor of *The Little Review*—Margaret Anderson and Jane Heap's experimental magazine had been forced to stop
publishing in New York because of *Ulysses* and they were planning to resume operations in Paris. Currently somehow restored in the editor's
graces, perhaps because Picabia was able to pay for most of the issue, Pound
organized a special Picabia issue. In it he included a calendar of his own
invention which began on his birthday. He had been telling his friends that

the Christian Era had ended and that they were then living in the Pound Era, a "fact" the calendar merely formalized. The declaration was, on its most innocent level, another sign of Pound's good humor, a joke at the expense of convention, a teasing rejoinder to the social order of things. On a deeper level it suggested a dissatisfaction with his own literary reputation, an awareness that the other modernists, Yeats, Joyce, and Eliot, would receive more acclaim than he would, even though he had helped engineer their successes.

Pound felt Picabia was a man of turbulent ideas. He called him an "anti-Socratic vacuum cleaner" negating conventions and routine responses. Picabia had become suspicious of the Dadaists and disassociated himself from the movement with a public letter. In mid-May 1921, André Breton confirmed Picabia's fears of increasing dogmatism with a mock trial of Maurice Barrès, a writer who had once seemed sympathetic to Dadaist approaches but who had repudiated them. Pound watched as Barrès was represented by a wax dummy and charged with "offence against the security of Mind." The trial was a burlesque of serious ideas. One witness appeared in a gas mask, Pound recalled in a magazine piece, representing a system of clichés that had broken down: but "a bit of stale gas had been left in the mask and the protagonist at a certain point nearly suffocated, could stand it no longer, and tore off the mask. One very red-faced real youth sputtering in the stage set." Louis Aragon, as defense counsel, wearing a white smock and a red clerical cap, demanded the death penalty for his own client, and Tzara finished testifying with a song. For Pound the trial was a demonstration of a liberatingly experimental attitude that started with letters but extended itself to life itself. Paris was a "laboratory of ideas," he declared, "where poisons could be tested, new modes of sanity discovered." But he also realized that the Dadaist group was disorganized, unreliable, and a possible source of treachery. Aldington, always the voice of sound English common sense, had warned him against consorting with the Dadaists, whose purpose was "to destroy literature by discrediting it."

In a café called the Dôme, Pound was introduced to Brancusi, who had worked for Rodin, and accompanied the Romanian sculptor to his studio off the rue de Vaugirard. He was immediately impressed by the simplicity and power of the oval forms he saw there, and he organized an issue of *The Little Review* around Brancusi's work, the attempt to purify sculpture by "getting all the forms into one form." Brancusi, Pound felt, was extending the attempts first suggested by Vorticism and Gaudier. Pound was so enthusiastic about Brancusi's work that he began attempting sculpture himself. Ford remembered visiting Pound's rooms and finding all over the floors egg-shaped stones which Pound had formed with hammers. His piece on Brancusi in *The Little Review* involved an extended comparison between the Romanian and Gaudier, who had first discriminated against the "beefy

statue" of the nineteenth century. Brancusi was extending the purification
process first begun by Gaudier. Gaudier had offered the world a "definite
appreciation of stone as stone: he had taught us to feel that the beauty of
sculpture is inseparable from its material and that it inheres in its material."
Gaudier had purged himself of every kind of rhetoric he had noticed:
"Brancusi has detected more kinds of rhetoric and continued the process of
purgation," having had the time to make statues where Gaudier had the
time to make only sketches. There was about Brancusi a kind of splendid
ideal detachment that Pound admired; Brancusi lived "in his atelier as a
Dordogne cavern sculptor may conceivably have lived in his rock-fissure,
content to let the world 'think' or not think in any way that it likes." Brancusi was outside the Vortex, the nerve center of the city, and was pursuing
something more basic and serene than Gaudier had, "a universe, a cielo, a
Platonic heaven full of pure and essential forms, and a cavern of a studio
which is, in a very old sense, a temple of peace, of stillness, a refuge from
the noise of motor traffic and the current advertisements."

Paris was a city of salons, and there was first of all Natalie Barney's on
the rue Jacob, near the Boulevard St.-Germain where in her garden with its
Grecian pavilion and her sumptuously furnished house she entertained the
Paris literati and managed to scandalize even the French with her band of
female admirers and her Wildean rejoinders to the old morality: "He who
confuses reproduction and love spoils both of them: the result of this mess is
marriage." Barney had been Apollinaire's friend, Proust's and Picasso's,
and she continued to show Pound her poems and to elicit his criticism.

William Carlos Williams, who visited Paris in 1924, was taken by
Pound to one of Natalie Barney's Friday afternoon gatherings in a well-
meaning effort to help sophisticate the New Jersey poet, and Williams described what he saw with a spirit of American bravado:

> It appears that there still existed a shred, a remnant of Remy
> de Gourmont's (badly accoutered) old salon, one of the wonders
> of the last century, presided over by a certain hardy character
> named Natalie Clifford Barney. You might think it was something
> preserved in amber from the time of the Renaissance. Ezra was full
> of homage for Natalie Barney, l'Amazone, as she was called at one
> time.
>
> But Ezra has always paid homage to old distinction: it is one
> of his handsomest traits. So we were to have tea with Natalie, a
> tremendous concession on her part toward me, one of the primi-
> tives of Ezra's earlier years.
>
> She was extremely gracious and no fool to be sure, far less so
> than Ezra under the circumstances. She could tell a pickle from a
> clam any day in the week. I admired her and her lovely garden,

well kept, her laughing doves, her Japanese servants. There were officers wearing red buttons in their lapels there and women of all descriptions. Out of the corner of my eye I saw a small clique of them sneaking off together into a side room while casting surreptitious glances about them, hoping their exit had not been unnoticed. I went out and stood up to take a good piss.

The story is told of some member of the Chamber of Deputies, a big, red-faced guy who had turned up there after a routine social acceptance. To his annoyance, as he stood lonely in the center of the dance floor, he saw women about him, dancing gaily together on all sides. Thereupon he undid his pants buttons, took out his tool and, shaking it right and left, yelled out in a rage, "Have you never seen one of these?"

In the liberated atmosphere of Paris, Pound became even more the figure of the poet in his dress. He wore a flowing black cape and cut his beard to a more pronounced point. John Gould Fletcher described his ebony cane, his pearl button velvet coats, and occasional sombrero; Margaret Anderson noted his large velvet beret and his "flowing tie of the Latin Quarter artist of the 1830s." Pound was brought to another salon by Cocteau. Coco Chanel, a peasant girl who became the leading courtesan of the era, began by designing hats and invented a new look in couture—stark and severe, flattening the buttocks and eliminating corsets and the curved bosom, the look austerely serious and perfect for the career woman. With the help of Misia Sert, the high-spirited wife of painter José Maria Sert, Chanel used her new profits to make her home on the rue Faubourg St.-Honoré into a gathering place for all kinds of artists.

Another important center for Pound, though a more reserved one, was a literary bookshop run by a young American woman named Sylvia Beach and called Shakespeare and Company. The shop was a place where writers could meet and it was stocked with the works of Pound, Yeats, and Joyce. Pound had just read the latest section of *Ulysses,* the Circe chapter, which he told his friend Agnes Bedford was "enormous—megascruptious-mastodonic." Joyce was writing "a new Inferno in full sail," he wrote his parents. Pound was forever trying to be useful to Joyce. He distributed copies of *A Portrait of the Artist* to French writers and critics and persuaded Ludmila Bloch-Savitsky, poet and publisher, John Rodker's mother-in-law, to translate it into French as *Dedalus.* Pound invited Sylvia Beach to a supper party at the home of a French poet, André Spire, so that she could meet Joyce. She received the impression of "a sensitiveness beyond any I had ever known," which may have been emphasized when Joyce, uncharacteristically, refused wine at the dinner table, and Pound prankishly lined all the wine bottles in front of him. After dinner, still embarrassed, Joyce retreated

to the library where Miss Beach pursued him. There was more than just a
hint of pathos about Joyce at this time. He needed a cane, he had to wear
dark glasses, his eyes were failing, and his teeth were rotting away. Joyce
visited the bookshop the next morning, in his blue serge suit and dirty
tennis sneakers, expressing his fears at not being able to find a publisher for
Ulysses when he completed it because of *The Little Review* prosecution in
New York. Without capital, facilities, or requisite experience, Miss Beach
offered to publish the book herself. Pound began a campaign of securing
advance subscriptions to help subsidize the costs of printing a book as large
as *Ulysses*. When he wrote to Shaw, the playwright replied that he was not
obligated to share Pound's tastes: "As for me, I take care of the pence and
let the Pounds take care of themselves." The quip stung Pound, who since
childhood detested puns on his name. When the *Tribune* journalist Wambly
Bald shared a Paris cab with Pound and remarked that they had in common
surnames that were easily punned upon, Pound glared and demanded that
Bald leave the cab. As for Shaw, he answered him in *The Dial*, commenting
that Joyce's picture of Dublin was "so veridic that a ninth-rate coward like
Shaw dare not look it in the face."

2. IL MIGLIOR FABBRO

Pound had begun composing the music for an opera, *Le Testament*,
based on the life and work of François Villon, using Villon's poems in their
original French as a libretto. His life was as busy and crowded with friends
as it had been in prewar London, and his work was frequently interrupted.
One of his visitors was Alfred Kreymborg, William Carlos Williams's friend
who had published *Des Imagistes*. When Kreymborg showed Pound a list of
possible future contributors to his magazine *Broom*, Pound began disqualify-
ing name after name: it was a sign of the superiority he felt to most poets
and the absoluteness of his convictions and taste as far as poetry was concerned. Scofield Thayer, editor of *The Dial*, appeared in Paris during the
brutally hot summer of 1921. Thayer felt Pound was less the enfant terrible
of criticism and more qualifying in his judgments than his letters had led
him to believe. Through Thayer, Pound met E. E. Cummings, a twenty-six-
year-old poet who while a Harvard undergraduate had read and admired
Pound's poems—especially "The Return"—and had been influenced to
abandon the early influences of Shelley, Swinburne, and Rossetti in favor of
modernism. Nine years younger than Pound, Cummings had a seasoned
skepticism that Pound liked—while working for the Harjes-Norton ambu-
lance corps in France in 1917, Cummings had been arrested because of
letters he had written criticizing the war and was interned for the duration

in a prisoner-of-war camp, an experience he described in *The Enormous Room.*

John Quinn was becoming highly irritated with Pound; in one eleven-page letter he complained of being too rushed, busy, and harassed to help him or any of his friends. He did have a moment for gossip and told Pound that Eliot had begun a long poem. Quinn warned Pound that he could not be expected to be his literary agent, he was not a seven-headed Hindu statue with fourteen eyes and seventy-seven arms. When Quinn visited Paris that summer he was more conciliatory, advising Pound that he had spent too much time helping others and that Pound should "play his own game" without permitting the strain of things to endanger his health. Pound's income was again precariously low and Quinn offered him a loan of $200 which Pound refused; a few months later Quinn sent him $250 and told him not to worry about repaying it.

That August, Agnes Bedford, an English musician and friend, came to Paris to assist Pound with his opera. Natalie Barney lent him a piano, but Pound felt picking out tunes on it was insufficient and purchased a bassoon, a choice that seemed odd to a number of his friends. There was something incongruous about Pound's decision to create opera, which the choice of the bassoon merely underlined. What had been merely marginal with the English Vorticists now seemed like a vain, foolish prancing, with Pound parading his love of sound in an arena for the deaf. Lewis, who visited later that month, wrote to Bedford, wondering if she had pushed Pound to buy the bassoon and asking whether this was "an action justified by the facts of existence, as you understand them?"

But the facts of existence for the artist set in Paris were as strange as the sounds of the bassoon. *The Dial* for August printed three cantos, and the New York *Evening Post* a piece by Pound on the Parisian scene that focused on Picabia. In the afternoons Pound would frequently drop into Picabia's studio which was located on his street. He felt Picabia had a "genius for handling abstract concepts" and the two men would talk for hours. Cocteau and Duchamp lived a few doors away and so did the painter Léger, who became another good friend. There were also regular tennis outings with Natalie Barney and continued visits to Brancusi, who would invite friends in the early evening and in a clay oven he had constructed bake chickens for them while they drank, smoked, and talked at his long stone table. Afterward, Brancusi might play Romanian folk tunes on his violin while dancing in heavy sabots as Duchamp beat a drum. At midnight, with flashlights, Brancusi would photograph his guests and then lead them out to the streets of Paris, with perhaps Tzara suggesting that they go to the Opéra to tear down the statues and replace them with Brancusi's. They would go instead to the cafés to drink, and by dawn end up in the Bois de Boulogne to watch the rising sun, or at Les Halles for onion soup, or on a boat down the Seine to Rouen to lunch at a provincial inn.

Pound had been working on a translation of Remy de Gourmont's *Physique de l'amour: essai sur l'instinct sexuel,* which was published under the title *The Natural History of Love.* In his book de Gourmont, who was not writing at all from practical experience, but very theoretically because he lived like a secular hermit, exalted the naturalness of sex and argued that it should pass beyond moral boundaries and the circumscriptions of Christianity, which were basically fetters for pagan energies. For de Gourmont, the one true sexual perversion was abstinence. His book was an advertisement for sexual liberation, which Pound endorsed and embellished in a postscript for the English version of the book. De Gourmont had suggested a correlation between a "complete and profound intercourse and cerebral development," an idea that Pound extended by viewing the brain as a "great clot of genital fluid held in suspension or reserve," a sort of sperm bank of mind. How such theories affected women is unclear, but the suspicion is that women were relegated to a secondary and passive role in the sexual and creative process. A year later, when reviewing a book on glandular systems, a curious kind of book for him to be assigned, Pound tried to develop his theory, urging that the two sides of the brain mutually magnetized themselves into "great seas of fecundative matter." Following de Gourmont, Pound said that women were the conservators of tradition, practical and clever but not inventive, not even suited to abstract projection. Man, the "phallus or spermatozoide charging head-on, the female chaos," was the inventor and originator because his brain was bathed in residual sperm which caused "the original thought, as distinct from the imitative thought." Pound compared his introduction of new ideas into the "great passive vulva of London" to the male sensation in copulation and argued that genius depended on a special interaction of testes, pineal gland, and brain.

While such theories may seem at best peculiar rationalizations for Pound's own life—his wife was spending her summers regularly in England and generally permitted Pound latitude in extramarital matters—they were widely discussed in Paris in the early 1920s. The de Gourmont book was successful and printed in several editions. Pound was attempting to live with the freedom de Gourmont espoused. Besides Agnes Bedford, another visitor to whom Pound was attracted that summer was Bride Scratton, an English writer whom he had met in 1910 at one of Yeats's evenings. Married and bored with her husband, she sought the company of other writers as a distraction from the ordinary. In Paris, Pound helped her find a publisher for her book *England,* which described her marital unhappiness and which was printed under her maiden name of Adams in 1923, the year her husband sued for divorce, naming Pound as corespondent.

Dorothy returned to Paris in September and together with her husband encountered an American sculptor, Nancy Cox-McCormack. An acquaintance of Harriet Monroe's in Chicago, McCormack knew of Pound by reputation and had read some of his work in *Poetry.* The meeting was spontaneous and McCormack's memory of it is instructive:

> He came along accompanied by a slimly tailored, commanding young woman. Her beautiful curly chestnut hair binding a broad brow above strikingly large serious dark eyes and fine features reminded me of paintable English beauties. Her entire personality bespoke the quality of an English lady. I was never more astonished and pleased than when this extraordinary couple turned into the restaurant where I sat. They came directly towards me, asking permission to sit at my table. Once seated, E.P. eventually introduced himself and then presented his wife. He told me later that I had looked too much like news from the U.S.A. to let me get away.

According to McCormack, Pound seemed to address his wife in all his conversation "as if he were in the habit of crystalizing his thinking through the intellectual channels of their mutual understanding." Pound brought Nancy McCormack to meet Picabia, then to Brancusi's studio, and then to see Zadkine, who was carving agonized shapes in tree trunks. McCormack did a plaster "death mask" of Pound's face which she then photographed. Pound decided to mail a copy to the literary critic of the Chicago *Tribune,* Fanny Butcher, who had been less than kind to him, as a notice of his own demise.

T. S. Eliot came to Paris in the fall on his way back to London after spending the summer recuperating in a sanitorium in Lausanne. He had suffered a breakdown before the summer brought on by his own worrying and compounded by his wife's increasing incapacities as well as her other complaints: migraines, colitis, a lingering low-grade fever, and exhaustion. The nervous collapse may have opened the way for "The Waste Land"; he himself had written:

> It is commonplace that some forms of illness are extremely favorable, not only to religious illumination, but to artistic and literary composition. A piece of writing meditated, apparently without progress for months or years, may suddenly take shape and word; and in this state long passages may be produced which require little or no retouch.

Eliot brought Pound the forty-page first draft of his long poem, and Pound realized immediately that it had the same sweep and power of conception that he had felt were in the opening sections of *Ulysses.* He thought that the poem was too long, that there were sections (like a sixty-nine-line imitation

of Pope) that failed to contribute to the poem's real movement, and he
began marking the manuscript, recommending huge cuts, and cutting the
poem to half its original size. Eliot had returned to London and his job at
Lloyd's Bank, but by December he had incorporated most of Pound's
changes and completed the poem. It is quite clear, especially after the publication years later of the original manuscript with Pound's marginal comments and emendations, that had Pound not clarified the poem with what he
called his "Caesarian operation," it could not have had nearly the impact it
did have. In fact, Pound had saved Eliot's poem and honed it into a master-
piece, a fact of which Eliot was fully aware. He dedicated the poem to
Pound as "il miglior fabbro," the greater craftsman, the words that had
been used for Dante by one of his contemporaries. Pound was quick to
acknowledge Eliot's accomplishment:

> Complimenti, you bitch. I am wracked by the seven jealousies, and
> cogitating an excuse for always exuding my deformative secretions
> in my own stuff, and never getting an outline.

Pound was referring in his curiously worded note to his continuing difficulties with *The Cantos*, his inability to chart their course and plan their purpose. But his readings of *Ulysses* and of "The Waste Land" were to be
invaluable, first as inspiration, but also as examples that myth could be used
as narrative, a connective tissue binding and relating the parts of a whole.

Pound was still concerned about Eliot's stability; he was afraid that the
pressures of returning to the bank and his wife's continued aggravations
could precipitate an even more serious collapse. By early spring he had
revived the idea he had originally broached to Quinn that a fund be guaran-
teed by patrons interested in the future of good writing who would each
contribute ten pounds "for life or as long as Eliot needs it." Natalie Barney
agreed to be one of the patrons and named the project "Bel Esprit." Aldington, May Sinclair, and Pound signed up as life subscribers. Pound believed that once the fund got started, it could grow to the point that other
artists could be supported. Pound had a leaflet printed describing Bel Esprit
and wrote an article for *The New Age* relating it to Douglas's idea of the
importance of leisure and of freeing artists from drudgery to allow energy
for invention. Eliot's bank employment was the "worst waste in contemporary literature," Pound asserted. "The only thing one can give an artist is
leisure in which to work."

Quinn offered to take seven shares, even to "bind myself for $300 a
year for five years." On Eliot's behalf, Pound thanked Quinn for his generous offer, adding that no one had ever provided him, Pound, with such an
amount and that he was more prolific. Pound wrote William Carlos Williams to tell him that Eliot was at his "last gasp," a prisoner who needed to

be released. There was no organized civilization left, he wrote, no aristocracy whose function it had been to select the best: "Only those of us who
know what civilization is, only those of us who want better literature, not
more literature, better art, not more art, can be expected to pay for it. No
use waiting for the masses to develop a finer taste, they aren't moving that
way." The response from the pediatrician from Paterson, New Jersey, was
less than positive, possibly because Williams felt Eliot's influence as a poet
was invidious, that Eliot was bookish, evasively impersonal, and without
guts. "Why don't you get yourself crucified on the Montmartre," Williams
teased, "and will the proceeds to art. What the hell do I care about Eliot?"
Williams, a hardworking physician, who had to write his poems between
office visits, scribbling them in prescription pads, had little patience for the
idea that Eliot should be relieved of all obligations so that his time would be
free for writing. For Williams, poets worked in the world, as Wallace Stevens was working as a lawyer for the Hartford Insurance Company, or
Mayakovski on advertisements for the new Russian Communist state. Pound
had urged Williams to come to Paris for a visit, but Williams complained
that he could not abandon his practice for so long and hope to keep it. He
added in a characteristic observation that he had been watching black men
in the Paterson brickyards make and pile bricks. (Did he know Eliot's father
owned a brick plant in St. Louis and could easily have helped his son?) In
the end he sent a check for twenty-five dollars made out to him by a man
named Katz who owned a steam laundry and whose third son had just been
delivered—Mrs. Katz defecating in the process, Williams added wryly, always careful to delineate to Pound the conditions of his world, which he
knew differed from the artistic ambience of Paris.

Pound had wanted to formulate the Bel Esprit plan without Eliot's
knowledge, but too many people had been involved for it to remain secret
for long. "I think you will agree," Eliot wrote to Aldington, "that the
method proposed by Ezra is rather bordering on the precarious and slightly
undignified charity." At his bank, at least, he would not be dependent on
his friends and on a doubtful income to be gained by literary work. Eliot
was mortified when a truncated and garbled version of Bel Esprit was
printed in the Liverpool *Daily Post* and subsequently refused to have anything to do with it. The newspaper account claimed that Eliot had received
eight hundred pounds from Bel Esprit, taken the money, and returned to
the bank. The article then described his nervous breakdown. Eliot thought
this account would jeopardize his standing at the bank. He suddenly began
a paroxysm of worry about providing for himself in his old age, and there is
little question that he felt humiliated and exhausted as a result of the article.

Boni & Liveright proposed to Pound in the beginning of 1922, as a
result of the success of the *Natural History of Love,* an arrangement whereby
he would be paid five hundred dollars annually for two years for more

translations. They had published in America at the end of 1921 *Poems, 1918–21,* including the Provençal translations, "Propertius," "Mauberley," and three cantos. Pound had sent the book to his former professor at the University of Pennsylvania, Felix Schelling, who chose to review the book in the Philadelphia *Public Ledger,* focusing on the translations from Provençal. The originals were romantic, insouciant, fluidly lyrical, and natural but these qualities had all "evaporated" in Pound's hands and all Schelling felt was rigidity, effort, and awkwardness. *The Cantos* were like the leer of a trained fencer intending to hurt his opponent; their best quality was the trenchant manner of satire, but worst was the "itch to wound respectability and decency." Schelling was touching a sore point. To Pound, Schelling was respectability with its head twisted to face only the past. Schelling represented the humorless university which had denied Pound admission to the club because he was insufficiently genteel. As Schelling saw it, Pound had been too outspoken for the university; there was a brazen, challenging quality to his convictions which could be interpreted as abrasiveness, and a corrosive defiance about the poetry. Pound replied in a letter that he had learned from Yeats an "absolute intransigence," that in *The Cantos* he was trying to preserve the remaining elements of civilization in his time and doing it didactically: "It is rubbish to pretend that art isn't didactic, only the aesthetes since 1880 have pretended the contrary and they aren't a very sturdy lot." Humanity, Pound added, "is malleable mud, and the arts set the moulds it is later cast into." Pound had abandoned the apolitical stance of Imagism, his literary priorities were shifting from a Jamesian concern with manners to a political, Whitmanesque perspective that concentrated on mores. Pound's remarks to Schelling suggest that he was becoming more elitist and more messianic at the same time, certainly a difficult combination to maintain.

In February of 1922, *Ulysses* was published by Shakespeare and Company. Joyce had noted in his manuscript that the huge novel had been completed on October 30, 1921, Pound's thirty-fifth birthday. It was an occasion of the synchronicity in which Joyce rejoiced. Pound had seen Joyce develop as a writer from the restrained and understated realism of the *Dubliner* tales, to the poetic realism of *Portrait,* and then to the modernist extravaganza of *Ulysses,* with its stream-of-consciousness exploration of the mind and its formal implosions and brilliance. He used a "Paris Letter" to *The Dial* to praise Joyce for his "epoch-making report on the state of the human mind in the twentieth century." He also described the novel in French for the *Mercure de France.*

Eliot then proposed that Pound do another quarterly letter from Paris for a new magazine to be backed by Lady Rothermere which he wanted to edit. Lady Rothermere was a friend of Natalie Barney's who had been interested in Bel Esprit but had conceived a more practical way of assisting Eliot. The magazine would be called *The Criterion* and Eliot pointed out that

Pound would be able to print his cantos in it as well as whatever translation of French material he found exciting. "This venture is impossible without your cooperation," he advised. Pound's reply was rigid and dismissive, perhaps colored by the fact that no magazine had been found by Quinn or others for him to edit. He told Eliot he was uninterested in the "fortune of any writer in England save yourself" and in this case was interested only if the compensation proposed by Lady Rothermere was sufficient to get Eliot out of the bank. He warned Eliot that Ford had been betrayed after starting the *English Review.* He surmised that Eliot's magazine would not be able to pay him Thayer's rates for the "Paris Letters," reminding Eliot that he had "beggared myself, and kept down my rates for years by contributing to any free and idealistic magazine that has appeared." He expressed his "absolute distrust" of anything English: "I don't want to appear in England. I have no belief in their capacity to understand anything. They still want what I was doing in 1908. They want imitations and dilutations."

Pound's distrust of Lady Rothermere's possible future attempt to control the magazine was not mere paranoia. Her husband, Lord Rothermere, was the Hearst of British newspaper publishing. Pound's apprehension was increased when he received a hysterical note from Eliot's wife, who claimed Lady Rothermere was becoming offensive: "She goes to La Prieure [Gurdjieff's monastery], that asylum for the insane where she dances naked." Eliot's position was that remaining at the bank filled him full of dread and abomination and that his situation was different from Pound's. Dorothy, he pointed out, had good health and a family that could help her, and prospects of enough money to live on afterward, but his wife, Vivien, had none of these possibilities. Were it not for her antipathy to the idea of living in the United States, he would have returned to a professor's life and probably never written another line of poetry. He thought that if the magazine succeeded, he would be able to leave the bank and thus have more time for his own work.

The Criterion became respected and successful. Eliot published "The Waste Land" in it and much of his own literary criticism. He later became an editor at Faber & Faber and his fame as a poet grew. Aldington, who also worked on *The Criterion,* compared the two poets from America:

> Tom Eliot's career in England has been exactly the reverse of Ezra's. Ezra started out in a time of peace and prosperity with everything in his favour, and muffed his chances of becoming literary dictator of London—to which he undoubtedly aspired—by his own conceit, folly, and bad manners. Eliot started in the enormous confusion of war and post-war England, handicapped in every way. Yet by merit, tact, prudence, and pertinacity he succeeded in do-

ing what no other American has ever done—imposing his personality, taste, and even many of his opinions on literary England.

With his pale ascetic face, his punctilious manners, and his deliberate air of
reserve, Eliot looked like the perfect assimilated Englishman. He struck
Douglas Goldring as having "brains without bowels," the perfect "ecclesi-
astical dignitary." Eliot did have an ingratiating ability to fit in, to accommodate himself for the sake of acceptance. His own emotional insecurity almost
made this a necessity. He could mix with people for whom he had little
regard and about whom he would be scathing in his letters. Exceedingly
cautious and circumspect when dealing with others, he had an instinct for
making the right impression, for appearances and proprieties, and he understood the social mechanics of making a literary reputation in England. In
short, he was everything Pound had not been in England.

3. THE MODERNIST YEAR

Nineteen twenty-two was a year of accomplishment for modernism
because of the publication of *Ulysses* and Eliot's poem. "It is after all a
grrrreat littttttterary period," Pound had exclaimed to Eliot. Quinn in New
York had convinced Thayer to publish the poem in *The Dial*, and to award
Eliot a two-thousand-dollar prize, after which Boni & Liveright later published the poem with notes in a book, *The Waste Land and Other Poems*. Eliot
was satisfied with these arrangements but told Quinn he felt Pound should
have received the prize as a recognition of his share in the making of the
poem. Nineteen twenty-two was also the year of Proust's death, the year
when Benito Mussolini led a legion of black-shirted men into Rome to
establish the Fascist order, and the year when Cocteau opened his nightclub,
Le Boeuf sur le Toit (the Ox on the Roof), a large room with a dance floor
and a bar, where artists would go for champagne, caviar, and celebration.
Cocteau had fallen in love with a sixteen-year-old prodigy, Raymond
Radiguet, who quickly wrote a novel, *The Devil and the Flesh*, in which he
attacked the modernist obsession with originality. The novel was sold with a
new emphasis on public relations—what Pound had done for Joyce, sending
copies to influential reviewers, was at this time being done in a more organized fashion—and Radiguet was soon touted as another Rimbaud.
Radiguet was a product of clique and advertising but also of the myth of
artistic creativity that made Paris in the twenties such a magnet for disaf-
fected artists from all over the world. The atmosphere at this time was one
of hectic flush as the young American Gerald Murphy described it:

> There was a tension and an excitement in the air that was almost
> physical. Always a new exhibition, or a recital of the new music of

Thaddeus Pound.
(Library of Congress)

Ezra Pound and
his mother, Isabel Pound.
(Idaho Historical Society)

A college production, September 1903. Pound is second from the left.

Left to right: Victor Plarr, Sturge Moore, William Butler Yeats, Wilfrid Scawen Blunt, Pound, Richard Aldington, F. S. Flint, January 18, 1914. *(Photography Collection, Harry Ransom Humanities Research Center, University of Texas at Austin)*

Pound at Shakespeare and Company. *(Sylvia Beach Papers, Princeton University Library)*

Right: portrait of Pound.
*(Photography Collection,
Harry Ransom Humanities Research Center,
University of Texas at Austin)*

Below left: Dorothy Pound.
*(Photography Collection,
Harry Ransom Humanities Research Center,
University of Texas at Austin)*

Below right: Olivia Shakespear.
*(Photography Collection,
Harry Ransom Humanities Research Center,
University of Texas at Austin)*

Above: Pound in his Paris studio, 1923. *(National Archives)*

Left: Pound in Paris, 1922. *(Photography Collection, Harry Ransom Humanities Research Center, University of Texas at Austin)*

Left to right: Ford Madox Ford, James Joyce, Pound, John Quinn, Paris, spring 1923. *(Photography Collection, Harry Ransom Humanities Research Center, University of Texas at Austin)*

Pound and two companions. *(National Archives)*

Above: A portrait by Wyndham Lewis.
(Courtesy of the Tate Gallery.
© *Estate of Mrs. G. A. Wyndham Lewis)*

Left: another rendering
of Pound by Lewis.
(Photography Collection,
Harry Ransom Humanities Research Center,
University of Texas at Austin)

Drawing of Pound by Gaudier-Brzeska. *(Photography Collection, Harry Ransom Humanities Research Center, University of Texas at Austin)*

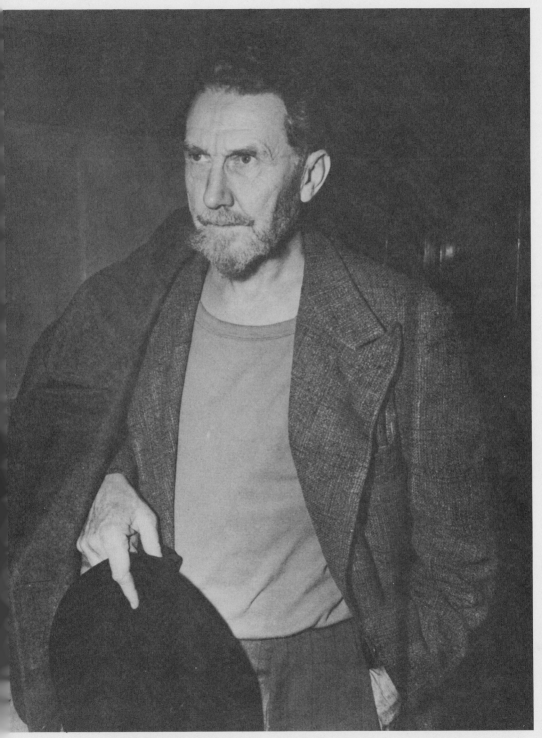

Pound in 1945 at the time of his arrest. *(Wide World Photos)*

Shortly after the arrest, Rapallo, Italy, May 1945. *(Wide Word Photos)*

Pisa, Italy. The security cages where Pound was held in 1945. *(Photography Collection, Harry Ransom Humanities Research Center, University of Texas at Austin)*

On deck of the liner *Christoforo Colombo,* on arrival in Naples, Italy, July 9, 1958. *(Wide World Photos)*

At Sant Ambrogio, March 24, 1965. *(Wide World Photos)*

In Venice. *(Copyright © Horst Tappe)*

Pound and Olga Rudge, Sant Ambrogio, 1969. *(Courtesy of Olga Rudge)*

Venice. One of the final photographs. *(Idaho Historical Society)*

Les Six. or a Dadaist manifestation, or a costume ball in Montparnasse, or a première of a new play or ballet, or one of Étienne de Beaumont's fantastic "Soirées de Paris" in Montmartre—and you'd go to each one and find everybody else there, too. There was such a passionate interest in everything that was going on, and it seemed to engender activity.

Early in the year Pound met a young American reporter named Ernest Hemingway who had come to Sylvia Beach's bookshop with a letter of introduction and praise from Sherwood Anderson. The son of a physician, he had learned a tremendous concision in writing by working on newspapers rather than attending universities. Hemingway had an earthy immediacy and boyish charm that Pound found irresistible. Radiant with an air of robust health and vigor, Hemingway was slim, but he had the back and shoulders of a football player. He rarely spoke about books or writing, but about sports and fishing and his love for woods and streams. When Pound tried to interest him in Eliot's difficulties, Hemingway's response was characteristically abrupt, hard, and facetious. If Eliot would strangle his wife, he suggested, rob the bank, and bugger his brain specialist, he might write an even better poem. Pound was impressed by Hemingway's avoidance of sentimentality or affectation in his writing, the economy and lack of superfluous language, a kind of Imagism in prose, and he tried to show Hemingway how to make his style even more sparse and unadorned. Later Hemingway remembered that Pound had taught him more "about how to write and how not to write than anyone else." Pound was the man, he claimed, "who had taught me to distrust adjectives as I would later learn to distrust certain people in certain situations." Soon Hemingway was teaching Pound how to box, a practice he described to his friend Howell Jenkins:

> We have a hell of a good time. I'm boxing regular with Ezra Pound, and he has developed a terrific wallop. I can usually cross myself though before he lands them and when he gets too tough I dump him on the floor. He is a good game guy and has come along to beat hell with the gloves—some day I will get careless and he will knock me for a row of latrines. He weighs 180.

Hemingway liked Pound and was more than generous in his account of Pound's pugilistic promise. On one occasion Pound complained to Dorothy that Hemingway treated him like a piece of Dresden china. Another impression, characteristically more astringent, was recorded by Wyndham Lewis, who knocked on Pound's door one morning that summer and received no reply. Lewis pushed the door open himself and saw "a splendidly built young man, stripped to the waist, and with a torso of dazzling white, standing not far from me. He was tall, handsome, and serene, and was repelling with his boxing gloves—I thought without undue exertion—a hectic assault of Ezra's. After a final swing at the dazzling solar plexus (parried effortlessly by the trousered statue) Pound fell back on his settee." In *A Moveable Feast,* Hemingway's sometimes maliciously recalled memoir of his Paris years, he recorded his own impression of Lewis's visit. He felt Lewis waited in the hope that Pound would get hurt. Lewis's face reminded Hemingway of a frog and his eyes, under his wide black hat, were the "eyes of an unsuccessful rapist."

In the spring of 1922 Hemingway had gone to report on an economic conference in Genoa and there interviewed Mussolini, whom he found was merely "the biggest bluff in Europe." At the conference Hemingway met another reporter, a tall, angular, reserved American named William Bird, who told him that he had recently established a small press on the Île St.-Louis in Paris and was searching for publishable material. Hemingway mentioned that Pound might be willing to let Bird publish some part of the cantos, and Bird visited Pound when he got back to Paris. Pound proposed that Bird allow him to edit a series of six books by himself, Hemingway, Ford, and Williams, a series that would constitute an "inquest" into the state of contemporary writing in English. Bird had been thinking of reprinting the classics, but Pound's argument that such a strategy would have little impact and Pound's suggestion that he should do the moderns appealed to him. Each book would be hand-printed by Bird, who would set the type and run his seventeenth-century press, using fine paper and issuing three hundred or fewer copies of each work. Pound's contribution would be *Indiscretions,* the experimental autobiographical chapter about his childhood that had already appeared in *The New Age.* By this time Robert McAlmon had come to Paris and Hemingway introduced him to Bird. Married to Bryher for over a year, McAlmon was planning to use some of her money to continue his Contact Press in Europe. McAlmon realized that the books he wanted to publish might make profits if proper business methods were applied, and he persuaded Bird to act as his distributor. Bird's cramped print shop became McAlmon's Paris headquarters and the two men set up an informal partnership, the books they published sometimes bearing the imprint of both Contact and Bird's Three Mountains Press.

Later that spring Pound went to Italy with Dorothy. In the ancient town of Sienna, trying to cultivate a medieval appearance, he shaved a straight line from the sides of his forehead over his ears to the nape of his neck, which was the way Malatesta Novello, one of the historical personages re-created in *The Cantos,* had been modeled by Pisanello. Pound was also translating the short fiction of Paul Morand, "Fancy Goods" and "Open All Night," with Dorothy helping with final corrections and changes. Pound had praised Morand in *The Dial* as one of a group of French writers under forty who were "writing without humbug, without jealousy, and without an eye on any market whatsoever," and he noted that Morand in particular had "the first clear eye that has been able to wander about both ends of Europe looking at the wreckage." When Pound learned that his English publisher, Guy Chapman, had rejected his translation as unsuitable, on the grounds of vulgar language and sexual frankness, Pound wrote Chapman an angry letter, pointing out that he saw no point in doing a verbatim translation and that Morand himself had gone over his work and approved the changes in idiom. Chapman still refused to accept the work, wary perhaps because of the contention caused by D. H. Lawrence's novels, and paid Pound twenty-five pounds to settle the matter. For Pound it was another case of the artist being victimized by the moral prurience of the Victorian hangover.

In June, Dorothy returned to England to spend the summer with her family. After a decade of marriage the Pounds had become more companions than lovers. H.D. commented on their relationship at this time:

> Yes, Ez is "married" but there seems to be a pretty general concensus of opinion that Mrs. E. has not been "awakened." . . . She is very English and "cold" and I personally like her although she is unbearably critical and never has been known to make a warm friend with a man or woman. She loathes (she says) children! However that may be a little pose. She is a bit addictive to little mannerisms. I don't think she can be poignantly sensitive or she would never have struck Ezra. Ezra is kind but blustering and really stupid. He is adolescent. He seems almost "arrested" in development.

Iris Barry had seen Dorothy as "a young Victorian lady out skating" and a number of other observers, including Pound, had noted her ladylike decorum and control, her quiet reserve and her delicacy. Pound remarked to Daniel Cory, George Santayana's secretary, in the 1930s that he had married a "beautiful picture that never came to life." Much earlier, in a letter written while Pound was teaching at Wabash College and sent to Mary Moore, Pound scrawled and then scratched over that it had been proven in Provence that love and marriage were incompatible. Pound meant romantic love; marriage was more a sustained friendship. Dorothy, on her part, had experienced a very liberated mother who had many male friends, some of whom had been lovers. This had been tolerated by Henry Hope Shakespear, so Dorothy grew up with the understanding that artists were special cases who could be expected to have many deep friendships. All during the time of their courtship, Pound was meeting other women, and on one occasion when Pound was in France he insisted that Dorothy entertain Mary Moore, who was visiting London. Edgar Jepson, one of Pound's friends in the London years, noted that because of his posture as a warrior for the arts, women "ran after him with commendable pertinacity."

Pound felt a connection between his creativity as a poet and his ability to attract and seduce women. They were always artists or attempting to become artists; Pound was always the troubador winning them through language and song. If genius depended on bathing the brain in seminal fluid, as Pound had convinced himself it did, then sex was necessary for poems to be conceived and made. Pound continued to woo and win women through his sixties and the years at St. Elizabeths, and Dorothy continued to maintain a ladylike indifference to his flirtations.

Pound had translated *The Natural History of Love* and had taken a trip to Verona, the city of *Romeo and Juliet,* with Bride Scratton. He had written a letter to Picabia which in turn Picabia openly printed along the margin of a page in his magazine *391:* "Why Paris? Paris is the centre of the world: Why? And I am here for three months without finding a congenial mistress." In the summer of 1922 he found the congeniality he was seeking when he met Olga Rudge, a petite twenty-six-year-old brunette, a violinist from Youngstown, Ohio. Olga Rudge's grandfather had come to Ohio from Limerick, Ireland, because as a sheep rancher he could no longer bear the competition from Australia. Her father went into real estate. Her mother, an opera singer named Julia O'Connell, had three children in Youngstown, which handicapped her operatic career. Before the First World War she decided to raise her children in Europe and was able to do this because her husband sent generous remittances and visited every summer. Julia O'Connell began her daughter's European musical education when Olga was three. After the war Olga continued her studies in Paris with the violin teacher Carambat. Pound had seen her perform in London in 1920 when he was still writing music criticism for *The New Age* and had favorably reviewed her playing while criticizing her accompanist. At an afternoon gathering in Natalie Barney's garden, Olga had seen Pound conversing in an animated manner, dressed in his usually colorful style. She found him remarkably handsome. They shared an immediate compatibility, and they continued to see each other for another half a century.

Pound was spending more time in the sometimes rambunctious company of Robert McAlmon, whose stories, *A Hasty Bunch,* he had favorably reviewed in one of his "Paris Letters" to *The Dial.* The collection was titled as a tribute to McAlmon's impatience, his refusal to revise any of his work, a trait Pound felt demonstrated "little skill." Pound remembered that his friend Ford had said there are always forty ways to say anything and the first one is usually wrong. But he praised McAlmon's ability to present small-town American values in a "hard and just light," with "no nonsense, no overworking, or overloading." Pound called McAlmon's use of actual spoken language an example of "tough realism" and noted the parallels to

Hemingway. Even more than Hemingway, however, McAlmon symbolized for Pound a generation that seemed more driven to expend energy on pastimes and talking than real work, a condition that Pound realized affected him as well as long as he lived in Paris. McAlmon was a man with a "violent dissatisfaction with himself," his friend Kay Boyle observed. Caustic and irreverent, he was capable of a devastating honesty verging on cynicism, a quality he could apply to other writers in the Gypsy Bar or Le Boeuf sur le Toit or the cafés of Montparnasse whenever he felt their pretensions. The hardness of McAlmon's strictures appealed to Pound. Williams wrote him that "no one is quite as *clean* about the truth as Bob is." He might have been a little less enthusiastic had he known that McAlmon would turn his sharp critical sensibility on Pound as well, calling him "too much the poet poetizing," "the pedagogue yearning for pupils to instruct," a "thwarted comedian," and finally "the martyred schoolmaster." McAlmon did, however, favorably contrast what he saw as Pound's health and vitality to the moldiness he felt in Eliot, whose "snob governess" attitude and "liverish wail" affected McAlmon in the same way it did Williams. But what Pound appreciated most in a friend was zeal for letters. McAlmon would proceed from bar to bar through the Paris night, perpetually on the prowl, friendly with prostitutes, jockeys, and a sportsman's crowd but still soliciting subscriptions for *Ulysses* as he went on. At one point he was rerouting $150 a month of Bryher's money to Joyce.

McAlmon wore a broad-brimmed hat that seemed to express his debonair disregard for what others thought of how he lived, or what he wrote. He was a drinking man, the sort who could drive to doom with a Western song and a smile on his lips if something about the destination appealed to him. For McAlmon, gaiety was the posture of courage. Williams once claimed that McAlmon had a "genius for life," but McAlmon replied that along with his gregarious but not always loving inclinations, he had a large capacity for indifference and despair and "long and heavy spells of ennui which takes bottles of strong drink to cure." During the twenties Contact, as well as printing books by Pound, Hemingway, H.D., Williams, Djuna Barnes, Nathanael West, and Gertrude Stein, brought out seven books of poetry and prose by McAlmon himself. By spending time with McAlmon, Pound knew he was helping to shape the publication of avant-garde writing, the group McAlmon called "the Bunch." With Bird, however, Pound's impact was to be even more immediate. By the end of 1922 Bird had prepared a printed notice of his Three Mountains Press series as edited by Pound, including *Indiscretions,* Ford's *Women and Men,* Williams's *The Great American Novel,* Bride Scratton's *England,* and Hemingway's *In Our Time,* a work Pound scoured with Hemingway, searching for any possible linguistic fat deposits and unnecessary words. These books set out from very different perspectives, Pound explained in a postscript to Bird's notice, to tell the truth about comtemporary manners "without fake, melodrama, or conventional endings."

In December of 1922 the Pounds, the Joyces, and the Yeatses enjoyed a farewell dinner. Pound had developed an aversion to cold weather, and he was complaining of a digestive disorder, perhaps related to his continuing struggle to shape the cantos he was writing. To escape the cold, Pound and Dorothy traveled to Rapallo, a small town on a sheltered curve on the coast south of Genoa on the Italian Riviera where Yeats at this point chose to spend his winters. Pound continued his work on *The Cantos,* gathering information on Italian Renaissance figures whom he would describe. One of these men was Sigismondo Malatesta, a fifteenth-century warrior who shrewdly traded his capacities for military leadership from city to city. Malatesta ruled in Rimini for thirty-five years and redeemed his despotism, for Pound at least, by his sustained art patronage and the remodeling of a thirteenth-century Gothic church into the Tempio Malatestiano, which celebrates his military and amorous conquests. Pound had also developed a fascination with the more recent career of Gabriele D'Annunzio, an Italian poet who had turned to political activism in the drive to unify his country. Pound received a letter from Hemingway, who announced that he and his wife, Hadley, wanted to join the Pounds but teasingly wondered whether he could "preserve my incognito among your fascist pals." Hemingway claimed that, because of his interview with Mussolini at the Genoa economic conference, he had been told that he could not live in Italy again. After two months in Rapallo, the Pounds met the Hemingways to visit battle sites in central Italy, a subject in which Hemingway was expert, and the town of Cesena, home of the Malatestine Library, which Pound called "a unique monument to the culture of the best decades of the Renaissance." The Pounds then traveled to Sicily with Yeats and his wife, the two couples forming a sort of extended family because of past histories and Dorothy and Georgina's friendship, which long antedated Yeats and Pound's.

By the end of February the Pounds were in Rome, where they found Nancy McCormack modeling a bust of Giacomo Boni, an influential Italian archaeologist. Pound wanted introductions to the Vatican librarian in connection with his researches for *The Cantos,* and Boni helped with personal notes. Through Nancy McCormack they met members of the Bosis family in Rome and were introduced to Professor Vacca, a leading Italian scholar of Oriental languages. Pound wanted to meet Mussolini as Hemingway had but was unsuccessful in arranging an interview at that time.

4. A "VILLAGE EXPLAINER" AMONG THE INTELLECTUALS

Pound returned to Paris in the spring to a mixture of bad and good news. Thayer wanted a fresh voice to capture the Parisian art scene and had chosen Paul Morand to do it. The "Paris Letters" had represented a steady source of good income for Pound and a certain amount of prestige. *The Dial* had also paid for cantos, and there were signs that this would not continue when Kenneth Burke returned three cantos in June. But by then William Bird had agreed to publish a limited edition of cantos, a quality production with large type and large format with capitals designed by Hemingway's friend, an American named Henry Strater. The book would be, Pound wrote, "one of the real bits of printing," a "modern book to be jacked up to something near the level of medieval manuscript."

More good news arrived in the person of Ford Madox Ford. He had arrived in Paris to edit a new magazine, the *transatlantic review,* an attempt to extend the high standards of early modernism as Ford had demonstrated them in the *English Review,* but in a more international setting. When Ford experienced difficulty finding suitable working space, the redoubtable Bird offered him a corner in his already cramped facility on the Île St.-Louis. Now Bird, McAlmon, and Ford could together hum with the literature of the future. Pound was also delighted to hear that Joyce was planning a new project. He assumed it would be a continuation of the pyrotechnical virtuosity of *Ulysses* and announced to his father, "J.J. launched on another work calculated to take the hides off a few more sons of bitches." Later, when he read examples of what Joyce was doing in *Finnegans Wake,* the poet who himself would face charges of increasing obscurantism in *The Cantos* was baffled: "Nothing short of divine vision or a new cure for the clapp can possibly be worth all the circumambient peripherization," he wrote to Joyce.

At the dinner at André Spire's where Pound had brought Sylvia Beach to meet Joyce, a Frenchman named Julien Benda had been present and had dominated the evening with his ideas and devouring talk. Benda's book, *The Treason of the Intellectuals,* was published in the late spring of 1923. Benda's subject was the artist-intellectuals like D'Annunzio or Barras who had been tried by the Dadaists. In their thirst for the immediate results caused by direct action, they had sacrificed an essential critical distance which allowed them to evaluate political and social realities with some semblance of objectivity. To the extent that the intellectual organized action, Benda suggested, he betrayed the sort of balanced inquiry that determined his authenticity as an intellectual. However, the real quandary, as the existentialists would discover a generation later, was that unless they could be actively engaged in creating the changes about which they were theorizing they would not be taken seriously. The effect on certain writers was a state of anxiety. The age was one in which the "intellectual organization of political hatreds," Benda asserted, would become a dominant characteristic, forcing the artist to affect aristocratic values and to appeal to arbitrary authority, encouraging the artist to scorn societies that pretended to be ruled by justice and civic equality. This happened to be the historical moment when the French were occupying the Ruhr valley, when Hitler succeeded in his Munich putsch, and a fascist coup occurred in Spain. Benda's book, soon translated into English by Aldington, influenced an entire generation of European artists to declare a political position. The Dadaists in France, among them Breton and Aragon, realized that their artistic escapades had failed to make any sustained impression on the middle classes. With their evolution in the direction of Surrealism, they became more activist, less abstract, more oriented to the political left; Aragon, in fact, declared himself Communist. Writers on the left and on the right believed passionately in their art, glamorizing it with the notion that it could be a route to salvation, a way to teach mankind and to save it from folly. Writers like Céline and Pound were influenced to move in the other direction, seeking the security of central authority and the strong state to be found in fascist organization. They believed that Benda's disparagement of the ideal of progress, which had been a mainstay of nineteeth-century politics, was not cynicism but realism; they expressed their contempt of the followers of Rousseau, who still hoped for the perfectibility of man, and they agreed that an active pessimism was the only antidote to false hopes.

Pound's interest in political and economic questions became intense in the summer of 1923. His friend Mary Colum recalled one instance that reveals some of the heat of his commitment:

> Ezra insisted on taking us to a lecture by Lincoln Steffens on Soviet Russia, the Russia of Lenin, in the apartment of one of his friends. The lecture seemed to me of an appalling dreariness, and I hated being dragged to it, with all the interesting things in Paris one could go to. But Ezra listened to it with rapt attention, his eyes glued to the speaker's face, the very type of a young man in search of an ideology, except that he was not so very young. He seemed to have an intense interest in new political and economic ideas, and after Steffens was finished he rose to his feet and started talking about the Douglas plan, to which he had tried to convert Arthur Griffith and through him the new Irish state.

Pound and Steffens had become friends, sharing a native American cracker-barrel grass-roots radicalism, a populism that hungered for drastic solutions while chastising governments. Steffens, along with Hemingway, had seen

Mussolini at the Lausanne Peace Conference and had been impressed by the strength of Mussolini's scorn for the old game of politics and diplomacy, and his contempt for democracy. Mussolini had flatly announced at a press conference that his group "had seized power, we possess power, and we will use our power." When asked what he would do if challenged by the opposition, he smirked and replied, "Whatever is necessary." When pushed to define exactly what he meant, and asked whether he would dissolve the Italian parliament, he repeated his enigmatic, "Whatever is necessary," prefacing it with "Dissolve them, shut them up, shoot them—whatever is necessary." This was just as much the sign of a new order as the Russian Revolution had been, and in its resort to brute force to settle political differences, very similar. It was a drastic solution to the squabbles of democratic disorder but it had particular appeal for Steffens, and he passed along his praise of Mussolini to Pound.

There were other distractions for Pound. Dorothy had taken her annual pilgrimage to England, and her father's sister had died, leaving her two thousand pounds. Olga Rudge was in Paris ready to meet Pound at teas or parties. John Quinn had come to visit, Pound having arranged this with a view to future acts of patronage. It was Quinn's first opportunity to see Joyce, the man whose book he had defended, but a man who felt little gratitude, since he thought Quinn's defense had lacked sufficient drama and brilliance. There is a photograph of Quinn standing with the men he had helped, Joyce poised next to a statue but looking very much like a statue himself, top-heavy and jovial Ford with his lower jaw jutting downward, and Pound, one hand in his pocket, looking warily at the camera as if history had caught him in a bad moment. Interestingly enough, of the four men only Quinn is standing straight—and he died of liver cancer three months later.

During the summer of 1923 Pound was seen doing the rhumba with Caresse Crosby at the Boule Planche dance hall, and he was visiting Kitty Cannell, estranged from Skipworth Cannell, in the late hours of the night. Hemingway, who had gone to Toronto, where his wife, Hadley, was going to have their first child, was writing special features and doing interviews for the Toronto *Star* at what seemed the munificent salary of $125 a week. In a letter he warned Pound not to consider returning to the United States to live. He had encouraged him to visit Gertrude Stein and her companion, Alice B. Toklas, who had an intimate salon in their large apartment near the Luxembourg Gardens which was decorated with the Cubist paintings Stein's brother, Leo, collected. Independently wealthy, an indomitable sort who had earned a medical degree at Johns Hopkins, she had begun writing while taking a postgraduate course at Harvard with William James. She often expressed herself in a clipped, repetitive, bare style that had a curious childish rhythm and sometimes sounded incomprehensible. As pugnacious and feisty as Pound, Stein had the same potential to dictate and pontificate. The Jews had only produced three original geniuses, she was given to announcing—Christ, Spinoza, and herself. When she had worn her hair in a bun she looked like an Italian peasant, Hemingway observed, but then she cut it mannishly short and she looked like a Roman emperor. "Ezra was right half the time," Hemingway wrote, "and when he was wrong you were never in doubt about it. Gertrude was always right." Such a combination was bound to end in conflict. When Pound visited, he began to lecture on his literary preferences from Catullus to Provence, interspersing his remarks with comments on Stein's collection of paintings. Stein found Pound's tone unpleasantly aggressive and responded with an air of stolid indifference, but what she found difficult to tolerate was the way Pound kept leaning back in her favorite antique chair, balancing it on its two back legs until one of them snapped. The situation perfectly exemplifies Pound's place in Paris, living frugally but lingering as well in drawing rooms of the rich like Natalie Barney's, feeling arrogant and cocky in the presence of bourgeois comforts in Stein's rooms, and with Toklas's taciturnity, feeling invulnerable and perhaps unconcerned with what they thought of his manners, wanting himself always to be on the dangerous edge between an artistic bohemia and literary respectability. So he rocked back to the edge on Stein's chair until he fell, breaking the chair. She never invited him back, and she hence disparaged him as a village explainer, "excellent if you were a village if not, not."

For Pound, Stein was only a representative of the ineffectual Paris art scene, and there are signs that he was beginning to tire of it, that he could easily dissipate all his power talking or in the service of others. Paris was the social whirl that was supposed to stimulate work, but it often left him too irritated or fatigued actually to do it. Something had curdled Pound's gaiety, soured his cheerfulness. The critic Malcolm Cowley reported in *Exile's Return* that Pound had broached the subject of his departure from Paris:

> Now he was thirty-seven years old and it was time for him to stop
> doing so much for other men and for literature in general, stop
> trying to educate the public and simply write. It would take years
> for him to finish the *Cantos;* he wanted to write an opera and he
> had other plans. To carry them out it might be best for him to
> leave Paris and live on the Mediterranean, far from distractions, in
> a little town he had discovered when he was in villeggiatura.

That he had not, however, been able to stop organizing and doing for others is evident in a letter he wrote to Nancy McCormack shortly after the Stein visit, a letter in which he reiterates his fantasy of an artistic community in a university setting, this time to be located in the benevolent presence of Mussolini's Fascist state. Pound's idea was to make Italy the intellectual center of Europe by gathering fifteen of the best artists and writers and persuading them to join such a community:

> The experiment would be expensive; the whole thing depends on the selection, and on the manner of the invitation. I shouldn't trust any one's selection save my own. There is no use going into details until one knows if there is or could be any serious interest in the idea; that is to say if the dictator *wants* a corte literaria; if he is interested in the procedure of Sigismundo Malatesta in getting the best artists of his time into Rimini, a small city with no great resources. I know, in a general way the fascio includes literature and the arts in its programme; that is very different from being ready to take specific action.
>
> You have to avoid official personages, and dead wood of academies, purely pedagogical figures. The life of the arts is always concentrated in a very few individuals; they invent, and the rest follow, or adapt, or exploit.
>
> Italy has an opportunity *now*, an opportunity she would not have had thirty years ago, or even ten years ago. Germany is busted, England is too stupid, France is too tired to offer serious opposition; America is too far from civilization and won't for a hundred years distinguish between the first rate and the second rate; she will stay content with copies.

5. A SQUATTER POISED FOR FLIGHT

In July of 1923, *The Criterion* published cantos IX through XII, the so-called Malatesta cantos. Pound had called Pope Pius II a son of a bitch in one of the poems, a reference that Richard Aldington, assistant editor on the magazine, decided to omit. Pound was outraged by the omission, and his term for the long dead pope was a sign of his own anger and intemperance, his complete disregard for the offense his words might cause. In July, Pound was visited by the novelist Glenway Wescott, who remarked that Pound did not appear normal. He seemed unable to complete a sentence, Wescott observed, interrupting himself, digressing constantly, "splintering his syntax into fragments." Wescott remembered that Pound seemed tormented, possessed: his face had "an unpleasant pallor. His eyes looked strange, like those of some old bird. His hair and beard were carrot-red. His expression was often tentative, dreamy, fatuous. He seemed unable to sit still, jumping from chair to chair, from chair to couch, throwing himself down flat on his back and kicking his legs in the air; and all these extraordinary acrobatics were going on in the middle of sentences."

That same month he was visited by Margaret Anderson and Jane Heap, who had finally moved their *Little Review* to Paris. Anderson found him agitated and nervously self-conscious and noted his "high Rooseveltian voice." An hour in Pound's presence made her feel like a human experiment in a behavioral laboratory. Pound had become, Anderson felt, "patriarchal" in his attitudes toward women, kissing them on the forehead and drawing them on his knee "with perfect obliviousness to their distaste for these mannerisms." Such acts were the expression of a condescension Pound felt for the editorial engineers of the new poetry who had not written any of it themselves. He arranged a meeting in his flat between Anderson and Heap and James Joyce, whose work they had championed, and on another occasion brought them to one of Brancusi's endless dinner parties.

Anderson introduced Pound to a young musician she had met in New York, George Antheil. Antheil was short, and he had a nose that had been flattened in an airplane accident and an unprepossessing, Chaplinesque air. He had studied with Ernest Bloch and was a composer of dissonant, experimental music. Pound had not yet completed his Villon opera and Antheil offered to help him notate the score. Olga Rudge had been helping, and Agnes Bedford. Pound had also deciphered and transposed a twelfth-century air he had found in manuscript form into "Plainte de Roi Richard, Coeur de Lion" and was writing a number of smaller pieces, most of them for Olga Rudge to perform on the violin.

He had written an essay on music called "A Treatise on Harmony," which Ford had printed in the *transatlantic review,* and he showed this to Antheil, who declared in the Paris *Tribune* that Pound "brushed away a world of imbecilities carefully cultivated and cherished by impotents since the time of Bach." Soon Pound and Antheil were collaborating to puff each other's reputations in Paris. Pound, of course, loved music, had been a music critic for *The New Age,* and had studied the clavichord with Arnold Dolmetsch in London. He also played the piano, recorder, and bassoon. Through Katherine Ruth Heyman he had met a number of musicians in London, and he had collaborated on editions of troubador poetry and music with his friend Walter Morse Rummel. Virgil Thomson, who knew both Pound and Antheil in Paris at this time, felt Pound's musical background was still sketchy and a bit on the elementary side.

It is possible that Antheil's energy and irreverence reminded Pound of Gaudier. For a time Antheil became part of the rage for things American that had swept Paris since the appearance of jazz. Pound assembled some of the music pieces he had done for *The New Age* and the *transatlantic review* piece in a book which William Bird later published called *George Antheil and the Theory of Harmony,* and Antheil helped him finish the Villon opera. Scored for clavichord, brass, violin, and *corne,* a medieval French instrument made of animal horn, and several ancient percussive instruments, and requiring only three vocal parts, the opera was an elegiac tableau, sparsely orchestrated, with a minimum of action, and bare sets influenced by Pound's study of Noh, and in general a reaction to the grand heaviness and sentimentality of Puccini. Virgil Thomson said that it might well be the best music by a poet since Campion, but that the music was subservient to the voice and not integrated sufficiently. Thomson also noted that Antheil played the piano more loudly than anyone else, and the noise of Antheil working through the Villon score caused Pound's upstairs neighbors to complain to the police. Pound visited the district commissioner and in turn claimed that his neighbors liked to dance at three in the morning and that anyway he was a composer and some noise was necessary.

Pound was interested in Fernand Léger's use of machinery and machinelike objects in his art, as he had been interested in a similar quality in Picabia's painting. A profound correspondence existed between Cubist painting and the spirit of war that had erupted in 1914; in fact, camouflage, introduced during the war to disguise troops from airplanes, had been inspired by Cubist painting. Léger said he had been "dazzled by the breach of a 75 millimetre gun" in the field. After the war he postulated that beauty in its ideal state was independent of any sentimental association or reaction, that it depended on form exclusively and could therefore be as apparent in a machine part as in a flower. Pound wrote an essay on Léger in one of his *Dial* pieces and pushed the idea a bit further, stressing that the intrinsic beauty of machines lay in their pivots or moving parts because that was where their energy was concentrated. Pound attended Léger's lecture on the aesthetics of machine art on June 1, 1923, where he met Léger's friend the poet Blaise Cendrars. Subsequently the three men discussed a notion Léger called simultanist art—using disruptive "cutting" effects as in film and "close-ups" or moments of intense focus on familiar objects which would then be spliced into the narrative without using any transitions or explanations. Such ideas had their effect on Pound's design of *The Cantos* on a line-by-line basis as he shifted from one culture to another without bridging.

Léger's simultanist art had been confined to the canvas but his terms were evidently more appropriate for cinema. He had met the filmmaker Abel Gance and wanted to make a film without a scenario or narrative structure to contain it which would use a prism in front of the camera to destroy perspective. Pound introduced Léger to Dudley Murphy, a cameraman who could work in this new manner. Léger supported the project with his own funds and called it *Ballet mécanique*. On Pound's recommendation, Antheil was chosen to compose a compatible score, and Natalie Barney was recruited to pay for Antheil's contribution. According to Léger, what Antheil did was a synchronized adaptation of what was shown on the screen —for instance, a shot of Christmas tree ornaments multiplied through the prismatic device and moving in syncopation to Antheil's music. The film was not for the millions, Pound observed in a supreme understatement.

Believing his music had an integral value of its own, Antheil separated his composition from Léger's film. It would be premiered two years later, in Paris ten days before the first performance of Pound's *Villon*. Antheil's score was for an unusual assemblage: four player pianos electrically operated and playing simultaneously, an airplane propeller driven by two electric motors, gongs and rattles, and xylophones. The literati of Paris were at the glamorous Théâtre des Champs-Élysées to witness it: Joyce with a patch on his eye, T. S. Eliot escorting a woman in black rumored to be royalty but actually Sylvia Beach's concierge, Diaghilev and Ezra Pound in the gallery screaming, "Silence, imbéciles," as the audience expressed their dismay by yelling and scuffling, setting the stages for a riot. The Vorticist past had come to Paris and Pound was still trying to force a public into admiring dissident artists.

The intense mix of influences and the different worlds that Pound encountered in Paris was unbalancing—his digestion continued to malfunction, he was more high-strung and nervous, he developed rectal piles that needed several operations, and there were false alarms with his appendix. But all the unbalancing, as with Eliot's release of "The Waste Land" after his breakdown, was beneficial as far as understanding how to establish an internal order and a means of progression in *The Cantos*. The lesson of Paris for Pound was drawn from the liberating impact of *Ulysses* and "The Waste Land," from the experiments of the Dadaist and Surrealist poets, from the worlds of film and music. Joyce and Eliot had unveiled new structures for fiction and poetry. The Dadaists had demonstrated a highly kinetic antilogic that permitted swift directional changes without signaling. Pound had composed his own Dadaist poems; one of them, written in French and called "Kongo Roux," appeared in a Paris underground publication and contained the phrase "Étas-Unis d'Amérique Diabetics Union for the suppression of sugar." Another one, published in *The Little Review* under a pseudonym, dedicated to Williams and the Baroness von Freytag-Loringhoven, was densely incommunicative and showed a complete departure from what poems were supposed to do:

> Godsway bugwash
> Bill's way backwash
> FreytagElse 3/4 arf an'arf
> Billy Sunday one harf Kaiser Bill one harf
>   Elseharf Suntag, Billsharf Freitag
> Brot wit thranen, con plaisir ou con patate pomodoro
> Bill dago resisting U.SAgo, Else ditto on the verb
> basis yunker, plus Kaiser Bill reading to goddarnd

>stupid wife anbrats works of simple
>domestic piety in Bleibtreu coner of
>Hockhoff'sbesitzendeecke before the bottom fell
>out. Plus a little boiled Neitzsch on the sabath.
>Potsdam, potsdorf potz gek und keine ende. Bad
>case, bad as fake southern gentlemen tells you
>everymorn that he is gentleman, and that he is not
>black. Chinesemandarinorlaundryman takes forgranted
>youwillsee he is not BookerTWashington.

Dadaist contortions, film, and Pound's own attempts to create music had all provided a new spatial dimension, and in *The Cantos* Pound's scope and reach were greatly enlarged, and he was much more cinematic and fluid than he had been in "Mauberley." In terms of Pound's expectations for his audience, he had seen the level of difficulty in "The Waste Land" and he would situate his cantos roughly somewhere between *Ulysses* and *Finnegans Wake* in terms of unexplained referents. "The Waste Land," as Pound had edited it, had become a sequential linking of four cantos with sufficient affinities of mood and theme to allow it all to cohere. In his *Cantos,* Pound attempted a far more ambitious, and perhaps impossible, linkage of 120 parts.

By the fall of 1923 all the necessary backing for the *transatlantic review* had been arranged and Ford was securing contributions from Pound, Hemingway, Joyce, Williams, McAlmon, Tzara, Gertrude Stein, Djuna Barnes, and E. E. Cummings. Ford was finishing his memoir of Conrad and working on *Some Do Not,* part of his quartet of novels about the war, *Parade's End.* Pound spent the end of his afternoons playing chess with Ford at the Dôme, trying to influence the shape of the magazine. Hemingway returned from Canada and found an apartment on the rue Notre Dame des Champs, a few doors away from Pound. Pound persuaded Ford to use Hemingway as an assistant editor, and Hemingway remembered Ford unsympathically in his memoir of the Paris years, *A Moveable Feast.* Ford was a "heavy, wheezing ignoble presence," Hemingway wrote, a man "breathing heavily through a stained moustache and holding himself as upright as an ambulatory, well-clothed, upended hogshead." Hemingway realized that Ford had not recovered from the war, but he had little patience for his pose of the country gentleman and the "elephantine absurdities" of his conversation. With Ford and Hemingway, Pound had been trying to bridge two generations that seemed incompatible. By January of 1924 the first issue of Ford's magazine appeared—it lasted only one year—and it included part of "Canto XII" and all of "Canto XIII." Beginning with February, Pound contributed a series of notes on music, some of which found their way into the Antheil book.

During this time Dorothy was complaining about the French and the long, dreary Paris winter with its all too brief periods of light. Pound's health had not improved—he came down with a touch of pneumonia—so the Pounds returned to Rapallo. Hemingway, addressing him as "Dear Prometheus," filled Pound in on the Paris gossip, telling him among other things that Basil Bunting, a young poet from Northumberland whose work Pound had admired, had been jailed in Genoa for some drunken disturbance. Pound returned to Paris in May, and in June, Hemingway, along with Jane Heap and Robert McAlmon, took him to see the prizefights. Two years earlier he had been Hemingway's sparring partner; this time he was an observer. During his recuperative stay in Rapallo, he had decided it was time to leave Paris for good. The city had become too popular with Americans who were there only as tourists, not as artists, and who were only interested in carnival. Some of Pound's artist friends had dispersed or no longer seemed quite as interesting. Cocteau, for example, had become addicted to opium after Raymond Radiguet had died of typhoid. Hemingway, Bird, and McAlmon were in Spain for the bullfights. His relations with Joyce had cooled since Joyce showed him a manuscript of poems later published as *Pomes Penyeach*. Condescendingly Pound had recommended that Joyce stuff the poems in a Bible or family photograph album. It was an example of a new brutal insensitivity, and Pound displayed a similar vein of it to Yeats a few years later.

Pound had gotten interested in the work of another poet, also an opium addict, Ralph Cheever Dunning, whose slender collection *Rococo* had won *Poetry*'s verse contest. Dunning, also an expatriate, had spent twenty years in Montparnasse and, according to Paris *Tribune* journalist Wambly Bald, had hardly spoken to anyone during this period. Williams wrote Pound that he thought Dunning's accomplishment was only technical and in the old style. He could not understand why Pound had "taken him up so." Joyce thought Dunning's work was "drivel" and wondered why Pound "defended him as if he were Verlaine." Pound's overly high estimation of Dunning's work was an early sign that his own ability to detect the best in others was no longer infallible. This was a condition he was to recognize in the fall of 1924, and it may have been a factor in his withdrawal from a literary center to Rapallo. When Pound was preparing to leave Paris in October, he procured a supply of opium for Dunning and gave it to Hemingway with instructions to deliver it if necessary. First, however, Pound who had already tried it, initiated Hemingway into smoking the drug. It was the ultimate act of Pound the helper, but also a note of the despair Pound felt at the end of his Paris years. Ironically, after Pound had left Paris, Hemingway tried to deliver the drugs. Dunning, a semirecluse who had spent years staring into space in the cafés of Montparnasse, barraged Hemingway with milk bottles and refused to allow him in.

Pound had been encouraged by Italian friends that Rome would be the place for him to stage his opera. He wrote Nancy McCormack, "Italy is my place for starting things." Italy was alive to every manifestation of modernism, he had told Harriet Monroe when he had finally met her just prior to his departure from Paris: "Italy has civilized Europe twice, and it may be that she has spiritual force enough in her to do it again."

The eulogy for Pound's Paris years was written by Hemingway, who recalled:

> So far we have Pound the major poet devoting, say, one fifth of his time to poetry. With the rest of his time he tries to advance the fortunes, both material and artistic, of his friends. He defends them when they are attacked, he gets them into magazines and out of jail. He loans them money. He sells their pictures. He arranges concerts for them. He writes articles about them. He introduces them to wealthy women. He gets publishers to take their books. He sits up all night with them when they claim to be dying and he witnesses their wills. He advances them hospital expenses and dissuades them from suicide. And in the end a few of them refrain from knifing him at the first opportunity.

Actually, Hemingway was not being overly generous. Pound was leaving Paris because its distractions were too great. And at a dinner organized by the Surrealists an assailant had attempted to stab him. The incident was spontaneous, haphazard, caused in a demented moment of panic that typified the confusion of Surrealist energies, and it was for Pound the clearest indication he could receive of the dangers of Paris. He had begun his stay in the City of Light with an intense admiration for the Dadaists, responding eagerly to the playfulness of their bizarre manifestations. The Surrealists who had succeeded them had moved many members of the artistic community to the left of the political center, but Pound had swerved in an opposite direction. Malcolm Cowley felt that Pound was running away from himself, unable or unwilling to see himself analytically. T. S. Eliot, recalling the "only a nomad" condemnation of Professor Doolittle, felt Pound was a squatter poised for flight with a "resistance against growing into any environment." As far as Pound was concerned, he knew the work he wanted to do on *The Cantos*, and he knew as well that he needed a quieter place than Paris in which to do it.

PART II

PART II

RAPALLO:
THE POLITICS OF ART

I consider myself a one-hundred percent American and patriot.
I am only against Roosevelt and the Jews who influence him.

Pound to Reynolds Packard,
United Press Correspondent

1. THE EXILE

If Paris had been the heart of Europe, Rapallo was the "navel of the world," Pound exclaimed. French is formal, clipped, precise, a haughty elegance for the ear. The language of Racine and Corneille, it was perfect for a dry, logical theater that appealed to the mind and the powers of reason. Italian is more lush, lyrical, more tonally expressive, depending more on broad open vowels and trilling consonants; it is earthier, more musically flourishing, operatic, more a language of the heart. By the "green clear and blue clear" of the almost motionless Tyrrhenian Sea, with its "thin line of broken mother of pearl shoreline," as Yeats put it, with its cypress and olive trees, its heath and ilex groves, its thermal baths and red-tiled roofs, and the background of calming mountains, Rapallo was idyllic. It had some literary tradition. Many English writers had sojourned there for the winter sun, and Keats had described the town in "Ode on a Grecian Urn," perhaps the ultimate romantic poem. Rapallo provided an interesting footnote to American history, as Columbus had returned and landed there after his momentous discovery. A small town with a population of only fifteen thousand, ten thousand were peasants living in the surrounding hills, Pound remembered.

At first the Pounds lived in a hotel. Before Christmas they left for another tour of Sicily, seeking warmer weather, and then visited Taormina, Siracusa, and Palermo. When they returned to Rapallo, they found an apartment facing the sea, with a large terrace, where Pound installed Gaudier's *Hieratic Head,* transported all the way along from Violet Hunt's garden. The

apartment was on the top floor of a small hotel, one hundred steps up.
Pound had brought along his homemade furniture—no one in Paris would
buy it—and devised an intricate system which completely circumvented having filing cabinets for his notes and manuscripts, hanging them from a series
of pulleys overhead to which were attached envelopes. Pound called it his
"active filing system" but it was a semaphore for the bizarre turns he would
take in the next two decades at Rapallo.

Olga Rudge had followed the Pounds to Rapallo carrying a child she
had conceived by Pound during the last month of his stay in Paris. She had
not been interested in the prospect of marriage or children, her music was
enough for her, but she realized the child could provide the possibility of a
continuing connection to the man she loved. The birth took place in July of
1925 in the Dolomite Alps of northern Italy, in Bressanone, a little town
with twelfth-century cloisters and cathedral and a history celebrated by
troubadors. The child, a daughter named Mary, was farmed out to a local
peasant woman whose own infant had died. There is no record of the effect
the birth of Olga's daughter had on Dorothy, who was in England on her
summer visit at the time; Dorothy still must have felt threatened by the fact
of Olga's child and realized that she could no longer be dismissed as one of
Pound's temporary fancies. But five months after the birth of Olga's illegitimate daughter, Dorothy conceived a child. Like Olga, she had been completely uninterested in children. Her son, Omar, was born in the American
Hospital in Paris in September of 1926. Shortly after his birth, Dorothy
deposited him with Olivia Shakespear, who raised him until he was old
enough to be boarded in schools. Dorothy continued her summer visits to
England for the purpose of seeing her son. Pound barely mentioned either
child to friends or in letters. Olga's father had bought her a little house in
Venice right in the area where Pound had lived in 1908. So, when Dorothy
went to England, Pound used to join Olga in Venice.

In Rapallo, Pound was accorded the respect Italians generally have
for scholars or writers, and he was called *il poeta*. It was a role he continued
to play by dressing the part. A journalist writing for *The New Yorker* observed:

> I had been walking about five minutes on the boulevard toward
> the baths when I heard a slight commotion behind me. All around
> people stopped moving. It was as if a fire siren had sounded and
> nobody could hear anything or even move until it had stopped. I
> leaned up against a balustrade and waited. They were all looking
> at a man advancing with giant strides. He was tall and broad, with
> a pointed beard. He had on a white suit that, large though he was,
> literally flowed from him. The spotless trousers wrapped around
> his legs as he walked, the shining coat billowed in the breeze.

There was a towel tied about his waist and the fringe from it bobbed rhythmically. His hat, which was white too, had been slapped on at a dashing angle. He marched by me, swinging a cane, ignoring the awed Italians, his eyes on an interesting point in space.

In January of 1925, *A Draft of XVI Cantos of Ezra Pound for the Beginning of a Poem of Some Length* was published by Three Mountains Press. Only ninety copies were printed because of Bird's policy of small editions that would appeal to collectors. Pound was pleased with the overall design and feel of the book. Glenway Wescott reviewed the book in *The Dial* under the heading of "A Courtly Poet" but the implication was that Pound had strayed far from court and capital to some far province for the forgotten:

> Not long ago Mr. Pound galloped up and down the frontier of criticism like an early American general, cursing the enemy, firing his recruits, and embarrassing the fearless with decorations of praise. The gallant fighter appears to have withdrawn from the hubbub; precocious children now mature in black ignorance, the makers of plaster casts grow rich, uncursed. He devotes his retirement no less than his notoriety to music and verse; the music is composed in forgotten modes, for the flute, and the poems have all been cantos.

When R. P. Blackmur, a young American poet, wrote inquiring about the high price of the book and the small number of copies printed, Pound's cryptic answer was that the American economy was at fault and that five men had been hanged with the poet Villon. Actually, Bird's press was just about paying its way. He published only one more book, Robert McAlmon's *Distinguished Air,* three stories about homosexual life in Berlin, and then sold the press to Nancy Cunard. McAlmon wrote to Pound reporting gossip about London. He had seen Eliot, who was currently worried that Vivien was spreading indescribable rumors about him, alleging that he was homosexual and impotent with women. Eliot, McAlmon felt, was a lost cause, an honest caterpillar, devitalized, his mind "Gosse-pompous" and sentimental; he had at last become Prufrock.

The sixteen cantos had all undergone changes since their original publication, and Pound had omitted three altogether. This opening group, Pound had informed his father, was like a map highlighting the routes he would use in the whole work. There were sections retelling the story of Odysseus, a tribute to Browning, pictures of Provence and the Renaissance of Sigismondo Malatesta where Pound raised the issues of art patronage and usury, the hell cantos describing England. All this was presented in a disjointed, fragmentary style, as in the opening lines of "Canto VII," the first of which line alludes to "The Waste Land":

> These fragments you have shelved (shored).
> "Slut!" "Bitch!" Truth and Calliope
> Slanging each other sous les lauriers:
> *That* Alessandro was negroid.

The difficulties were compounded by a thick texture of intricate reference to myth, fleeting visions of gods and goddesses that attempt to re-create an immediate experience of the pagan world, to ancient and medieval authors and their works, to history, and to a mythic view of Pound's own history as suggested by his allusion to Henry James in "Canto VII":

> And the great domed head, con gli occhi onesti e tardi
> Moves before me, phantom with weighted motion,
> Grave incessu, drinking the tone of things,
> And the old voice lifts itself
>   weaving an endless sentence

Perhaps the most significant of these opening cantos, as well as the most beautiful, is number XIII, the so-called Kung canto, which tells a story about Confucius's teachings. Pound's interest in the material to which he had been introduced by the Fenollosa manuscripts had not abated. He had continued his study of Chinese and his reading of Confucius had become an avocation. "Canto XIII" is important as the measure of a road not taken, the moderation that Confucius prized above all things but that Pound could not accept. Kung walks with his students past the dynastic temple, past the cedar groves and to the river, asking each student to project a future course of action. One says he would put the defenses in order, one imagines himself as the lord of a province and another as a priest in a mountain temple "with order in the observances." The principle is order, both for the state and in the individual:

> And Kung said, and wrote on the bo leaves:
>   If a man have not order within him
> He cannot spread order about him;
> And if a man have not order within him
> His family will not act with due order.

Disorder, the extreme or emotional response, violates the Confucian code of restraint and moderation:

>   "Anyone can run to excesses,
> It is easy to shoot past the mark,
> It is hard to stand firm in the middle."

Early in the spring of 1925, Pound learned of a new possible source of patronage for the modernists, a foundation established in New York by John Simon Guggenheim with a mission to support the arts and humanities. He wrote a twenty-six-page letter to the foundation, recommending that it assist Lewis, "who had invested more in modern art than any other living man save possibly Picasso"; Eliot with a lifetime endowment; and Antheil so that he could stop concertizing and start devoting himself exclusively to composition. Pound was also corresponding with Ernest Walsh and Ethel Moorhead, editors of a new magazine called *This Quarter*, determined to publish what seemed fresh and exciting. The editors warned all "critics, labellers, baptisers, slanderers, experts, reviewers and such" to be careful not to categorize them. They claimed that they were "fickle, wayward, uncommitted to respect of the respectable established armies strong because many." Pound thought the statement was spirited and that the magazine might continue the challenging traditions of *The Little Review*. The first issue, complete with tributes to Pound from Joyce and Hemingway, was dedicated to Pound for "his creative work, his editorship of several magazines, his helpful friendship for young and unknown artists." Pound had proven himself to be the one indisputable enemy of respectability, the editors asserted. The editors of *This Quarter* were peripatetic, disorganized, and desperately short of funds, but they printed cantos XVII through XIX and paid him forty pounds, as much as he would have received from a magazine like *The Dial*. Walsh and Moorhead visited Pound in Rapallo, where Pound made numerous editorial suggestions for *This Quarter*. Walsh also left Pound a group of his poems, but Pound made no offer to help him with them. One of Pound's suggestions was for a special issue on Lewis, but when he wrote to Lewis asking his approval, Lewis replied in angry tones that Pound had "no mandate to interfere when you think fit, with or without my consent, in my career. If you launch at me and try and force on me a scheme which I regard as malapropos and which is liable to embarrass me, you will not find me so docile as Eliot." Lewis had become paranoiac, McAlmon advised Pound. He was editing a magazine called *The Enemy*, the name a sign of his own antagonism. In it he freely ridiculed artists and writers including, D. H. Lawrence, Joyce, Eliot, and Pound.

Walsh was dying of tuberculosis but continued to give all his energies to his magazine. Three issues were printed in Paris, Milan, and then Monte Carlo, the first with a focus on Brancusi, the second organized around Antheil. Walsh died before the third issue, so Moorhead decided to include some of his poems and a number of tributes. She requested that Pound submit one, but he never sent it. In a final, fourth issue of *This Quarter*, Moorhead publicly rebuked Pound.

There were other poets who wanted his approbation. He was visited by Nancy Cunard, whom he had known in his London days as a tall, thin,

tawny blond teenager with a provocatively sexual sway to her walk and skin
as pale as bleached almonds. Nancy had sent him her poems when he was in
Paris, and he had advised her that she had to overcome an obsolete dialect
and her Tennysonian cadences. Recently she had been on a walking tour of
Provence with John Rodker and was eager to discuss what she had seen with
Pound. She also wanted to give him a copy of her book of poems, *Parallax*,
which Virginia and Leonard Woolf had just published. Pound received the
poems more generously than he had Walsh's poems. He realized *Parallax*
was not a major effort, but Nancy had purchased Bill Bird's press and might
be in a position one day to publish Pound or his friends.

By the summer of 1925, Pound seemed to have recovered all of his
high spirits. "Do yew know of any acts of high treason or anyfink that jess
OUGHTER be pulled off?" he wrote to Bill Bird. "Time to sink a ship or
bust a bank or sumfink." The reference to high treason, considering the
development of Pound's career, seems almost like a willful jinx, a taunt to
fate. Of course, Pound's comment was an exaggeration, a metaphor, not an
invitation to pass government secrets or commit espionage. If anything,
Pound always acted openly with the expectation of receiving the utmost
publicity for his acts. He knew he needed to keep his name alive in the
public consciousness, even though he despised that public, because *The Cantos* were so dense and difficult, and the audience they could expect was
getting smaller. The strong opinions would become Pound's volcanic tremors, and they became more central than *The Cantos* during Pound's years in
Rapallo. The style of the letter—slangy, disrespectful, and ornery, the
down-home philosopher who chews his tobacco while reading Plato—was
another way of seeking attention. It is a hillbilly voice, the sound of the
backwoodsman or the frontiersman, Natty Bumppo, not Henry James or
even Whitman. The frontiersman was free of the manipulations of government because he had willfully fled modern civilization, choosing a more
primitive possibility. But the frontiersman would not have given a whoop or
a hoot for the civilization Pound searched for in his cantos, for the columns
at San Zeno or the heavenly city of Dioce he imagined. In American fiction
the frontiersman is usually seen as hating government, which Pound knew
existed under every high form of past civilization, whether under the pha-
raohs or in the city-states of the Greeks. One Pound scholar, Wendy Stallard
Flory, has argued that the hillbilly style is a disguise for Pound's self-consciousness as he sought solutions for the problems of the universe, the comic
persona necessary to soften the pontificatory and authoritative thrust. A less
sympathetic way of looking at the style of his letters is to see it as reflecting a
raw center in Pound's sensibility. The cowboy disguise that he had affected
in London had become integral, and his need to throttle the world's compla-
cency was a willful compensation for the delicacies of poetry.

In the fall Pound was occupied by a number of minor matters and found it difficult to concentrate on the cantos. He was still reading widely but even that became desultory. He had met Carlo Linati, an Italian journalist interested in American writing. Linati wanted to organize a premiere of his opera at La Scala in Milan, but in the end Linati could not arrange the necessary backing. Pound recruited the assistance of Natalie Barney. He encouraged her to continue assisting Antheil:

> No. Go ahead with the Antheil—I don't need cash at the moment and anything that helps A helps me. As the sooner he gets control of some musical power—(I mean executive)—the sooner he will put on my opera. I don't know any other conductor who wd. take the trouble to understand it—and he does know what I want from the instruments. And *rhythmically.*

Barney was eager to start her own literary magazine, but on this matter Pound was not encouraging, feeling she might pack it with her friends, which would be an embarrassment. He asked her instead whether she could revive Bel Esprit for an Italian poet, Emmanuel Carnevali, who had worked as an assistant editor on *Poetry* and had been attempting to translate some of the cantos into Italian. Carnevali was now fatally ill in Bologna and without means. Pound, Barney, and a number of others helped him until he died. Writing to Harriet Monroe about Carnevali, Pound added an appraisal of Mussolini:

> I personally think extremely well of Mussolini. If one compares him to American presidents (the last three) or British premiers, etc., in fact one can NOT without insulting him. If the intelligentsia don't think well of him, it is because they know nothing about "the state" and government, and have no particularly large sense of values. Anyhow, WHAT intelligentsia?

Pound was still trying to help Dunning, who had put together the manuscript for another book, *The Four Winds,* but was unable to find a publisher. He wrote to Hemingway asking about Dunning's condition, to H. L. Mencken, and again to Harriet Monroe, who agreed to print one of Dunning's poems. In December, Pound received a letter from Hemingway, addressed to "Dear Duce." Dunning was "only puke," Hemingway asserted, not worth any more trouble. Hemingway had been boxing, swimming in the ice-cold Seine, and was then preparing to leave Europe for Key West. "You go on and learn everything," he said, referring to Pound's continued explorations of myth and history, the books he needed to read in order to write *The Cantos.* "I can't, I'm limited. But I'm going to know everything about fucking and fighting and eating and drinking and begging and stealing and living and dying." The letter was a characteristic example of Hemingway's own machismo, a statement of his preference for experience over idea, for sensation rather than mind, for activity over books and writing. But the letter was also a form of tacit rebuke. Hemingway believed writers needed to avoid political games. The cynical perspective of his generation was that politics was always poisoned by deceit and compromise, and the writer would inevitably be dragged down and somehow degraded by any involvement with dishonesty.

The winter and early spring of 1926 was a quiet, unsocial period, as Dorothy was pregnant, and for Pound a time when concentration was difficult. Except for a little piece for *The Criterion* on Antheil, he wrote no prose. He was working with "Canto XXIV," mired in his own extrapolations from myth and history and unable to forge ahead. There was, however, something to look forward to. Natalie Barney had helped Antheil produce his *Ballet mécanique,* and a selection from Pound's *Villon* was to follow. First Pound went to Rome with Olga Rudge, who performed works by Erik Satie and Pound's own "Hommage à Froissart," a violin piece that had never been heard in public. Pound then went to Paris to rehearse *Villon* with Yves Tinayre, who sang the leading role, during which he whistled and hummed his score to clarify it for the other musicians. The performance, ten days after the riotous premiere of Antheil's *Ballet mécanique,* was not given the same reception. Pound's spare orchestration and the complex and monotonous score were just not as disturbing or as diverting as Antheil's airplane propeller blowing a cold stream of air into the audience. Pound had seen his opera through, but he soon realized that it would not win him much acclaim. He had chosen to tell the story of a brigand poet who lived outside the social code with impunity, who was seen by those in power as a despicable worm. It could have been a vehicle for a very dramatic conflict, but Pound had used Villon's own poems as his libretto, making the opera more esoteric than it needed to be to reach an audience. Pound had identified with Villon because of the rugged lyricism he heard in the poetry, but it seemed as if he was making a martyr of a man who had lived badly, that the beauty of the poetry was sufficient excuse for any action.

By the fall of 1926, Pound was back in Rapallo. He wrote E. E. Cummings that he was thinking of starting his own magazine. He also wrote to Harriet Monroe, using the tone of admonition bordering on nastiness that *Poetry* had always provoked in him because of its catering to sentimental verse makers:

> Have been looking through your last 18 or more numbers, find many of 'em uncut.
>
> My impression is that you have tried ladies' numbers, children's numbers, in fact everything but a man's number. And that you tend to become more and more a tea party, all mères de

famille, only one fallen woman among them (and 'er with a sob of repentance).

You might as well admit that trying as you may to be catholic, you miss being any kind of arena for *combat;* you get a general air of mildness. . . . Fraid I will have to take the bad boys off your hands and once again take the hickory.

The new magazine was to be called *The Exile,* a word that Joyce had used to name his play and at the very end of *Portrait of the Artist* when stipulating the cautions that any artist would need to take: "silence, exile and cunning." In a circular Pound announced that the magazine would appear three times a year until he got "bored with producing it" and it would appeal to matters that interested him personally. It is possible that Pound had become jealous of Eliot's *Criterion* and the way in which that magazine had helped spread Eliot's reputation. But *The Criterion* was not set up as an organ reflecting Eliot's personal taste, nor was it especially designed to arouse controversy, and Eliot was ready to print the work of writers whom he deplored in private.

Eliot told Ford that he did not expect to agree with contributors to *The Criterion* but to print writers with whom it was worth disagreeing. He wrote Pound that finding contributors of whom they could both approve would be as likely as seeing eye to eye with a cross-eyed man. Pound's attitude was that most of the people Eliot published were not worth agreeing or disagreeing with. As usual he was elitist while Eliot was more centrist and accommodating. Eliot became an editor at Faber & Gwyer (which later became Faber & Faber) in 1927; it was a position he held with distinction until his death, and another reason for Pound to be envious—for Eliot had found a sinecure that put him in daily contact with the world of letters. He called Eliot's criticism "apple sauce" and accused him of bookishness, of writing about writing in order to "rise to his deserved position as arbiter of British opinion." Eliot had to cater to the "feeble and brittle mentalities" of the English with commentary and elucidation, writing about subjects that might easily drive a man like Pound, who preferred a more oppositional style, to the movies.

Joyce was being supported by a patron, Harriet Shaw Weaver of *The Egoist,* and Eliot had a magazine. A literary magazine of his own would give Pound a forum for his ideas and make his presence known. He saw that the literary success of his two fellow modernists was greater than his, and that knowledge served to color his relationship to them in the future. The satirist Max Beerbohm, who also lived in Rapallo, said that Pound often mixed praise with criticism when speaking of his friends: "The treacle of admiration, don't you know, was always strongly tinctured with the vinegar of envy." Beerbohm's remark is highly stylized, like his famous caricatures.

He had drawn Henry James as a huge fat man seen from the rear peeking through a keyhole. Had he done a drawing of Pound, it would have needed to combine Aubrey Beardsley's mood and Cubist angles.

He had been receiving letters from a young journalist in New York, John Price, offering to represent him and other expatriate authors in America. Pound liked the directness of Price's letters and tested him by asking him to intervene with an unscrupulous publisher, Samuel Roth, who was using Pound's name on the masthead of his magazine *Two Worlds* without permission and printing Joyce's work without paying him. When Joyce asked Pound to sign a petition denouncing Roth—a petition already signed by Yeats, H. G. Wells, Virginia Woolf, and Albert Einstein—Pound demurred, feeling that Joyce was using a "mountain battery to shoot a gnat." The real quarrel was with the "whole American people which sanction the state of the laws." Pound had vigorously protested in letters to the Paris *Tribune* a series of laws he felt interfered with individual liberties, in particular the postwar rule on passports governing international movement. Joyce, he felt, was putting personal advertisement ahead of the principle, which was the weakness of the copyright law and the invidious provisions of article 211 of the penal code applying to pornography. For Pound, Roth was symptomatic of an uncontrolled capitalistic evil, one that was entirely condoned and supported by a system that allowed the artist's work to be stolen. Always the firebrand moralist, Pound felt the system was more at fault than Roth was, and the "whole American people" more subject to blame than any particular scoundrel. The remark was only a small seismic tremor, but an advance warning as well of the time when he would take his case against his government to Radio Rome.

As of the end of November, Pound's magazine project was still in the theoretical stage, with Pound still writing long letters to Price outlining his expectations. He wanted to begin with pieces from writers he already respected, like Hemingway and McAlmon, who could provide enough "powder to fill the cartridge." Realizing that Pound's magazine would have too tiny a circulation for anyone to make money from it, Price still mailed out 350 circulars at his own expense notifying people of the enterprise. To capitalize and finance *Exile*, Pound was asking for personal contributions. Archibald MacLeish sent Pound a check for a hundred dollars, taking the opportunity to berate him for a petty, vituperative letter Pound had written to the American ambassador to Italy complaining about passport and copyright laws. It was only one of a stream of such letters, letters full of invective and hatred, that Pound began to send over the next fifteen years.

The correspondence with Price had made Pound realize that he had lost touch with his country and made him think of returning for a visit. He asked Price about the possibilities of arranging a lecture tour. He told Harriet Monroe that he was open to an invitation, but that he would have to be paid well enough to get "a few years free from worry after it." He also wrote a letter to the New York magazine *New Masses,* which it printed in December of 1925, entitled "Pound Joins the Revolution," in which he says, "For the first time in years I have gone so far as to think of making a trip to America." Another reason for the trip was the publication later that month by Boni & Liveright of a new version of *Personae,* a selection of the shorter poems exclusive of the cantos which Pound wanted to see reprinted.

By the end of January 1927, he had received a sufficient number of donations to begin *Exile,* and he had chosen his contributors. He wrote to Joyce, telling him that his installments, called "works in progress," were more suitable for Eugene Jolas's Paris-based *transition* magazine than for *Exile* because the former appeared more frequently. He solicited John Price's assistance in securing American copyright, warning him that it would be "necessary to treat official america as one wd. the inside of a mad house." Pound's plan was for Price to have printed a sample issue including part of "Canto XX" and part of John Rodker's novel, but the copyright bureau ruled this was insufficient. Pound's response to Price was to recommend the "complete annihilation" of all bureaucrats, a characteristic overstatement but alarmingly extremist in the light of the political direction he was to take. Pound considered writing out his rage against the bureaucrats and encouraged Lincoln Steffens to act in a similar manner:

> Is there any solid conservative review that will take an article on the rise of bureaucracy and the general gone-to-hellness of Murkn. life, administration, irresponsible govt. by pimps and placemen etc. Either from YOU (you ought to write it) or from me who might. . . . Or praps you're for having things rot as quickly as possible so that the dead fish will revolute (i.e., turn belly side up).

Pound told Price the magazine could succeed only if it sold enough copies to pay for cost, and he asked Price to find manuscripts in America but discouraged him from sending work by women, saying, "the whole of American publicationdom is submerged with females." Until a "female invents something," he added, "let us conduct this magazine by male effort." In his antifeminist mood, he received an inquiry from Marianne Moore, then working as an editor at *The Dial,* asking whether he had something to contribute. Still smarting from Scofield Thayer's hiring Paul Morand to replace him with the "Paris Letter," Pound archly replied that he did not "propose to do odd bits of journalism for the convenience of a review that throws out my best work."

2. THE REVOLUTIONARY SIMPLETON

Pound usually started his days in Rapallo by writing in the mornings, but his concentration span was short and he needed breaks, a walk by the sea, or if he had more time to spare, a game of tennis or an hour of rowing or swimming. The journalism he had to produce for income took more time than writing poetry. Then there was the reading he had to do without which he could not write *The Cantos*. In the afternoons the Pounds always had tea and sweets, which Pound loved.

While Pound was recovering from minor surgery, Yeats and his wife and Aldington came to Rapallo. Pound saw Yeats daily and Aldington almost as often. The poets would meet for a cappuccino before noon or with their ladies at a small hall where a band played dance music in the afternoons. Brigit Patmore, who had accompanied Richard Aldington, remembered that dancing with Pound was always unusual because he "danced according to no rules I understood." He moved to unearthly beats with odd steps, she claimed, but remembered that Dorothy, the "sweet faithful," loyally pretended that her husband had a wonderful sense of rhythm. Actually, Dorothy detested Brigit Patmore and defended her husband instinctively. The matter was all part of a sexual nexus, a tension for Pound because Brigit had been his lover, but now she was with Aldington, who had married H.D. The sense of liaison was in the warm Rapallo air. Aldington, watching from his hotel window, saw Yeats on the beach in total self-absorption, walking with "sublime unconsciousness" two paces behind a woman who kept looking at him over her shoulder "in an agony of impatience for the rich Irish senator to make improper advances." Yeats had completed his mystical book, *A Vision*, but was still working with his wife on receiving messages from the spirit world. On another afternoon at an outdoor café with Pound, when a perfumed prostitute strolled past, Yeats said he thought he had smelled an odor from another world.

Yeats did not understand the fierceness with which Pound was espousing his new political views. He told Aldington that Pound was a man "who produces the most distinguished work and yet in his behavior is the least distinguished of men." For Yeats it was an instance of what he had called in *A Vision* the "antithetical self," a self-destructive component in personality that subverts idealistic efforts. He had classified many of his contemporaries in astrological terms, and in a draft of the book ranked Pound with Nietzsche as an inhabitant of the twelfth lunar phase, a stage Yeats called the Forerunner, a man who gives advance notice to the world. But by the time the book was published Yeats had removed Pound's name.

Pound was still interested in lecturing in the United States, partly because he thought of it as a way to boost his flagging reputation, partly as a source of income. At the end of March he received a letter from Ford, who had spoken to a representative of the Lee Keedrick Agency and encouraged him to go, "for your star there is on the wax." Indications are that interest in Pound's poetry had diminished considerably. No doubt this had as much to do with the difficulty of *The Cantos* as with the unpopularity of his rash political opinions. In England, Robert Graves had observed that Pound's reputation was sinking. Joyce, in a letter to his patron Harriet Shaw Weaver, said that Pound was capable of "brilliant discoveries and howling blunders." Aldington had written that Pound "has wide knowledge, with strange gaps of ignorance, especially when he leaves the one subject he really knows—i.e. poetry. Possibly his credulity in matters of occultism and economics, for example, is due to a complete lack of the philosophical training so conspicuous in T. S. Eliot." In America, Harriet Monroe asked a young poet, Maurice Lesemann, to report on Pound's influence on the younger generation, and the findings were bleak:

> Miss Monroe has asked me to express what the younger poets now think of Mr. Pound. So far as I can tell they do not think of him. I find no curiosity about him among young people who read or write poetry. Only here and there one runs across some vague knowledge of him. But he is spoken of without enthusiasm.

Another young American poet, Yvor Winters, was to be even more categorically dismissive. In a letter to Pound, Winters said the younger poets of his generation admired him as a stylist but found that his "general mentality seems awfully fuzzy." His capering was scented with lavender and mothballs, Winters continued, but he was like the "village spinster who in spite of everything is still hoping for a husband." Archibald MacLeish had complained to Hemingway that he was "a bit fed up with the Ezraic assumption that he is a Great Man," adding that Pound was as full of fears "as a maiden schoolteacher and as full of shit as a cesspool." Hemingway agreed that interest in Pound's work had faded, arguing that "like all men who become famous very young, he suffers from not being read." In another letter to MacLeish he called Pound an "ass" who "makes a bloody fool of himself 99 times out of 100 when he writes anything but poetry." For Pound, Hemingway offered no recrimination, but he sent him the jawbones of a shark he had caught off Key West. Impressed by the power and tenacity he saw in these jaws, Pound hung them on his living room wall. It was a little lesson in Imagism, the concrete object acting as visible symbol and existing entirely without discourse. For Hemingway, the shark was another reminder of what he saw as the writer's true pursuit, an exact delineation of the struggle with nature.

The most sustained public attack came from an unexpected quarter, Pound's old Vorticist companion Wyndham Lewis, who in the fall of 1927 published his *Time and the Western Man*. Lewis praised Pound as a translator of dead idioms and as a preserver of the past but argued that Pound's "fire-eating propagandistic utterances were not accompanied by any very experimental efforts in his own medium. His poetry . . . was a series of pastiches of old French or old Italian poetry, and could lay no claim to participate in the burst of art in progress. Its novelty lay largely in the distance it went *back*, not forward; in archaism, not in new creation." Lewis admitted that Pound had felt the past as few of his generation had, but that was not in itself revolutionary: "He has really walked with Sophocles beside the Aegean. He has seen the Florence of Cavalcanti; there is almost nowhere in the Past that he has not visited. . . . But where the present is concerned it is a different matter. He is extremely untrustworthy where that is concerned." In terms of current affairs Lewis termed Pound a "revolutionary simpleton," a romantic type who flings open all doors—"whether there is anything inside or not"—for the sake of gesture. For Lewis the gesture had an adverse impact on Pound's poems: "Pound is the true child which so many people in vain essay to be. But some inhibition has prevented him from getting that genuine naif (which would have made him a poet) into his work. There, unfortunately, he always attitudinizes, frowns, struts, looks terribly knowing, 'breaks off,' shows off, puffs himself out, and so obscures the really simple, charming creature that he is." Three years later Lewis wrote a book full of praise for Hitler and his new fascist order, but in 1927 he found fault with Pound's poor intuitions. He saw this problem reflected in *The Cantos*, where Pound saw himself and his contemporaries through precedents in history. In *The Cantos* fragmentation and terseness prevented Pound from committing himself to any comprehensive embracing statement or principle. Clearly Lewis had a point, but he had become reactionary in his paranoia—what he was doing in his book was renouncing modernism, not only whatever was new and interesting about Pound and Joyce and Eliot, but himself as well.

Pound knew that *The Cantos* were problematic. His father wrote, having received the first issue of *Exile*, which included "Canto XX," and requested some explication.

Dear Dad:-/-/Afraid the whole damn poem is rather obscure, especially in fragments. Have I ever given you outline of main scheme::: or whatever it is?

I. Rather like, or unlike subject and response and counter subject in fugue.

A. A. Live man goes down into world of Dead

C. B. The "repeat in history"

B. C. The "Magic moment" or moment of metamorphosis, bust thru from quotidien into "divine or permanent world." Gods, etc.

In Canto XX, fragment in Exile. Nicolo d'Este in sort of delirium after execution of Parisina and Ugo. (For facts vide, I spose, the Encyclopedia Britan.)

    " 'And the Marchese
    was nearly off his head
    after it all.' "

Various things keep cropping up in the poem. *The original world* of gods' the Trojan War, Helen on the wall of Troy with the old men fed up with the whole show and suggesting she be sent back to Greece.

Rome founded by survivors of Troy. Here ref. to legendary founding of Este (condit (founded) Atesten, Este).

Then in the delirium, Nicolo remembers or thinks he is watching death of Roland. Elvira on wall or Toro (subject-rhyme with Helen on Wall). Epi puregos (on wall); peur de la hasle (afraid of sunburn); Neestho (translated in text: let her go back); ho bios (life); cosi Elena vivi (thus I saw Helen, misquote of Dante).

The whole reminiscence jumbled or "candied" in Nicolo's delirium. Take that as a sort of bounding surface from which one gives the main subject of the Canto, the lotophagoi: lotus eaters, or respectable dope smokers; and general paradiso. You have had a hell in Canti XIV, XV; purgatorio in XVI etc.

The "nel fuoco" is from St. Francis' "cantico"; "My new spouse placeth me in the flame of love." Then the remarks of the opium smoker about the men who said under Ulysses.

"Voce profondo": with deep voice.

And then resume of Odyssey, or rather of the main parts of Ulysses' voyage up to death of all his crew.

For Elpenor, vide Canto I

Ear wax, ears plugged so they couldn't hear the sirens.

Neson amumona, literally the narrow island: bull-field where Apollo's cattle were kept.

Ligur aoide: keen or sharp singing (sirens), song with an edge on it.

That gets most of the foreign quotations.

The first number of *Exile* included a two-line joke of a poem by Hemingway and a dull extract from John Rodker's undistinguished novel *Adolphe 1920*. There was a political commentary by Pound in which he noted that both Fascio and the Russian Revolution were interesting phenomena. Pound offered a definition of "republic" which he would repeat frequently in the future: "The res publica means, or ought to mean 'the public convenience.' When it does not it is an evil to be ameliorated or amended out of, or into decent, existence." Pound asserted that America was a "colossal monkey house" whose comic disasters were best captured by H. L. Mencken's *The American Mercury*. He attacked prevailing views of economics and added that the artist was always in advance of any revolution or social change, but no existing political platform considered the importance of art. *Exile* seemed more of an opportunity for Pound to puff his opinions in public than a quality publication. McAlmon had not contributed anything; he was bored with life and had lost interest in writing. Bryher had ended their friendship of convenience and called him fat and brutal. Neither of Pound's friends, Hemingway or McAlmon, had come through, had found the "powder to fill the cartridge," but then a Chicago publisher, Pascal Covici, who had agreed to reprint the Antheil book and who wanted Pound to write a book on machine art, expressed the desire to continue *Exile*.

Pound was at work translating Cavalcanti. A scholar from Seattle, Glen Hughes, wrote with some queries about the history of Imagism and proposed that Pound do another autobiographical piece of the nature of *Indiscretions* for a series he was editing. Pound answered but did not like the idea of autobiography. When Hughes pressed him for another publishing possibility, Pound suggested Confucius, an idea that Hughes responded to, and Pound began, with the assistance of previous translations, working on his version of Confucius's *Ta Hio* or *The Great Learning*. Pound also wrote an introduction to his translation, a piece attacking Western values and bureaucratic governance, but then withdrew it as an "impertinence," realizing he should not use Confucius to batter the State Department, the Wilson and Harding administrations, and the "goddamnability of all monotheistic Jew, Mohammeden, Xtn buncomb."

The second issue of *Exile* was a bit livelier, with poems by Dunning, more of Rodker's novel, a story by McAlmon, a section of Joe Gould's "Oral History" that was mostly about Cummings, and the work of one new poet, Carl Rakoski. There was also the inevitable declaration by Pound in which he argued that the decline of American freedom was due to a loss of distinction between private and public affairs and the tendency to interfere in other people's affairs before establishing order in one's own. Good had been established by Confucius and it consisted of establishing order within oneself—the principle animating "Canto XIII." There was also a page of quotations from Mussolini, Lenin, and de Gourmont, altogether a somewhat incompatible mixture. One new contact as the result of *Exile* was a young Jewish poet from Brooklyn, Louis Zukofsky, who had submitted a long poem called "The" which was the "first cheering manuscript I have read in months." Pound encouraged Zukofsky to meet with Williams and with Marianne Moore.

Moore, who had been helped by Pound with her first book of poems, had been working behind the scenes at *The Dial*, trying to convince her coeditors that Pound was the logical choice for the *Dial* Award, a prize that was not only prestigious but lucrative, since it came with two thousand dollars. Pound was informed that he had won the prize in October but insisted that he could accept the award only for his cantos or his poetry as a whole. In a note for the January 1928 issue an announcement to this effect was made, but in her own editorial note Moore made it clear that the award was just as much for general service to literature. She compared Pound to Anatole France, the French novelist and Nobelist, saying both had done so much to encourage other writers. But where Anatole France "encouraged mostly bad ones, it can be said that Mr. Pound has never made a mistake. When he was foreign editor of *The Little Review*, *The Little Review* was the most interesting magazine of a quarter century." In the same issue of *The Dial*, T. S. Eliot reviewed *Personae* under the title "Isolated Superiority." No one alive, Eliot suggested, had practiced the art of verse with such devotion and austerity; and no one alive had done it with as much success. These were terms of high praise indeed. Pound had had "an immense influence," Eliot maintained, but it was so pervasive and basic that he had no disciples or imitators.

Pound at this time was finding it easier to give himself to *The Cantos* and was encouraged by John Rodker, who agreed to publish a limited edition of cantos XVII through XXVII. In England, Eliot had persuaded his firm, Faber & Gwyer, to publish Pound's *Selected Poems*, which Eliot edited. Pound was busy with his Cavalcanti translations and was contributing again to *The Dial*, which in March printed his translation of Cavalcanti's medieval thought. In an introduction, Pound asserted that the modern world had lost a quality of radiance present in Cavalcanti's world which he had once articulated in *The Spirit of Romance* and now characterized as "the radiant world where one thought cuts through another with clean edge, a world of moving energies." The same words could be used to describe the fragmentation and kineticism of *The Cantos*.

Yeats returned with his wife to Rapallo for the winter and in February of 1928 had written to Olivia Shakespear that the Pounds seemed content and happy, "pleased with their way of life." He told Mrs. Shakespear that Pound was still helping him with revisions of his poems, and he compared his political extremism to that of his former lover, Maud Gonne, the Irish revolutionary. After almost twenty years of working with poems together, Yeats and Pound had developed deep mutual sympathies. Pound wrote to Archibald MacLeish in the fall of 1928 that no one except Yeats and Eliot had "ever stood up to my criticism for a protracted period." Others came "as to a chartered accountant. They are pleased by my statement of assets and displeased by my statement of liabilities." Yeats noted that Pound had a passion for feeding the stray cats of Rapallo who would wait for him at night "knowing his pocket is full of meat bones or chicken bones." In an essay called "A Packet for Ezra Pound," Yeats later chose to interpret the significance of the cat feedings, which he had found peculiar because Pound did not really like the cats. He fed them, all except the fat café cat, because they were oppressed creatures who were treated with contempt. Yeats implies that Pound saw himself as a parallel case and points out how much of Pound's literary criticism praised writers who had been pursued by bad luck or had found themselves in isolated positions.

The third issue of *Exile* appeared that spring with twenty pages of Zukofsky's long poem "The" and Yeats's "Sailing to Byzantium," one of the Irish poet's masterly late poems. Pound printed only a portion of his own "Canto XX," explaining that its opening section was too obscure for it to be separated from the main context of the poem. There was also an editorial comment by Pound in which he maintained: "Quite simply: I want a new civilization." In the April issue of *The Nation*, in a piece called "Where Is American Culture?" he suggested that what he was seeking would probably not occur because Americans had forgotten the best of their former civic values and the capacity for intelligent individualism. The new institutions, the Carnegie and Morgan libraries or the Guggenheim Foundation (which had not accepted any of Pound's fellowship recommendations), were only wasting large sums of money without really knowing how to affect civilization in America. In May, Pound went to Vienna to hear a concert by Olga Rudge and Antheil and met Count Albert von Minsdorff-Pouilly-Dietrickstein, who was an agent for the Carnegie Endowment for International Peace in Europe. With Count Minsdorff, Pound drafted and cosigned a letter to Nicholas Murray Butler, former president of Columbia University, then president of the foundation. The letter listed three principal causes of war which the endowment had failed to study: first, the munitions industry and its intense sale of weapons; second, the trade rivalries caused by "overproduction and dumping"; and finally, the "intrigues of various cliques." The foundation's reply was a cursory form letter of acknowledgment, a fact Pound was never to forgive. In the future he attacked Butler at every opportunity.

From Vienna, Antheil and Olga Rudge traveled to Frankfurt for another concert. Pound accompanied them, eager to meet Leo Frobenius, a German anthropologist whose works Pound had been reading with admiration. Frobenius had used archaeological and anthropological disciplines to study past cultures and had tried to identify revealing patterns, the active elements in an era that characterize it, the "tangle or complex of inrooted ideas," as Pound put it, that constitute *paideuma*. Frobenius suggested that race and culture were inextricably linked. *Paideuma* was useful in deciphering those salient traits defining a culture, the "mental formulation, the inherited habits of thought, the conditioning aptitudes of a given race or time," Pound wrote. Like Pound, Frobenius was an intellectual outsider whose doctoral dissertation had been rejected. Frobenius had only criticism for the German university system and he was never granted a professional chair. Like Pound, he was a wandering exile, spending half of his life as an active anthropologist in Africa. Frobenius had been used by Spengler in his study of the systematic rise and fall of cultures, and Pound felt that by going to Frobenius's writings, he was going to one of the sources of wisdom in his time. He continued to recommend Frobenius's work for years.

When Pound returned from Germany he began searching for an apartment for his parents, who having visited and found the cost of living very low, had decided to live in Rapallo. After thirty-nine years of working for the Mint Homer was ready to retire and since the Pounds had been unable to persuade their son to return to America, they decided to join him. In July the furnishings and the house at 166 Fernbrook Avenue in Wyncote were auctioned off. The proximity of his parents, however genial and loving, did present possible complications. Pound decided to protect his privacy from unexpected parental visits by fitting bookshelves on a door that led to an unused room, and putting the door on a pivot so that by unlatching the door from behind the books it would swing around, making a passage into a small private studio into which either he or Dorothy could disappear.

The fourth and final issue of the *Exile* appeared in the fall. Contributions included a disparaging piece on Gertrude Stein by McAlmon, a long section of poetry and prose by Williams, and another by Zukofsky. Through letters Pound had been attempting to form a new group of young poets around Zukofsky, Marianne Moore, Williams, and Cummings. These included Charles Reznikoff, who had his own press in New York, Carl Rakoski, George Oppen, Meyer Shapiro, who became an eminent art historian, and Whittaker Chambers, who became a Communist dupe and turncoat and testified against Alger Hiss after World War II. Reznikoff set up the Objectivist Press in Brooklyn and Pound tried to get him to translate Frobenius into English. He told Zukofsky he thought there was "capital" in the idea that the next wave of literature would be Jewish, as Joyce had discerned with Leopold Bloom. He also tried to persuade Harriet Monroe to let Zukofsky edit an objectivist number for *Poetry*, and after a year she relented, despite her fear that the material was too dense for her readers.

The last number of *Exile* also had a forty-page political commentary by Pound which touted Lenin for his supposed war on bureaucrats. "If we must have bureaucrats," Pound suggested, "let them be employed in making a concordance to *Hiawatha*, or in computing the number of sand-flies to every mile of beach at Cape May." The ideal official was lazy, well-mannered, and

timid, but the "job of America" would be to drive back the government
into its proper place, that is, "to force it to occupy itself solely with things
which are the proper functions of government." The position was tradition-
ally conservative, about as perennial in American letters as possible, and first
announced by Emerson and Thoreau. *Exile* had had a short life and it had
been intensely political because of Pound's running commentaries. Where
Eliot in his *Criterion* had tried to deal with political principles in a disinter-
ested way, and Eliot had, perhaps disingenuously, described himself as a
"political ignoramus," Pound had begun a raucous one-sided debate with
America.

3. TRUMPETING OF A TERRIFIED ELEPHANT

Pound's work was appearing regularly in *The Dial*, and he was receiving remarkably crisp, poised, and calculated comments from Marianne
Moore—a woman whose life was encapsulated, McAlmon told Pound, in
letters—explaining with a Jamesian fastidiousness of phrase what *The Dial*
wanted as well as the latest gossip about Williams or Wallace Stevens.
Pound's translation of a French biography of Stravinsky appeared in seven
issues of *The Dial*. In November he had a long piece on his friend Williams
called "Dr. Williams' Position." In it Pound tried to explain why a writer
like Williams could accept his country with such equanimity while Pound
raged. Williams was a product of polygot America, which Pound had criticized in "Patria Mia" in 1910. Williams was really European, Pound argued, coming from parents whose blood was mixed with traces of English,
Danish, Spanish, and French with the possibility of a Jewish strain. The
mixture somehow allowed Williams a more generously optimistic view of
American possibilities. "Where I see scoundrels and vandals, he sees a spectacle or an ineluctable process of nature. Where I want to kill at once, he
ruminates." Williams wrote thanking Pound for the sobriety of his essay:
"Nothing will ever be said of better understanding regarding my work," he
surmised. Pound had formulated the essential differences between the two
poets, which went far beyond Williams's earlier remark on how he represented bread and Pound caviar. Williams had spent his life in steady work,
without flashiness or thunder; Pound was the shark, poised and eager for
the ideological kill.

Pound also heard from his friend H. L. Mencken. A bullet-shaped man
with shoulders hardly broader than his head, Mencken's grating humor and
his explosively opinionated views of American life had organized *The Smart
Set* and *The American Mercury*. "Lolling in Italy," Mencken advised, Pound
had missed "the greatest show on earth," the presidential campaign of Al
Smith and Herbert Hoover, which Hoover would probably win, Mencken

predicted, as a "ninth rate country deserved a ninth rate president." Pound could not have felt more in agreement. He had just written that the "slime of bureaucracy" was reflected in the "execrable taste of the populace in selecting its rulers."

Pound's jaundiced reflection on popular taste was part of a piece he was writing for the New York *Herald Tribune* book supplement called "How to Read or Why." The function of literature was to morally cleanse and purify the material of thought and ideas, which depend on language. Whenever the medium of language begins to rot, to get "slushy and inexact or excessive and bloated, the whole machinery of social and of individual thought and order goes to pot." The health and vitality of the social order depended on language and could be measured by the work of the literary artist, his "feel and desire for exact descriptive terms, and it was just as important for the makers of thought to keep language efficient and clean as it was for the surgeon to keep the tetanus bacilli out of the patient's bandages." Pound was now exporting the principles of Imagism to the middle class. What he was saying was hardly original: Carlyle and Emerson had preached the same doctrine, and George Orwell offered a similar platform in England in "Politics and the English Language." But the idea that social problems could be alleviated or solved by purified language or great art was itself a rationalization for artists and dreamers. In Germany at this time, Walter Benjamin was writing that all efforts to make politics aesthetic only culminate in war. Pound classified writers as inventors, masters, or diluters, and his essay selected exemplars from each category, from the classics to the contemporaries, giving his readers what constituted his own literary canon, from Confucius to Homer to Dante to Villon.

Pound was immersing himself in his reading for *The Cantos,* more on the Renaissance, more Confucius, more Frobenius. Eliot had received a ten-volume set of the works of Thomas Jefferson from his father, which he did not want, so he sent it to Pound, who began reading Jefferson and then American Colonial history, all material that he would eventually incorporate in *The Cantos.* But the work was handicapped by Pound's health, which again became delicate with a recurrence of the digestive and rectal disorders he had suffered in Paris.

Yeats once again was in Rapallo in the winter of 1929, writing to Lady Gregory that he saw Pound daily and that they would "disagree about everything." In "A Packet for Ezra Pound" he admitted that he would quarrel more with a man like Pound than anyone else were they not so united by bonds of affection. Discussing *The Cantos* that had already been published, Yeats found he could not discern a plan or a principle behind them. Yeats "often found there brightly painted kings, queens and knaves" but could not understand why the various cantos could "not have been dealt out in a different order."

In his letter to Lady Gregory, Yeats mentioned the presence of Basil Bunting, a young poet from northern England who had become "one of Ezra's more savage disciples" and who was then living in Rapallo. Bunting had served a jail sentence for conscientious objection after the war and was a student of Persian. He spent parts of the next several years in Rapallo, his purpose being simply to talk with Pound and show him his work. He was one of the first acolytes in an informal "Ezuversity," a system of learning based on reading and a kind of loose tutorial discussion with Pound as presiding Confucian master. Except for Yeats, who left by spring, Bunting, and a brief visit from Antheil, there were no visitors in 1929. Pound heard from H.D., who called herself disembodied and said she was suffering from a betrayal of age and a spiritual fatigue. It led her in the thirties to Sigmund Freud in Vienna and sanatoriums in Switzerland. Ford wrote stating he had named a champion Angora goat after Pound. He heard also from Upton Sinclair, a radical novelist living in California who had vigorously protested against the economic injustices of the capitalist system, a system that seemed prepared to collapse because of the unprecedented rate of bankruptcies in America and the crisis in the stock market. Pound proposed to Sinclair the idea of a group of writers effecting a change in public consciousness if they could "all shoot simultaneously on certain definite infamies," by publishing essays or letters to editors in fifty different newspapers. Pound also received letters from R. P. Blackmur and Lincoln Kirstein, who were starting a new magazine, *Hound and Horn*, which would publish cantos XXVIII through XXX in 1930, but in general Pound's correspondence had tapered off because of his poor health.

In the spring, with Olga Rudge and his father, Pound went to Gais to visit his daughter. Mary, blond and blue-eyed, was being raised by German-speaking peasants on a farm in very simple circumstances. When shoes were necessary, the cobbler would come for a sizing. At bedtime Mary dipped her hand in holy water and touched her forehead. The only books in the house were lives of Christ and the saints. In the summer Pound accompanied Dorothy to London to be tested by doctors and to see his son, Omar, who was now four. Henry Hope Shakespear had died and Olivia was living in an elegant flat in Kensington which had in it three abstract stone sculptures by Gaudier. Omar was in the Norland, a nursery nearby, learning German and French along with English and being raised as a proper English gentleman, although without the advantages of a normal domesticity.

In the winter of 1930, Pound was visited by the anthologist Louis Untermeyer and his wife, Jeanne, who wanted to show Pound her poems. She described Pound still wearing his velvet jacket and open Byronic collar and a large beret. He was still his "voluble, exuberant, and exasperating self," but she found he lacked social grace, lolling back in his seat, interrupting her, and listening reluctantly. Pound typed out a cursory autobiographical statement for Louis Untermeyer which reveals how isolated he felt; in it he claimed that no American publisher had even taken a book on his recommendation, that no university had ever invited him to teach, that none of the candidates he had sponsored had ever received a fellowship, that he had never been asked to sit on a literary jury.

No one Pound knew came to Rapallo that winter except for Yeats, who was bedridden. The truth was that Pound did not even want to see Yeats and that he had become accustomed to his own isolation. Pound used the excuse of his fear of infection to postpone any visit to Yeats. When the two poets finally met in April, they argued about Confucius, whom Yeats did not admire, saying that he should have worn an eighteenth-century wig and preached in St. Paul's Cathedral. While Pound felt that Yeats's rejection of Confucius was stupid, it actually was symptomatic of the breach that had already divided the two men. In his last years Yeats had become ceremonial, magisterial, Olympian in his attitude toward the world. At the same time he seemed deeply unhappy, unfulfilled, and dissatisfied by his own accomplishments as a poet. Pound emphasized the discontent, reminding Yeats that though his diction had become modern thanks to their joint efforts at Stone Cottage, Yeats had never really become a modernist because he had never been able to break with the rhythms and harmonies of the nineteenth century.

Yeats did lack a certain magnanimity and the ability to learn from his peers. Pound had been the exception. The two men had connected profoundly. They had been practically brothers in poetry—because of the close friendship of their wives, if for no other reason. In the decade since the three winters that Pound had spent at Stone Cottage, he had been more intimate and comradely with Yeats than with any other poet. But Yeats could not help but notice Pound's developing intemperance, his abrasiveness, his insensitivity to the possibility of other perspectives, especially if they were political. Like Pound, Yeats had gone far beyond the Art for Art's Sake poetic narcissism of the 1890s exemplified by William Morris's notion of the poet as "idle singer for an empty day." Yeats had chosen a more public path, he had become a senator in the Irish Free Republic, he had been awarded the Nobel Prize, and he had been recognized—even though, and perhaps because, he had remained free of marked, ideological commitments. He had not proselytized or campaigned but was chosen as a man in whom one could have faith, a man who would do the right thing. As with Eliot and Joyce, writers whom Pound had "discovered" and certainly pushed, the coolness came as their recognition grew, and the excuse was politics.

And political questions were becoming more and more central. Pound was interviewed by a stringer for the Paris *Tribune* who reported Pound's attack on the Carnegie Peace Endowment. In letters Pound had called its

president, Nicholas Murray Butler, a "bloated crab" and a "muddle-headed
sandbag." To the readers of the Paris *Tribune,* Pound offered his theories on
the origins of war: "Usurers provoke wars to impose monopolies in their
own interests, so that they can get the world by the throat. Usurers provoke
wars to create debts, so that they can extort the interest and rake in the
profits resulting from changes in the values of monetary units." The statement had a nice, simple ring to it, but it was an oversimplification of history
and world events. In Germany the Nazi Party was about to win six and a
half million votes in the national elections, establishing itself as a force on
the European political map.

In France, Nancy Cunard had moved Bill Bird's printing presses from
the Île St.-Louis to Réanville, a small country town where she had established Hours Press and began to set type herself. Uninhibited, a compulsive
drinker, with a free life-style that had involved numerous lovers, probably
including Pound and Louis Aragon and a black American jazz musician
named Henry Crowder, she had remained faithful to Pound in friendship
and at the end of August published *A Draft of XXX Cantos.*

In the fall Pound returned to his cantos, working on the sections dealing with Colonial American history and Jefferson. He was also finding time
for angry letters to the Paris *Tribune,* attacking American magazines like
Harper's, Scribner's, and the *Atlantic Monthly,* and then the American Academy of Arts and Sciences, which he claimed had done nothing to advance
art in America. He received a personal reply from Henry Seidel Canby,
editor of the *Saturday Review* and a member of the Guggenheim Foundation
governing board, answering what he felt were scurrilous attacks. Pound was
too dogmatic, Canby claimed. He was frequently right but often extrava-
gantly wrong, and more capable of saying foolish things than was any other
writer he knew. But some dam of anger and resentment in Pound seemed
to have burst and he could no longer hold back his rage. In a letter to *Our
Nostrum,* a little New York magazine, Pound complained about the "stink"
caused by the Harding administration, *The Saturday Evening Post,* prohibi-
tion, passport regulation, and the "saccharine of our 'leading magazines.' "
He noted a principle which became a keynote for him in the 1930s: "Dis-
gust is a very valuable emotion. . . . Personally, I experience a strong desire to annihilate certain states of mind and their protagonists. Even so
distinguished a critic as Eliot mistakes my expression of hate for humor."
He sent the *American Mercury* a vituperative little essay on bureaucracy,
passports, and American culture which Mencken immediately returned,
warning Pound that he was describing "an imaginary United States. All you
say or can say has been said 10,000 times before and by better men." If he
published the piece, Mencken advised, Pound would be disgraced. Instead,
he suggested that Pound return to see the country for himself. Pound seems
to have been aware of the element of paranoid fantasy in his prose declara-

tions. "It may be that my weekly writings are no more articulate than the trumpetings of a terrified elephant," he wrote. But the elephant's blare serves its purpose, he added, "to warn its contingent herd."

For a leftist publication from New Mexico called *Front* he wrote a "Credo" in which he called Eliot a corpse, recommended Confucius and Ovid, and announced his belief that "a light from Eleusis existed through the middle ages and set beauty in the song of Provence and Italy." The "Credo" was brief, disjointed, and almost incoherent, and the reference to Eleusis was offered without any context, like a surrealist thrust. It was a sign of how desperate, erratic, and marginal Pound had become.

Pound started writing to congressmen and United States senators, promulgating the theories of Social Credit, which he believed could be used to alleviate the Depression. He asked Senator Bronson Cutting of New Mexico for the names of others who might be sympathetic to his views and Cutting recommended half a dozen names. He found out that Senator Smith Brookhart of the Committee on Interstate Commerce had attacked the Federal Reserve System and began writing to Brookhart, quoting part of one of his speeches in a canto, telling him his speech was one of the most important historical documents of the time.

The Dial had ceased publication after the Wall Street crash in 1929 and afterward Pound tried to convert the imperturbable Marianne Moore to his views: "Wot yeh don't see IZ that surrounded by the desolate waste barbarism of our unspeakable fatherland, you are so thankful for a scrap of kulchuh no matter how scrofulous the container, that you lose sight of main issues." To Williams he wrote of the illusion of American "freedumb."

In the spring of 1931, Pound was corresponding with several editors who were interested in his writing. Caresse Crosby, who with her husband, Harry, had run the Black Sun Press until his suicide, sought to change its focus from a small press printing finely produced books to a more commercial house specializing in cheap reprints of avant-garde literature. Pound had contributed an essay of tribute to a book of Harry Crosby's prose, and Caresse asked him what writers he thought were worth publishing, a question that delighted Pound because it made him feel he was back at the center of a literary situation. Pound recommended volumes of short stories by Wyndham Lewis (even after Lewis's attack on him in *Time and the Western Man*), McAlmon, and a new writer, James T. Farrell. He also recommended Joyce's play *Exiles*, Cummings's *The Enormous Room*, and Mike Gold's *Jews Without Money*. The editors of *Pagany* wanted a contribution and Pound gave them cantos XXX through XXXII, which present extracts from Jefferson's letters and prose. In *The New Review*, a Paris magazine begun by Samuel Putnam, he contributed a note on obscurity in poetry that applied to the most recent cantos, remarking that the ideal poem should "swallow its own

notes," which might make obscurity more likely but which would increase
the poem's possible depth.

Pound was also encouraging Louis Zukofsky, who had been teaching at
the University of Wisconsin and needed to publish a critical piece, to expli-
cate *The Cantos*. Zukofsky found the going much rougher than he had anticipated, but Pound pushed him to continue: "So far as I know no one else has
writ. a crit of me AFTER reading the work. This method has advantages.
Also, so far as I know you are the first writer to credit me with an occasional
gleam of intelligence or to postulate the bounds or possibility of an underlying coherence." While Zukofsky was finishing his essay, Pound sent him
quatrains in mock Yiddish. At one point Zukofsky spent a night in New
York City at the New Weston Hotel—"the drain wot swallered all the
fambly forchoons"—once owned by Pound's Aunt Frank, the woman who
had introduced him to Europe at the age of twelve. When the essay was
finished Eliot published it in *The Criterion* and Carnevali translated it for an
Italian publication.

4. THE MESSIANIC WARRIOR

On October 30, 1931, Pound reached his forty-sixth birthday. There
was no celebration: he read and worked on a canto and had tea with Olga
Rudge and a quiet dinner with Dorothy at the Albergo Rapallo. The day
was not set aside for reflection or self-assessment; that was not part of
Pound's nature. Wyndham Lewis had remarked that he had never known "a
person less troubled by personal feelings." But a study of Pound's own
paideuma, the salient clues in the geography of a region or a personality, the
habits of mind and feeling that constitute a person, shows that in Italy he
had changed. He was still thinking about poetry as a connection to the
Eleusinian mysteries practiced by the Greeks in their nomadic stage, now
obscured by history and part of myth, a combination of sexual release and
god worship. He had argued that the troubadors were the last group to
have remembered the Eleusinian mysteries and his long study and translation of their poetry had been profoundly formative. Essentially the
troubadors' poems projected two possible prototypes for male action: the
lover and the warrior. As a young man in London and Paris, Pound had
delighted in the lover role; he had loved women like H.D. and Bride
Scratton and Brigit Patmore, and he had been a lover of letters and of the
past. This love was perpetuated in *The Cantos*. But in Italy the warrior role
was becoming more central. Of course, the combative urge was not new—
this was a quality that Pound demonstrated in college with debating and
fencing. By choosing in his early poems figures like Bertrand de Born, or
like Sigismondo Malatesta in *The Cantos*, Pound was projecting the myth of

the superior individual who has no fixed scruples, a Nietzschean figure who is all thrust and action without guilt or reflection. De Born and Malatesta as warriors who fought on the field of battle knew the motivating power of hatred. Another of Pound's masters was Dante. Commenting on how much of Dante's work was compounded of gossip about his contemporaries, Ford Madox Ford observed that he was "propelled by a deep, an almost venomous hatred for what he did not stand for in his civilization." The same words could be used to describe Pound through the thirties. Dante's cruel and often nasty obsession with justice was part of a tactlessness that led to his own exile. It was the reflection of an idealized devotion to a past that he had invented, just as Pound chooses to emphasize the glory in a Malatesta rather than the unscrupulousness that allows him to sell his services to the highest bidder. By choosing a figure like Villon, Pound shifts his persona to that of the literary warrior who because of his creativity is in touch with ecstasy, not "the whirl or madness of the senses," as Pound described it in *The Spirit of Romance,* but "a glow arising from the exact nature of the perception." Villon becomes the exemplar of Pound's idea of the literary warrior because he never lies to himself; he is the only poet without illusions, Pound tells us in *The Spirit of Romance.* Speaking with "unvarnished intimate speech," he writes what he sees with "the stubborn pertinacity of one whose gaze cannot be deflected from the actual fact before him." As thief, panderer, and possibly murderer, Villon preaches the wisdom of the street and also puts himself, like Malatesta, beyond the accepted moral code. Unlike Pound, however, Villon had no literary ambitions or consciousness of fame; he never sought a persona or a role—he was it.

Pound's concept of the literary-prophetic warrior was a graft based on multiple possibilities. He had maintained in one of his earliest poems, "Histerion," that all poets could speak through him, that the bardic tradition of the past, of Li Po or Confucius or Browning, could resonate once again through his voice. Thus, the timelessness of *The Cantos* is set in a historical present where Tiresias or Dante can become active, existent, and believed in. And belief is particularly important: Pound needs to believe in the power of his pagan deities to make them live in his poem. He had a rare capacity for belief in an era of increasing pessimism because of the catastrophes of war and economic depression. It was an essential part of his naïveté. But he also believed he was a Master of Understanding, that he could learn the intricacies of any subject through sheer mental exertion, and he turned to political theory, economics, government. On the one hand, his legacy had been government because of his Wadsworth ancestor who had protected the Connecticut charter, and his grandfather Thaddeus Pound; on the other hand, there was the memory of horse thieves in the Loomis family on his maternal side that allowed him to rebel from existing law if it did not suit his purposes. This was the frontier side of Pound, his own identification with his birth in Hailey, Idaho, and the code of Western independence and freedom from government. The myth of the frontier was that a man could take matters into his own hands when frustrated by impeding law. It was a time of sudden, direct action, whether that meant a lynch mob or a raid into Indian land. Pound could accept the contradictions of lawgiver and lawbreaker. His father had been a land agent in Hailey who had represented government control; Social Credit involved total government control of the money supply as well. And before long Pound was advocating control of working hours, and government programs for eugenics and birth control.

A few days before Pound's birthday, BBC Radio in London did a broadcast of the complete *Villon*, now rearranged for violin accompaniment. Set in a cathedral and a brothel, the fourteenth-century vagabonds expressed themselves in the dialects of Chicago gangsters. The opera drew mixed notices, though Pound's friend John Rodker wrote that it would take its place in the operatic repertory. Pound was paid fifty pounds and he was excited about the format of radio, feeling it would allow him to reach large audiences who had never heard of the poets who interested him. The potential of radio was just beginning to be appreciated. Pound himself did not even have one in his house, but it appealed to the messianic fever that was beginning to flame in him. Radio was a way to take poetry and ideology off the printed pages where they had failed to move an audience to action and into the air as the troubadors had done with their songs—it was the machine age reinterpretation of the thirteenth century. Pound was encouraged to begin another opera, now using the Cavalcanti material. As with *Villon*, Cavalcanti's poetry was used autobiographically and for its insights into the social and political nature of the times. Unlike the *Villon*, however, the Cavalcanti was not produced in Pound's lifetime.

Shortly after his forty-sixth birthday, Pound began dating his letters according to the Fascist calendar, which began with the year 1922 and the march on Rome. He had expressed the greatest contempt for the English but he observed the spread of the fascist movement there, the result of the inspiration of one man, Sir Oswald Mosley. Mosley was a member of the British ruling class whose first marriage to the daughter of Lord Curzon, foreign secretary and formerly viceroy of India, was attended by King George V. Adolf Hitler attended his second wedding and his sister-in-law fell in love with the German Chancellor; at the outbreak of the war, she committed suicide. Mosley had been wounded twice in the First World War and at twenty-three had become the youngest member of Parliament. He called for nationalization of the banking system at the start of the depression and government control of currency and credit, ideas all compatible with Douglas's Social Credit. In 1932 he formed the British Union of Fascists and his followers, wearing black shirts and some carrying rubber truncheons, marched through London. Later, Mosley's men launched physical attacks on London Jews, looting their stores and smashing windows in an attempt to imitate the sort of terrorism Hitler had used so effectively in Germany. But the British did not sympathize with such tactics, and an important supporter, Lord Rothermere (whose wife had backed Eliot's *Criterion*), began to withdraw his support.

Pound was writing to Zukofsky again, urging him to visit Europe. When Zukofsky's application for a Guggenheim grant was denied, Pound blamed it on a "capitalist syfilization" which would not support the arts. He explained that he himself was short of money because he had subsidized the publication of his Cavalcanti translations when a publisher went bankrupt with only one half of the book set in type. He could not hope to employ Zukofsky and "it was a mystery how I bloody live ennyhow. Mebbe on imagination." Actually, since 1914 the Pounds had relied on Dorothy's income, which had at least during the 1920s been supplemented by dividends from stocks in Valvoline Oil, Colgate-Palmolive, Gillette Safety Razor, Curtis Publishing, and the Savoy Plaza Corporation—a modest but still quite capitalist portfolio.

Pound was beginning to hear reports of hard times in the United States, which he accepted as a confirmation of his admonitions since "Patria Mia" in 1913. Mencken wrote that all the optimists were in breadlines, that Hoover had been "unbearably offensive," and that the country "begins the New Year in the depths of despair." From Morton Dauwel Zabel, who was currently editing *Poetry*, he was informed that he had only a "remote idea of the economic desolation and horror which deepens all over America. The stagnation and hunger get steadily worse." In a magazine called *Contempo*, published in South Carolina, Pound offered a solution to increasing misery based on Douglas's formula. Douglas, he asserted, had discovered that what was called the necessary price of any given article was a "fake, a superstition of bookkeeping." By selling goods below what traditional bookkeeping calculated as their cost, "you can release all the tied up food, clothes, etc., all the tied up goods that everybody can't buy, provided you arrange to have credit (government paper) distributed in some way that will temporarily cover the paper losses incurred in sale." The deep contradiction here is that Pound was asking for more and more government control while preaching on the soapbox of individual freedom, which was incompatible with such controls. Pound's scheme would be financed by deficit financing, which is Keynesian, what Pound deplored and railed against.

In January of 1932 Pound's translations of Cavalcanti appeared. He described the book on its title page as "pieced together from the ruins." He had tried a number of times to convince authorities at the University of Pennsylvania to award him the doctorate he felt he deserved, and he submitted the *Guido Cavalcanti Rime* in lieu of a dissertation, but he was told he was still missing requirements that could only be fulfilled on campus. This

provoked Pound into writing to Felix Schelling, his former professor, who
had been partly responsible for blocking Pound's academic career twenty-
five years earlier. Schelling was harsh in his refusal to help: "If you had not
expatriated yourself long since, but had remained in deplorable America to
help somewhat in the realization of at least an approach to better ideals, you
would not find yourself so hopelessly embittered toward the mediocrities
which after all so make up the world." Schelling's letter was signed, "Your
one time teacher who failed to communicate to you anything like liberal-
ity." Pound's reply was that Schelling had been one of the least tolerant
men he had ever met. He denied any bitterness, adding that "everyone
marvels at my good nature" and that he had expatriated because the "country would not feed me."

That Pound could so blithely deny his anger shows either a strategic
deviousness or a marked lack of self-awareness. He had been invited to a
dinner in New York honoring his old friend Lincoln Steffens, whose autobiography was being published, and Pound's ungracious reply to Steffens's
editor is acidic:

> The problem whether a country that does not provide me
> with $50 a month in regard to my literary work should be re-
> garded as a country or a shit house is one that I cheerfully leave to
> posterity.
>
> But I certainly shall not spend money on congratulatory
> cables until the situation has changed.
>
> I have great respect for Mr. L. Steffens but until you or some
> of the god damned plods can run a publishing house that will use
> at least 1% of its profits in printing literature that I care to read I
> can not see that I need to assist you in your prandial celebrations.
>
> I am perfectly willing to go further into detail on proof from
> you of interest in starting an intellectual life in our devastated
> fatherland.

Pound's letters had turned rancid and some of his friends told him so.
When he abused English publishing to his old friend Ernest Rhys, Rhys
responded that Pound was too good a poet and man to be "crying Rotten
Fish in the literary Billingsgate" and how "inevitably the man with a grievance misses his contemporary dues." Rhys pointed out that Pound had put
enough energy and profanity in his letter to kindle a new inferno, implying
that such energies should be directed to his own creative work.

Pound was working on "Canto XXXIV," reading *The Diary of John
Quincy Adams* and Allan Nevins's edition of *American Political, Social and
Intellectual Life.* He extracted thirty-four pages of material from the Adams
diaries and reduced them to eight for the canto. The presentation is dense.
There is no narrative thread to provide context, and though it becomes

apparent that most of the material revolves around the War of 1812, in general the accumulation of fact quenches any possible fire. Pound was also interested in the career of Martin Van Buren, who had been president of the United States in 1837–41. He bought a copy of Van Buren's autobiography and began basing a canto on it. He was also writing his *ABC of Economics,* in which he presented two sensible ideas. One was to reduce unemployment caused by the depression by having a twenty-five-hour workweek, and the second was Jefferson's principle that "no nation has the right to contract debts not payable within the lifetime of the contractors," which would be about nineteen years. He was also writing letters to Treasury Secretary Henry Morgenthau. They were answered by polite notes of acknowledgment from Herbert Gaston, Morgenthau's assistant. He told Morgenthau that Keynes and the London School of Economics were a pack of knaves. He advised Morgenthau to read Douglas and recommended that Nicholas Murray Butler be incarcerated. He warned that if the New Deal brings "in the dole and filthy idiotic British methods" to combat the depression, "some hygiene expert will shoot the lot of you."

Joyce had been asked to lecture at an international gathering in Florence and declined, suggesting Pound because he had translated Cavalcanti, who was Florentine. Pound was elated at the invitation, writing Zukofsky that "Merejkowsky, Stefan Zweig, Pirandello, yours very truly and some lesser lights are asked to orate at the gran Fiera del Libro in Firenze this month, representing internashunal licherchoor . . . Me first offishul Honours." He added that he had also seen Marinetti in Rome and had returned with a supply of Futurist and Fascist literature. He had once distrusted Marinetti in London and found him a fool, but in Italy relations were different. Pound had brought his daughter on his visit and Marinetti had given her a treatise on how to transform milk into synthetic wool, a sign that his mind was still working in peculiarly incoherent patterns. At this time there was a plan to publish Pound's collected prose, but it called for the cooperation of several small publishers, one of whom went out of business before the project could get any momentum. In New York the Objectivist Press considered attempting a twenty-volume edition, but that proved too expensive a venture, and it was all the press could do to publish Williams's *Collected Poems.*

Another old friend then offered opportunity. A. R. Orage had returned to England to begin a new review, *The New English Weekly,* which became an organ for Social Credit and a forum for Pound, who contributed 180 items between 1932 and the beginning of the war. He continued writing letters to newspapers and began writing in Italian for *Il Mare,* the Rapallo newspaper which printed sixty of his pieces over the next seven years and translated earlier essays by Pound. Pound also joined with Ferruccio Cerio in writing a filmscript on the history of fascism, but the film was never made. He was reading about armaments manufacture, and he wrote to William Bird in Paris asking about the rumor that much of the press in Paris was controlled by an armaments group known as the Comité des Forges. Bird thought that his fear was groundless and that he had been the victim of conspiracy theories.

Another writer given to belief of conspiracy in Paris who had the same fixated hatred for the world that became Pound's obsession in the thirties was Louis-Ferdinand Céline, whose *Journey to the End of Night* was written with uninhibited vernacular bitterness and an exasperation that led to invective, rage, and explosion. Céline's personal journey would a few years later bring him to the courtroom to face treason charges. And another enraged Frenchman who influenced Pound, and Eliot as well, was Charles Maurras, who had formed the L'Action Française, an anti-Semitic right-wing political movement. Maurras believed that international financiers governed by Jewish interests, particularly those of the Rothschild family, represented a basic social evil. Jews were dangerous because since biblical times they had based their culture on egalitarian principles. For Maurras, equality was poison and he believed Jews should be deprived of their political rights.

Farrar and Rinehart had decided to publish *A Draft of XXX Cantos* in New York with Eliot's firm, Faber & Faber, bringing out the English edition. An editor at Farrar and Rinehart named Ogden Nash, a humorous versifier, was an admirer of *The Cantos.* He had pushed the publishing house into accepting the work and saw the volume through the press. Ford wrote to John Farrar, offering to contact a group of Pound's friends to solicit testimonials because Pound "is not half as much recognized in his own country as he should be." Farrar agreed to publish an accompanying pamphlet and Ford gathered the testimonials from Hemingway, Eliot, Joyce, H.D., and Archibald MacLeish. Joyce acknowledged Pound's "generous campaign on my behalf," noting that "it is probable that but for him, I should still be the unknown drudge that he discovered—if it was a discovery." Hemingway was more sweeping in his comments: "Any poet born in this century or in the last ten years of the preceding century who can honestly say that he has not been influenced by or learned greatly from the work of Ezra Pound deserves to be pitied rather than rebuked. . . . The best of Pound's writing—and it is in *The Cantos*—will last as long as there is any literature."

5. IL DUCE IN FEATHERED BOA

But Pound was prepared to receive a more insidious and unfortunately intoxicating sort of testimonial. Olga Rudge had performed for Mussolini, and had described Pound to him. Pound had written to Mussolini's private secretary expressing the desire to meet Il Duce and enclosed a copy of *The Cantos*. At the end of January 1933, Pound took the train to Rome and was ushered into the grand room at the Palazzo Venezia where Mussolini received distinguished visitors, and he saw *The Cantos* on Mussolini's large desk. He presented Mussolini with an eighteen-point digest of his economic theories, a document that Mussolini brushed aside, remarking instead that he had found *The Cantos* "divertente"—entertaining. It was perhaps the last thing one would expect to hear about a work so swollen with the gravity of history. Instead of accepting Mussolini's comment as a graciously dismissive compliment, Pound found it an evidence of his discerning ability. He became an instant believer in Mussolini's genius and his favor for the arts. Like Malatesta, Mussolini was a strong man, a man of order who would organize Italy. Of course, many other Americans were enthusiastic about Mussolini, especially in the business community, because he made things work. The American ambassador to Italy during the twenties, Richard Washburn Child, was one of Mussolini's biggest supporters and wrote an enthusiastic introduction to a biography of Mussolini. Churchill's *Memoirs* reveal that he too was full of admiration for Mussolini until the invasion of Ethiopia. In a book Pound began writing comparing Mussolini to Thomas Jefferson—surely the most maladept parallel in the history of American writing—Pound wrote that Mussolini was "an OPPORTUNIST who is RIGHT, that is, has certain convictions and who drives them through circumstance, or batters and forms circumstance with them." Mussolini's concern was not for the machinery of the state, the bureaucracy, but for "Italy organic, composed of the last ploughman and the last girl in the oliveyards." Mussolini was a great man, Pound believed, because of the swiftness of his mind; his honesty was reflected in the speed with which his real emotion was shown in his face. Mussolini, in one of the flourishes that disguised his real purposes, had once proclaimed that poetry is a necessity for the state, and Pound seized on the remark, convinced that Mussolini was a new Confucius. But Mussolini's master was Machiavelli, and Pound remained astonishingly oblivious to his duplicity. The essential theory of the Corporate State which even Lenin admired had been that the trade union organization would be integrated as a responsible part of the state's machinery of government; in fact, however, Mussolini had gained power by burning the offices of the unions in 1922. But for Pound, Mussolini was a man with ideas for improvement, with plans for combating crime, usurers, and munitions makers, a man who would fight the money hoarders and aristocrats, drain the swamps, start restorations, new buildings, and an artistic as well as political revolution. Pound admitted that any full appraisal of Mussolini was partly based "on an act of faith, it will depend on what you believe the man means, what you believe he wants to accomplish."

In his forty-first canto, Pound eulogizes his meeting with Mussolini:

> "Ma questo"
> said the Boss, "è divertente."
> catching the point before the aesthetes had got there;
> Having drained off the muck by Vada
> From the marshes, by Circeo, where no one else would have
>   drained it.
> Waited 2000 years, ate grain from the marshes;
> Water supply for ten million, another one million *"vani"*
> that is rooms for people to live in.

The meeting with Mussolini increased Pound's interest in economic and political questions. He wrote C. H. Douglas that he had "never met anyone who seemed to GET my ideas so quickly as the boss." He promised to try to arrange a meeting for Douglas. He wrote to Senator L. J. Dickson complaining about the "syphilis of capitalism," a phrase he often repeated in the thirties, and sent a lecture on economics to Senator Lynn Frazier of North Dakota. He wrote the monetary reformer and Fascist sympathizer Arthur Kitson that he was more concerned "with getting ideas into the heads of a few men near the center of power in the U.S. than with saving England, which seems to me the blackest country in Europe, and the last where intellectual and social progress is going to occur." He wrote to John Gould Fletcher, then back in Arkansas, exhorting him to become politically more aware and to write a column of American notes for *The New English Weekly*. He heard from Eliot, who complained about the "obsxurity" of Pound's "episstlary stile" while suggesting that *The Cantos* could be made more humanitarian. Eliot was lecturing at the University of Virginia, offering his own contemptuous dismissal of American civilization, a society "worm-eaten by Liberalism" which had been "invaded by foreign races" and had lost its valuable homogeneity and was now being corrupted by "free-thinking Jews."

In early spring of 1933, Zukofsky came to Europe, with Pound and Williams contributing to his expenses. In Rapallo he slept at Homer and Isabel Pound's, had his meals with Bunting and his wife, and took tea with Pound every afternoon. Pound had corrected proofs for his *ABC of Economics*, which Faber & Faber published later that spring, and was working on his *Jefferson and/or Mussolini*. At the end of March he delivered a series of ten lectures on economic theory at the Luigi Bocconi University, a commercial college near Milan. His subject was the material on which he had based his cantos—the economic principles of the American founding fathers. There were separate talks on Jefferson, Adams, and Van Buren, on the history of economics, and on the function of literature. He was publishing letters and articles on economics in virtually any organ that would accept his thoughts. In a little magazine in Cincinnati, Ohio, called *The Outrider* he argued the advantages of Douglas's Social Credit over Marxism; capitalism had failed to distribute purchasing power and Douglas showed how it could be returned to the people. In the New York *World-Telegram* he published "Some Thoughts on Fascism" and a series of letters in the London *Morning Post*. In *The Criterion*, in the summer of 1933, he had a piece called "Murder by Capital" in which he praised Mussolini for defending quality in national production and Douglas as the first economist to consider the importance of creative arts in his economic scheme. With all this prose, he was still writing his cantos, working on numbers XXXI to XL. A considerable amount of energy was being devoted to his correspondence and he had designed a new letterhead with a drawing of himself by Gaudier and various slogans like Mussolini's Liberty Is a Duty, Not a Right.

Pound was also organizing a concert series in Rapallo. It was a way to charge his relationship with Olga Rudge, who had moved to Rapallo, renting her house in Venice from fall through spring and living on the profits in an apartment on Sant'Ambrogio, a hill outside Rapallo. The apartment, the top floor of a two-story house whose first floor housed an olive press, and full of Pound's homemade furniture, was reached by a forty-five-minute climb along an old hill path made of stone, and several hundred stone steps. Pound began spending several nights a week with Olga. Together they decided on programs and arranged for performers and publicity, balancing works of classical composers like Telemann and Pergolesi with the more experimental contemporaries like Antheil, Stravinsky, and Satie that Olga liked to perform. Dorothy Pound had by this point completely accepted her husband without conditions. She was happy doing her sketching and watercolors, but in a more conventional style, never returning to the Vorticist attempts of her earlier years. Modest in her talent, she refused to show her work, feeling that her husband was the artist. Nancy McCormack saw her at this time and noticed that she shunned cosmetics and presented herself very plainly. Pragmatic, more methodical than her husband, she kept the family accounts and managed a separate literary fund which had been capitalized by the two-thousand-dollar Dial Award and was used to help Carnevali, Cournos when Pound heard he was having an operation, and other artists in desperate circumstances.

In April, Hemingway sent a check for twenty pounds in return for some sketches that Dorothy had meant as a gift, and a letter disparaging Mussolini. Pound replied that Hemingway was "all wet" on the subject, that Mussolini had finally brought together contending and disputatious segments of Italian society as no one had since D'Annunzio. Pound's letter was choked with economic speculation and Hemingway retorted, "Since when are you an economist, pal? The last I knew you you were a fuckin' bassoon player." Calling Pound a "natural patriot," Hemingway said that he disbelieved in all government and hated the very conception of the state.

Hemingway could be as brutally uninhibited as Pound in his letters and used terms like "wop" and "kike" freely—a reflection of the easy access to such terms before World War II. At the end of July he wrote Pound again. He had caught fifty-four big marlin and the biggest of them had leaped forty-four times. Implicit in this boast was that a man had better things to do with his time than wonder about economics, that the brain existed to reorganize the senses, not to theorize. In his letter, however, he acknowledged once again that he had "learned more about how to write and how not to write from Pound than from any other son of a bitch alive" and had always said so.

In September, Faber & Faber published *A Draft of XXX Cantos* and in October, Pound's *Active Anthology,* which included poems by Williams, Cummings, Hemingway, Marianne Moore, Bunting, and Zukofsky. Pound was represented by a selection of cantos chosen by John Drummond, a young Englishman who had written about them in *The New English Weekly,* and there was a note on methods by Zukofsky. Zukofsky's comments inspired a letter from a reader who was troubled by the difficulties of reading *The Cantos.* Pound's answer seemed like a method for reading his poem: "Skip anything you don't understand and go on till you pick it up again. All tosh about foreign languages make *[sic]* it difficult. The quotes are either explained at once by repeat or they are definitely *of* the things indicated." Pound was receiving letters from a group of old sweethearts, from Iris Barry, from Mary Moore, now Mary Cross, who apologized for being a suburban housewife submerged in domesticity, and Viola Baxter Jordan, whose letter included an astrological profile: Pound was a man of great passion whose sensitivity made him withdraw at the slightest rebuff, a man with a bitter eagerness in his speech whose words had a demonic capacity to wound. Marianne Moore, more chastely, wrote warning him not to "root out the wheat in a mad desire to destroy the hares." Pound's reply was dogmatically assertive; capitalism had "perverted every craney of mind," and his own exposures and economic revelations were being held back from the public just as his poems had been in 1912. Economics, he told her, was a simple subject which he would "clear up and put right within three years." Ironically, he reflected on Scott Thayer, Moore's former employer at *The Dial,* then in a mental institution: "I suppose itz a judgment that the titular editor of America's leading magazine was crazy."

That fall he received a letter from a young man at Harvard, James Laughlin, one of the heirs of the Laughlin steel fortune, an editor of the *Harvard Advocate* with connections to the Yale literary magazine *Harkness Hoot.* Laughlin told him he was in a position "to reach the few men in the two universities who are worth bothering about, and could do a better job with your help." Writing again, this time from Lausanne, he described himself as never having missed a meal, thrown a bomb, or worn a pink coat, but full of "noble caring for something as inconceivable as the future of decent letters in the United States." For Pound the letter was an encouragement, a sign that now "les jeunes" might gather around him. Another helper at this time was Archibald MacLeish, who tried to place *How to Read* and *ABC of Economics* with the Yale University Press. When Pound complained to MacLeish of "twenty five years of being sabotaged by American publishers," MacLeish replied that in his view Pound was "wrong as hell about America."

By 1934 Pound himself had become aware of the amount of time he was giving to his "hysterical crusade on economics." He published over a hundred letters and articles in periodicals in 1934, mostly relating to economic matters, in places like *The New English Weekly*. Pound was proselytizing for Douglas with white heat, but Douglas himself was a model of British decorum and reserve, much calmer, more deliberate and self-contained than his follower. To encourage debate, Pound began sending a printed statement called "Volitionist Economics" along with his correspondence:

WHICH of the following statements do you agree with?

1. It is an outrage that the state should run into debt to individuals by the act and in the act of creating real wealth.

2. Several nations recognize the necessity of distributing purchasing power. They do actually distribute it. The question is whether it should be distributed as favour to corporations; as reward for not having a job; or impartially and per capita.

3. A country CAN have one currency for internal use, and another good both for home and foreign use.

4. If money is regarded as certificate of work done, taxes are no longer necessary.

5. It is possible to concentrate all taxation onto the actual paper money of a country (or onto one sort of its money).

6. You can issue valid paper money against any commodity UP TO the amount of that commodity that people WANT.

7. Some of the commonest failures of clarity among economists are due to using one word to signify two or more different concepts: such as, DEMAND, meaning also responsible.

8. It is an outrage that the owner of one commodity can not exchange it with someone possessing another, without being impeded or taxed by a third party holding a monopoly over some third substance or controlling some convention, regardless of what it be called.

When Pound sent a copy to Hemingway, the novelist replied the statement lacked clarity and asked when a report on Pound's interview with Mussolini would be published. Pound answered that no one in the United

States wanted to hear about Mussolini (Hemingway, of course, had published his interview disparaging Mussolini ten years earlier) and protested Hemingway's charge that his statement lacked clarity, saying that the difference between his writing and Gertrude Stein's and Joyce's ("Chimme Jheezus") was that "they want to wrap up something simple in a lot of feather boas, whereas ole EZ is constantly trying to get wot he means into woidz of one syllable so az even the simple minded pubk CAN understand 'em. Only the god damn pubk is too god damn dumb to understand anything." That summer Pound was in Paris for a brief trip and wanted to see Joyce. Sure that Pound was maddened by his political involvements, and feeling he needed a buffer, when Joyce learned that Hemingway was in Paris he invited him for dinner with Pound. It was the last time Hemingway and Pound met. Hemingway remembered that Pound was erratic and distracted, speaking during the entire evening of economic questions and the imminent collapse of Europe. Writing to Harriet Shaw Weaver, Joyce said that "I am afraid that poor Mr. Hitler-Missler will soon have few admirers in Europe apart from your nieces and my nephews, Masters W. Lewis and E. Pound." Joyce had seen that Pound's interests had shifted from art to politics. Later that year when Pound was asked to write an article about Joyce he refused, stating, "There is too much future, and nobody but me and Muss/ and half a dozen others to attend to it."

For his part, Pound felt most art was uninspired: his experience as music and art critic on *The New Age* had taught him so, and much of what he had seen in Paris simply confirmed the view. Furthermore, Pound felt one had the ability to judge only one's own generation as far as art was concerned. Before the first war, he had been the finest scout for literary talent in English, and that had led to his association with Yeats, Ford, Joyce, Hemingway, and others. But these friendships had failed to help him become a literary power, a writer who set taste and helped determine what would get published in his own day. Pound had just never been taken seriously enough by the general public for that to occur. Rather than becoming a literary kingpin, he became seduced by the Confucian notion of the writer as political adviser to a ruler. But it was an illusory notion. Confucius had been regarded as a quirky, rambling talker in his time; he was not taken seriously by those in power, he was never given political office, and he never enjoyed any real power.

6. PLAYING WITH LIONS AND WASPS

Following a recommendation of Hemingway's, Pound wrote to Arnold Gingrich, editor of *Esquire,* and proposed a piece on Mussolini. His letter expressed what for him was the central delusion that with politics he could

do what he had done for art twenty years earlier: "More and more people
are being made to recognize that I see just as straight in matters outside art
and letters as I did when I was picking winners inside the gawden of the
muses." Mussolini was more alive than Gaudier or Picabia: "As a MIND
who the hell else is there for me to take an interest in?" Pound asked. At
this moment, in the fall of 1934, Adolf Hitler was leaving to make his first
state visit to Italy, and Mussolini had ordered the last mile of railway track
to Rome lined with false apartment blocks to impress him.

Gingrich, who said he had been reading Pound since 1918, was uninterested in Mussolini but proposed that Pound do Gaudier and Brancusi.
He did write these pieces and several others, but the obscurity of some of
his references and an increasingly polemical tone presented a problem for
Gingrich. Pound had warned Gingrich in his first letter that "Hemingway
may shoot lions; but he don't play around with 'em in the domestic cage."
Economics was a "factor in world villainy," he told Irving Brandt, a journalist who had written a book called *Dollars and Sense,* which Pound had favorably reviewed. "To Hell with the lillylivered aesthetes who can't EVEN
write because they are too piffling silly to SEE the bearing of econ/factor on
every bloody human activity," he told John Gould Fletcher. Pound recommended that Gingrich use Williams and Cummings but also new, nonliter-
ary spokesmen, right-wing journalist Westbrook Pegler and radio agitator
Father Coughlin, who read on the air anti-Semitic propaganda written by
Joseph Goebbels, Hitler's propaganda minister, without acknowledging its
source.

Pound's work days were long but he still found time for swimming,
tennis, and going to the cinema. When James Laughlin wrote from Paris
intending to visit, Pound's reply was euphoric: "Visibility high!" Laughlin
joined the "Ezuversity" for part of the summer of 1934, sharing meals with
the Pounds at the Albergo Rapallo, taking long walks with Pound, and
discussing history in Pound's study. When he returned to America, Laughlin began editing the literary section of the American Social Credit magazine *New Democracy,* calling the section "New Directions." In Rapallo,
Pound had advised Laughlin to start a small publishing company to print
writers like Williams and himself who did not have sufficient commercial
interest for the large presses. Using his own inherited capital and ingenuity,
Laughlin did this and called his press New Directions.

Also that summer there was a visit from Yeats, then sixty-nine years old
and afraid that he was losing his creative powers, as he had not written
poetry for the past two years. He showed Pound the script for his play *The
King of the Great Clock Tower* and took Pound to dinner to hear what he
thought, but Pound was uninterested in any literary discussion. Without a
context to provoke him, Pound exclaimed that former British foreign minister Arthur Balfour "was a scoundrel," and from that point on in the evening

he would only talk politics. According to Yeats, Pound argued that all modern statesmen except Mussolini and Hitler were scoundrels. He told Yeats
that Dublin was "a reactionary hole" and the next day returned his play
with the word "Putrid" slashed across its front page. The episode shows
how far Pound's mind had departed from the sources that had formerly
sustained him. What he had written across Yeats's manuscript was gratuitous, the unsympathetic and unforgivably ugly result of hateful scorn. The
remark showed Pound's new myopia with regard to beauty, for when the
work was produced, it turned out to be the most successful of Yeats's plays.

In September, Pound visited Venice, staying with Olga Rudge and
their daughter. Mary was nine and found the difference between her sophisticated parents and her foster parents difficult to reconcile. In Gais she could
herd sheep; in Venice there were books and rules. Her father inscribed a
batch of them for her to consider, including a rule on the advantages of
suffering, which he considered a manifest sign of misunderstanding the universe that exists "in order to make people think." The rule later presented
an ironic parallel to Pound's own suffering. In the mornings Pound worked
in a studio provided by a friend while Olga practiced the violin. Often in
the afternoons the three took the ferry to the Lido, the beach where they
could row, walk, and swim. Mary recalled her father's periods of concentration in her book *Discretions:*

> It seemed as though he were visibly fighting a wasps net in his
> brain. Quite different from when he was merely pensive. That
> occurred often, and I knew immediately that he wanted me to
> refrain from talking. Inherent in his silence was suspense, a joyous
> sense of expectation, until he broke into a kind of a chant that
> sometimes went on for hours, interrupted and picked up again, no
> matter whether he was sitting at table or walking in the streets.
> Hard as I tried to imitate this humming, I never could. No words:
> sounds bordering on ventriloquism, as though some alien power
> were rumbling in the cave of his chest in a language other than
> human; then it moved up to his head and the tone became nasal,
> metallic. Athena banging in her glistening helmet inside Jupiter's
> skull, clamoring for release. A hasty scribbling on a piece of paper,
> a tearing off of newspaper clippings, a frantic annotation in a book.
> Something had clicked, some truth revealed, a new thought, a new
> line, a new melody.

Pound's "chant" was the voice of *The Cantos,* a voice that was difficult to
summon because to hear it clearly a writer would have to tap into his deepest being, a place so wound in the psyche that when it was reached and it
spoke through him, it could almost seem independent of volition, autonomous, resonating through the brain and fingers.

From Venice, Pound wrote to Eliot, whom he addressed as the Right Reverend Possum Prodigious Wunkadorus Dogwasher, urging the economics of Social Credit. The moral basis of Pound's argument that money should not be a commodity manipulated by financiers and bankers appealed to Eliot. When Orage died in November of 1934, Eliot agreed to serve on the editorial board of *The New English Weekly* and over the next decade contributed a number of articles on Social Credit of his own. Feeling some success because of Eliot's interest, Pound wrote to T. E. Lawrence at Oxford, who told him that Gandhi would prescribe "a daily wrestle with the spinning wheel" as a way to assuage his anger. "In your filthy country," Pound replied abusively, "every man in high office is a thief's accomplice." Oxford was a "pervertery" and an "inculcator of slaves and bureaucrats." "The only way to get an Englishman to say anything," Pound wrote the English director of the Imperial Fascist League, "is to insult him," and the comment underlines his own bellicosity.

He wrote twice to Roosevelt, a bit more temperately, and with his second letter he enclosed an example of his grandfather Thaddeus Pound's Union Lumbering Company private scrip. He reminded the President that money was only a ticket that represented work done "before the bank swine got the monopoly." To back money by gold or silver instead of work was "merely to favour the owners of that metal and by just that much to betray the rest of the public." He wrote to Professor J. H. Rogers, a member of Roosevelt's Brain Trust, who was attending an economic conference in London: "I don't care what you DO, so long as it isn't on my conscience that you are an Abroaded innocent/trusting in British vipers, General mandrakes, and ignorant of Douglas, and ras moneta(stamp script). I am prob/ younger'n you are, tho' not by much, but by god I'll spit on yr/tombstone if some attention isn't given to contemporary economics." Writing to Huey Long, the governor of Louisiana who was interested in Social Credit, Pound facetiously proposed himself as secretary of the Treasury. In a letter to Senator Bronson Cutting of New Mexico he called Wilson a skunk, Harding a slob, and Hoover a crook. In other letters he argued that the American government had the right to issue its own currency, but since 1913 was instead borrowing money at interest from the Federal Reserve Bank, a private source, and that part of the taxes collected by the government went to pay the interest charges. He quoted from the seventeenth-century Charter for the Bank of England, which states that the bank has the "benefit of the interest on all moneys which it creates out of nothing." Pound also preached Jefferson, quoting him as one might the Old Testament. But Pound was not alone in this admiration. William Randolph Hearst, trying to rally the resistance to Roosevelt, appealed to conservatives among the Democrats to split by forming a Jeffersonian Democratic party as opposed to what he called the Socialist Democrat party of Roosevelt. In support of this program, Hearst made sure that there were features on Jefferson in most of the newspapers under his control in 1935.

Writing to the historian W. E. Woodward, a member of Roosevelt's Industrial Advisory Board and another Brain Truster, Pound claimed that John Maynard Keynes was an "imbecile, a crook, a pusillanimous louse." He added a dangerous aside on Jews: "The kikes, right up to Einstein, run like pigs from all economic discussion regurgitating in orthodox Zionistic communism as preached on Sinai." Along with his letter, Pound enclosed articles on economics which he wanted Woodward to pass to Roosevelt. One of the articles was on the stamp scrip theory of Silvio Gesell developed in a book called *The Natural Economic Order,* which Pound saw as a "counter-usury" system. Gesell had proposed that paper money require monthly stamps to maintain its par value so that taxation would be based directly on the money one acquired and so that people would be encouraged to spend rather than to save. Gesell's idea was tried in a small town in Switzerland, sending "shivers down the backs of all the lice of Europe, Rothschildian and other" until the Swiss banks learned about it, forming a conspiracy, Pound later alleged, to eradicate the practice. Pound wanted Woodward to convince Roosevelt to try such a scheme as a way to counter the effects of the depression. In a letter to Hemingway he suggested that he would like to join the Brain Trust, and that it might be as easy for Hemingway to recommend him to Roosevelt as it had been to Arnold Gingrich. He reviewed Paul de Kruif's *Hunger Fighters.* Since de Kruif worked for the government and supposedly was listened to by Roosevelt, Pound sent him a series of letters on what Pound considered the real causes of poverty—the banking interests. Later, de Kruif introduced Pound to Henry A. Wallace, Roosevelt's secretary for agriculture, who commented, when he received a copy of Pound's "Volitionist Economics" questionnaire, that the questions took emotional half-truths and distorted them.

Woodward wrote back that he had gone to hear Douglas speak in New York and had been disappointed. Neither in his tepid talk nor in his muddled book had Douglas explained how his system would arrange Social Credit dividends without terrible inflation. Pound disregarded Woodward's objection and instead wrote that "Jew power in England is enormous, that New York City had been invaded by Jews, and that everybody in Europe with any knowledge is convinced that there is a continual drive toward war worked by international finance, banks and gun sellers." Pound's remarks at this stage sounded extremely populist, in the interests of the exploited victims of banking interests, and reminiscent of the oratory of his grandfather running for Congress in Wisconsin a half century earlier. But at the same time Pound had on every possible occasion expressed the greatest contempt for the people, the "damned dumb pubk," and his populism was a matter of mind, not heart.

In 1935 Pound began writing the "American Notes" section for *The New English Weekly,* gathering his information on economic matters in the United States from newspapers and correspondents like Zukofsky—who himself was uninterested in Social Credit and consequently berated by Pound—and members of the American Social Credit movement, which had formed two years earlier. The American proponents of Social Credit, men like Gorham Munson and writers for *New Democracy* magazine, however, refused to accept either the political doctrine of fascism or the anti-Semitism which had become more pronounced among Mosley's group in England and in Pound's letters. They also regarded Pound's advertisement of Gesellite stamp scrip as little more than quackery. John Hargrave, an English writer on Social Credit, thought that Pound's incessant lobbying with American senators was worthless and compared Pound's impact to a "series of explosions in a rock quarry."

But Pound had launched a one-man crusade. In 1935 he contributed 150 articles and letters to periodicals. He was writing regularly to Mussolini, in one letter informing him of fourteen American senators who were interested in Social Credit, in another sending him a copy of his grandfather's Union Lumber Company private scrip, just as he had sent it to Roosevelt. Mussolini would have been delighted to learn that Thaddeus Pound had been, of course, a double capitalist, making a profit on the labor of the lumbermen who felled the trees for him and then a second profit when they used the scrip that he had paid them to purchase items at the company store. It was a corporate state in miniature. Altogether, there were fifty letters retrieved by the Federal Bureau of Investigation after the war. Written in Italian, they were unwieldy, ungrammatical, and at times indecipherable. Some of these letters were forwarded to Mussolini by Count Galeazzo Ciano, his son-in-law, who was minister of propaganda from 1934 to 1936, and after that minister of foreign affairs until he was shot by the Germans in 1944 for leading a plot against Mussolini. One of the letters bore a memorandum by an administrator in Ciano's office: "One thing that is clear is that the author is mentally unbalanced."

Pound was becoming predictable to his friends, an irritant whose anger surged without substantial insight. He wrote to William Bird in Paris, stating that he divided men "into the good guys and the shits." His position was that "a drop of water in baby's bottle will dilute the milk," a condition Bird could accept because he knew with his liberal prespective that "the kid will die in time anyhow." He added that Mussolini had drained the swamps, and a comment on the validity of his grandfather's currency. In a sharply worded reply, Bird pointed out that Thaddeus's scrip was good only in his store, where he could charge what he pleased, exploiting the worker and the fact that he lived in an isolated frontier. Furthermore, Bird argued,

Mussolini had drained the swamps as a grandstand play with unemployables living in barracks and paid an infinitesimal wage.

In Paris on Bastille Day in 1935, a crowd of almost half a million Communists and socialists had marched, the "Internationale" was sung, and the Soviet red flag displayed. On the same evening thirty thousand members of the right-wing Croix de Feu goose-stepped down the Champs-Élysées in uniform. The atmosphere was revolutionary and incendiary, and Bird was worried about the instability of the situation. He felt Pound had assumed a simplistic position. Bird did his best to correct it, but the fact is that Pound had stopped listening. He ranted in a letter to Williams, who saw some sense in Social Credit, "May God blot out yr eyes if you will not look into the cancer of financial iniquity. May God rot all men like you who to avoid reform at home preserve the damnable usurers." Williams commented in *New Democracy,* "Pound's mind is clogged with a curious sort of idealism which trips him up at every step."

There is some indication that Pound, feeling isolated and neglected in Rapallo, chose a more and more extremist path as a way to get notice which —whether favorable or not—was something on which he had become emotionally dependent since his early success in London. In a letter to Nancy Cunard he declared that "any man's honesty in 1935 is measured by his curiosity as to the nature of money and his willingness to have it examined." In an unpublished essay called "Clean It," he wrote that he had been "patient during the long drawn infamy of F.D.R.'s four predecessors. There is a time for all things and the time for patience has ended." In a letter to a Harvard law professor, a distant cousin named Roscoe Pound, he claimed that he "realized the scandal caused by a living versifier barging into a subject which poets have neglected since Dante and Shakespeare looked into it, but that can't be helped."

He continued to admonish Zukofsky, whom he had regarded as one of his leading American disciples, for ignoring Social Credit, threatening to omit him from any future anthology he might edit. Coolly, Zukofsky responded that no one in America was interested in Mussolini draining the swamps, that the Romans had tried that shortly before their empire collapsed, to little avail. Pound inquired why Zukofsky didn't have any of the "god damned pestilent adaptability (of your tribe) which produces the rabid forms of anti-Semitism in Aryans *after* they've been had?" In subsequent letters he would use economic theory as an excuse to abuse Zukofsky, calling him a Marxist fool, his mind a "gormy mess" because as "a damned foreigner" he had never bothered to learn English.

On the pathway to scandal, Pound continued with a relentless and fanatical insistence to write to influential Americans. He told Paul de Kruif that Roosevelt was a fool if he "thinks he can borrow the nation out of debt. . . . And if he knows he can't and goes on as if he could, he is a traitor."

He reminded Senator A. H. Vandenberg that war is caused by finance, not by guns, and told Vandenberg to investigate the Carnegie Endowment for Peace. He asked Senator J. P. Pope "to tear right through the activities of the munitions makers INTO the financial forces that drive on the gun-buzzards." Pound did not know that at this time the technology of aerial warfare had been advanced with the development of the giant Boeing "Flying Fortress," a fifteen-ton death machine capable of carrying one ton of explosives at 250 miles per hour. And aerial warfare was to be tested in the fall of 1935 by Mussolini in the invasion of Ethiopia, revenging the humiliation of the defeat of the Italians who had tried unsuccessfully to subdue that part of Africa forty years earlier.

Winston Churchill warned Italy against the invasion, calling Ethiopia a "deadly trap," an arid region that no conqueror in four thousand years had found worthwhile to subdue. But by 1935 every classroom and most public spaces in Italy paraded the slogan Mussolini Is Always Right. And Mussolini believed in war as a means of expressing national identity: "War alone brings up to its highest tension all human energy and puts a stamp of nobility upon the peoples who have the courage to meet it," he declared in "The Political and Social Doctrine of Fascism." Writing to Senator William Borah of Idaho, Pound's home state, Pound tried pathetically to justify Mussolini's aggression, a brutal attempt to expand Italian Somaliland. Pound's rationalization for the war was that Ethiopia was a backward region still trading in slaves and fortunate to be receiving the civilizing influences of colonial settlement. It was an embarrassing version of Kipling's White Man's Burden. In his confused mind, the war had something to do with a British desire to grab Africa. He pointed out to Borah that Anthony Eden, a leading English younger statesman, was the son-in-law of the president of the Westminster Bank, one of England's largest financial institutions, and in Pound's eyes that determined conspiracy. Borah had been chairman of the Senate Committee on Foreign Affairs, he was a man who distrusted big business, an isolationist who, like Pound, did not believe in the League of Nations. After Pound's letters defending the invasion of Ethiopia, Borah wrote him off as a crank and would no longer reply. When Ethiopia appealed to the League of Nations, Pound described that body as "born rotten," an assembly of "bank pimps" without honesty. To V. Adams, a member of the British Parliament, he wrote that "no decent man wants to die for a lot of city jews" who ostensibly were the real cause of English interest in the war.

Pound published one book and two pamphlets in 1935, both issued by Stanley Nott, who printed Social Credit propaganda in London. One was a collection of political doggerel written under the pseudonym of Alfred Venison. The second pamphlet, *Social Credit: An Impact,* repeated the ideas on money and finance that Pound had been tirelessly urging for over a decade.

The book was *Jefferson and/or Mussolini*, which in two years had been rejected by forty publishers, Pound claimed. In it he stated Mussolini was a genius who had to be appreciated as one does an artist, which sounded strange after the bombardment of Ethiopia: "I don't believe any estimate of Mussolini will be valid unless it starts from his passion for construction. Treat him as *artifex* and all the details fall into place. Take him as anything save the artist and you will get muddled with contradictions." With the successful invasion of Ethiopia, Mussolini had boosted the Italians' image of themselves, and the country was an excitement of patriotic ferment. Pound insisted that his daughter wear the Fascist uniform to school in Gais, though the only others who did were the children of government functionaries.

Pound had become an ardent supporter of Mussolini and had lost the ability to see the facts as they existed. "The Duce's aphorisms and perceptions," he declared in his *ABC of Economics*, "can be studied apart from his means of getting them into action." The statement was incredible: Pound was arguing that Mussolini should be appreciated as some sort of Confucian master whose intentions could in some mysterious aesthetic manner be separated from the actions that accompanied them. To call this naïve idealism, as his friend Williams did, seems much too generous: the myopia had degenerated to blindness. Pound was no longer able to evaluate history; he had become another hero-worshipper.

It was clear that Pound's literary interests had subsided. He wrote to Paul Chauvet, editor of the *Revue Anglaise* in Paris, asking for a report on the events of the First International Congress of Writers for the Defense of Culture, presided over by André Gide in Paris during the summer of 1935, with Louis Aragon and André Malraux organizing for the fight against fascism. When he heard from Chauvet, his reply was that "our gangsters never shoot the right people" and that Europe had "suffered 30 years under the black infamy of the usurers touts and plutocrats (dressed in professorial and editorial robes)." In France a Jew named Léon Blum, a former literary critic, had been elected to head the Popular Front, which he would use to obtain advantages like the forty-hour week and annual paid vacations for workers. Pound detested Blum because he was both a socialist and a Jew.

7. DYNAMITE AND DOGMA

The tone of Pound's letters had turned from a semblance of reasonable inquiry to imperious condescension and vituperative impatience. What may have seemed eccentric or humorous a decade earlier at this point seemed abrasive, cantankerous, and mean-spirited. The letters were full of puns and private references—the *Ladies' Home Journal* became the Ladies' Home Urinal, *Harper's* became Harpie's. In *Jefferson and/or Mussolini* Pound had written that "it takes a genius, charged with some form of dynamite, mental or material, to blast away human preconceptions and dogma," which was the role Pound thought his letters could play. At the end of 1935, Count Ciano, sensing that Pound could be useful to his own propaganda machine, invited him to use the airwaves of Radio Rome to voice his political observations and economic theories. Pound had been impressed by the power of radio since his opera *Villon* had been broadcast, and he had heard of the way Roosevelt was using radio to rally public opinion. Ciano was the serpent in the Garden of Eden and Pound could not resist. He began to broadcast in 1936, sporadically and intermittently at first, his comments as abrupt, nonconsecutive, digressive, and fragmented as his cantos or prose.

He began to intensify his anti-Jewish remarks. In 1922 he had attacked Harriet Monroe for the "damn remnants in you of Jew religion, that bitch Moses and the rest of the tribal barbarians. Even you do still try at least to leave the reader in ignorance of the fact that I do NOT accept the current dung and official opinions about the dregs of Xtian superstition, the infamy of American Laws, etc." In the years just before the beginning of World War II, Pound was writing that "the Jewpart of the Bible is black evil," that "Jewspapers" had poisoned the world, that the music business was "Jewed," that the Jew was unable to accept civic responsibility because he had no nation of his own. In a letter to Cummings he called Trotsky a "kike blockhead" and claimed that the Rothschilds controlled American news agencies. He carried on correspondence with a number of virulent Jew haters, among them Arnold Leese, an Englishman interested in monetary reform who regarded Mussolini as a tool of the Jews and Mosley as a "Kosher Fascist" because he did not push for their extermination, only wishing to resettle all European Jews in Madagascar. Referring to "Jew York," Pound told McAlmon that Jewish arrivistes were taking the city over and that "I'm off on Jewish publishers—can't cope with the race." In a letter to Peter Fanning he wrote that the journalist Walter Lippmann was enough to "justify all the Heil Hitlers, Goebbels and pogroms," an obvious exaggeration which appeared nevertheless as the grossest sort of bad taste when it was continued after the war. When he referred to the "Jewnited" States and said Roosevelt was "Jewsfeld" and "Rosenstein," he had crossed the boundaries of humor that someone like Mencken might have understood into the no-man's-land of ugly, coarse vilification unrelated to fact.

Pound himself vigorously denied being anti-Semitic, pointing to his many Jewish friends, stating that he dedicated *Guide to Kulchur*, which he was writing in 1936, to a Jew, Zukofsky, and a Quaker, Bunting. During the war, however, he wrote Ciano that of all the Protestant sects the Quakers were the least "Jewified" because they did not sing in worship, and commenting in Italian on Eliot's book *After Strange Gods*, he observed that

Eliot had not "come through uncontaminated by the Jewish parson." Pound claimed the charge of anti-Semitism was a red herring used to create a distraction from the real issue of the economic basis of war. He attacked Jews partly because he believed they conspired to finance the war through usury (though except for the Rothschild family there were few Jews in British or French banking), but even more because he saw monotheism historically as a Jewish development that had ended the pagan era and introduced a narrowness of perspective. His anti-Jewish remarks must be seen in the context of his anti-Christian and anti-American diatribes, especially the insulting terms he used for American presidents. They serve as a reminder, too, that anti-Semitism was normative in Europe and America at the time. Coolidge had written an essay on race pollution for *Good Housekeeping* and sponsored restrictive legislation in the early twenties. At least two American heroes of that era, Henry Ford and Charles Lindbergh, made no attempt to hide their anti-Semitic attitudes. Pound, however, persisted beyond the point when it was fashionable to openly despise Jews. As late as "Canto LXXIV" he could state:

> The yidd is a stimulant, and the goyim are cattle
> in gt/proportion and go to salable slaughter
> with the maximum of docility.

In 1936 he continued to examine old books and newspapers for evidence to confirm his economic biases. He was an intuitive rather than a scientific investigator, and he often did not have the patience to verify his findings. He began a series of six essays on economics, called the *Money Pamphlets,* half of them written in Italian, and he contributed over twenty articles to the *British-Italian Bulletin* mostly in defense of Italy's invasion of Ethiopia. He was also working on cantos XLIV through XLVI. In "Canto XLV" he presented the case against usury bitterly, listing medieval and Renaissance art that would not have been possible in a system that permitted usury where "no picture is made to endure" but rather to "sell quickly." With usury and modern capitalism, bread had become "stale rags" and "dry paper" and there was no meaning to craft:

> Usura rusteth the chisel
> It rusteth the craft and the craftsman
> It gnaweth the thread in the loom
> None learneth to weave gold in her pattern;
> Azure hath a canker by usura; cramoisi is unbroidered
> Emerald findeth no Memling
> Usura slayeth the child in the womb
> It stayeth the young man's courting
> It hath brought palsey to bed, lyeth

between the young bride and her bridegroom
CONTRA NATURAM
They have brought whores for Eleusis
Corpses are set to banquet
at behest of usura.

"Canto XLV" is one of the most concentrated and emotional sections of the
entire work. At the end of the canto Pound included a definition of usury as
"a charge for the use of purchasing power, levied without regard to production." In one of the money pamphlets, he put this definition in a more
sinister political context: "USURY is the cancer of the world, which only
the surgeon's knife of Fascism can cut out of the life of nations."

With the concerts at Rapallo, Pound had been trying to create conditions simulating the Renaissance. When the concerts were temporarily discontinued when Gerhart Münch departed, Pound began a study group on
Vivaldi where he would lecture and Olga Rudge would demonstrate on the
violin. Vivaldi's reputation had been in eclipse and his music was in danger
of being forever buried in archives. In Dresden, Münch photocopied some
ninety Vivaldi concerti and sent them to Pound; Olga Rudge went to Turin
to examine their collection of over three hundred concerti and began preparing a comprehensive catalogue. In 1937 she organized a series of Vivaldi
concerts in Venice, and the following year a regular Vivaldi festival was
begun in Sienna under the auspices of the Accademia Musicale Chigiana
where Olga Rudge worked as a public relations secretary.

In his letters Pound continued his running commentary on world
events. War had begun in Spain, a war "that the kikes were financing on
both sides," he wrote to Nancy Cunard. To Cunningham Graham, an English novelist, he said that the British Parliament was a collection of six
hundred apes and that British universities were full of "dozens of hired
pimps." He told Bertrand Russell he was glad "you know your lousy country has paralysis," adding that he regretted not "kicking a little manhood
into you when I met you." The attack on Russell was unfortunate because
the English philosopher was in essential agreement with Pound on a prime
cause of war. Only a year earlier he had argued that magnates of industry,
not statesmen or the masses, manipulated nations into war. Hitler, Russell
had declared, was merely a megaphone for the Krupps, the German iron
and steel industry, and the next war, he feared, would destroy civilization in
Western Europe. Pound sent copies of *Jefferson and/or Mussolini* to FDR and
to "Her Excellency" Eleanor Roosevelt, including a note urging her to get
rid of Treasury Secretary Henry Morgenthau. In "Canto XLVI" he set
down his impression of the debacle of the Great Depression as the fault of
Roosevelt and usury economics:

FIVE million youths without jobs
FOUR million adult illiterates
15 million "vocational misfits," that is with small chance
of jobs.
NINE million persons annual, injured in preventable industrial
accidents
One hundred thousand violent crimes. The Eunited States ov America
3rd. year of the reign of F. Roosevelt.

He contributed an article on Social Credit to the *Fascist Quarterly,* whose editor wrote to him in thanks, signing his note "Yours in fascism." He heard from Congressman Amos Pinchot that Douglas had spoken again in New York with "unique lack of clarity and definition" and that the Social Credit movement in America was distrusted as a sort of "religious fermentation."

At this period a number of Pound's former friends were back in the United States. McAlmon was living in El Paso, Texas, working at mundane jobs and no longer able to write or care about life. Antheil, whose brilliant career Pound had predicted, had been writing background music for Hollywood films but was currently conducting an advice-to-the-lovelorn column. Ford was living in Michigan and began teaching at Olivet College in the fall of 1936. He warned Pound that his letters were becoming incomprehensible and that his insults would end only by making him a pariah. Yeats was writing his introduction to the *Oxford Book of Modern Verse,* and his comment on Pound largely determined the world's view for years to follow:

> When I consider his work as a whole, I find more style than form; at moments more style, more deliberate nobility and the means to convey it than in any contemporary poet known to me but it is constantly interrupted, broken, twisted into nothing by its direct opposite, nervous obsession, nightmare, stammering confusion; he is an economist, poet, politician, raging at malignants with inexplicable characters and motives, grotesque figures out of a child's book of beasts. This loss of self-control, common among uneducated revolutionists, is rare—Shelley had it in some degree— among men of Ezra Pound's culture and erudition.

After their final meeting in Rapallo, when Pound had savaged his play by writing "putrid" on its first page, it is a wonder that Yeats bothered to consider his former friend at all. But his remarks were quite accurate, especially if applied to the work Pound was then doing on his *Cantos.* The sense of "nervous obsession" and "stammering confusion" were qualities that most readers recognized in Pound at the time. The key phrase, however, was "loss of self-control," which was reflected in *The Cantos* as in the letters, and later in the radio broadcasts.

No matter what Yeats or the world thought, Pound had come to see himself as a master of history and culture, and he set out to display that mastery in a book called *Guide to Kulchur,* the spelling an indication of the unconventional nature of his views and the peculiar sources of his tradition. Written with a sense of harried desperation in the spring of 1937, it was more digressively impulsive, more disorganized than anything Pound had done previously, a barrage of ideas without sequence or attempt to develop relationship. In a letter written while he was working on the book, he declared that Thomas Aquinas was an "empty noise" in a barrel, the propagator of a "kind of non-thought that one would expect of a class dunce." St. Augustine was only a "drunken African." The comments were closer to the spirit of insult than iconoclasm, and Pound included them in *Kulchur* only because they had occurred to him, not to satisfy any turn of argument or organic necessity. Essentially, this had become the method of *The Cantos* as well, the grab bag of his consciousness, whimsy, or spite. It was as if he had the need to defame and antagonize history itself. Pound knew that more writers fail from lack of character than from lack of intelligence, and *Guide to Kulchur* exists as the testament of a man struggling unsuccessfully with himself, politics, and history. Pound had chosen a political "pathway to scandal" as a desperate means of calling attention to himself at a time when his work was being neglected. But politics was a treacherous route. Yeats, who had been elected to the Irish Senate, declared his horror of modern politics: "I see nothing but the manipulation of popular enthusiasms by falseness." Joyce, who was consistently apolitical, had announced that history was a nightmare from which he was trying to awake. For Pound, the nightmare was his own paranoia. Donald Hall in his memoir, *Remembering Poets,* has told the story of the man who visited Pound at Rapallo at this time. As they were playing tennis, Pound confided that the hills above were filled with spies from Wall Street with binoculars who were watching Pound because they knew his economic program could ruin the banker's conspiracy to control the world's wealth.

In June, Nancy Cunard sent Pound and other writers a questionnaire on the Spanish Civil War, publishing the results as *Authors Take Sides.* For Pound it was a "sham conflict," organized by the international usurers and armament manufacturers. In a letter to Cunard he explained that he disliked the questionnaire because it neglected the economic basis of war, and he thought little of its signatories, Aragon, Stephen Spender, Wells, Auden, and Pablo Neruda, all writers associated with the left: "Your gang are all diarrhoea," he wrote, "sap-headed dilettantes."

Early in 1937 Faber & Faber published his *Polite Essays,* a collection of pieces—mostly literary—including "How to Read." *The Fifth Decad of Cantos,* Pound's documentation of the history of usury, was released by Faber in June and by Farrar in New York in the fall. Pound had been working again on Confucius, summarizing the *Analects* in a book called *Confucius. Digest of the Analects*. Part of Confucius's continuing appeal was related to his belief that the masses could be pushed in any direction that the skillful leader determined as right. It was a strong aristocratic bias. "The gentleman's essential quality is like the wind," he suggested in the *Analects*, "and the common people's like the grass. And when the wind is on it, the grass always bends." That summer and fall Pound was reading the Confucian philosopher Mencius and wrote an essay on him which Eliot published in *The Criterion*. In the essay Pound found occasion to attack Jewish influences in Christianity, what he called "semitic insanity," and he began to call for a new paganism uninfluenced by "semitic immoderation." Such attitudes, of course, were being advocated as well in Nazi Germany.

In February of 1937, Pound had received a long letter from Ford stating that there was a position available for him at Olivet College:

> In short, you are invited to stroll for eight months of a year—or several years—about the philosophers' groves of Olivet. I personally give a couple of lectures a week to classes because I like lecturing. You would not have to if you did not want to. You would be conferring obligation if you talked to any youth or youths you thought intelligent. There the duties would—or could—stop. The real point is that you would have complete leisure to write while earning a living wage.

Ford pointed out that Olivet would pay him boat fares from Europe and back, that it had an orchestra he could use, library facilities, and a "working model educational machine to play with." Ford remembered that Pound had several times proposed ideal universities in London and in Italy, but Pound was reluctant to go, afraid that at Olivet he would not be able to continue to work effectively for Social Credit and Mussolini. Nor was he in need of money. In 1939 he received an offer of five thousand dollars to give a series of twenty-five lectures for the Lee Keedrick Agency and refused the chance. Pound had succeeded, Williams observed, in never holding down a full-time job since the abortive experience at Wabash, making him one of the last men who could give all his time to poetry and other writing; besides Olivet seemed too remote a place, and in the winter too cold. A year later Ford was still remonstrating, actually pleading that Pound come:

> The situation is this: I am offering to give up my job at Olivet to you because you have been making noises about Universities for a long time and it would give you a chance really to do something. I have already answered your question about a press. They have already a press at Olivet. They print a paper. They would no doubt do any necessary scholastic printing you needed. But they proba-

bly would not print Mussolini-Douglas propaganda for you. They might. But it would be up to you to persuade them. They do not, as I have already told you, use your books as text books because "They" are I and I do not approve of the use of text books.

Ford said that the college paid him fifteen hundred dollars a year, but that he had supplemented that with outside lectures bringing in another twelve hundred. Pound could probably demand a higher salary and do more lecturing. He would probably turn the college into a "disastrous sort of hell" but Ford said it could be a stepping-stone to the Charles Eliot Norton Professorship at Harvard, which he knew would appeal to Pound. Pound refused the offer, writing directly to college president Joseph Brewer, *"All you blighted American College Presidents ought to be boiled in oil."* The colleges were "perverteries and aids to betrayal of the nation." He did not care to surrender his freedom of inquiry to any college board of trustees, no matter what the salary: "Certain facts are facts and certain lies are lies. This is a different distinction from that between one theory and another."

8. THE TOTAL DEMOCRACY BILGE

Early in 1938 Pound heard from Henry Seidel Canby that he had been elected to the National Institute of Arts and Letters. His response to Canby was in the form of a reprimand—he remembered Henry James telling him of taking great care to write for his friend William Dean Howells's installation, but the letter was never read. For Pound, the incident revealed the institute's disregard for the artists they supposedly honored. Pound immediately nominated Eliot, Williams, Hemingway, McAlmon, and Zukofsky, and the philosopher George Santayana to the "otiose" body, and he presented a series of sensible criticisms calling for regular meetings, a published bibliography, a formal declaration of aims. When Canby informed him that no funds were available for such procedures, Pound proclaimed that the institute was a joke: "U.S.A. so damnably organized that its chief cultural institution can not raise funds for the most elementary activities of such institutions in other countries." The institute, he said, should be used to "lead dead universities into contact with the present," it should fight the "unutterably slack standards of American publishing," and it should publish on its own inexpensive editions of Jefferson, John Adams, and the founding fathers whose works were difficult to find.

During this year Pound made a concentrated effort to push his *Cantos* forward. Out of his rereading of Confucius and Mencius and a French history of China by Mozriac de Mailla, Pound began making extracts and using them in cantos LIII to LXI. He devoted another ten extracts to the writings and career of John Adams, second president of the United States. Pound was writing articles for Oswald Mosley's newspaper *Action* and the *British Union Quarterly,* and he helped A. Raven Thompson, one of Mosley's subordinates, revise a pamphlet called "The Coming Corporate State." Pound also wrote to Willis Overholser, a lawyer in Libertyville, Illinois, for a copy of his *History of Money in the United States,* asking him to write a history of the Rothschild interests and their agents in America, and recommending a book written in 1880 by Osman Bey on Jewish world conquest.

In September, Hitler and Neville Chamberlain signed their nonaggression pact. T. S. Eliot wrote that he felt a "deep personal guilt and shame" and that "national life seemed fraudulent." However, Pound told Kay Boyle and Laurence Vail, two visiting young writers, that the pact signaled the beginning of the end for America and England, that now the international Jewish conspiracy would be exposed, and that Hitler and Mussolini were the two greatest statesmen alive. In an unpublished piece called "National Culture—A Manifesto" he wrote about "the total democracy bilge, by which I mean the clichés, the assumptions, the current cant about 'the people' arose from sheer misunderstanding or perversion. Perversion of ideas by means and by misuse of words. The disequality of human beings can be observed. . . . There is no more equality between men than between animals." Pound had become more than simply an apologist for fascism making an occasional broadcast on Rome Radio for Mussolini. He believed Fascist propaganda about combating international bankers, and he tacitly approved of the effort to subjugate the Jews.

In October, Olivia Shakespear died and Pound went to London to settle matters of her estate and dispose of her furniture and possessions. When Herbert Read saw him, he felt Pound was "a man who had become agitated and elated to a dangerous degree." He saw his twelve-year-old son, Omar, for the first time in eight years—Pound had expressed almost no interest in him. He visited T. S. Eliot and Wyndham Lewis, who did a portrait in oils of Pound reclining. Pound also helped Lewis by purchasing several drawings. Lewis was a bad journalist, disastrously wrong in his projections and predictions, careless with facts, and awkward when he attempted to be personal, but he had revised his earlier opinions of Hitler and wrote a new book reneging his earlier praise. He also wrote a book with the clumsy title *The Jews, Are They Human?* in which he denied charges of personal anti-Semitism. "The views of any writer, if his mind develops and matures, will change or be modified by events," Eliot wrote in his little book on Pound. But Pound's views, unlike Lewis's, did not change after the war or even after his long internment.

Pound wrote to Congressman George Tinkham that a former British secret agent had told him in a pub that any British politician, excluding Chamberlain, could be bribed and that there were many Russian agents in Britain. The letter was a sign of how indiscriminately Pound was receiving information—a barroom conversation is hardly the basis for a political theory—but Pound stubbornly used such information to buttress his beliefs and inserted them in *The Cantos.* As for the American Constitution, he told Tinkham, it had been betrayed by every administration since Jackson. Pound was corresponding with Hjalmar Schacht, head of the German banking system, and Gottfried Feder, one of Hitler's top economic advisers. He wrote to Senator Robert Taft and to historians Charles Beard and Davis Dewey, including with the latter letters a mimeographed "Introductory Text Book" for the study of American history with questions from Adams, Jefferson, Lincoln, and George Washington. He heard that Yeats had died and he received a letter from Zukofsky, who was finally ready to break with Pound but added that he "had gone on respecting your integrity ever since you drowned in the butter of credit economics." Another young Jewish poet named Delmore Schwartz, who had been asking intelligent questions about *The Cantos.* wrote, "Ready to resign as one of your most studious and faithful admirers." Schwartz had been offended by the remarks associating Jews with usury in *Guide to Kulchur* and argued that a race cannot commit moral acts, only individuals could.

Pound left for the United States on the Italian liner *Rex* in the middle of April 1939. With a suitcase and a rucksack, he booked second-class passage but was placed in a first-class luxury suite; later, he said the boat was half empty and it was a sign of Italian courtesy, but others alleged the suite had been provided by the Italian government. In New York, lounging on a deck chair and wearing a tweed jacket with a wide-collared shirt open at the neck, he answered questions posed by reporters eager for a story. According to Pound, Mussolini wanted only peace:

> Nothing but devilment can start a new war West of the Vistula.
> I'm not making any accusations against anyone. But the bankers
> and the munitions interests, whoever and wherever they may be,
> are more responsible for present talk of war than are the intentions
> of Mussolini or anyone else.

Later, when asked by a friend why he advertised Mussolini in an atmosphere bound to be hostile, Pound replied, "They won't pay attention to me unless I say something sensational."

Pound had come to America because he wanted to personally convince Franklin Delano Roosevelt that war was not in America's best interests. Pound was not doing this exclusively out of Fascist sympathies: his world had broken because of the First World War and there was nothing he dreaded more than war. And his fear of war underlined much of his hysteria during the thirties. His daughter, Mary, who saw him just before his departure, argued in her book *Discretions* that her father's desire to confront FDR was "not megalomania but a sense of responsibility carried to the extreme."

Roosevelt, of course, had no intention of meeting Pound, whom he would have considered disreputable. No American president since Buchanan had expressed the desire to meet an American poet, and even Buchanan changed his mind when Edgar Allan Poe arrived at the White House in soiled clothes. Instead, Pound saw Agriculture Secretary Henry Wallace, Congressman Tinkham, Senator William Borah, and several other members of the House and Senate, including the right-wing isolationist representative Hamilton Fish, Jr., and Martin Dies, the Texas congressman who was the chairman of the House Un-American Activities Committee. For Pound it was a frustrating experience, for these men offered little encouragement. In *The Cantos*, Pound quoted Borah in two poignant lines that show how out of place and awkward he must have felt:

> "Am sure I don't know what a man like you
> would find to do here."

Ford, living in New York, wrote to Allen Tate that Williams had seen Pound in Washington and found him fearful and depressed because he had made no real impression and because he felt Roosevelt was prepared to evade the Constitution, bending it to his will. Senator Burton Wheeler had warned him that Roosevelt had "packed" the Supreme Court so that it would support any action he took. Williams, in a letter to McAlmon, described Pound as disoriented, afraid of the cold dampness of the spring, looking "like Henry VIII," wrapped in "sweaters and shirts and coats until I thought him a man mountain."

Pound returned to New York City in early May, visiting Cummings and Ford and Wyndham Lewis, who was seeking portrait commissions and was to spend the war years in Canada writing *Self Condemned*, his best novel. He saw Iris Barry, who was the curator of the film library at the Museum of Modern Art, visited Katherine Ruth Heyman on Perry Street in the Village, and for the first time, met two longtime correspondents, Marianne Moore and H. L. Mencken. He had tea with Mary Barnard, a more recent correspondent, who had sent him her poems and with whom he had conducted a tutorial by mail. Barnard remembered him with a brown paper parcel which Pound explained was his overnight bag. Mary Barnard's awe for the poet prevented her from seeing the incongruity of the man who had come to advise the President of the United States and carried his clothes in a brown paper parcel. Pound was out of his element. The younger poet with the dashing flamboyant appearance had been replaced by the dissident bohemian who believed he could become a political force. But political power requires support, not simply ideology. Pound lacked support, not even getting it from the Social Credit group. The grace in his style, his cane and cutting remarks, had been replaced by something sheepish and awkward— the "man mountain" that Williams saw.

Pound took Barnard to see Iris Barry, hoping she would be able to help Barnard find work in New York, perhaps in the museum. He gave a poetry reading at Harvard, where he stayed with poet Theodore Spencer and met Archibald MacLeish, now librarian of Congress, who wrote an article on Pound that appeared in June in the *Atlantic Monthly*. He visited New Haven to meet James Angleton, editor of a new magazine called *Furioso*, and from there went to Clinton, New York, in a return to Hamilton College. He had been in touch over the years with several faculty members at Hamilton, who persuaded the college to offer him an honorary doctorate, a turn that flattered Pound. He was awarded the doctorate on June 12, along with journalist H. V. Kaltenborn, but the two men argued loudly over politics and Mussolini at an alumni luncheon afterward.

Before he left the United States he visited Williams in New Jersey, who wrote to James Angleton at *Furioso* that Pound was interested only in political attack and that his "youthful faults are creeping up on him fast." He hoped Pound would watch his step lest he "trip over the hem of his skirt" but feared there was trouble ahead: "Even the lion finally gets a horn through his guts." Then Williams wrote to James Laughlin, his publisher and Pound's at New Directions, remarking that Pound seemed to have acquired a habit of evading direct questions:

> The man is sunk, in my opinion, unless he can shake the fog of fascism out of his brain during the next few years, which I seriously doubt that he can do. The logicality of fascist rationalization is soon going to kill him. You can't argue away wanton slaughter of innocent women and children by the neoscholasticism of a controlled economy program. To hell with a Hitler who lauds the work of his airmen in Spain and so to hell with Pound too if he can't stand up and face his questioners on the point.

Williams had known Pound since they had met at the University of Pennsylvania when Pound was still an undergraduate. He had seen the problems of Pound's excessive pride and the postures he could assume to compensate for his self-consciousness. After having practiced medicine for thirty-five years, Williams had become an even sharper judge of character, and his comment had diagnostic and prescriptive truth.

9. THE FOG OF FASCISM

Pound returned to Europe to hear that Ford had died in France. He wrote a memorial essay which he contributed to a London magazine, *The Nineteenth Century and After*, and he sent to Faber cantos LII through LXXI, which he had corrected in America and on the ship home to Genoa. Publication in the United States seemed doubtful because John Farrar was incensed at the letters he had been receiving from Pound and wanted nothing more to do with him.

In Italy he began writing for newspapers like *Corriere della Sera* and the *Meridiana di Roma,* publishing a particularly offensive piece called "The Jews, Disease Incarnate." He was reading anti-Semitic tracts and pamphlets like "Britain and Jewry," which blamed international tensions on Jewish financiers and at the same time claimed that communism was part of a Jewish plot. He wrote James Laughlin that in his view "Roosevelt represents Jewry" and signed his letter "Heil Hitler." To Cummings he wrote that "Germany is 90% right in the present show." He wrote Congressman Horace Voorhis that if war began it was the fault of "international usury" and England's attempt to seize African territory mandated to Germany. He was still writing to American political leaders, hoping to discourage American participation should war occur. He heard from Mencken, who predicted that Roosevelt would find a way to involve America in any ensuing war. Pound switched his and Dorothy's investments from stocks in American companies to Italian government bonds. He condemned America, its institutions, and values even more stridently to his American correspondents, yet he suggested he would like to return again if possible.

In August of 1939 he was working on an essay on religion, calling for a Christianity unpoisoned by Jewish or non-European influences. The only legitimate holidays, he speculated, were those that could correspond to pagan celebrations of nature, the sun, the harvest, and the gods and goddesses of love. In letters he started referring to Pan, to the relation between coition, clarity, and creativity, and the need to purify Christianity, all of which possibilities he felt were being fully explored in Germany: "The function of Germany, as I see it, in the next forty years' art is indispensable. Nowhere else is there a force toward a purgation. The Italians are too easygoing. Spain is African and Christian, and you cannot trust Christianity for ten minutes." In Oswald Mosley's newspaper *Action* he lauded the Third Reich as "the natural civilizer of Russia. No less gutsy and active people would bother about educating the Mujik." In Washington, Pound had had lunch with the Polish ambassador, Count Jerzy Polocki, and had cautioned him not to trust Winston Churchill or the English. In the dawn hours of September 1, 1939, German Panzer tanks rolled over the Polish frontier headed for Warsaw and the second international catastrophe of the century had begun.

Pound had written over a thousand letters a year for the past decade, most of them motivated more by his economic theories and his fear of a new world war than by his literary concerns. He had presented his views tirelessly in sections of *The Cantos* and in hundreds of articles. No American or English poet had been as actively political since Blake had been tried for sedition, since Wordsworth and Shelley had written their political pamphlets, and Byron had died fighting for a political cause in Greece a century earlier. The British romantic poets had defended progress and change, inspired by the success of the French and American revolutions. Though Pound stood with the forces of reaction, his political criticism was not without substance. The history of modern capitalism has been one of periodic cycles of recession, depression, and expansion. Armaments manufacturers, traders, and financiers did begin to play a larger role in the economic game plans of nations after Napoleon when the organization of war became more complex and the battlefields bigger. What Pound feared was an economic structure dependent on an armaments industry, when the profit motive becomes a lever controlling war and peace.

At the same time, Pound's own hatred of an America that had failed to support him as a poet or had insufficiently admired his work had blinded him to the obvious differences between the American and fascist systems. By 1939 in Germany, Jews had already been horribly victimized, publicly humiliated, beaten and defiled in the streets, their stores and homes looted and burned by thugs encouraged by the Nazi system. All this was front-page news. The Germans could rationalize their barbarities on the grounds that the Jews were an inherently inferior people; could Pound do the same on the grounds that the Jews were conspiring to control the world's economies?

He began reading *The Law of Civilization and Decay* by Brooks Adams, Henry Adams's brother and a descendant of two presidents. In part, he took the book as a justification of his own stand. Adams had argued that "at times of economic competition the capitalist and the usurer become predominant in society, and the producer of goods falls into debt and servitude." Both Brooks and Henry Adams were disillusioned men, disgusted by modern culture, and blamed bankers for much of what seemed pernicious in modern life. This was, it should be noted, a perennial Americanism: Jefferson had declared in 1816 that he believed "that banking establishments are more dangerous than standing armies," and Jackson, a generation later, warned a group of powerful financiers that they were a collection of vipers and thieves whom he intended to rout.

Pound sought further confirmation of his views from the Spanish philosopher and former Harvard lecturer George Santayana. Santayana had lived in Italy as long as Pound had, and though Pound had met Daniel Cory, Santayana's personal secretary and assistant, he had never met Santayana. The two men did meet in Rome early in 1939, and Santayana told Daniel Cory that Pound reminded him of certain friends of his youth who had been what he termed "spasmodic rebels, decent by tradition, imitators of Thoreau, full of scraps of culture but lost, lost, lost in the intellectual world." Pound saw more of Santayana during the Christmas season of

1939–40 in Venice. His interests were gradually shifting from the polemics of economic theory to the larger, more philosophical questions of *The Cantos* and he thought Santayana might be able to help him. Santayana wrote to him not to expect too much: "You must not count on my philosophy to answer your questions, because questions are apt to imply a philosophy and don't admit of answers in terms of any other; so that you had better find your answers for yourself." But, Santayana added, he would be glad to see Pound again, and happy if Pound could show him some of the beauties of Venice which he might have missed. Santayana was staying in the Danielli, the most expensive and luxurious hotel on the Grand Canal while Pound, Olga, and their daughter, Mary, were comfortably installed in the modest Pensione Segusa near Olga's house, which was rented as usual. Olga was busy copying music, correcting proof for the *Accademia Chigiana*, a newsletter published where she worked, and arranging a series of concerts at the home of some former English diplomats attended by some of the foreign-service officers who were living in Venice in retirement. Pound had fully recovered from the disappointments of his American trip and his spirits were animated. He loved seeing movies in the evenings and one night, his daughter remembered, he returned from a Ginger Rogers–Fred Astaire film and began to leap and tap dance in his room to the distraction of the other guests at the *pensione*. Mary claims that her father was equally enthusiastic about seeing Santayana, who shared certain basic attitudes such as the belief that Mussolini was a humane man with good intentions. Pound gave Santayana his essay on Fenollosa and began instructing him on the "Ideogrammatic method" and Confucius. Sensing the possibility of a new convert, he began to describe a mode of thought that avoided abstraction but instead was based on mental leaps connecting particulars. This was the exact method Pound had chosen for *The Cantos*, and Santayana's comments can be taken as a basic criticism of that method: "When you ask for jumps and other particulars, you don't mean (I suppose) *any* other particulars, although your tendency to jump is so irresistible that the bond between the particulars jumped to is not always apparent? It is a mental grab-bag. A *latent* classification or a *latent* genetic connection would seem to be required, if utter miscellaneousness is to be avoided."

Cantos LII through LXXI were published by Faber at the end of January 1940, and James Laughlin agreed to publish them in an American edition eight months later. Recognizing the density of the material, Laughlin suggested that Pound write an explanatory preface to help the reader through the Chinese sections and the mysteries of John Adams, but Pound felt he might be compromising if he did it:

> The new set is not incomprehensible. Nobody can summarize what is already condensed to the absolute limit. The point is that

with Cantos 52/71 a NEW thing is. Plain narrative with chrono-
logical sequence. Read 'em before you go off half-cocked.

When the American edition appeared, it included an introductory pamphlet
written by Laughlin and a comment by Delmore Schwartz on versification.

Work on *The Cantos* diminished during the war years, but his correspondence and articles continued to flow. The articles were sometimes
poorly conceived diatribes which appeared wherever they were accepted.
Pound felt compelled to get his ideas into print no matter where or in what
publication. In the Japan *Times* he wrote: "Democracy is now currently
defined in Europe as a 'country run by Jews' " and in a piece for *Meridiana
di Roma*, called "The Jews and This War," reprinted in the Nazi publication
News from Germany, he used the fictitious *Protocols of Zion* to explain the
origins of the war. He was convinced of a Jewish conspiracy to control the
world. He wrote in *Action* that he did not "think the native races of Europe
should be annihilated for the Jew . . . or kike millionaires to make the
world safe for Lazard frères," but he feared this would occur because the
English were a slave race governed by the House of Rothschild since Water-
loo. He wrote friends that Henry Morgenthau, Roosevelt's secretary of the
Treasury, was half-Jewish, that Cordell Hull, the American secretary of
state, was married to a Jewess. In a letter to Fascist economist Odon Por, he
called Roosevelt "Jewsfeldt," and in a subsequent letter, "Stinkie Rooosen-
stein." Harold Ickes, Roosevelt's secretary of the interior, responding to
one of Pound's letters said he could not tell whether it was "a lyric or
merely modernist prose." On the sea voyage from New York to Italy a year
earlier, Pound had heard the name William Wiseman, a New York banker
with political influence. Later he learned that Wiseman had once been an
officer in British intelligence, and he wrote to Wyndham Lewis: "America is
damn well to keep out of the war/BAD enough to have european aryans
murdering each other for the sake of Willie Wiseman and . . . a few bug-
garin' kikes." Lewis's reply was that he heard that Mussolini had "a screw
loose due to syphilitic poisoning." Pound then wrote attacking Lewis's apos-
tasy in *The Hitler Cult*, asking whether it was done for money to escape
"judaea," his name now for England, which he believed was controlled by
Jewish financiers. "Of course you couldn't have printed or been paid for the
truth about the war," he told Lewis. The war was for usury, for the gold
monopoly, for the vengeance of the Rothschild family, and the "yidd influence has never been anything but a stinking curse to Europe from A.D. 1 to
1940."

Most of Pound's letters continued to be sent to Americans whom he
hoped would exert pressure to keep the United States from becoming involved in the war: among them, H. L. Mencken, Pearl S. Buck, Charles
Beard, Congressman Tinkham, Dr. D. G. Mathews of the House Un-Amer-

ican Activities Committee, and Senators Robert A. Taft and Burton
Wheeler. He sometimes commented in these letters on what he was reading: Henry Adams's *The Degradation of the Democratic Dogma*, an attack on
plutocracy, or Brooks Adams's *The New Empire* and *The Theory of Social
Revolutions*, and Davis Rich Dewey's *Financial History of the United States*, in
which he learned that President Andrew Jackson had paid off the existing
national debt in 1837 and distributed a surplus of twenty-eight million dollars to the states, which Pound took as an illustration of the national divi-
dend idea of Social Credit.

10. HUMAN INFERNO

While Pound was reading the books by the Adamses and Dewey in the
spring of 1940, Germany had invaded Norway, Holland, and Belgium, the
natural and predictable corridor to France. By June France had fallen, besieged by both the Germans and the Italians, who had by then declared war
on England and pushed into North Africa and Greece. The English had
been forced off the beaches at Dunkirk, and London was being blitzed. Of
the many civilian casualties, one was H.D.'s friend Frances Gregg, who had
served as a sort of anodyne for H.D.'s pain when Pound left her for Europe
in 1908. H.D. had given Frances the only copy of *Hilda's Book*, the youthful
poems Pound had written to celebrate their love. Frances was killed in the
Nazi bombings of Plymouth, but the book survived. On May 8, 1940,
Pound's old friend and publisher, William Bird, spoke on WNBC radio in
New York to urge American entry in the war, describing the Nazi menace
and a fifth column of French collaborators who sympathized with the German occupation. One of the most infamous of these collaborators was another friend of Pound's Paris years, Jean Cocteau, who anticipated the Nazis' arrival and immediately sought the official license for the staging of his
plays. Pound decided to return to the States once again to promote isola-
tionism. Books, drawings, and sculptures were packed and stored by his
friend Ubuldo degli Uberti, chief of the Rome Navy Press Office. The
Uberti family all liked Pound, and after the war, Uberti's son wrote an
impassioned defense of Pound for a Rapallo newspaper, *Corriere della Ligu-
ria*, in which he argued that the American depression, with six thousand
bank failures and "spreading communism under the cloak of Roosevelt's
demagogic policies" justified Pound's action. Pound never did manage to
leave Italy, however, partly because the clipper ships were only taking mail
from Italy, and travel to Lisbon through the French war zone seemed too
dangerous. Uberti put Pound in touch with Cornelio di Marzio, director of
the Fascist Confederation of Artists, who introduced Pound to officers of the
Italian Ministry of Popular Culture, which administered a program on Ra-

dio Rome called The American Hour. Most of the men Pound met were eager to help him express his views, especially if they might help prevent or delay American intervention. Soon he was publishing articles in the Fascist newspaper of Genoa, and in the *Libro e Moschetto,* a journal published by Fascists in Milan for university people, in which Pound maintained that the duty of Italian intellectuals was to support Mussolini and to savor the artistic values inherent in fascism. He was writing regularly for *Meridiana di Roma,* comparing Hitler and Mussolini to Confucius, whom he claimed they understood perfectly because their intuitions were so developed. In an article in the Japan *Times* he described the "essential fairness of Hitler's war aims" and said that Churchill was senile and mentally deranged, merely a front for the Rothschilds. Such articles were not read by many Americans, but they were being collected by agents of the Federal Bureau of Investigation.

Pound had been eager to resume broadcasting for Radio Rome on a regular basis. He had written to Ronald Duncan, an acolyte who edited a magazine called *The Townsman* in London, that his old friend Natalie Barney had just given him a present:

> Dear Ron: -/-/Blasted friends left a goddam radio here yester.
> Gift. God damn destructive and dispersive devil of an invention.
> But got to be faced. Drammer has got to face it, not only face
> cinema. Anybody who can survive may strengthen inner life, but
> mass of apes and worms will be still further rejuiced to passivity.
> Hell a state of passivity? Or limbo??
>
> Anyhow what drammer or teeyater wuz, radio is. Possibly the
> loathing of it may stop diffuse writing. No sense in printing until it
> gets to finality? Also the histrionic developments in announcing.
> And the million to one chance that audition will develop: at least
> to a faculty for picking the fake in the voices. Only stuff fit to hear
> was Tripoli, Sofia and Tunis. Howling music in two of 'em and a
> cembalo in Bugarea.
>
> And a double sense of the blessedness of silence when the
> damn thing is turned off.
>
> Anyhow, if you're writin for styge or teeyater up to date, you
> gotter measure it all, not merely against cinema, but much more
> against the persanae now poked into every bleedin' 'ome and
> smearing the mind of the peapull. If anyone is a purrfekk HERRR-
> kules, he may survive, and may clarify his style in resistance to the
> devil box. I mean if he ain't druv to melancolia crepitans before he
> recovers.

Barney had given Pound the radio because she wanted him to listen to a regular series of anti-British broadcasts made by a William Joyce, called

Lord Haw-Haw, who delivered his attacks in a flawless Oxford accent with a "far sweeping view that no Islander in Britain seems to possess."

Radio was a way to get news during wartime. One consequence of the war was the curtailing of Pound's correspondence, especially with America and England. Letters came infrequently when they came at all and Pound suddenly felt out of touch. Some of his excess energy went into the translation of the economic theories of Odon Por, a Hungarian resident of Italy who fully subscribed to Mussolini's ideas and whom Pound had known since 1934 when he reminded Por never to lose sight of "the AIM of Fascism, and its great elasticity." By translating Por into English, Pound was assured at least a minimal income for a year. Dorothy's income was stopped during the war, and after the American entry, any royalties Pound had earned from American publishers or stocks were blocked as well.

Another way of earning income was by speaking on the radio. Pound's daughter, Mary de Rachewiltz, and Olga Rudge have asserted that the radio broadcasts began in an almost accidental fashion, that Pound was in Rome in connection with his Vivaldi work when he accepted a casual invitation to do a broadcast explaining his views. This was not true during the war, however. Pound later told his friend Harry Meacham that he had been permitted to begin broadcasting only after repeated requests: "It took me, I think it was, TWO years, insistence and wrangling etc., to GET HOLD of their microphone." The broadcasts were a form of direct action for him, an attempt to shape events in the tradition of his heroes Bertrand de Born and Sigismondo Malatesta. Pound had been proposing projects to various sectors of the Italian propaganda apparatus for several years. His style, once he became convinced of the merits of an idea, was to organize his own response, whether it be a new literary movement, a magazine, or an ideal university. He had suggested to Mussolini a plan to replace the League of Nations. The plan never reached Mussolini, but members of his staff characterized it as extremely eccentric, "conceived by a foggy mind, lacking all sense of reality." Pound had also tried to convince the Ministry of Popular Culture to publish a series on great American political thinkers whose ideas paralleled those of fascism, an English-language magazine and a weekly bulletin summarizing the best Italian articles. None of these plans was approved. When Pound proposed resuming his broadcasts on a regular basis, certain officials of the government-controlled radio broadcasting agency demurred, and there was some fear that he might have been a double agent transmitting information through code. Given the abruptness and incomprehensibility of some of the remarks he subsequently made on Italian radio, these fears seemed justified. He was investigated by the Military Information Services, which concluded that he was a dubious risk; he had met with American ambassador William Phillips and with Herman Moss, a consular officer in Genoa known to be an anti-Fascist. Despite this investigation, and other reports such as one by the director of the National Institute of Cultural Relations with Foreign Countries, who asserted that in his opinion Pound was pleasantly insane but potentially dangerous because of an inclination both to gossip and to speak nonsense, Pound was permitted to contribute to a program called "The American Hour," which was transmitted to England, parts of central Europe, and the United States. His initial broadcast was on January 23, 1941, and it lasted for seven minutes.

The opening remarks of the broadcast characterized his goals: "The United States should try to understand the last twenty years of European history, before going too far in finding themselves involved in the war. Democracy was created in America and this is the place where it must be saved. The peace of the world is set forth through good government from the interior." The intention to dissuade American participation in the war because that might in some never explained manner weaken democratic institutions was a frequent assertion of Pound's, but it was soon overshadowed by some of the harshest invective of his career. By the time of the first broadcast, the Germans had advanced through Yugoslavia and Greece and had moved to within thirty miles of Moscow after having taken almost half a million prisoners.

His talks occurred every three days, and he traveled to Rome one week a month to prerecord them. He also wrote scripts for others, edited them, and wrote press releases for broadcast. Whatever he wrote had to be approved by the Fascist hierarchy. Pound was friendly with a number of the other broadcasters, particularly with Olivia Rossetti Agresti, who was the English poet Dante Gabriel Rossetti's daughter, and with several of the station officials. Another friend was Camillo Pellizzi, who for nineteen years had been on the faculty of the University of London and was director of the National Institute of Fascist Culture. Pellizzi asserted to agents of the FBI after the war that Pound saw Italian fascism as a means to reform American government, not as an ideal that could be useful for America. At no time did he ever consider himself a traitor, but always a patriot exposing the Roosevelt administration.

In an unpublished piece called "How I Lost Ezra Pound's Letters," Pellizzi claimed few Italians understood why Pound went on radio either before or after the Americans entered the war. He stressed that Italians could not in any event, understand what he was saying, and that what they heard seemed a register of the confusion of the times. Pound was assured in his Americanism, there was always an aura of suspicion about him, and he was distrusted all the more by Italians because of his habit of saying anything he had on his mind to anybody. Pellizzi's impression was that Pound was using the microphones to continue an old feud between himself and his country. Pound's point of view in his radio talks was extremely personal, as if the war was some kind of affront, an attack on all the values and civilization he cherished. His persona would shift according to accent and diction, and he would use a folksy western twang, a southern drawl, an ironic cockney whine, a flat toneless rage. Sometimes he slurred, often he seemed to be ranting. A representative example of the mixture of bile and personal complaint in Pound's remarks occurs in his broadcast of October 6, 1941:

> Mr. Churchill, even Mr. Churchill hasn't had the brass to tell the American people why he wants them to die to save what. He is fighting for the gold standard, and monopoly. England is trying to starve the whole of mankind, and make it pay through the nose. . . . His gang, Churchill's with a kike, gentile, or hybrid is not fit to govern. And the English ought to be the only people ass enough and brute enough to fight for him. . . . And Mr. Churchill and that brute, *Rosenfeld*, and their kike postal spies and obstructors distress me by cutting off my normal mental intercourse with my colleagues. But I'm not going to starve, I am not going to starve mentally. The cultures of the Occident came out of Europe, and a lot of it is still right here in Europe, and I don't mean archaeology either.

This ravaging of Churchill was followed by an attack on Roosevelt, one of a series that intensified as the months passed:

> Will you look at the age of the chief war pimps? Roosevelt now says he saw war coming back in 1937. In 1937 there was no necessity of war. Roosevelt did all he could to make it inevitable. There is no record of a single act of Roosevelt's [made] in the spirit of staving off war. Ignorance of Europe. Government in charge of pigs. . . . Don't say that I affirm what he did. What I affirm is that he never showed the faintest inclination to learn the facts and come out for a just solution. That is a very conservative statement. He has never been neutral. But get down to this one point of age. How old are the blokes who are trying to throw America into the conflict? What is their business? What is their civic record?

Very few people in America other than the FBI were aware of Pound's activities, but Williams received a letter from Pound in which such attacks were summarized. At first Williams was charitable, writing Laughlin, who was disturbed by such diatribes, that Pound's "stupidities" should be forgiven though not excused:

> I do, no matter how much he riles me. But I prefer not to have to do with him in any way. He wants to patronize me. Don't tell me this isn't so, for I know better. His letters are insults, the mewings of an 8th-grade teacher. That's where he thinks I exist in relation

to his catastrophic knowledge of affairs, his blinding judgments of contemporary values.

But even Williams's charitable attitude had its limitations. Later he got furious over Pound's continued defense of Mussolini's invasion of Ethiopia.

Soon Pound was claiming on the radio as he had formerly in letters that Roosevelt was "more in the hands of the Jews than Wilson was in 1919." This remark occurred in a radio broadcast made on December 7, 1941, the same day that Pearl Harbor was suddenly attacked by waves of Japanese bombers. On the night of December 7 in the Chelmo woods in Poland, nine hundred Jews from the township of Kolo were the first to choke with the poison gases of the Final Solution.

After the American entry into the war, Pound refrained from broadcasting for a month. He met American news correspondent Reynolds Packard and told him he intended to remain in Italy. Packard warned him that his actions, especially the broadcasts, could later be interpreted as treason. According to Packard, Pound gave the Fascist salute and claimed he believed in fascism, wanted to defend it, and could not see how it was contrary to American philosophy. He considered himself 100 percent American and was against only "Roosevelt and the Jews who support him."

Americans had been instructed by the American Embassy to make preparations to leave Italy. Pound's passport had expired and in Rome he was told it would be extended for only six months. He had freely and fiercely criticized the postwar system of passports and visas as a control inhibiting what he regarded as the natural right of freedom of movement. To Pound, consulates represented the entrails of bureaucratic evasiveness and dishonesty. Richard Rovere, writing for *Esquire,* claimed that Pound was denied permission to board the last train carrying diplomatic personnel from Rome to Lisbon. There may have been an earlier outburst by Pound in the American Embassy in Rome, and a State Department memorandum signed by George Wadsworth, chargé d'affaires at the Embassy, refers to Pound as a "pseudo-American." Ironically, some of Pound's venerable ancestors were Wadsworths. Pound was reported to have made "undignified remarks" at both the Embassy in Rome and the consular offices in Genoa, offering the Fascist salute in each place on his departure. He may have been enraged at his inability to get a visa for his daughter, Mary; Olga Rudge charged that her illegitimacy had been used as an excuse to deny her one. His parents, too, presented a problem; Homer had fallen and broken his hip, his pension payments had stopped coming, and Italian banks were no longer changing or accepting American checks.

Suddenly Pound, who had barely ever earned enough to support himself, who needed his wife's income to maintain his respectability, was surrounded by dependents. The radio broadcasts paid the equivalent of seventeen dollars for writing and reading a broadcast of about ten minutes. There were the articles for *Meridiana di Roma* and translations: the Odon Por book, Confucius, and a novel by Enrico Pea, *Moscardino.* He met frequently with Pea, trying to find idiomatic parallels for the dialect Pea used in his novel. On one occasion Pea accompanied him to the Rome train terminal. The barrier was down and the train for Rapallo had started to move off. Pea recalled that Pound, gripping his typewriter in his left hand, leaped "over the barrier and jumped onto the moving train with all the agility of an American cowboy who vaults on the back of a fleeing horse."

Mary had been in a convent school but was then living with Olga in Sant'Ambrogio on the hill above Rapallo. Pound was directing her education, choosing books from his library for her to read, helping her to translate a Hardy novel, *Under the Greenwood Tree,* into Italian. He wanted her to become a writer and to translate his *Cantos* into Italian, and as a beginning they worked together on the Chinese poems he had done in *Cathay.* Often, he would take her to Rome with him when he did his recordings for the radio programs. Pound seemed sobered by the war, and once when he was invited to lunch by some Italian friends he refused the champagne they provided for dessert, remarking to Mary as they left that it was no time for frivolity. Mary noticed a change in her father which she blamed on the "usury of time" and a metaphysical war at work inside him. Pound had lost his sense of humor and his "grip on what specifically he should have been able to control, his own *words."* His tongue was "tricking him, running away with him, leading him into excess, away from his pivot, into blind spots." Mary's observations echo less sympathetic remarks made by Virgil Thomson, who had known Pound in Paris fifteen years earlier. Pound, Thomson argued, was always "jumping ahead of himself," saying "foolish things" which he would then begin to believe only because he had said them.

At the end of January 1942, Pound was notified by the Italian Supreme Command that he could remain in Italy with his family for the duration of the war. He made 125 more broadcasts until his indictment by the U.S. Department of Justice. The talks were now prefaced by a carefully worded preamble:

> Rome Radio, acting in accordance with the Fascist policy of intel-
> lectual freedom and free expression of opinion by those who are
> qualified to hold it, has offered Dr. Ezra Pound the use of the
> microphone twice a week. It is understood that he will not be
> asked to say anything whatsoever that goes against his conscience
> or anything incompatible with his duties as a citizen of the United
> States of America.

"Dr." Pound's first transmission centered on an attack on Roosevelt, who had, according to Pound and many others in the United States, planned the American entry into the war long before:

> The United States has been for months . . . illegally at war through what I considered to be the criminal acts of a President whose mental condition was not, so far as I could see, all that could or should be desired of a man in so responsible a position or office. He has, so far as the evidence . . . available showed, broken his promises to his electorate. He had to my mind violated his oath of office. He had to my mind violated the oath of allegiance to the United States Constitution which even the ordinary citizen is expected to take every time he gets a new passport. It was obviously a mere question of hours between that day and time when the United States would be legally at war with the Axis. I spent a month trying to figure things out. Well, did I? Perhaps I concluded sooner. At any rate I had a month clear to make up my mind about some things. I had Confucius and Aristotle, both of whom had been up against similar problems, both of whom had seen empires fall, both of whom had seen deeper into the causes of human confusion than most men.

According to Pound, the country had been misinformed, traduced by incompetent advisers, pushed into a war that would drain it for the next thirty years, one that might have been avoided "if anyone had the unlikely idea of sending me out there [to Japan] with any thought of official powers." The talk ended with a reflection (exceedingly ironic considering subsequent circumstances) on madness and Roosevelt's "weakness of mind": "Whom God would destroy, he first sends to the bughouse."

Pound's voice in the broadcasts had begun to assume a rasping, buzzing quality like the sound of a hornet stuck in a jar. Dr. Charles Upson Clark, an American scholar in Rome and a friend of Nancy McCormack's, reported that Pound's conversation was frequently obscene and his appearance unkempt, that he looked dissolute. Pound was commuting between Rapallo and Rome with a pass for the national railway given to him by an official at the Ministry of Popular Culture, and he took a room in a hotel across from the radio station. When he met Italian writer Romano Bilenchi, he was surprised to learn that Bilenchi was not a Fascist and that many Italians disapproved of the war. Pound told Bilenchi he thought the Italian people had wanted the war and wanted to win it, but Bilenchi argued that no war had been less popular, that Pound's impression was absurd, that most Italians were disillusioned by Mussolini and particularly by the men around him. Instead of destroying the structures of the old bourgeois state, Bilenchi claimed, Mussolini had become the main buttress for those structures.

Pound replied with a lecture on the genealogy of fascism, tracing it through
Confucius, Cavalcanti, and Frobenius. Bilenchi told him of an old woman he
had seen hurling a bag of potatoes at an officer, denouncing the Fascists, but
Pound waved his hand as if bothered by a disturbing insect and claimed the
Axis was too powerful to lose the war even if there were temporary inconveniences. He admitted that there was a scarcity of butter, but that problem
could be easily solved by planting peanuts in the Alps. He planned to discuss this idea with novelist Enrico Pea and then take it up with Mussolini
himself. After the war Pea told Bilenchi that Pound had indeed proposed
his peanut scheme and that "the fellow is crazy, crazy, completely crazy."

The radio talks showed his increasing disorientation as they lurched
randomly through a panoply of Pound's favorite hatreds. He spoke with
absolute conviction in a manner that Daniel Pearlman, in *The Barb of Time,*
has seen as an "unconscious parody of the style of the fascist 'Leader' whose
power in the final analysis rests on nothing more than the spellbinding force
of his personality." He attacked the Rothschilds, Bernard Baruch and
Henry Morgenthau, J. Pierpont Morgan and Franklin "Finklestein" Roosevelt with a shrieking fanaticism. He recommended the *Protocols of the Elders
of Zion* and *Mein Kampf.* Occasionally he reminisced about his literary
friends Joyce, Eliot, Lewis, or Cocteau, he quoted from *The Cantos,* and he
discussed Frobenius and Confucius. All through the disordered rhetoric of
the talks he sustained the notes of chaos, hysteria, and exacerbated outrage:

February 3, 1942:

> You are at war for the duration of the German's pleasure. You are
> at war for the duration of Japan's pleasure. Nothing in the Western
> world, nothing in the whole of our Occident, can help you to
> dodge that. Nothing can help you dodge it.

March 15, 1942:

> No Rothschild is English, no Streiker is English, no Roosevelt is
> English, no Baruch, Morgenthau, Cohen, Lehman, Warburg,
> Kuhn, Kahn, Schiff, Sieff or Solomon was ever yet born Anglo-
> Saxon. And it is for this filth that you fight. It is for this filth that
> you have murdered your Empire. It is this filth that elects, selects,
> elects your politicians.

April 23, 1942:

> The drift of Mr. Archibald MacLeish's remarks toward the end of
> March seems fairly clear. He has been given a gangster's brief and
> he has been entrusted with the defense of a gang of criminals and
> he is a-doing his damndest. I object and have objected to the
> crime, regardless of who may be related to the men who have

committed it, and I accept the conditions of the debate, namely that the Morgenthau-Lehman gang control 99% of all means of communication inside the United States and that they can drown out and buy out nearly all opposition, on top of which Roosevelt has, characteristically, resorted to blackmail. Any man who does not accept the gigantic frauds perpetrated by the Morgenthau-Roosevelt treasury is to be held up as a traitor to the United States. The reply is that any man who submits to Roosevelt's treason to the public commits a breach of citizen's duty. There is no connection between submittin' to the Roosevelt-Morgenthau frauds and patriotism. There is no connection between such submission and winning this war—or any other. There is no patriotism in submittin' to the prolonged and multiple frauds of the Roosevelt administration and to try to make the present support of these frauds figure as loyalty to the American heritage, is just so much dirt or bunkum. Doubtless the tactics of evasion will be used to the uttermost—but if the American people submit to either or both of these wheezes the American people will be mugs.

April 30, 1942:

Don't start a pogrom. That is, not an old-style killing of small Jews. That system is no good, whatever. Of course, if some man had a stroke of genius, and could start a pogrom up at the top. I repeat . . . if some man had a stroke of genius, and could start a pogrom up at the top, there might be something to say for it. But on the whole, legal measures are preferable. The 60 kikes who started this war might be sent to St. Helena, as a measure of world prophylaxis, and some hyper-kikes of non-Jewish kikes along with them.

May 5, 1942:

The kike, and the unmitigated evil that has been centered in London since the British government got on the Red Indians to murder the American frontier settlers, has herded the Slavs, the Mongols, the Tartars openly against Germany and Poland and Finland. And secretly against all that is decent in America, against the total American heritage. This is my war all right. I've been in it for twenty years—my gran'dad was in it before me.

May 8, 1943:

There is not one ounce or atom of honesty in either Churchill or Roosevelt. Most of the reasons for England and America being in the war are unconfessable and indecent. . . . A clean England

and a clean United States might collaborate in a new world, but it will take a hell of a lot of Sapolio to wash off the mess made by Roosevelt and Churchill. I'm telling you, I'm not giving you the Axis point of view.

May 9, 1943:

The Jew is a savage, his psychology is . . . may the stink of your camp drive you onward—herders—having no care but to let their . . . herds grouse and move onward when the pasture is exhausted.

11. LORD GA-GA

Treason, especially in wartime, is not a narrowly defined technical term. It does not apply exclusively to the sale of military secrets or to sabotage or espionage but broadly means giving aid or comfort or support of any kind to an enemy. During 1941 and 1942, Pound vilified American leaders, policy, and institutions while the war raged in North Africa, Asia, Russia, and Europe. He seems to have given all his time to the propaganda effort. When not preparing his own talks he wrote them for others with the same obsessive zeal he had once devoted to Social Credit. During the war, he wrote only two cantos, those in Italian. Out of argument with ourselves, we make poetry, Yeats once observed; out of argument with others, rhetoric. According to an FBI investigation after the war, Pound usually used the Fascist salute when greeting people in Rome. Except for the fall and winter of 1942, his voice was on the airwaves every third day. By then the FBI had begun questioning anyone in America who had known him; he may have heard about this and stopped for several months. There is speculation that he may have been in Germany for part of this period or that he may have been ill. An FBI agent visited William Carlos Williams and asked him to help identify Pound's voice on the radio broadcasts. Williams had chastised Pound for his talks in an article, calling him Lord Ga-Ga, a "pitable spectacle," a fool, and a "spoiled brat." E. E. Cummings and others offered information. Archibald MacLeish, then assistant director of the Office of War Information, said, "The real question seems to me to be a question of how the government should treat as tragi-comic a figure." James Laughlin told visiting FBI agents that "Pound's plight is the case of a man never adjusting himself to society, although having vast ambition and ego." As a result of that ego, Laughlin added, Pound felt himself "the greatest poet since Dante. He, however, believes that people have persecuted him over a period of years. Therefore, he is now anxious to persecute the Jews." Laughlin remembered that when Pound had read at Harvard, he had included anti-

Semitic poems because he felt there were Jews in the audience. He also believed that FDR was Jewish.

On July 26, 1943, the District Court of the United States for the District of Columbia handed down an indictment for violations of the Treason Statute. Seven other Americans were indicted along with Pound, the others for broadcasting from Germany. Attorney General Francis Biddle told reporters at a press conference that the indictments were based not only on the falsifications inherent in their respective propaganda efforts, but on their free choice in wartime to devote their services to the enemies of the United States. Pound heard of the indictment on the BBC. He had felt great freedom on Italian radio, he claimed later, because he had been sure that he was understood by no one (but in that event why even bother to broadcast?). More than a decade earlier, in his essay on Cavalcanti, he had praised another Italian poet, Leopardi, as the only living writer who had helped take a city at machine-gun point—which gave him more authority than a "batch of neurasthenic incompetents" who were incapable of action and who had never swerved from routine expectations. For Pound, the broadcasts had been an occasion when he could move, as Emerson had advised in his "American Scholar" essay, from the position of "man thinking" to that of "man acting," from the reflective arranger of sounds and words to the doer of deeds.

But Pound's analogy of his own experience to Leopardi's is imperfect. Edmond de Goncourt, a French writer whom Pound admired, has a passage in his journals describing a gathering of intellectuals at Brebant's in Paris in 1870 as the German armies were besieging the city. It was a gloomy moment for France and for her intellectuals. At this gathering the historian Ernest Renan chose to speak, praising German intelligence and culture and arguing that it was superior to French culture. It was a moment of arrogant bad taste in French history and de Goncourt registered his surprise at how absurd a great man can be when dealing with matters beyond his capacity.

By the summer of 1943, the war fortunes of the Axis powers had shifted. In North Africa the Germans had been routed, and Sicily had been successfully invaded, making Italy extremely vulnerable. There were peace demonstrations in several cities, and the day before Pound's indictment had been handed down in Washington, King Victor Emmanuel asked Mussolini to resign. Mussolini was imprisoned and a new government outlawed the Fascist party and all its organizations.

Pound immediately wrote Attorney General Biddle a long, reasoned, and temperate defense of his position which showed that he understood the gravity of the charges and the possible consequences:

I understand that I am under indictment for treason. I have done my best to get an authentic report of your statement to this effect. And I wish to place the following facts before you.

I do not believe that the simple fact of speaking over the radio, wherever placed, can in itself constitute treason. I think that must depend on what is said, and on the motives for speaking.

I obtained the concession to speak over Rome Radio with the following proviso. Namely that nothing should be asked of me contrary to my conscience or contrary to my duties as an American citizen. I obtained a declaration on their part of a belief in "the free expression of opinion by those qualified to have an opinion."

The legal mind of the Attorney General will understand the interest inherent in this distinction, as from unqualified right of expression.

This declaration was made several times in the announcement of my speeches; with the declaration "He will not be asked to say anything contrary to his conscience, or contrary to his duties as an American citizen" (Citizen of the U.S.).

These conditions have been adhered to. The only time I had an opinion as to what might be interesting as subject matter, I was asked whether I would speak of religion. This seemed to me hardly my subject, though I did transmit on one occasion some passages from Confucius, under the title, "The Organum of Confucius."

I have not spoken with regard to this war, but in protest against a system which created one war after another, in series and in system. I have not spoken to the troops, and have not suggested that the troops should mutiny or revolt.

The whole basis of democratic or majority government assumes that the citizen shall be informed of the facts. I have not claimed to know all the facts, but I have claimed to know some of the facts which are an essential part of the total that should be known to people.

I have for years believed that the American people should be better informed as to Europe, and informed by men who are not tied to a special interest or under definite control.

The freedom of the press has become a farce, as everyone knows that the press is controlled, if not by its titular owners, at least by the advertisers.

Free speech under modern conditions becomes a mockery if it does not include the right of free speech over the radio.

And this point is worth establishing. The assumption of the

right to punish and take vengeance regardless of the area of juris-
diction is dangerous. I do not mean in a small way; but for the
nation.

I returned to America before the war to protest against particular forces then engaged in trying to create war and to make sure
that the U.S.A. should be dragged into it.

Arthur Kitson's testimony before the Cunliffe and MacMillan
commissions was insufficiently known. Brooks Adams brought to
light several currents in history that should be better known. The
course of events following the foundation of the Bank of England
should be known, and considered in sequence: the suppression of
colonial paper money, especially in Pennsylvania! The similar
curves following the Napoleonic wars, and our Civil War and Versailles need more attention.

We have not the right to drift into another error similar to
that of the Versailles Treaty.

We have, I think, the right to a moderate expansion including
defence of the Caribbean, the elimination of foreign powers from
the American continent, but such expansion should not take place
at the cost of deteriorating or ruining the internal structure of the
U.S.A. The ruin of markets, the perversions of trade routes, in fact
all the matters on which my talks have been based is *[sic]* of importance to the American citizen; whom neither you nor I should
betray either in time of war or peace. I may say in passing that I
took out a life membership in the American Academy of Social
and Political Science in the hope of obtaining fuller discussion of
some of these issues, but did not find them ready for full and frank
expression of certain vital elements in the case; this may in part
have been due to their incomprehension of the nature of the case.

At any rate a man's duties increase with his knowledge. A war
between the U.S. and Italy is monstrous and should not have occurred. And a peace without justice is no peace but merely a pre-
lude to future wars. Someone must take count of these things. And
having taken count must act on his knowledge; admitting that his
knowledge is partial and his judgment subject to error.

Pound's defense rested on a free speech argument. In "Patria Mia" he
had argued, "The artist is free. The true artist is the champion of free
speech from the beginning." Now Pound claimed the right to "protest
against a system which creates one war after another, in series and in system." In the preface to *Kulchur* he had written, "Given my freedom, I may
be a fool to use it, but I would be a cad not too." Pound's defenders have
argued that whatever he said would have been permissible had he said it in

the United States, but of course it is exactly to the point that he did not. And what radio station would have allowed him to condemn Roosevelt more than once in wartime? Cocteau had told Pound in Paris in the twenties that "the tact of audacity consists in knowing how far to go too far." Pound, writing after the war to his friend Ingrid Davies, phrased the aphorism a bit differently: "In art and in life, one has to go too far before one can learn how far is far enough." Cocteau, as he proved masterfully in wartime Paris, was able to pander to the Germans and their French collaborators without outraging those in the Resistance: after the war his face was on a French postage stamp celebrating the peace. Pound, less politic and more impetuous, had plunged into a situation from which there would be no safe retreat even had he wanted one. Near the end of the war he could see his predicament in almost mythic terms, writing, "Forty years I have schooled myself, not to write an economic history of the U.S. or any other country but to write an epic poem which begins, 'In the Dark Forest' crosses the Purgatory of human error and ends in the light. . . . For this reason I have had to understand the NATURE of error."

12. THE DARK FOREST

In the fall of 1943, as the Allied armies were preparing to invade Italy, the Germans tried to secure and fortify the coast around Rapallo and Pound and his wife were ordered to evacuate their waterside apartment. Homer Pound had died and Isabel's apartment was small, so Ezra and Dorothy decided to move in with Olga at Sant'Ambrogio. Mary was sent back to Gais, and Pound, as Mary put it in *Discretions*, "was pent up with two women who loved him, whom he loved, and who coldly hated each other. Whatever the civilized appearances, the polite behavior and the façade in front of the world, their hatred and tension had permeated the house." Food was scarce; there was little or no meat, milk, eggs, or sugar available; there was no coffee or butter, barely any wood or charcoal for heat or cooking; there were no letters, no newspapers, no telephones, and few trains. People were seen begging for food, and air raids had begun in northern Italy. There was also considerable tension between German and Italian troops.

Pound was in Rome when General Badoglio, hero of the invasion of Ethiopia and head of the new government, agreed to capitulate and declared an armistice. Rome was immediately occupied by German troops. There was an atmosphere of panic as Fascists and former government officials began to flee. Borrowing a knapsack, a pair of heavy hiking boots, a map, and a few provisions, Pound prepared to leave but then decided to head to Gais to see his daughter. The poet who had walked through Provence a quarter of a century earlier seeking reminiscences of troubador culture was now tramping in a landscape of nightmare. On his way north he slept in fields and was fed by peasants. He spent a night in an air raid shelter in Bologna, where he found a train that took him as far as Verona. He walked the remainder of the way, his feet blistered and swollen because the boots did not fit properly. When he arrived in Gais, Mary did not at first recognize the dirty and soiled traveler, taking him for one of the many beggars that passed by asking for food. Pound had come to Gais with the express purpose of telling Mary about Dorothy and Omar, the circumstances of his other family, a situation about which she, at nineteen, was completely unaware. She seems to have accepted her father's news without rancor or bad feeling. The disorder of the moment and the upheaval of the war meant that shattering news was commonplace, and her father's almost penitent journey to Gais inspired pity rather than anger.

It is also true that Pound had always felt much closer to Mary than to Omar. Mary had been the love child, the child of illicit romance; Omar was Dorothy's and as such more associated with routine and convention. Pound had chosen his daughter, he had seen much more of her because of the time she spent with Olga, he had consciously tried to educate her and develop her sensibility even if he had agreed to shift her daily responsibility to the peasant family at Gais.

While Pound was in Gais, Mussolini was abducted by German commandos. Flown to Germany to consult with Hitler, he returned and established a Fascist republic at Salo on the southern end of Lago di Garda, not far from Sirmione, where Pound had sojourned when he first came to Italy. The new government was a puppet state with Mussolini guarded by Nazi SS troops and more inclined to spend time with his mistress than with matters of state. From Gais, Pound went to Salo, where he met with Serafino Mazzolini, the new minister of foreign affairs.

In Rapallo he continued to write articles and pamphlets in support of the new government, mostly for a newspaper called *Il Popolo,* in which he described the Fascist "freedom to express an opinion on the part of those qualified to hold an opinion" and chose to remind his readers of one of the "eternal laws of nature," namely, that the strong shall dominate the weak. In another piece he warned that Italy has been poisoned by the wrong books imported from England. He wrote thirty-five articles for *Il Popolo* and many others for Fascist papers and magazines. They had become little more than random collections of old ideas, presented like buckshot with little internal order or logic. The editor of Milan's *Corriere della Sera,* Ermanno Amicucci, refused to print Pound's material—though he was encouraged to do so by government officials—because he found it incomprehensible, simplistic, and propagandistic. Pound seemed completely unaware that the tide of the war had turned, that the Fascist forces were on the defensive and retreating, that in Italy they had lost most of their popular support and remained in power in the north only because of their guns and terrorism. While Sigismondo Malatesta's temple at Rimini was being bombed by Allied planes, while children were being sent out of the cities into the countryside, Pound began sending copies of his articles to the Salo Republic's new minister of popular culture, Fernando Mazzasoma, along with a stream of letters on educational reform, on maintaining the level of intellectual life, suggestions for improving the propaganda machine, even on new bus and train routes, and a proposal that the ministry publish a book of his three hundred-plus radio talks. He was also writing letters of advice to many of the other leading Salo officials, to Mussolini's new private secretary, and to Mussolini himself.

On December 1, 1943, the Salo Republic established a new radio propaganda station in Milan, which Pound visited during the first week of its operation. On December 10, he spoke on the radio on the subject of Italians accused by the Germans of betraying the Fascist cause, a group for whom Pound had no sympathy. Count Ciano, who had sponsored and assisted Pound in his attempts to reach a wider public with his version of the political situation, was one of those being tried for the attempted assassination of Mussolini: Pound recommended that Ciano be executed. He ended his talk with a characteristically hateful reflection: "Every human being who is not a hopeless idiotic worm should realize that fascism is superior in every way to Russian Jewocracy and that capitalism stinks." By February 1944 he was being used as a paid, regular broadcaster and was submitting short pieces, slogans, anti-Semitic caricatures, and skits for a humorous character named Mr. Dooley. Much of this material was used on a program called "Jerry's Front Calling."

Later, psychiatrists, literary critics, and some of Pound's friends would wonder why he continued to work for the Fascists when it was evident they would fall. Of course, Pound, his wife, his mother, and to some extent his mistress were then all dependent on the small income he earned as a propagandist. Douglas Goldring, who had known Pound in London before the First World War, wrote in a letter to the Paris *Tribune* in February of 1944 that Pound had been an early admirer of Charles Maurras, the French poet and reactionary. Most of Pound's ideas, Goldring asserted, seemed "barmy" and Pound a bit of a poseur. Though he was a romantic and a "misguided ass," however, he was "never a rat," never the type to "leave a sinking ship while the going was good." For Goldring, Pound was clearly acting from principle; others came to see it as unregenerate stubbornness, the certainty that if Pound was pushed he would push back twice as hard. Pound's friend William French has described this as Pound's kamikaze tendency, which he attributed to his "reckless driving Scorpionic nature." Aristotle, the first theoretician of tragedy, might have considered Pound and his indomitable resistance, the conviction that he was always right and his eagerness to defend his actions, as a case of "hubris"—the blinding pride of figures so confident that they can never even admit to the possibility of error.

During 1944 and for the first months of 1945, Pound continued with his radio propaganda pieces and his newspaper articles. He was no longer speaking on the radio himself, but he made frequent trips to Milan and was asked by the station officials to resettle there so that he could do even more and presumably speak again on a regular basis. The question of treason must have occurred to him, and in a discussion at Salo he compared himself to Socrates. Even if he was not fully concerned about the consequences of his acts, his friends in America were. Williams wrote McAlmon that he would defend him if called as a witness in a trial. "It is a pathological business," Hemingway told MacLeish, adding that it would surely come to a trial in which they would be asked to testify after the war. Hemingway asked MacLeish to send him the transcripts of Pound's broadcasts, which he did with the following comment: "Treason is a little too serious and a little too dignified a crime for a man who has made such an incredible ass of himself, and accomplished so little in the process." Hemingway's response was that the transcripts showed that Pound was "obviously crazy." Angrily Hemingway suggested Pound deserved punishment, disgrace, and ridicule but not the death penalty because that would make him a martyr. The broadcasts were "vile, absolutely idiotic drivel" and Pound was a "crazy and harmless traitor" who belonged in the "loony bin," a man who had foolishly swallowed fascism whole because he felt respected as a poet in Italy, something no one "but an idiot with Ezra's type of ego" would do. One of MacLeish's old friends was Harvey Bundy, assistant secretary of war under Henry Stimson. MacLeish told Bundy that Pound was "a half-cracked and extremely foolish individual" and that the broadcasts were the "product of a completely distracted mind" which "seems to have gone to pieces under the pressure of a swollen and dropsical ego." MacLeish urged Bundy to have Stimson issue orders to the military protecting Pound from any summary disposition of his case and the risk of martyrdom. Attorney General Biddle issued an order for Pound's arrest and distributed a photograph with a description, asking to be immediately notified on his apprehension.

Rome had fallen on June 4, 1944, and the invasion of Normandy began two days later. By the end of the summer, the Allies had liberated Paris and in October they were in Germany, moving toward Berlin. In Rapallo bombers flew overhead, a church was exploded, but damage and disruption was slight.

13. "EVEN THE LION FINALLY GETS A HORN THROUGH HIS GUTS"

At the end of April 1945, Benito Mussolini was caught trying to flee into the Italian Alps. His corpse as well as that of his mistress was desecrated and hung by the heels in a square in Milan. There was virtually no resistance on May 1 when the Americans occupied Rapallo. Pound walked down the hill from Sant'Ambrogio prepared to surrender and offer his services to the Americans with the curious idea that he could somehow help them with his knowledge of Italy. He found a few officers in a café who were totally uninterested in him. An infantryman tried to sell him a bicycle.

Pound was alone in Olga Rudge's house on the next day. Olga had gone down the hill looking for a newspaper and Dorothy was visiting Pound's mother. Two partisans appeared believing there was a reward for Pound's capture. The poet was working on his Confucian materials when they rapped on his door with machine guns. He slipped a Chinese dictionary and his Confucius into his pocket, gave his keys to the woman who lived downstairs, and made a sign with his hand to her signifying that he was going to be hanged. As he walked down the hill path he paused before a eucalyptus tree, bent down and picked up one of its seeds, and put it in his pocket.

The partisans drove their handcuffed prisoner to their central headquarters, where Pound demanded to be taken to a United States command post. Escorted by two MPs, he was driven to the Counter Intelligence Center in Genoa on May 3, where Olga Rudge found him a day later, still handcuffed, waiting in a large room full of people who were going to be interrogated. Pound was questioned for two days and Olga Rudge was told by special agent Amprim of the FBI that she should return to Sant'Ambrogio and be ready to testify in the event of a trial. Amprim appeared himself at Sant'Ambrogio a few days later to examine Pound's private papers and to question Olga and Dorothy. He left with over seven thousand letters, typescripts, and articles seized as evidence.

In Genoa, Pound was interviewed by Edd Johnson, an American reporter to whom he stated that if a man valued his beliefs, he would die for them. In a fit of omnipotence, he declared that if he would be allowed to meet President Truman or Stalin he could help resolve the political complications that would surely ensue because of the war. He had a series of other comments: Mussolini was an imperfect man who had lost his head, Churchill a man who stood for the "maximum of injustice enforced with the maximum of brutality," and Hitler was a saint like Joan of Arc, a martyr who failed only because he had not followed Confucius closely enough.

Several weeks later, after a flurry of cables between Genoa and Washington, Pound was handcuffed to a soldier accused of rape and murder and transferred under guard to the Disciplinary Training Center near Pisa. Instructions from the War Department in Washington were to "exercise utmost security measures to prevent escape or suicide." There were to be no more press interviews or any preferential treatment. Pound was manacled and driven in an army jeep under the command of Captain A. T. Moore, who, in a letter printed in the *Saturday Review of Literature,* claimed that "Pound vilified the Americans and derided the Military Police" during the entire ride. Pound's new quarters were in a penal center, a barbed wire stockade surrounded by fourteen guard towers and illuminated at night by searchlights. The Disciplinary Training Center was designed to punish and contain the most vicious criminals in the American army, a collection of some thirty-six hundred deserters, brawlers, rapists, murderers, and maniacs. Some of these men were waiting for trials, others were already paying for what they had done with hard labor days that lasted fourteen hours. Most of the men lived in tents which were housed within the barbed wire compounds, but there was also a group of ten wire-and-concrete cages for the most dangerous prisoners or those who had been sentenced to death by court-martial. Pound was placed in one of these isolation cells, a so-called death cell that had been reinforced on the night before his arrival by men working with acetylene torches who welded galvanized mesh and heavy airstrip steel onto the wire grid of the cell. It was a fact that made Pound figure in the speculations of the other prisoners, who must have wondered about the extra precautions and the dangers presented by this new inmate.

Dressed in army fatigues but without a belt or shoelaces to prevent any attempt at suicide, Pound paced his six foot by six foot "gorilla" cage. Protected from dust, sun, and rain only by a tar paper covering, he was tortured by the constant glare of a reflected light set up to shine directly into his cell at night while he tried to sleep on the cold cement floor. No one, not even the guard who delivered his food or who emptied his refuse bucket, was allowed to speak to him. "They thought I was a dangerous wild man and were scared of me," Pound said later. "I had a guard night and day. Some of them brought food. Old Ez was a prize exhibit." He was mistaken. The precautions were not taken because of the dangers he presented, but because of the possibility that Fascist sympathizers might try to free him. For three weeks the fifty-nine-year-old poet paced his cell, exercised as best he could, sat staring, or read his Confucius and his Chinese dictionary which he had brought with him from Sant'Ambrogio. His eyes were red and inflamed from dust. After a downpour one day, the guards gave him a pup tent and a military cot. But by then the strain had proven intolerable and Pound collapsed, stricken with violent and hysterical terror, nightmares, hallucinations, and cold. He suffered memory loss and lost the ability to identify his surroundings. He stopped eating.

In later years he characterized the experience by saying, "The World fell in on me." Actually, the breakdown was a wordless catharsis, a sudden recognition of the peril of his situation and the price he might have to pay. Hemingway had once told him that a writer needed to feel terrific pain before releasing his subject. The breakdown was an admission of such pain. Pound, the man of words, was now caught in the most overwhelming moment of his life without the power to summon language. But he might have realized, in some silent corner of his being, that language was merely the artistic fiction of tragedy, the rationalization of pain, and that the flow of words would be invented by the novelist or playwright, or Pound himself in the cantos he would soon begin to write, to stylize and heighten and explain the conjunction of superior forces and the puny human who could dare to defy them.

Pound's reference to himself as a "prize exhibit" is suggestive. His pain becomes most intense when he is absolutely separated from the world, his guards forbidden to speak to him, the poet himself isolated in a cage as a specimen of evil. At that point, he could communicate only as a sort of a totem like Antonin Artaud, another writer who despised psychiatry as an agency of social conditioning, who resisted social institutions with his entire being, and who argued that the writer should be like the victim being burned in the Inquisition, signaling his message through the flames. For Artaud, this was the archetypical and ultimate role for the writer, one that caused tremendous pressure, heat, and pain, so that one could no longer even imagine an audience, but the writer would have to keep on writing, telegraphing his message with his arms and gestures in a final dance of annihilation. In a very central sense, Pound had always longed to be the "prize exhibit" and in London and Paris he had done his best to surprise the world into believing he was that. Pound was always volcanic and, as such, responding only to deeply felt intuitive urges that would explode to the surface unpredictably. But now the volcano was solitary. Such a situation is, of course, basic to philosophical inquiry and phenomenology. If the volcano erupts, no matter how powerfully, has it *really* erupted if there is no one to suffer its consequences, to measure its devastation? Any human volcano fears such a predicament and feels its peril. The abyss of meaninglessness which it represents is a canceling quality which can lead to madness or at least breakdown. Pound had become a literary monster (the word deriving from the Latin *monere*, to warn), and as a monster, he had gone beyond the human community, joined the forces of the dark forests, become an untouchable, stigmatized, outcast, a pariah unable to reach his audience with his voice.

The breakdown was the culmination of a long process of exile. He had spurned his country as lacking civilization and now he was being treated by its army as no better than an animal. Pound was a man who had pursued beauty until the First World War had turned him to a more political route, his anger making him into a biblical Ezra or Jeremiah scourging those whom he felt were responsible for the catastrophe. His own faith had been a curious amalgam of paganism, bits of Renaissance culture, and a messianic belief in the saving grace of art. His politics had been confused by a central contradiction: while it was necessary for an artistic-elect to rebel against convention in the search to "make it new," the masses needed direction and the sort of authority best provided by fascism, which only regimented "those who can't do anything else without it." He invested his faith in the Nietzschean idea of a Master Leader, Mussolini, whom Pound could advise in the Confucian tradition of savant-poet guiding his ruler. But one of the last books Mussolini had been reading at Salo before his desperate flight was Plato's *Republic,* which points to the danger to the state presented by artists who are governed not by reason but by passion. Pound may have felt that in his letters on economic theory and in his radio exhortations he was fulfilling the role of adviser, but his sensibility had none of the moderation Confucius said was necessary for balance and thus wisdom, and Mussolini would have dismissed him as he did when he met him as merely a diversion for entertainment, not someone to be taken seriously. But Pound's enormous self-confidence, which had made him a leader among poets, had deluded him into believing he could also be a leader of men, as Thaddeus Pound to some extent surely had been. This confidence only grew with his work on *The Cantos,* whose method he did not question once he had gotten started until the end of his life.

As Malcolm Cowley had observed in Paris in 1924, Pound was in flight from himself. His friend Lewis had observed that no man had less of a recognition of the personal, and his letters never mention his feelings about Dorothy, Olga, or his daughter, Mary. In London he had been the prankster eating tulips to gain attention; in Italy he had turned into the crank, and even Douglas began to find him a hindrance and an embarrassment. His economic strategies were extremely simplistic, but they released his potential for fanaticism—he was warped by the excesses of his own zealousness. As he poignantly recalled in a later canto, "I lost my center/fighting the world."

After the collapse, Pound was moved to the Disciplinary Training Center medical compound, a large tent. As soon as some of his strength returned, he was interviewed by the camp psychiatrists, Richard Finner and Walter Bates. He was in the hands of those whom he had always regarded as enemies. He had systematically derided Freud and the psychiatric profession. Pound was an intuitionist who had avoided introspective processes; he preferred leaping to luminous conclusions to discursive reasoning and analysis. Freud and Marx were only examples of the world's "kikery," he wrote in "Canto XCI," and Freud in particular was a "sex crank," the "flower of a deliquescent society going to pot." Psychoanalysis did not work, Pound had conjectured, because the average human head needed something removed from it rather than having something inserted. It was the "Viennese sewage," he wrote to Lewis just before the war, a "hoax for paralyzing the will of its victim, like the wopse or whatsoam that lays its eggs in a caterpillar, thus providing MEAT for its progeny." Freud and Proust, he added, were simply "unmitigated shit" passing for "inteligenzia because their shit is laid out in most elaborate arabesques."

Doctors Finner and Bates concluded that Pound was suffering the effects of claustrophobia and noted a lack of personality resilience, an inconsistency in his thought patterns, a frequent shifting of mood, and a general discontinuity. They, of course, had not read *The Cantos*. The confusion, the anxiety about his own fate, the feelings of frustration and fatigue were not surprising given the enforced circumstances of his confinement. The psychiatrists warned that Pound had suffered a "spell," an attack of panic plus anxiety which could be an advance warning of a more complete mental breakdown, and they recommended transfer to an institution in the United States with better facilities. Essentially, however, the psychiatrists found him sane, despite his boasts that he would never be tried because he "had too much on several people in Washington." He vigorously denied that his broadcasts had been treasonous, and he continued to denounce the "usuring cutthroats" and the political leaders who had swindled the American people.

Considering the psychiatric report, Lieutenant Colonel John Steele, the base commander, ordered that Pound be accommodated in the medical compound. Pound was put in a section for officers, given a cot, a table, and a few packing crates, and he had some freedom of movement within the compound. The camp psychiatrists decided to permit him to write, since it was both therapeutic and preventive medicine. He was keeping aware of current developments through *Stars and Stripes, Time,* and *Newsweek.* He knew that the war with Japan had ended after the atomic bombing of Hiroshima and Nagasaki, though perhaps he was unaware of the irony in the fact that the navigational plane accompanying the *Enola Gay*, which dropped the Hiroshima bomb, was called the *Great Artiste.* He was also reading during that dreary and rainy fall about a series of treason trials in various parts of Europe for those who had collaborated with the Nazis: Marshal Pétain in France, who was sentenced to life imprisonment, and his second in command, Pierre Laval, who was sentenced to death by firing squad; Vidkun Quisling, who had made wartime broadcasts urging his fellow Norwegians to accept the Nazi occupation, was sentenced to death; William Joyce, Lord Haw-Haw, a supporter of Oswald Mosley who had broadcast from Berlin and was sentenced to hanging. Of special significance was the trial of a seventy-seven-year-old Frenchman, Charles Maurras, whose writing Pound had admired during his London years. Even a relic like Maurras was sentenced to jail, where he spent the remaining seven years of his life for his support of Pétain. Pound had either admired or, in the case of Joyce and Quisling, corresponded with all these men. The case, though, that most impressed him was Pierre Laval's. Laval conducted his own defense, and he dominated the proceedings with his oratory and eloquence, complete with three-hour monologues in which he tried to prove he had been a superpatriot and demanded that his judgment occur in terms of the whole of his policies. It was a dramatic last stand that Pound identified with, if only in fantasy. Soon he was discussing economics with Colonel Steele, whose name he found appropriate for his position and who had taught economics in college. He began talking to various detainees about the American Constitution and usury. He also started to exercise more vigorously, starting each day with a brisk walk which wore a circular path in the grass of the compound. With a broomstick he played imaginary games of tennis and baseball. In the evenings he was granted permission to use the dispensary typewriter on which he would often type out letters for other detainees who were allowed only one letter a week.

Pound needed the typewriter because he was again working on his Chinese translations and had resumed *The Cantos.* His crisis of spirit, his nervous breakdown, seemed to have opened a doorway to the personal and all the wandering and prophetic personae who had appeared and reappeared in his long poem. The poems he wrote at the Disciplinary Training Center are known as *The Pisan Cantos.* They express a tremendous resurgence of plenitude and poetic power, mixing memories of his own past, his friendships with Yeats, Ford, and Joyce, with sharply observed details of prison life. But they differ from the previous cantos in their release of feeling. Earlier, the attitude had been one of Jamesian restraint; feelings were qualities other people had—"One never spoke of them or showed them," Mary explained in *Discretions.* In the past, the Dantean hell Pound imagined in his cantos—Eliot had observed it was "a hell for other people" —was not rendered with sufficient depth; it was unconvincing. Now, in the final inferno, Pound's pain and his openness about it made that hell full of dimension and reality. Pound had become the man "on whom the sun has gone down," an isolated, broken figure who had not known the taste of his food in three months, and on a more mythic level the man in Africa described by Frobenius "whose mouth was removed by his father/for having said too many *things."* Only shadows enter his tent, he is a "caged panther" tormented by the images of his defeat like the picture of Mussolini hanging from his heels that begins the section:

> The enormous tragedy of the dream in the peasant's bent
> shoulders

> Manes! Manes was tanned and stuffed,
> Thus Ben and la Clara a Milano
>   by the heels at Milano
> The maggots shd/ eat the dead bullock
> DIGENES, *Siyeves,* but the twice crucified
>   where in history will you find it?
> yet say this to the Possum: a bang, not a whimper,
>   with a bang not with a whimper,
> To build the city of Dioce whose terraces are the colour of
> stars

The poem swings wildly from ideology—"free speech without free radio speech is as zero"—to myth, the world of "Circe's swine sty"; but the balancing factor restoring sanity and soothing pain is the natural world the poet sees from his place of detention, the smell of mint under the tent flaps, a white ox on the road, dark sheep in a drill field, a lizard, a spider, or some ants:

> When the mind swings by a grass-blade
> an ant's forefoot shall save you.

Pound sees himself as a diamond in an avalanche who cannot be destroyed unless he destroys himself, and who will not surrender his dream of Dioce, the heavenly city built by man, and who insists in a refrain that paradise exists only in fragments like the smell of the mint and that nothing really matters anyway except the quality of affection:

> What thou lovest well remains,
>   the rest is dross
> What thou lovest well shall not be reft from thee
> What thou lov'st well is thy true heritage.

In *The Pisan Cantos* natural beauty becomes the dramatic reminder of what Pound has lost. For one stripped of everything, caged like a beast, true value becomes measured by the elemental in nature. It is a reminder that Pound's greatest strength as a poet was his lyricism, an ability to register sharp pictures of nature which evoke feeling.

After five months of separation, early in October, Pound was finally permitted a visit from Dorothy, who was living with Pound's mother in Rapallo. The meeting, however, was in an office in the presence of guards. Two weeks later Olga Rudge and Mary came to see Pound. In *Discretions,* Mary remembers that her father had aged considerably. His eyes were inflamed, he was allowed no laces on his shoes, and a sheepish guard was still at the tent entrance.

In New York, James Laughlin had heard about Pound's internment and in September he had asked a friend, Julien Cornell, a Hamilton graduate and an attorney who specialized in civil rights cases, to consider defending Pound. Pound himself was thinking of a court trial and wanted to defend himself; had that happened the exhibitionism that had in part prompted the radio broadcasts would have been repeated and perhaps reached a larger audience. In more sober moments he considered retaining Lloyd Stryker, a well-known criminal lawyer and son of Hamilton College president Woolsey Stryker. He had also written to Arthur Moore at Shakespear & Parkyn, Henry Hope Shakespear's old firm, which had previously handled his legal problems. In his letter he mentioned using Stryker and possibly Archibald MacLeish, who had resigned his position as assistant secretary of state and was also a lawyer, certainly one with the right connections. He insisted that in his broadcasts he had not been voicing Axis propaganda but his own ideas and those of others like Brooks Adams, all reflecting the monetary researches of twenty-five years. He was concerned about what segment of the public might have heard his broadcasts or if "hearing they understood one single word of my talks." Pound also asked Moore to contact Eliot about the possibility of Faber printing *The Pisan Cantos* and the Confucian translations: he had been sending his hand-corrected versions of his new cantos to Mary, who then retyped them and sent them back, alarming the authorities at the Disciplinary Training Center, who felt the poems might be coded messages.

In November the United States War Department notified Colonel Steele to prepare for Pound's transfer to Washington, D.C. In *Stars and Stripes* Pound read that seven Italian radio technicians and former station officials were being flown to Washington to testify. The case was receiving wide publicity in the American press along with that of Tokyo Rose, who was already in prison awaiting trial. Finally on the evening of November 16, 1945, Pound was informed by two young lieutenants that he was being flown to Washington. As he walked through the door of the prefab where he had been reading Joseph E. Davies's *Mission to Moscow*, he turned with a half-smile and put both hands around his neck to form a noose, jerking up his chin. It was the same gesture he had used after being taken by the partisans. Once again he was handcuffed and placed in a jeep for the drive to Rome.

WASHINGTON:
THE BEDLAM OF ART

Nor may the weary-in-mind withstand his fate,
Nor is high heart his helping.
For the doom-eager oft bindeth fast his thought
In blood-bedabbled breast.

"The Seafarer"

The word I have translated "doom-eager" is "domgeorne." And
"dom" is both "fate" and "glory." The "Dom georne" man is the man
ready to pay the price.

If a man has this quality and be meagre of speech one asks little
beyond this.

"Patria Mia"

1. THE DOMGEORNE MAN

Pound arrived in Washington two days before the Nuremberg trials, on November 18, 1945. The newspapers were full of stories about the atrocities in German concentration camps, the previously unpublicized horrors of the Final Solution. After stories on the Dachau and Belsen camps, the Washington *Post* headline blared the news POET EZRA POUND FLOWN HERE TO ANSWER TREASON CHARGES. As Pound left the army 0-54 transport, he was greeted by newspaper reporters, who found him debonair though a bit frazzled, an incongruous apparition in baggy gray suit over a soiled army sweatshirt and GI shoes that seemed too large for his feet. He reminded the reporters that they had ignored him on his visit in 1939. Pound denied that he was guilty of treason: "If that damned fool idea is still in anybody's head, I want to wipe it out. . . . What I want to know is whether anybody heard my broadcasts, and, if so, how they could have any earthly idea of what I was talking about."

Taken to the District of Columbia jail, Pound was brought the next day before Chief Judge Bolitha J. Laws. When he requested permission to conduct his own defense, Judge Laws refused, stating that the charge was too serious. On the next day he was visited by Julien Cornell, who wrote to James Laughlin:

> I found the poor devil in a rather desperate condition. He is very wobbly in his mind and while his talk is entirely rational, he flits from one idea to another and is unable to concentrate even to the extent of answering a single question without immediately wandering off the subject. We spent most of the time talking about Confucius, Jefferson and the economic and political implications of their ideas. I let him ramble on, even though I did not get much of the information which I wanted, as it seemed a shame to deprive him of the pleasure of talking, which has been almost entirely denied to him for a long while.

Cornell found the poet still under a "mental cloud," claiming that certain government officials would assist him if they could only be persuaded of the soundness of his economic views. He repeated what might be called his Confucian delusion that he could be of great assistance to Truman. Finally, he wryly told Cornell that being hanged could be the greatest benefit for a poet—undoubtedly he was thinking of Villon, one of the poets with whom he had most closely identified himself.

Cornell raised the possibility of using an insanity plea as his defense strategy, a proposal to which Pound had no objection, remarking that it had naturally occurred to him already. It was apparent to Cornell, as he stated in his affidavit before Judge Laws, that Pound was in no condition to stand trial, that he was in fact insane and needed medical care and hospitalization, and that if he remained in prison he might never recover "and not only will [he] be unable to stand trial under this indictment, but one of the greatest literary geniuses of these times will be permanently eclipsed."

In pursuing a defense based on the plea of insanity, Cornell was following the course advocated by Hemingway, Laughlin, and MacLeish, who wrote Eliot that a civil rights defense would not work, since "a calculated campaign of anti-Semitism . . . is hardly an expression of the right of the intellectual to tell the truth as he sees it." James Laughlin wrote to Eliot: "I think you and I both realize that Ezra is 'sane' and the world is 'insane' but since it is the world which habitually hangs or torments men of genius or vision this solution seems the most practical."

Dorothy Pound wrote to Cornell in alarm because she had heard of newspaper accounts of "violent insanity." Cornell's reassuring reply reflects the way Pound would be regarded by his friends:

You need not be alarmed about the report on your husband's mental condition. While, no doubt, his difficulties were aggravated by the ordeal of his imprisonment, he has been resting comfortably in a hospital for some time now, and I believe that his condition is just about normal. However a state which would, no doubt, appear to you to be normal, is defined by the doctors as paranoid in character, to an extent which impairs your husband's judgment of his predicament and renders him unable to properly defend himself.

While the doctors are agreed that he is to this extent mentally abnormal, I feel quite sure that you will find, when you see him again, that he is his usual self, and the mental aberrations which the doctors have found are not anything new or unusual, but are chronic and would pass entirely unnoticed by one like yourself who has lived close to him for a number of years. In fact I think it may be fairly said that any man of his genius would be regarded by a psychiatrist as abnormal.

Even before Dorothy received this letter, Cornell had used the insanity defense successfully. On November 23 Pound was taken to Judge Laws's courthouse and kept in a "bull-pen" with other prisoners because a grand jury was preparing a new indictment. The law required at least two witnesses to any act of treason, but since the Italian radio technicians did not know English, they could not attest to what Pound had said, only to the fact that he had spoken. On the next two days Pound was kept locked in his cell, deprived even of outdoor exercise because of an attempted escape in another part of the jail. On November 25 he suffered another claustrophobic attack and spent that night and the following one in the jail infirmary. On the morning of November 27, Cornell saw Pound "in a state of almost complete mental and physical exhaustion." After an hour spent hearing Pound trying to read his *Pisan Cantos,* Cornell explained to him that he was going to be arraigned that afternoon and would have to plead to the indictment: "When I asked him whether he wanted to stand mute or would prefer to enter a plea, he was unable to answer me. His mouth opened once or twice as if to speak, but no words came out. He looked up at the ceiling and his face began to twitch. Finally he said he felt ill and asked if he could not go back to the infirmary."

That afternoon Pound appeared with Cornell before Judge Laws in a crowded courtroom and heard the new indictment read. It consisted of nineteen counts, each one a different broadcast witnessed by two of the technicians, supporting the contention that Pound had violated his allegiance to the United States by "knowingly, intentionally, willfully, unlawfully, feloniously, traitorously, and treasonably" supporting the Kingdom of

Italy while employed as a radio propagandist. Answering the charges, Cornell summarized his own affidavit, emphasizing the seriousness of his client's condition while Pound stood silent, hands folded, head downcast, shuffling his weight from one foot to the other. According to Charles Olson, a young poet covering the trial as a journalist, Pound kept taking off his glasses and rubbing his eyes, which seemed full of pain. After a short recess, Judge Laws ordered Pound to be removed to Gallinger Municipal Hospital, where he was to be examined by four psychiatrists, three representing the government and a fourth selected by Cornell. These doctors were Winfred Overholser, superintendent of St. Elizabeths Hospital, the federal asylum for the insane in Washington, Marion King, medical director of the Bureau of Prisons, Joseph Gilbert, head of psychiatry at Gallinger, and Wendell Muncie, Cornell's choice, associate professor of psychiatry at Johns Hopkins.

During the first two weeks in December, the psychiatrists each interviewed Pound at Gallinger Hospital. According to Fuller Torrey, a psychiatrist himself, two members of the team were not eminently qualified and were excessively influenced by Dr. Overholser. Dr. King had spent most of his career in medical administration and had practiced psychiatry for only a year. Dr. Gilbert was competent but hardly outstanding. Torrey contends in *The Roots of Treason* that Overholser had his own ideas about how Pound should be treated. Another psychiatrist, Thomas Szasz, reviewing Cornell's *The Trial of Ezra Pound* in the New York *Times Book Review* in 1966, had first raised this possibility, arguing that the insanity defense had been forced through by Overholser, that Pound was not insane and was not excessively paranoid. Overholser was a man with considerable power. He knew from the beginning that Pound would have to pay for the broadcasts after Pearl Harbor. He wanted to protect and patronize Pound. Eventually he had Pound placed in a ward adjacent to his own apartments in St. Elizabeths—so Pound was as close as a couple of walls. As secretary-treasurer of the American Psychiatric Association and president-elect of that organization, Overholser was particularly concerned with the professional image of psychiatry and deplored trials in which psychiatrists for the defense contradicted psychiatrists for the prosecution. He had been published in many journals and was an outstanding authority in forensic psychiatry. A relativist, he understood that between the normal and the abnormal lay a "vast no-man's-land of deviations." People were not simply sane and responsible for their acts or insane and not responsible. Overholser had written about the condition of genius and felt that though it usually resulted in abnormality, it was quite different from psychosis or derangement. A Harvard graduate who had majored in economics, Torrey proposed that Overholser was part of an "old-boy" Harvard network formed to assist Pound. The guiding figure in this network was Merrill Moore, a poet and psychiatrist who had been a research fellow at Harvard for six years and who was friendly with Laughlin and MacLeish.

The examining board issued a joint report, even though Dr. Muncie was able to see Pound on only one day for three hours because of his other obligations. It recognized that Pound had long been considered "eccentric, querulous and egocentric" but found that by then he had become "abnormally grandiose, expansive and exuberant in manner, exhibiting pressure of speech, discursiveness, and distractibility." The board concluded he was suffering from a paranoid state complicated by recent events and that he could not be expected to participate reasonably or intelligently in his own defense. The psychiatrists agreed he was "insane and mentally unfit for trial, and in need of care in a mental hospital."

While the psychiatrists were deliberating, Cornell had returned to New York in an attempt to free Pound's assets. His American account was in the hands of the Custodian of Alien Property, his wife's funds had been seized by British authorities (the United States Consul had refused to renew her expired passport so that she could visit her husband), and the family safe-deposit box had been sealed by the Allied Command in Rapallo. Laughlin advanced some money for trial expenses and E. E. Cummings, who had just sold a painting for a thousand dollars, claimed he did not need the money and turned it over to Cornell to assist in the defense. He had become much more sympathetic to Pound's predicament than he had been two years earlier when he was interviewed by agents of the FBI. In the New York newspaper *PM*, which had excerpted and printed some of Pound's broadcast commentary, Cummings declared: "Every artist's strictly illimitable country is himself. An artist who plays that country false has committed suicide; and even a good lawyer cannot kill the dead. But a human being who is true to himself—whoever himself may be—is immortal; and all the atomic bombs of all the anti-artists in space time will never civilize immortality." Cummings's remark was emotional, extravagant, and anarchistic, a perfect illustration of why Plato feared artists in *The Republic*.

Cornell's plan had been to offer a motion for bail so that Pound could either be treated privately or eventually freed on the grounds that he was incurably insane but not in need of hospitalization. Cornell felt he might have to carry his case as far as the Supreme Court, where he hoped to prevail because "a man cannot be shut up indefinitely after being indicted when he cannot be tried because of illness." This motion was denied by Judge Laws. The government had made a considerable effort to establish its case—the radio technicians had received a two-month paid holiday in Washington until they were flown back to Italy on a government plane—and many hours had been spent in the attorney general's office planning strategy. Despite popular sentiment against Pound, the case was never certain because of the difficulty in establishing treasonous intent and the two-witness rule. By putting Pound in St. Elizabeths, the government avoided a trial altogether and placed Pound in a situation where he could be released only at the discretion of the psychiatrists, in effect giving him an indeterminate sentence.

2. THE HELL-HOLE

A few days before Christmas of 1945, Pound was transferred to Howard Hall, the prison ward at St. Elizabeths, a grim, dilapidated building with locked wards and barred windows, which Whitman had visited during the Civil War when it was used as a hospital for Union soldiers. In Howard Hall he was in what he would describe as the "hell-hole." There seemed to be little sympathy for him in the outside world. The *Saturday Review of Literature* printed a piece about his case stating that there were no alibis for treason. Henry Seidel Canby, whom Pound had insulted and attacked in numerous letters, wrote that "the false scholarship, the excessive eccentricity, and the confused thought of much of his poetical work show something less than greatness" but that the real problem was what Pound had done during the war, "Pound of the broadcasts, the prose pamphlets and private letters, signs of a muddled and mediocre mind, easily deluded by childish fallacies in government and economics." The magazine *New Masses* asked five writers to express their opinions and they all felt Pound should be made to pay. Playwright Arthur Miller argued that Pound's vilifications were worse than Hitler's, Norman Rosten said he was a Fascist hireling who had contributed to the murder of the innocent, screenwriter Albert Maltz pointed out that if Pound had been a businessman, a factory worker, or a physician, no voices would be raised on his behalf.

Pound's case was the first American treason case after the war; there was broad public interest and demand for vengeance. There were also allegations that Pound was simply feigning insanity to escape the death penalty, that he was no less insane than any war criminal being tried at Nuremberg. In support of this position there was his calmly reasoned letter of 1943 to Attorney General Biddle, his equally controlled letter to Shakespear & Parkyn sent from Pisa, and his initial appearance before Judge Laws, when, according to newspaper reports, he pleaded for ten minutes in a scholarly manner to conduct his own defense. The Department of Justice requested Judge Laws to summon a jury for a sanity hearing. On the day before the hearing, February 12, 1946, Cornell visited Pound at St. Elizabeths to inform him about the procedure, and then he stopped in to see Dr. Overholser. Overholser was still of the opinion that Pound was mentally unfit to stand trial, but he told Cornell that a number of the younger psychiatrists on his staff disagreed with him and believed Pound was merely eccentric, not insane. This, of course, had been the finding of the two psychiatrists at Pisa.

During the first seven weeks that Pound was in St. Elizabeths, he was examined by a number of psychiatrists at the facility. Some of these psychiatrists were aware that Pound's case was the most complex and interesting they would ever get to hear. On Pound's part, it was the beginning of a contest of wits with many opponents, a sort of chess game played by a grand master against a crowd of experts who change off after every move. Pound remembered that at Pisa the word around the center had been that he had outsmarted the psychiatrists. At St. Elizabeths he tried to do it on a larger scale, not realizing at first how long the game could last.

He there had found a tragic arena for his resistance. He depended on his cleverness, his wit, his ability to project a role and manipulate an audience—essentially the poet's task as he pushes image and sound across a page to create a place of his own choosing. But the contest was with the new secular priesthood, the scientific mind-agents of the all-powerful state. Pound had committed an ultimate heresy by challenging the state in a time of war. Caged, broken psychically in his cage, he refused still to recant, to admit any weakness. Had his confidence warped itself into an illusory omnipotence; and was he convinced that he was invulnerable and could always outwit his tormentors? Eight staff psychiatrists recorded impressions in his hospital chart, all of them aware that Overholser had proclaimed Pound paranoid, and all of them equally aware of Overholser's enormous power in the psychiatric profession at the time, and the fact that when they completed their residency at St. Elizabeths they would need a letter of recommendation from him. Most of the psychiatrists, as well, believed that Overholser was doing the right thing, that Pound was a special case because he was a great poet.

In his evaluation of Pound's initial "mental examination," Dr. Jerome Kavka noted Pound's rambling manner, his explosive anger, and his complaints of fatigue. He refused to follow orthodox methods of questioning and would "ramble on in a devious fashion, skipping rapidly from one point to another." Pound would "soliloquize," Kavka observed, stringing together disconnected thoughts and commenting on whatever distracted him, the birds outside, organ music from the chapel, the howls of another inmate. Kavka felt Pound displayed considerable egocentricity and that in fields other than poetry his attitudes bordered on the delusional. When Kavka questioned him on his sanity, Pound replied, "No, I don't think I am insane, but I am so shot to pieces that it would take me years to write a sensible piece of prose. I think I am of unsound mind, and I don't think I have been shown good treatment here. I am absolutely unfit to transact any business." Pound told Dr. Kavka that "his main spring had gone haywire" at Pisa, and he told him and the other doctors that he felt a hollowness in his head, an emptiness, as if part of his brain had been dissipated by his ordeal. Pound admitted questioning his sanity at times in his past and noted that certain early poems like "La Fraisne" and "Pierre Vidal" are poems about madness. He mentioned being interested in palmistry at one time and pointed to a line in his palm which was revealed to him as a potential sign of madness. He said that he had "definitely decided at that time 'not to go crazy.' "

Subsequent psychiatric evaluations by the other seven members of the staff showed that Pound showed signs of being fully oriented and having superior intelligence. Everyone noticed his egocentricity, and one psychiatrist commented on his "haughty, boastful and dogmatic" manner, but his thinking pattern was seen to be coherent and clear. The only psychiatrist who noted delusions of grandeur and persecution during this period was Dr. Overholser. At a psychiatric case conference held on January 28, 1946, six staff psychiatrists denied he was delusional despite his economic theories.

Dr. Torrey in *The Roots of Treason* argues that Pound was quite capable of "faking symptoms" to strengthen his case or to prevent being tried. He observes a pattern of "selective memory loss," which he calls lying, and suggests that Pound's frequent claims of excessive fatigue were acts of convenience or part of a "grand performance." When Marion King interviewed him at St. Elizabeths, he reported that Pound was tense and emotional, weeping at one point while discussing economics. He complained of a partial memory loss, insomnia, fatigue, and a "queer sensation on the top of my head." In an interview with Dr. Arthur Griffen, Pound was disheveled, his shirt open in front and his shirt tail protruding from his trousers. His talk was punctuated by "cursing and vile language." He complained that his ideas had been suppressed for thirty years and that he was excessively fatigued because "all Europe on my shoulders." On one occasion he was interviewed by Dr. Addison Duval, later to become president of the American Psychiatric Association. Pound requested that he be allowed to lie prone on the floor during the examination. Duval began the interview with the assumption that Pound was a psychotic because of Overholser's diagnosis, but "I couldn't elicit any symptoms of psychosis at all. There were no delusions, no thought disorder, and no disturbances of orientation. He definitely did not seem to be insane." None of the psychiatrists who saw Pound during this period felt that he was in a paranoid state or that there was any evidence of psychosis. Most of them agreed that he had a psychopathic personality with strong neurotic tendencies, a diagnosis which fit a large part of the so-called normal world, but they were afraid or unwilling to challenge Overholser. When Duval reported to Overholser on the difference of opinion, he was told "that we didn't need to disturb the practicalities of the situation by making it public and that we should just keep it to ourselves. So that's what we did, so as not to embarrass our boss."

During this period Pound had few visitors, except for the psychiatrists. Two aged spinster sisters, Ida and Adah Lee Mapel, whom Pound had originally met in Spain in 1906, lived in Washington and began to come regularly, even though they could barely comprehend the reasons or the circumstances of Pound's internment. He was also receiving weekly visits from Charles Olson, an exceptionally tall thirty-five-year-old man who had just finished writing *Call Me Ishmael,* a highly charged book on Melville, but whose important work as a poet, *The Maximus Poems,* was still to come. Coming to offer comfort and compassion and the respect he felt was due Pound as a great poet, Olson was still ambivalent and uncertain because of Pound's fascism and treason. He wrote Malcolm Cowley that he wished "to be of use if there is anything to do to save the scoundrel's skin" and he was able to help in small ways such as retrieving Pound's personal effects from the District of Columbia jail. In larger ways he gave Pound an audience, a reason to release his word flow, though it sometimes was hard for Olson to accept. Questioned by Pound about his own genealogy, Olson told Pound his maternal grandfather's name was Lybeck, and Pound asked him if he was a Semite. The question must have caused a peculiar tension. Pound stood with those who took pride in the Anglo-Saxon heritage of the early Republic and who actively discriminated against the waves of immigrants who came later. During the war Olson had worked for the Office of War Information and had been responsible for getting news to Americans of foreign origin. At the end of the war Olson had worked for the Democratic party in the effort to recruit voters of foreign extraction. The son of an immigrant who was raised in Massachusetts towns with large immigrant populations, Olson had always identified with exactly the minorities Pound had pilloried since "Patria Mia." For Pound, Olson was an example of the loss of racial purity; for Olson, Pound was the poisoned poet, confused, depressed, exhausted, living in his own past, his "eyes worried and muddy, his flesh puffy and old."

Olson was important to Pound as evidence that at least some segment of the literary community was not ready to ostracize him for what he had said during the war. The two men talked about the war, economics, Pound's friendships with Yeats, Ford, and others in London thirty years earlier. For Olson, whose mind worked with a similar rapidity, Pound's "jumps in conversation are no more than I or any active mind would make." The final sanity hearing was on February 13. Before the hearing, Pound was visited by William Bird, who found him uncommunicative and nervous. At the hearing the four psychiatrists, Muncie, King, Overholser, and Gilbert, again testified on Pound's incompetence. Throughout the day-long trial Pound sat subdued, clenching and unclenching his hands, nervous, head down. At one moment he loudly cursed one of the attorneys for the Department of Justice, at another point he shouted that he had always been opposed to fascism. According to Albert Deutsch, a journalist who was particularly eager to see a treason trial actually occur, the Department of Justice attorneys acted as if they were simply going through the motions, as if the case had already been decided. The jury needed only five minutes to return with the decision of "unsound mind." After the decision, Pound was congratulated by James Laughlin, who presented Pound with an advance copy of *The Pisan Cantos*, which he was to release only two years later.

Olson saw him on the day after the trial, and Pound seemed reanimated. Wearing a new blue suit that Caresse Crosby had brought when she had come to visit, he greeted Olson with an aggressive forward movement, a thrust of the upper body, all chest and head, Olson remembered, a restlessness to get on with his work that Olson compared to "a loaded gun" and the "blind swing of a battering ram." The therapeutic significance of Olson's visits cannot be underestimated, as a note written two weeks earlier to Cornell in the form of a canto reveals:

> Problem now is
> not to go stark
> screaming hysteric . . .
> relapse after comfort of
> Tuesday= & mute.
> olson saved my life
> young doctors absolutely
> useless.
> must have 15
> minutes sane
> conversation daily . . .
> velocity after
> stupor tremendous.
> enormous work
>   to be
> done.
> & no driving
>   force
> & everyone's
>   inexactitude
> very
> fatiguing.
>
>   Dungeon
>   Dementia
> mental torture
> constitution a religion

a world lost
grey mist barrier impassible *[sic]*
ignorance absolute
anonyme
futility of might have been
coherent areas
constantly
invaded
aiuto [help]
Pound

Pound's life may have been saved by Cornell's strategies, but he was still very much in the "hell-hole" of Howard Hall, a building without windows, in a room with a thick steel door whose nine peepholes allowed doctors to observe him at their convenience and isolated him to a certain extent from tranquilized inmates, criminals, and patients in straitjackets who roamed the overheated halls of the ward with its smells of sour sweat and urine. Eliot felt Howard Hall was like a medieval prison, a place where rapists and killers screamed day and night, foamed at the mouth, tried to choke one another, or wallowed in their own filth. Pound had been questioned by one psychiatrist after another for months and would continue to be so questioned. The interviews began with Pound's protests about the intolerable conditions of Howard Hall, and his complaints about his excessive fatigue. As the interview proceeded, according to one of the psychiatrists who saw him regularly, he would ignore his "obviously feigned infirmities," jump up from his reclined position, raise his voice, become flushed, and speak for about an hour in sentences of extreme economy, compressing a volume of thought into a brief expression, a style not related to schizophrenic condensation, the psychiatrists soon realized, but quite similar to the telegraphic urgencies of his cantos and letters. In these interviews Pound would act histrionically, responding to certain questions in a low subdued tone, sighing and gasping "as though they were a man's last words." Then, with a sudden outburst of energy, he would express an anger or enthusiasm that seemed totally inconsistent with the weakness and the fatigue of which he complained. Pound was aware that the treason charges against him could be pressed were he to be declared sane and released from the hospital. For the time being St. Elizabeths was his sanctuary. Visitors invariably raised his spirits, but they were allowed to remain for only fifteen minutes and they were all, even the hard-boiled Mencken, invariably appalled at the conditions of Howard Hall and unable to disguise their dismay.

In June of 1946 Dorothy Pound finally succeeded in having her passport renewed and her funds released, and she sailed for the United States.

In Washington she stayed with the Mapel sisters and wrote to Julien Cornell after three visits to her husband. He was nervous and jumpy, she found, extremely scattered and unable to concentrate on any subject for more than a few minutes. Dorothy wanted Cornell to try to get Pound into a private sanitorium, stating that on each of her visits he had declared he could never get better in St. Elizabeths. Cornell replied that the time was not yet propitious for any sort of plea, that they would wait at least until after the November elections, adding that a transfer to a private facility would occur only if Overholser could be persuaded to testify that such a move was necessary for Pound's health.

Pound's friends were reconsidering his status. Laughlin wrote Eliot that he approved of the psychiatric diagnosis, reporting that Pound had told him after the sanity hearing that he could not understand why the Jews wanted to hang him, since he had worked out complete plans for rebuilding the old temple in Jerusalem—a project that had been organized over two thousand years earlier by his biblical namesake. Eliot wrote to A. V. Moore at Shakespear & Parkyn that Pound's behavior was what was to be expected, that he seemed disoriented only to those meeting him for the first time. In July of 1946, Eliot, in delicate health and holding himself together (as his friend Lady Colefax recalled) as if he were "a piece of riveted china," came to visit Pound. Eliot had separated from his wife, who had subsequently been institutionalized for her maladies. Feeling the guilt and loneliness that his earlier poems had so magnificently dramatized, he later married his secretary at Faber, who would afford him the emotional security and support his first wife had been unable to provide. Eliot's impression was that, above all, Pound needed to be calmed.

Some of his other friends were less protective in nature. H.D. wrote him a very placid letter from her sanatorium in Lausanne. Malcolm Cowley told him that Hemingway was shooting ducks in Gardiner's Island. Cummings sent an article on the closing of the renowned Sphinx brothel in Montparnasse, the result of a law making prostitution illegal in France. Marianne Moore announced her intention to visit. "Misfortune does not alter friendship," she declared, while warning Pound against embitterment, a subject in which she claimed to be expert. Wyndham Lewis, who was still feeling the privations of the war, getting only two eggs a month, and having trouble keeping warm, jocularly wrote: "I am told that you believe yourself to be Napoleon—or is it Mussolini? What a pity you did not choose Buddha while you were about it, instead of a politician." Dorothy would send him a package that included some tinned butter, which he declared a rare luxury. One of the harsher correspondents was Nancy Cunard, who called him a scoundrel, stating she believed him in "perfect possession of your faculties." There had been other letters comparing him to Tokyo Rose or Axis Sally, but Cunard, who had worked for the Free French Radio during the war, had

heard Pound's broadcasts and had been shocked. She reminded Pound of
his defense of Mussolini's invasion of Ethiopia on the ground that the Ethi-
opians were only black Jews who deserved conquest. Ironically, she noted,
until that time she had believed Pound himself was Jewish. At the end of
her nine-page handwritten letter, she related the destruction of her house in
Normandy. All its windows had been smashed, her books thrown into a
well, a copy of the vellum edition of *The Cantos* she had printed "crucified"
against a window frame. Pound's reply was belligerent: "What the buggar-
ing HELL are you talking about. I had freedom of microphone to say what I
liked—namely the Truth that your shitless friends were afraid to hear, your
friends who busted the Tempio at Rimini. Swine on both sides but Truth
suppressed for 40 and for 200 years."

Pound ended his letter to Cunard with a reference to William Carlos
Williams, "an ass who won't face historic fact." Williams had been one of
the first of his friends to write, declaring that he did not "for one moment"
believe that Pound was crazy. "You might as well realize," Williams asserted, "that there is a point in all controversy beyond which a man's life
(his last card) is necessarily forfeit." Williams was recovering from a hernia
operation in the spring of 1946 when he sent Pound a copy of *Paterson*, his
American epic counterpart to *The Cantos*. Pound admitted he could not then
read it—"Can't clamp mind on anything so closely packed . . . . main
spring is busted." Later that summer Williams wrote to Dorothy Pound,
stating that he saw no release for her husband unless it came through executive clemency, which was unlikely because Pound's broadcasts had been
inescapably treasonous. Williams's position was that civil disobedience was
"only justifiable when we pledge our very beings to the moral cause which
motivates us." To escape the issue after the event is just ignoble. Ezra, he
advised, should stand up like a man and accept a trial no matter what the
consequences. Such a position was difficult for Williams to take, he added,
but though Pound was his oldest friend he felt he could not really exculpate
him. In the fall he wrote Pound that his attacks on Roosevelt had been
particularly stupid, that it had been contemptible to have slurred
Roosevelt's wife and family, that his broadcasts had put him on the side of
the "most vicious and reactionary forces" in America seeking to discredit
Roosevelt. Pound's reply was to resume the offense. He knew he had completely failed to arouse any real interest in the American Constitution because of "foreigners" like Williams who "don't give a damn if it is thrown
on the dung heap." Williams had a mind that was informed only by newspaper headlines, he was frivolously ignorant of the real issues, still the provincial in the pasture. "Between us lies the sea" was Williams's answer,
scrawled in a notebook pad in pencil on his desk when he received Pound's
letter. He had just seen a five-year-old boy who was recovering from menin-

gitis, an affirmation for Williams which in some way was partial compensation for the loss of a friendship he knew he could never really recover.

As he had promised, after the November elections Cornell began his
new strategy for securing Pound's release, a motion for bail on the grounds
that Pound's confinement would not improve his mental state and that no
one should be incarcerated in violation of the Fifth Amendment to the
Constitution unless there was some prospect of a trial: "I do not believe a
man can be shut up indefinitely after being indicted," Cornell wrote Pound,
"when he cannot be tried because of illness." At a hearing on January 29,
1947, Dr. Overholser testified that Pound might benefit by being transferred from Howard Hall, but that he could be cared for as well at St.
Elizabeths as anywhere else. A year later Cornell applied for a writ of
habeas corpus in a final attempt to secure Pound's freedom, and to avoid the
possibility of imprisoning for life a man who had not the "sufficient mental
capacity to meet the charge." This writ was denied in March of 1948 and
Cornell appealed immediately, explaining to Dorothy Pound, who had
been appointed as Pound's legal guardian, that he might have to take his
case as far as the Supreme Court. Dorothy, knowing that her husband no
longer even had a passport and that the State Department could not be
forced to issue one, and perhaps fearing the exclusive responsibility of caring for her husband, instructed Cornell to withdraw his appeal: "My husband is not fit to appear in court and must be kept as quiet as possible; the
least thing shakes his nerves up terribly."

3. THE MARTYRED SCHOOLMASTER

St. Elizabeths is situated on a hill over Washington on some four hundred acres with wide lawns and flowering trees. Pound was moved to his
own small room, a doorless cubicle with a high narrow window where
through hemlock trees he could see the Capitol and the Library of Congress.
He was in Chestnut Ward of the Center Building, where Dr. Overholser
had his private quarters. He was allowed more liberal visiting hours and
could go outdoors. At the end of the corridor outside his room there was a
screened alcove with a round table and several wicker chairs which he
converted into a sitting room for his visitors. Dorothy came every day,
having found a small, Spartan basement apartment within a short walk of St.
Elizabeths. Life was hardly easy on Chestnut Ward with the distractions
presented by blaring radios and drooling, muttering, wandering patients,
but it was a vast improvement over Howard Hall. Pound resumed working
on *The Cantos* and his own correspondence. Afternoons there was Dorothy
bringing books and magazines and there were the visitors. Olson was still
coming, caught in his own ambivalence, charmed by Pound but resenting

his bigotry. The charm had betrayed him, however, as Olson began to feel that Pound was using it to manipulate people. The rigidity with which Pound held to his prewar views during his long period of incarceration at St. Elizabeths amazed and disturbed a number of his friends. Olga Rudge, writing to Ronald Duncan in England, commented: "The Absolute refusal to face facts is a very strong family trait, both his mother and Mary share it in a marked degree; Dorothy I should imagine has acquired it." Olga Rudge's reference to Isabel Pound came just before her death at eighty-eight. When Dorothy left for Washington, Isabel had moved to the Tyrol to live with her granddaughter. By then Mary had married a descendant of Austrian nobility, Principe Boris de Rachewiltz, and the couple had managed to buy an old ruined castle in Schloss Brunnenburg which they were slowly restoring.

There were other visitors—a young University of Maryland lecturer in Greek named Rudd Fleming, who started working with Pound on translations from Greek plays, and two professors from Catholic University, James La Driere and Giovanni Giovannini, whom Pound had visited on his 1939 trip. Cummings traveled to Washington from New York several times, feeling a special kinship because of his own imprisonment by the French during World War I. Williams came, noting that Pound's unruly gray hair made him resemble the beast in Jean Cocteau's experimental film *Beauty and the Beast*. Williams remembered the restless twitching of Pound's hands, his "shifting his shoulders about as he lay back in the chair studying me, the same bantering smile, screwing up his eyes, the half-coughing laugh and short, swift words, no sentence structure worth mentioning." Privately, Williams was dismayed at his absolute lack of contrition, his refusal to admit that his ideas had been wrong:

I can't understand how Pound has been so apparently unmoved by his incarceration, guilty or essentially innocent as he may be. His mind has not budged a hair's breadth from his basic position, he has even entrenched himself more securely in it—recently finding precedents in the writings of a certain Controller of the Currency sixty or seventy-five years ago, who held similar views on our official perfidies. Pound has privileges, it must be acknowledged, and is kindly treated by the hospital personnel. But he does not waste them. He works constantly, reads interminably. The curator of the Oriental Library in Washington brings him the texts he is interested in when he wants them; he has the Greek of whoever it may be to decipher and understand. He may translate; he has his typewriter; his erudition is become more and more fearsome as time passes, whatever the outcome is to be.

Williams agreed to Dorothy's plan to try to get Pound released in his care, writing to Overholser to suggest this. He was also constantly advising Pound on minor ailments, a troublesome hangnail, a swollen eyelid, a persistent stomachache—"Swallow a bottle of coke and let it fizz out of your ears." He told Pound that he had read his eighty-third canto at a writers' conference at the University of Utah, which caused a long dispute on treason. Driving home he detoured to El Paso, Texas, to visit McAlmon, thinner, tubercular, discouraged, now slovenly as a writer, but also still discerning with his "biting way of destroying fake and overblown emptiness."

In 1947 Pound received letters from three young poets who became important voices in the postwar American literary scene: Robert Lowell, John Berryman, and W. S. Merwin, who wrote that he was fascinated by the Fenollosa material. Another young poet, Robert Duncan, wrote sustaining certain of Pound's more rabid views, commenting that "minorities of any kind are symptoms like boils, cancers," signs of the breakdown of the body politic. His recurrent paranoia was fed by other correspondents like Berenice Abbott, the photographer, who wrote that fluoride in the water supply was causing deformed children, and that there was cobalt in milk and grains. There was also a joint letter by two young writers, Guy Davenport and Christopher Middleton, comparing Pound to Richard the Lion-Hearted in his captivity. There was a letter from George Santayana, to whom Pound responded: "Trouble with your Xtianity is that it is a sham cult cut off from agriculture. Steam roller no substitute for plow." Referring to Santayana's own philosophy, he warned of the "awful mess of trying to hitch greek and latin horse sense to epilepsy from alien source."

In 1947 New Directions published Pound's Confucian translations as *The Unwobbling Pivot and The Great Digest.* A number of the cantos were also beginning to appear in *Poetry,* the *Sewanee Review, The Yale Poetry Review,* and *The Quarterly Review of Literature,* which in 1948 devoted an entire issue to assessing Pound's reputation. The publications were a good sign for Pound. He had heard from one of his correspondents that the New York Public Library system had removed all copies of his books. Furthermore, Bennett Cerf had decided to eliminate Pound from the Random House anthologies, a very controversial position which Cerf later changed after Cornell threatened a libel suit, since Pound was presumably innocent of any crime unless brought to trial.

Poets, critics, scholars, and friends continued to come in person as part of a curious pilgrimage of the literary tribe to a man they were making into an icon: Thornton Wilder, Allen Tate, Conrad Aiken, Stephen Spender, Katherine Anne Porter, Elizabeth Bishop, Langston Hughes, Louis Zukofsky, Archibald MacLeish, Paul Blackburn, Robert Lowell. Marianne Moore brought peanuts for the squirrels on the lawn. The scholars came as well, Achilles Fang, the Chinese expert at Harvard, Norman Holmes Pearson of

Yale, Marshall McLuhan, who had started his career as a Joyce scholar and who brought with him on one of his visits a young student, Hugh Kenner, who was to write one of the first intelligent books on Pound's poetry. Greek scholar and novelist Edith Hamilton, tiny, eighty, and nearly deaf, came once a month with homemade chocolates. One of her conversations with Pound was recorded by Eustace Mullins and stands as a record of the intellectual quality of the Chestnut Ward salon. Pound was showing Miss Hamilton Confucian ideograms:

POUND: This ideogram means respect, the root of respect, respect for the kind of intelligence which enables the cherry tree to grow cherries. Now, this other ideogram represents the man carrying a lance and the spoken word from the mouth, meaning the crusade to find the rightly-aimed word. Yeats said to me that if they knew what we thought, they'd do away with us. They want their poets dead.

EDITH HAMILTON: A Chinese friend of mine was told in the examination halls at Nanking of a great Confucian scholar, such a scholar that he wrote a letter, and there was only one man in all China who could understand it. That is not very democratic, I'm afraid. That is aristocratic, like you, Mr. Pound.

POUND: But it is democratic as long as it provides that anyone may have the opportunity to learn enough to read that letter.

EDITH HAMILTON: You always puncture my balloons, Mr. Pound.

POUND: You haven't been out since my latest theory that Dante was a real democrat and Shakespeare a bloody snob.

EDITH HAMILTON: I'm no Shakespearean, Mr. Pound, but I must quarrel with you there. I don't believe Shakespeare ever had that fixed an idea.

POUND: In the *Inferno*, Dante doesn't pay any attention to the class from which the characters sprang.

EDITH HAMILTON: But he didn't have any common men in his *Inferno*. They were all important people. He didn't portray the torturing of the common man.

POUND: Shakespeare was propounding this idea of a limited monarchy in his twelve histories.

EDITH HAMILTON: I don't think so. I think he was too careless a man to do anything like that. And I think that Mr. Dante was more

aristocratic than Mr. Shakespeare. [She quotes Hamlet's soliloquy.] The soliloquy was Mr. Shakespeare coming through—the
only time I know where he really came through. By the way, is
that Rouse translation of Homer a good one?

POUND: It doesn't have the movement or the sound or any ap-
proximation of one. Edwards in the *Hudson* has done the best
translation, but it hasn't got the right quantities *[sic]* in it.

EDITH HAMILTON: Is anyone doing a good translation?

POUND: There are probably fifty or sixty people doing bad translations, and I know of five or six incompetent young men doing
better translations that will not be good enough, but they are trying to make a good translation.

EDITH HAMILTON: Mr. Pound is such a naughty fellow (to Mrs.
Pound). What do you do with him when he's like that? Does
scolding do him any good?

DOROTHY POUND (Laughs): Oh help, I gave that up long ago.

T. S. Eliot came to the United States annually on business for Faber &
Faber and would always discuss Pound's situation with James Laughlin and
Joseph Cornell. After a visit to St. Elizabeths in November 1948, he wrote
Cornell, inquiring whether Pound might be allowed more freedom of
movement within the hospital grounds and whether there was any possibility of his being transferred to a ward with patients who were less visibly
insane than on Chestnut. Cornell forwarded a copy of Eliot's letter to Overholser, who replied that he hesitated about accepting Eliot's suggestions
because Pound was still "under indictment for the most serious crime in the
calendar" and at present he already had more privilege than any other
patient. Overholser added that it did not much matter what ward Pound was
on, since he had "supreme contempt" for the other patients and was "inclined to be rather supercilious in his views of practically everyone with
whom he comes in contact." Much of this superciliousness was directed to
the psychiatrists who were still interviewing him regularly. One of his visitors, George Kearns, a young army private in uniform, asked Pound what
he talked about with the psychiatrists. Pound answered, "Honor," paused
for a minute, rolled his eyes, and then added, "It AIN'T that they don't
believe in it. It's just that they never HURRRRRRD of it!"

One of the doctors who saw Pound at this time, J. M. Langford, observed that on one occasion Pound went out walking with a group of other
patients, lay down in the road, and complained that he needed his wife, that
"it was too much for him alone." Another psychiatrist, a Dr. Small, noted
that Pound kept his room messy, had lots of visitors, and wrote several

letters every day. The room, which was lined with metal shelving for books from floor to ceiling on one wall, was the space in which Pound organized his creative endeavor. The floor was littered with boxes and papers, and one wall was a giant bulletin board where Pound would tape other papers, memos, pictures, schematic drawings. Pieces of paper and envelopes with quotations and excerpts from books that he was going to incorporate in *The Cantos* were hung on strings attached to the ceiling, clothing was strewn everywhere, and most of his drawers were left open, revealing the complete disorganization of his personal effects. Dr. Small observed that Pound stayed in his room most of the time, almost always humming as he worked his typewriter. He complained chronically, but never caused any real trouble, and appeared quite normal, except perhaps for his dress. Pound's carelessness with his clothing was part of a new statement. In his London days he had been a dandy, but during this time he was dressing the role of his madness, wearing a scarf in summer, never buttoning his shirt, and often leaving his fly unzipped, especially for the psychiatrists.

In a sense Pound was perfectly in his element on Chestnut Ward. He had always criticized the fact that as a poet he could never earn a living in America, but here he was being provided for. He was reading omnivorously and writing on the average of three letters a day. A young scholar named D. D. Paige was editing his earlier letters for publication. He was working on translations of Sophocles's *Women of Trachis* and *Electra,* assisted by Edith Hamilton and Rudd Fleming, and he was attempting some new translations of Chinese poetry with a young woman studying at Catholic University. He was also writing the "Rock-Drill" section of *The Cantos,* named after the sculpture by Jacob Epstein he had seen in 1913 that showed man fusing into and being absorbed by the machines of his creation.

The Pisan Cantos had been propitiously held back by Laughlin, but at last he felt the time was right for their release. In June of 1948 he met with a group of Pound's friends—Eliot, Cummings, W. H. Auden, Allen Tate, and Joseph Cornell—to discuss strategies to free Pound. According to Archibald MacLeish, these men conceived a plan to award Pound the first national prize for poetry, the Bollingen Award, which was to be administered by the Library of Congress with the one-thousand-dollar prize money to be contributed by the Mellon family. The expectation was that awarding the prize to Pound would put the Department of Justice in an "awkward if not untenable position" and force it to drop the charges against Pound, or at least permit his release. Laughlin published *The Pisan Cantos* in the summer of 1948 and the book was widely reviewed. The awards committee of fifteen Fellows of the Library of Congress included a number of Pound's friends and supporters—Eliot, Aiken, Tate, Lowell, Katherine Anne Porter, and Theodore Spencer. The committee voted to award its prize to Pound, aware that the choice might provoke some controversy and pointing out that it had been asked to select the best book published in the preceding year: "To permit other considerations than that of poetic achievement would destroy the significance of the award and would in principle deny the validity of that objective perception of value on which civilized society must rest."

There were two dissenting votes, one by Katherine Garrison Chapin, the wife of Francis Biddle, who had first indicted Pound in 1943, and the other by Karl Shapiro, who argued that Pound's political views vitiated his poetry and that as a Jew he could not vote for an anti-Semite. Shapiro criticized the award in *Partisan Review*, and a further attack was launched by Robert Hillyer, president of the Poetry Society of America, in a heated series of articles for *The Saturday Review of Literature*. There was another attack by Dr. Fredric Wertham, a noted psychiatrist, who denied that Pound had ever been insane, blaming the psychiatrists at the sanity hearing for not choosing to distinguish between delusion and political conviction. The ultimate delusion, Wertham concluded, was national: "We have let ourselves be deluded—into a belief that responsibility is not responsibility, guilt not guilt, and incitement to hate not incitement to violence." Later Harry Levin, an influential critic, charged that the psychiatrists had served to absolve Pound's responsibility for his antisocial behavior. The result was that Congressman Jacob K. Javits of New York demanded an investigation of the award, and the Library of Congress allowed Yale University to assume all future responsibility for administering it. A number of literary magazines broadened the scope of the controversy, concerned most of all by the line separating dissent from treason in a free society. Allen Tate in *Partisan Review* defended the award. Even if Pound had been convicted of treason, he asserted, in his revitalization of language he had performed "an indispensable duty to society."

When the award had been announced, Cummings telegrammed Pound: "Hearty congratulations to Capitalist system and to Andrew Mellon in particular." While Pound may have enjoyed the notoriety of what he disparagingly called the "Bubble-Gum Prize"—it was quite clear he would have preferred the Nobel Prize and thought he deserved it—it evidently was not considered embarrassing by the attorneys in the Department of Justice, and the arguments that had been raised about Pound's fascism and anti-Semitism were only adverse publicity for him, a reminder of the reasons for his being in St. Elizabeths in the first place. While Pound then found it convenient to deny that he had sympathized with fascism or that he had ever intended to commit treason, and while in public he repudiated the idea that he was anti-Semitic, in practice he continued to vilify the Jews. He distrusted and often refused to talk with psychiatrists who had Jewish sounding names and told Olson he was for pogroms because of what he had experienced in St. Elizabeths. He referred to visitors whom he personally

did not like as Jewish whether or not this was in fact the case. In a correspondence with Seymour Krim, a young writer who happened to be Jewish
but refused to judge Pound because of his anti-Semitism, Pound quickly
managed to irritate Krim with anti-Semitic slurs which terminated the correspondence. Krim later visited Pound and remembered him driving off some
of the ward wanderers with a rolled newspaper. Some of Pound's correspondents were equally scornful of the Jews: one of them, Eustace Mullins,
writing on the Aryan League of America letterhead, said, "THE JEWS ARE
BETRAYING US." In another letter Mullins joked about burning a synagogue and boasted of friendship with a neo-Nazi circle. Pound urged certain of his visitors to read the *Protocols of Zion* and continued to denounce the
influence of the Old Testament: "the jew book is the poison/that since A.D.
has bitched everything it got into." His Jewish obsession had clearly intensified, and he continued to blame the Jews for everything from the ruination
of the publishing industry to World War II. He frequently insisted that he
had never been anti-Semitic, that he had enjoyed many Jewish friends. But,
as critic Irving Howe has argued, it is the abstract quality of his views that
makes them so terrifying—the expression of a "theological hatred that
never sought a particular victim or even envisaged the consequences of its
rhetoric" but resulted nevertheless in "a blind complicity in the twentieth
century's victimization of the innocents."

Despite his capacity for vitriolic outburst, all signs indicate that Pound
had adjusted to life on Chestnut Ward. During the 1950s he had a procession of acolytes to whom he assigned different visiting days. Some of these
younger visitors started little magazines with decidedly Poundian biases
where he would publish short political pieces, often anonymously. The first
of these was Dallam Simpson's *Four Pages,* which Simpson published from
his hometown of Galveston, Texas; another was *Strike,* published in Washington, D.C., by William McNaughton, a Washington cab driver. Pound,
who was sixty when he was interned at St. Elizabeths, also had a number of
female companions, the first of whom was Sheri Martinelli, a former model
and painter of sorts who later explained her attraction to Pound in a lively
and unpredictable letter:

> I was going around t/world with the/clouds and t/air like Chief of
> all The Chiricahuas Apache: Cochise—when Ezra Pound (known
> to us as: "E.P.") "spoke to my Thoughts." I, too, "carried My Life
> on My Finger Nails" and they were each & all a different colour
> because I was a working painter—a Fighter in The Ethical Arena
> wherein you KNOW what's Really Wrong because you did that
> yourself and you found out by The Way of Being There. Artist.
> Maestro.

Martinelli contributed to a growing legend of Pound as a rakish lover, and once again he became the subject of sexual rumors. By 1952 Pound was allowed visitors at any time during the day or evening, and he was seen on numerous occasions, sometimes in Dorothy's presence, either caressing or being caressed by Martinelli. In a letter to Overholser, Dorothy explained that Pound regarded Martinelli as a daughter. Pound, it should be noted, saw it differently, praising his wife's "respectable allergy to the affairs of others." Later, Marcella Spann, a naïve young English teacher from a small town in Texas who had originally come to interview Pound about his poetry, replaced Martinelli.

When his daughter, Mary, arrived at St. Elizabeths to visit and to discuss plans for his release, Pound refused to discuss the subject. Olga Rudge visited twice, in 1952 and 1955, and could not understand why Pound did not take more assertive steps toward his release. She wrote to Peter Russell that "E. P. has—as he had before—bats in the belfry but it strikes me that he has fewer not more than before his incarceration." She collected signatures on a petition in Rapallo attesting that Pound had never been a Fascist and issued a pamphlet of his radio broadcasts which were all literary in scope called *If This Be Treason*. Overholser noted in an interview with Pound in 1956 that Pound made no attempt to be released. Eliot also observed that Pound would object to any scheme that offered the possibility of release. Most suggestions, however, involved the probability of trial. Basil Bunting urged that Pound present himself as having been duped by the Fascists, flattered by them into making the broadcasts. In the spring of 1948, the Nazi collaborator R. H. Best, an American journalist who had broadcast from Berlin, was found guilty of treason and sentenced to life imprisonment. Another American, Douglas Chandler, received the same sentence for his broadcasts. These cases were sober reminders of why Pound needed to remain in St. Elizabeths. D. D. Paige sent Wyndham Lewis the draft of a petition he planned to circulate and present to Truman. Lewis was very busy with his own painting and writing and also gradually going blind, but he never lost interest in Pound's situation. He wrote Paige in October of 1948 that some of Pound's friends thought it was better for his reputation in the long run that he remain in St. Elizabeths so as not to be able to outrage people with his public remarks. Pound was the scolding schoolmaster, a "pig-headed dominy" who, though benevolent, would invariably cause trouble. Lewis felt that Pound deserved special treatment because of his "cultural importance." In 1952 Lewis wrote to his old friend: "It wearies me you remaining where you are. To take up a strategic position in an lunatic asylum is idiotic. If I don't see you make an effort to get out *soon*, I shall conclude either that your present residence has snobbish appeal for you, or that you are timid with regard to Fate."

4. MANIC TERRITORY

Pound's mainstay during his twelve years at St. Elizabeths was his wife, who organized her life around the afternoons she spent with him. Dorothy sometimes typed his letters for him if he was too nervous or distracted, and she generally exerted a calming, soothing influence. According to William French, one of the young men who gathered around Pound at St. Elizabeths, Dorothy was attuned to her husband's needs and adept at shielding him from grating guests. She had the ability to gracefully guide conversations to safety zones whenever she suspected Pound was in danger of entering what French calls "manic territory." Representing probity and propriety, patience, detachment, and equanimity, she was the socializing and stabilizing factor in Pound's salon, his most trusted and empathetic confidante. And there was a good deal to support, from the drabness of her own dark studio on Brothers Place in southeast Washington, set in a line of uniform row houses with fake fluted columns, to the irascibilities and infidelities of her husband. The descendant of a line of British generals, Dorothy was the stalwart soldier, uncomplaining and loving.

Much as Dorothy tried, however, the one person she could not protect Pound from was himself. His friend Wyndham Lewis had pointed out that Pound's excesses were really an outpouring of exuberance. But Lewis had also predicted that Pound was ending his career with a parallel to Villon's, who died on a gibbet surrounded by other criminals, while the more politic Eliot—who received a Nobel Prize in 1948 and was enjoying the height of fame—would end his days as a sort of Tennyson, sanctimonious and revered. The Villon parallel seems accurate in the light of Pound's friendship and sponsorship of John Kasper, a young man who had taken a course in modern poetry at Columbia University's School of General Studies, where he was introduced to Pound's work. In a term paper at Columbia, Kasper had written: "I thrilled at Niccolo Machiavelli, Friedrich Nietzsche and the political Ezra Pound. Hitler and Stalin are clever men and Wilson a fool. The weak have no justification for living except in service of the strong. What is a little cruelty to the inocuous when it is expedient for the strong ones who have the right to alter the laws of life and death before their natural limits." Kasper's remark is reminiscent of Pound's, on his 1939 visit, that fascism coerced only the inferior man, that the superior man knew how to use any system for his own ends. Kasper first visited Pound during the summer of 1950. According to Kasper, at the end of their meeting Pound shouted, "Bravo for Kasp!" and a bond was formed. Kasper became a regular correspondent and a frequent visitor, offering to devote himself to whatever cause Pound inspired, sure that Pound was a great man whose ideas could be used to lead others. Kasper then opened a bookstore in Greenwich Village—long known as a center of tolerant liberalism—that specialized in Nazi literature, memorabilia, and anti-Semitic tracts. He had met another young follower of Pound's at St. Elizabeths, David Horton, a Hamilton graduate, and together they bought a printing press and began a publishing imprint called the Square Dollar Series to print books that Pound approved of, including his translation of the Confucian *Analects*.

After the Supreme Court decision of 1954 ordering integration in the schools, Kasper found his cause. By 1956 he had organized the Seaboard White Citizens Council, a neo-Klan pressure group formed to terrorize blacks and rally whites. One of his organizational fliers was a direct imitation of the Lewis-Pound *Blast* manifesto of 1914, which Pound must have shown him:

> JAIL NAACP, alien, unclean, unchristian
> BLAST irreverent ungodly LEADERS
> HANG 9 SUPREME COURT SWINE
> (this year domine '56)
> BANISH LIARS
> Destroy REDS (ALL muscovite savages)
> rooseveltian dupes
> EXPOSE BERIA's "psycho-politics"
> DEATH TO USURERS

In the same announcement Kasper harangued southerners to "hate mongrelizers," damning the "stink: Roose, Harry & Ike" as "race-mixers," and warning against "the pink punks, flatchested highbrows, homos, perverts, freaks, golf players, poodle dogs, hot-eyed Socialists, Fabians, scum" and "degenerate liberals crying for the petrifaction of putrefaction." The phrases in his publicity had a distinctly Poundian ring, and it was clear that Kasper had been counseled by his mentor. He began requesting material from Pound, whom he addressed as "Dear Boss," that could be used in his campaign against Jews, integration, and miscegenation, on occasion signing his letters with a swastika. Pound was again in the position of publicist for a dark cause, and the parallels with his work for the Salo government of Benito Mussolini are clear. In East Tennessee, Kasper started a small newspaper, a propaganda outlet for his ideas. In it he criticized Claire Booth Luce, the American ambassador to Italy, for disregarding "the countless pleas of Italian intellectual, religious, academic and political leaders demanding the immediate release from an eleven year political imprisonment of Ezra Pound." Except for the petition organized by Olga Rudge in Rapallo, the "countless pleas" were a fiction. Like Wallace Stevens's poem on the abandoned jar in Tennessee, the probability is that very few in that state had ever heard of or cared about Ezra Pound or his "struggle against deadly usury." Kasper began speaking publicly around the South—in Louisville he declared he had heard of blacks with tails, in Charlottesville he alleged Communist influence in the NAACP. His appearances in South Carolina were sponsored by the Ku Klux Klan, and in Alabama by George Lincoln Rockwell, who founded the American Nazi party. Integration was a plot instigated by the Jews, Kasper claimed, and in Clinton, Tennessee, in September of 1956 his remarks provoked a riot and landed him in jail. Out on bail, he resumed agitating and was arrested a few months later, suspected of having organized the bombing of an elementary school which was about to be integrated. Sentenced to jail in Tennessee in May of 1958, Kasper entered a penitentiary with a copy of *Mein Kampf* under his arm. Though the involvement with Kasper may have been the result of what Lewis had called Pound's "exuberance," a riot had taken place and children's lives threatened in the bombing. Kasper was no better than one of Mussolini's thugs, a rabble-rouser whom Pound had encouraged. The effect on Pound was a delay of his own release, since Kasper showed that Pound's influence was far from harmless.

In the early fifties, when Pound had first met Kasper, the St. Elizabeths salon was a place of perpetual ferment. Pound was being visited by the literati, the scholars, the Social Creditors and right-wing sympathizers, and cranks like the Chinese-American David Wang, who tried to organize segregationist groups on Ivy League campuses. Several of the resident psychiatrists at St. Elizabeths complained about the fawning sycophants who came to adulate. There were also visits of a more social nature: Elizabeth Winslow, for example, a Washington resident who had worked as an official for the Housing Reconstruction Administration and who visited with gifts of delicacies, or the millionaire art collector Huntington Cairns, whose wife, Dorothy, tutored in drawing, and whose annual Christmas gift was a huge supply of caviar. The cynosure of these visits was Pound himself who had been seeking a circle of admirers all his life. Pound was chief entertainer and resident sage—thirty years earlier in Paris McAlmon had called him a "martyred schoolmaster," a perception that proved prescient, given the circumstances. Pound's boisterous good cheer was the mask he chose to disguise his suffering. He knew few would want to visit him if he were morose and depressed; and as he explained in a later canto, "A man's paradise is his good nature." For entertainment there were the anecdotes of Pound's literary past, the ample memories of London and Paris, and his mimicry, his ability to imitate the accent and mannered tone of a Henry James or a Henry Adams, an Idaho maverick or a Kentucky hillbilly.

The hillbilly accent which Pound had perfected was an ironic rebuke to his own reputation as cultural guardian. It was contagiously disarming and many of Pound's followers, like the lawyer Robert M. Furniss, Jr., began imitating it in their letters. On Pound's part it was an expression of a core of

Americanism and an ear for regional dialect that was as finely tuned as Mark Twain's. Some of his other accents may not have been as felicitous. When raging against Roosevelt, he would often assume a "Jewish" accent. He told Michael Reck that his hatred for Roosevelt was enough to dam up the Potomac River, and he could spend twenty minutes defaming Roosevelt and the New Deal. Pound also claimed that the insanity ruling, which, as Hemingway pointed out, had been his protection, had in fact been used to discredit him with the young, that the government was afraid to try him because he would tell the truth about Roosevelt in court. There were other views on this matter. Dr. Overholser noted that Pound could have had the insanity ruling changed by changing his own behavior at St. Elizabeths, implying that Overholser was fully aware of the game Pound had chosen to play to avoid trial. Though St. Elizabeths was a sort of prison, it was a secure place, and on several occasions Pound had expressed fears of being assassinated were he to leave.

Pound played chess in the evenings with a patient who had been an engineer, and tennis during the day with members of the hospital staff. He was allowed to sit outdoors till 8 P.M., and for six months of the year, despite the dampness and humidity of Washington, which adversely affected a chronic arthritis of the neck and back, he would hold court outside under a large Japanese pine tree among the blue jays and squirrels, which he tried to train with peanuts on strings. Eustace Mullins described these gatherings as set in a kind of pastoral academy:

> During these afternoons, Ezra's manner was that of a deservedly popular professor at a small but highly-regarded school, who was having some of his star students in for tea. His *bonhomie* was always perfect for the occasion; he was a benevolent Socrates who as yet had no intention of drinking the cup of hemlock which his fellow citizens had offered him. Dorothy Pound was also as apt and self-effacing as a professor's wife, as she poured tea, murmured "Shush" when the bluejays became too noisy, and produced little paper bags for the shells of hard-boiled eggs, so that we should not litter the lawn.

Pound was always appropriating leftover food, which he would distribute to visitors like Mullins or MacNaughton, perhaps imagining that he was feeding a community of future poets. These outdoor meetings, too, were perhaps reminiscent of the café culture Pound had so enjoyed in Paris and Rapallo where he had conversed with friends in public. In Paris he had been known to leave a café suddenly without formalities. At St. Elizabeths he suddenly lapsed into silences, long periods where he would recline and stare at the sky and not answer questions—an ominous sign.

According to William French, Pound saw the "Ezuversity" which had been transplanted from Rapallo to St. Elizabeths in terms of wheels and cubes. Wheels were people like Kasper, who could act quickly and get things done. But they were not reliable: "You can't lean on 'em. They'll roll out from under you," Pound would say. Cubes were foundations one could build on. The "Thrones" section of *The Cantos* partly relates to this, the ideas and values Pound could rely on without seeing them collapse in his time. The "scum floating on the surface," a phrase Pound used in a letter to French to describe the category for a European journalist he knew, were the betrayers, those he had once described in excremental terms in the English hell cantos.

Pound was pleased by the seriousness of some of his acolytes. A young man named David Gordon started the *Accademia Bulletin;* David Horton, *Mood;* Eustace Mullins, *Three Hands.* In Australia another young admirer, Noel Stock, was editing *Edge,* and in England Henry Swabey had begun a Social Credit paper called *Voice.* Pound began publishing notes and commentaries in these and similar journals, often using pseudonyms. He had become convinced of an "evil conspiracy" in America organized by liberal leftists to degrade the Constitution and vitiate it. He began to insist that the American Communists had tried to prevent him from publishing and depressed his reputation since 1928. The atmosphere of these years, of course, was dense with imagined conspiracies, most flagrantly proclaimed by Senator Joseph McCarthy, who chose to see a Communist in practically every teapot and a legion of them in the State Department. The scowling senator from Wisconsin offered little proof but considerable rhetoric, and the newspapers publicized his accusations. Alger Hiss was tried and defended by Lloyd Stryker, Pound's Hamilton classmate and his original choice for his own defense. Hiss was convicted mostly on testimony offered by Whittaker Chambers, who had been a member of the Objectivist circle of poets that Pound had helped organize, through Zukofsky, from Rapallo. The Cold War had created an internal freeze in America. "America seems clenched and somehow nervous and muscle bound," Robert Lowell wrote to Pound in 1951. Suspicion and fear were endemic and the newspapers were full of innuendos and contentions that treasonous spies were giving strategic secrets to the Soviets. The House Un-American Activities Committee had been investigating labor unions, universities, and Hollywood, and a blacklist of former leftists was in effect in advertising and many other industries. Pound was visited by the young poet-critic A. Alvarez, who found him surrounded by disciples questioning him on currency reform, Communist plots, and the use of drugs for political ends. Alvarez said he sounded rhetorical, his speech disorganized and full of improbable theories, and he seemed at moments "faintly embarrassed by his followers' zeal." Alvarez's impression of Pound was "a sense of terrible loneliness, and also of great courage and resilience." In fugitive publications like *Strike* and *Four Pages,*

Pound added to the hysteria of rabid anticommunism that defined the political tenor of the early fifties.

5. "HE JUST TALK TOO MUCH"

In Rapallo, Pound had been the forgotten exile, but in St. Elizabeths he was attracting more and more notice. In the fall of 1950, D. D. Paige's edition of selected letters appeared. In it Paige attempted to document Pound's position as the seminal modernist, the man who had pushed the interests of his friends, Yeats, Joyce, Ford, Eliot, and Lewis, before his own. The letters were reviewed by Malcolm Cowley, who felt that Paige's edition was cosmetic, an attempt to suppress Pound's obsessions and aberrations. Cowley noted that he had read some of the broadcasts, which were "heartbreaking to me as revelations of how far a gifted poet could travel toward substantive evil simply by riding a hobby horse." Cowley had always been sympathetic to Pound. In 1943 in *The Saturday Review of Literature* he had tried to explain Pound's broadcasts as resulting from "a succession of literary attitudes and the habit of trying to amaze his readers." Both Paige and James Laughlin, who had published the book, hoped that the ensuing publicity would be more favorable and perhaps lead to Pound's release. Paige wrote Hemingway in Cuba, asking whether he would sign a petition for amnesty being organized by the South American poet Gabriela Mistral in the name of Nobel Prize winners. Hemingway's reply was that it was an election year and he doubted that any Democratic president could offer such amnesty, especially since the Democrats were being charged with permitting Communist control or influence in forming foreign policy and such a move would open them to showing favoritism to Fascists as well. He reminded Paige that whenever Pound was declared sane, he would have to stand trial on the treason charges, that being in St. Elizabeths was his only "protection from the charges against him." Hemingway also wrote a letter to Dorothy Pound, asking her to tell her husband how much Hemingway admired *The Pisan Cantos.* Pound seems to have accepted Hemingway's position and its seriousness. He was delighted, however, when Michael Reck showed him an advertisement for Rheingold that featured Hemingway in his shorts, hairy, happy, burly, with a glass of beer in his hand. According to Reck, Pound folded the ad over so that it showed only Hemingway and the slogan Purity, Body, Flavor.

In 1951 Hugh Kenner's book on Pound's poetry appeared, extending his audience. In the six months from July through January 1 of 1951, Pound had earned $2,315.92 from the eleven of his books that were still in print with New Directions—certainly much more than he had ever earned previously in the same period. *The Hudson Review* was printing his Confucian

Analects, and it later published his version of the *Women of Trachis* and seven cantos. In England, Peter Russell formed a Pound Society and began publishing his work in his magazine, *Nine.* Pound at this time was working on the "Thrones" section of *The Cantos* and studying the thought of a neglected American historian named Alexander Del Mar, a civil engineer who had written several books on the history of money which had disappeared from public consideration, Pound believed, because of "usocracy." Horton and Kasper were issuing the first six of the Square Dollar books. Two were by Del Mar; another two, translations of Confucius by Pound; the fifth, Kasper's edition of Louis Agassiz, the Harvard naturalist, whom Pound admired; and the last, a history of the Bank of the United States. Pound wrote to Wyndham Lewis, encouraging him to contribute to the Square Dollar series, and his letter is a fairly coherent illustration of what Hemingway categorized as U. T., or unknown tongue:

> The Sq/$ pair are ready to be of USE. it don't mean much spondooliks, but it does mean 10% royalty AND personal distribution to the best grade of peruzer, and of course grade A. company/no cigarette butts of the late J[ames] J[oyce] or other spent rockets. AND as a lot of the early stuff is NOT covered by cawpy rite in this kuntry, it wd/be clear gain, and thin edge of wedge. . . . Curiosity, damBit, KU-RI-osity/as to source of lies/of slanders/ W. L. has occasionally stimulated thought/let him steer the good guys onto CURiosity. Hownd-dawgz on trail.

A number of correspondents began referring to Pound as "Dear Maestro." There were more inquiries from scholars and young writers: Gil Orlovitz, Chandler Brossard, and Lawrence Ferlinghetti, who offered his projected magazine, *City Lights Journal,* as a "mouthpiece to the West" for Pound. Ferlinghetti was organizing the publishing company that printed many of the Beat writers, especially Allen Ginsberg, and the Beats admired Pound for his resistance, took him as the type of the overpowered artist struggling with mind and body against the tyrannous modern state. William Burroughs echoed the savage hatred of Roosevelt and New Deal bureaucracy. Despite Pound's fascism and anti-Semitism, Ginsberg gleefully nominated him as his secretary of economics in a poem. "If you can see this guy Ginsberg, do so," Williams wrote in a letter of introduction. Ginsberg had been raised in Paterson, the town where Williams lived and worked and the two had become good friends. Ginsberg was "whatever you want to call him," Williams added, "but hidden under as fine a heap of crap as you'll find blossoming on any city dump is a sensitive mind. I like him in spite of himself. See him if you can."

From one of the former overseers of his war propaganda, Carlo Pellizzi, Pound heard of the transience of postwar Italian politics. "We Italians live in fright with no sense of nation," Pellizzi asserted, "under the rule of the parish priests and led at the top by a group of unknown men." From Marshall McLuhan, he heard about the consequences of the war for American intellectuals. The literati, McLuhan wrote, were refugees from Buchenwald whose "only fare has been soup made from straw." Universities were places where timid and prudent professors planned ambushes. "In a mindless age," McLuhan said in a subsequent letter, "every insight takes on the character of a lethal weapon."

Pound was receiving letters from unknown writers and ordinary citizens, some of whom used titles like "Dear Fatigued Prophet." One such correspondent, twenty-year-old Charles Shuts of New Jersey, sent nearly two hundred effusive letters:

> I hold your meanings/ your every subtlety/
> in the palm of my worship of your beauty/
> I adore/
> Will you see the course of what I hope to be?
> and more
> Tell me be he em-er-ald.

Shuts made regular visits to St. Elizabeths, noting in his final letter that he had contracted poison ivy after sleeping in Rock Creek Park.

Early in 1951 Pound was visited by Richard Cassell, a doctoral student preparing his dissertation on Ford's work. Pound had recently written to Peter Russell urging him to devote an issue of *Nine* to Ford as a way of beginning a Ford revival in England. Pound saw Cassell in his alcove, carrying in his own blue canvas deck chair and stating, as he had so frequently to many of the psychiatrists who had seen him, that he could not think unless he was flat on his back. The psychiatrists chose to dismiss this as eccentricity, but it may have had to do with his chronic arthritis. Cassell questioned Pound for two hours as patients wandered by in institutional gowns or casual dress. Pound seemed plump and affable and considerate of Cassell's nervousness. He was not always coherent and sometimes distracted Cassell's thought, and at times he showed energy but then a few minutes later seemed terribly fatigued. He mixed the memories of Ford with commentaries on Social Credit and economics, interspersing several anti-Semitic remarks, and near the end of the interview his thoughts became incomplete.

Pervading Cassell's account is a brooding sense of the suffering Pound endured while on Chestnut Ward. On certain warm afternoons he might host a dozen admirers under the trees outside, but there were other times when only Dorothy came, and when he must have wondered why former friends like Hemingway never did. There were expressions of dejection and long silences that would occur spontaneously, sometimes in the middle of a conversation. He had adjusted to St. Elizabeths; the psychiatric visits became much less frequent and routine, the evaluations programmed by earlier reports. Pound complained to the psychiatrists and to his friends that something had gone wrong with his neck, that he had difficulty holding his head up straight. The complaint was revealing both of his aging and as a reflection of a quality of humiliation that this proud spirit must have realized over the years with the loss of his independence. He had become the subject of what Eustace Mullins called "the rank dead odor, the atmosphere of futility as the blank-faced old men paced up and down the hall." These men were afflicted with a sense of purgatorial hopelessness, and as Pound soon realized, one could not escape the effect of their despair.

At the same time he shouted and sang and paraded his ebullience. Once he was visited by musician Frank Ledlie Moore and sculptor Michael Lekakis. After the meeting Moore remembered hearing a shout as they walked away from the Center Building at St. Elizabeths. Pound was at his window, leaning out and happily singing Greek verse at the top of his lungs. On another occasion he shouted down to Robert Lowell that Lowell belonged in St. Elizabeths rather than himself—Lowell was later institutionalized. The manic enthusiasm was one register of Pound's spirit. As he brazenly declared to Eustace Mullins, "The insane asylum is the only place I could have lived in, in this country."

The visitors continued to arrive—Frederick Morgan, who edited *The Hudson Review,* Jaime de Angular, an anthropologist from California who wrote fables about American Indians which Pound admired, the Spanish novelist and later Nobelist Juan Ramón Jiménez, who was teaching at the University of Maryland, Rex Lampman, a fellow inmate, a Washington journalist who had had a nervous breakdown and who invented a mock epitaph for Pound: "Here he lies, the Idaho kid, only time he ever did." Pound scrawled a note to John Gould Fletcher, one of his old Imagist collaborators, that he was no longer fit enough to write letters. He told Eileen Kinney, a friend of Brancusi's, "I can't hold two sides of an idea together but can live on memory if someone *BRINGS* it." The British novelist John Wain recalled that Pound "talked on and on in connected sentences and with perfect logic and persuasiveness; but if anyone interrupted him with a question it simply threw the needle out of the groove, and he fell silent for a moment, passed his hands wearily over his eyes, and then went on talking, starting from a different point."

On other occasions his words were still sharply to the point. When Michael Reck asked him about what he thought of the current condition of contemporary poetry, Pound's truculent reply was that it did not exist. Reck, Meacham, Mullins, Cornell, Olson, and others were inspired to write books about Pound, centering on what they saw at St. Elizabeths and all-admiring of the quality of Pound's teaching and conversation. He had been forced into the Confucian situation where he could only reflect and not act, and the result was the tyranny of talk. Robert Lowell recorded in his *Note-books* Eliot's complaint of how on one occasion he had visited Pound for two hours and Pound had not permitted the Nobel laureate to say anything. Pound at last asked Eliot what was on his mind, but "by then he had absolutely nothing to say." In a very peculiar way, Pound's talk was both the disease and its cure. The talk was what made the poetry as well as the prose and, of course, the broadcasts. If it was often recklessly irresponsible, highly imaginative, perhaps deluded or distorted or excessively removed from reality, it had to be released, even if volcanically. William Carlos Williams tells in his autobiography that after one of his first visits he confided in the cab driver who was taking him back downtown. He told the cabbie, a black man who had not graduated from high school, about the broadcasts and the circumstances of Pound's imprisonment. The cabbie's diagnosis was that Pound was not crazy: "He just talk too much." And this was how Pound's friends saw him as well. Robert Frost asked Omar Pound, who had come to visit him, whether his father was really crazy, and Omar shrugged and replied, "Like always." But after a decade in St. Elizabeths, Pound may have talked himself out.

His talk was at this time becoming periphrastic, convolutedly Jamesian. Dorothy observed that he often omitted his main point while circling around it. For St. Elizabeths was the labyrinth, the place of chaos. Pound had always had difficulty concentrating, which is why poetry came more naturally to him than prose: *The Cantos* could be written in short bursts. In 1952 a large number of televisions had been contributed to St. Elizabeths which would blare through the halls all the insanity that Pound hated in America and make St. Elizabeths seem all the more like a medieval madhouse.

Pound read a story by James, "The Jolly Corner," about Spenser Brydon, who leaves America as a young man and returns thirty years later to be told by his friends that he has lived a "selfish, frivolous, scandalous" life in Europe. Brydon speculates on what his life might have been like had he stayed in America and worked to gain power. Instead of money and influence, Europe had helped him develop culture and sensitivity and, as far as America saw such matters, overrefinement. Brydon dreads that he will meet his double, the man he might have been. One dawn, in his empty family house, he sees his double. The figure has a mutilated hand—sensitivity traded for power. He feels in it something "evil, odious, blatant, vulgar," but when it advances on him, he also feels "a roused passion of life larger than his own, a rage of personality before which his own collapsed." It was a story with considerable appeal for Pound.

In the passing time he still had his work to do. In 1952 Laughlin decided to reissue *The Spirit of Romance*. When the galleys arrived, they were checked by Dorothy and William French, with Pound spot-checking. He was also reading galleys for the Chinese poetry he had been translating which Harvard University Press was to publish as *The Classic Anthology Defined by Confucius*. David Gordon remembered Pound at his work:

> And on a warm afternoon in early autumn of 1952 in a spare moment he would sit upright in his deck chair in shorts and leather sandals on the lawn of St. Elizabeth's with a sheaf of galleys in his lap; face and eyes serene; shoulders and back broad and straight but supple and easy and begin chanting the Chinese sounds of the Odes. Deep and resonant to soft and high, every vowel sound and consonant pitched, regulated, and rehearsed. . . .
>
> I had heard him recite Sappho's ποικιλόθρον, Arnaut Daniel's bird songs, bits from Homer and long passages of Dante and they were unforgettable performances. But when he sang the Odes he could draw on all the technical resources of these musicians; this was where it "all cohered," and yet produce [sic] something entirely different. This was the pleasure he always had time for. The whole man and mind so responsive to the word, sense, sound, beat and pitch, the modulating tonalities, a pervading hymn to the pine trees overhead; and you would become aware of a most incredible sensation, that this singing man and the song had joined undividedly into one.

6. THE NATIONAL SKELETON

In 1953 Pound suffered from a severe bronchial condition that refused to improve. He was still writing regularly to Natalie Barney and Agnes Bedford, friends of forty years' standing, and to Bedford he admitted that "it is time that a little more intelligence was used to get Grandpa out of the Bughouse." Mary had had two children whom Pound had never seen. Bedford wrote to Wyndham Lewis, who in turn wrote to Eliot proposing a new plan to petition President Eisenhower. Wary and cautious, Eliot was aware of how difficult Pound could be, that he was still unprepared to admit any guilt for his wartime activities, that he could be arrogant and angry. When Pound criticized Eliot's Christianity as "lousy," Eliot returned his letter as offensive and insulting. Hemingway at this time provided more direct assistance. When he was awarded the Nobel Prize in 1954, he declared that the prize might well have gone to Pound and that it "would be a good year to release poets."

It also seemed like the right time to release some of the poet's books. New Directions published *The Translations of Ezra Pound*, followed by *The Literary Essays* as edited by Eliot. Pound's *Women of Trachis* was performed on the BBC in London and later published in book form. There were documentary broadcasts on the BBC and at Yale University and a conference on *The Cantos* at Columbia University. A campaign to free Pound was begun in Italy by a number of his friends, including Carlo Pellizzi and his Italian publisher Vanni Schweiwiller, who was in the process of publishing a series of Pound's books. Claire Booth Luce, the American ambassador, took the matter of Pound's release up with the State Department and spoke to the attorney general. *Life* magazine, owned by her husband, Henry Luce, ran an editorial early in 1956 calling Pound a "national skeleton" and publicizing the strange legal circumstances of his case.

Pound was visited by Merrill Moore, the psychiatrist and poet who may have first suggested the strategy of St. Elizabeths. Merrill found that Pound was quite psychotic, bristling with hostility, making wild and extravagant remarks, asserting that there was a plot to keep his ideas from being printed. According to Merrill, Pound was still suffering from paranoid schizophrenia; the real question was whether he could be dangerous to others.

There is reason to believe, however, that Moore's official evaluation was only the latest installment in the efforts of the psychiatric community to shield Pound. Moore wrote William Carlos Williams a week after seeing Pound that he had a "delightful visit with Cousin Ezra. He is a most fascinating human being. There are many shade trees there that will shade his head but best of all his friends will contain him and save his neck. If he were out scotfree, the hounds would get him." Shortly after Merrill's visit, Pound was visited by Archibald MacLeish. For several hours MacLeish and Pound calmly discussed the state of literature and the arts. MacLeish was terribly moved by the encounter, dismayed by the fact that so civilized a discussion could occur in such circumstances, that a "conscious mind capable of the most complete awareness" could be "incarcerated among minds that are not conscious and cannot be aware." He was impressed by Pound's patience and kindliness and knew he was suffering, and he determined to do what he could to help get Pound out.

In England two poet disciples, Dennis Goacher and Peter Whigham, helped form a society to work for Pound's release. Eliot's attitude to Pound was a bit distant at this point. "In everyone's relations with Mr. Pound there comes a coolness," Cummings had observed. Eliot was still hurt by Pound's comments about his religion and by remarks about some of his friends like the Protestant theologian Reinhold Niebuhr, whom Pound called Eliot's "dirty talmudic pal." Eliot complained that Pound's letters to him had turned abusive and incomprehensible. William Carlos Williams was equally offended because of Pound's continued insults to Roosevelt. He admonished Pound once again sternly:

You are incapable of recognizing what you mean to present and to
hide your stupidity resort to namecalling and general obfuscation.
Do you think you will get anywhere that way—but in jail or the
insane asylum where you are now? Mussolini led you there, he was
your adolescent hero—or was it Jefferson? You still don't know
the difference.

Wyndham Lewis was ill with the brain tumor that had already blinded
him and his contribution was as usual eccentric and artistic. He had been
pondering Pound for years, his portrait of Pound had been shown in a
major show of his work at the Tate Gallery. In his novel *Self Condemned* his
character René Harding suffers from a perfectionism that motivates his contempt for the world. In an essay Lewis had attributed this same quality to
Pound: "He demands *perfection* in action, as well as in art. He even appears
to expect perfection, or what he understands as such, in the world of politics." Lewis repeated his view in a story called "The Doppelgänger," in
which Pound's personality is divided between two characters, a sage and a
fool. The foolish character is Thaddeus Trunk, a great poet with a perfect
devotion to literature which is marked by an extreme detachment. Living in
a mountaintop cabin, Trunk takes on the persona of a rugged Yankee. He
needs solitude for his work but is soon surrounded by a group of disciples
and betrayed by his own childish mania for publicity. There was "always the
itch to offer advice, to tell others what to do with their lives, to teach them
how to Write, to teach them how to Read." At this point an unnamed
Stranger appears, Trunk's alter ego, who knows more than he does about
whatever subject Trunk raises but offers what he knows in a rational, calm
manner. When Trunk's wife, Stella, who is based on Dorothy, sees that the
Stranger is everything Trunk pretends to be without the hysterical theatricality, she leaves with the Stranger and Trunk stays on his mountain with his
disciples. Trunk's persona had been believed in so intensely that it had
consumed him "like the extraordinary grimaces some men affect, until, two
thirds of the way through life, the face integrally includes the grimace."
Pound could never admit he was wrong in St. Elizabeths, Lewis was suggesting; he had entered spheres that seemed within his grasp but actually
were not; he had been the fool and should be forgiven.

Pound's resistance to superior forces was folly. Most heroic action includes elements of such folly, but to excuse Pound because he may have
been a fool seems tautological. The fool is neither idiot nor child; he must
also accept responsibility for his actions. Was Pound simply the fool, as
Lewis claimed, or was he also a knave, as some of his detractors argued? The
difference depends on the motives for action. The fool can act out of love,
constructively, perhaps honorably inspired by some ideal of perfection; the
knave acts maliciously and destroys more out of spite and angry denial.

Pound's resistance combined elements of the fool's naïveté and the knave's hatred. He had played the fool in London and in Paris with the Surrealists, and it had been the subject of his projected doctoral dissertation. When he was first brought to Washington, he had insisted that no one could have understood his radio broadcasts. Did he suppose that the world could accept them as another prankster stunt, a surrealism persisting over five years? Was the poet still munching tulips as he once had done in the hope that he would be noticed even when what he had to say was nonsense? More likely, the broadcasts were a calculated step on the pathway to scandal. In "The Doppelgänger" Lewis suggested that Pound had become consumed by his own persona and that such a transformation was the tragic consequence of his own passionate delusions. But tragic protagonists are rarely reprieved as one forgives a child: usually their eyes are blinded or their hearts broken before they can be again accepted by the community.

In 1957 Pound was visited by David Rattray, who published his "Weekend with Ezra Pound" in *The Nation:*

> Before we had a chance to talk about anything, Pound jumped up again: "You'll have tea, won't you?"
>
> I said that I would, and immediately he was everywhere at once, in a frenzy of activity, loading himself with jars of various sizes, tin boxes of sugar and tea, spoons and a saucer. I stood up in embarrassment, not knowing what I ought to do, but Mrs. Pound beckoned me from her corner: "Let's sit here and talk while he makes the tea." She was sitting behind a ramshackle old upright piano, so as not to see the people in the hall or be seen by them. Miss Martinelli was making sketches for a portrait of her.
>
> Suddenly Pound was standing before me, holding out a peanut butter jar filled with hot tea. When we settled again, he glared up at me and said, "Well, what specific questions have you? Or did you just come to talk? I'd just as soon talk."

Rattray's portrait stressed that Pound had not lost all of his energy and ebullience. But Rattray claimed, in a letter to Sheri Martinelli, that the article had been composed from a private letter written to a friend which reached *The Nation* when he was traveling in Europe and that it was published against his will. While such instances of energetic activity could still occur as late as 1957, they were rare. Pound was often depressed and fatalistic about his long confinement. "I seem to be born to be jailed," he told Malcolm Bradbury, a visiting scholar from England. He was visited by Katherine Anne Porter, who wrote that she had never doubted that "Ezra Pound was even for a moment insane. He was just a complete, natural phenomenon of unreason." Porter found Pound friendly, talkative, and still calling Mussolini "Old Mussy" with affection and loyalty.

There is another report on Pound in the summer of 1957, written by Marcella Spann, the Texas teacher who became part of his entourage. In bad weather, she explained, Pound would meet his guests in the alcove on Chestnut Ward with all its peculiar odors and sounds:

There was constant clamor and motion: E.P.'s ghostly companions, never at rest, were in aimless parade up and down the hall in front of the alcove where we were seated. Some of them had vacant eyes; Homer's hell gives us the measure for the pitiful state they were in. Others had eyes so full of anguish, we would need to read Dante's *Inferno* for their story. Such tortured souls never stopped their aimless walk to come near; but the others, those who lacked life, were often drawn to us by the laughter and energy emanating from the small alcove. On several occasions, before E.P. could get out of his chair, one of them would bend down in front of me and peer into my face. His hands gripping the arms of my chair cut off any escape. I could see the effort his eyes made to focus, the angry disfiguring scars on his forehead, and the gaping mouth trying so hard to form words.

Such moments, recalled in *The Cantos* as "where the dead walked/and the living were made of cardboard," had become commonplace for Pound, but each incident left its scar. As a poet, Pound had described the exploits of wandering heroes and he had imagined the gods of antiquity. But he had been brought down to the demented company that repelled Marcella Spann. As a ward of the welfare state he had once feared, criticized, and abhorred, he had lost control over his circumstances and dignity. As a poet he had always clamored for freedom. It had been an Emersonian, perennially American cry for independence and individualism, a cry that warned of the power of the state and its drive to conformity. Even in St. Elizabeths, locked into the very citadel of the state like some medieval heretic in his tower, Pound had continued his tragic resistance. But was it indeed "tragic" or is it necessary that all tragic heroes voice general values and ideals? Aeschylus, Euripides, Sophocles, the Greeks who invented the tragic form, never saw it this way. For them, the tension of dissent and the minority view provoked tragedy. And Pound's resistance, though born of blind folly and a stubborn sort of self-righteousness, was tragic because it caused a man of great sensibility, a great musician of the mind, to suffer great pain. Suffering itself is a private matter; tragedy is something that can touch us all. Pound, in his challenge to the state, had made himself a public man, an archetype of the rebel artist, and his pain was a matter that people would continue to consider.

Popular sentiment in the United States was changing on the question of war crimes, and the feeling among many was that Pound had already paid sufficiently for his political views. MacLeish wrote Hemingway that his visit had made him sick: "I made up my mind I wouldn't rest until he got out. Not only for his sake but for the good name of the country: after ten years it was beginning to look like a persecution and if he died there we'd never wash the stain out." He asked Senator J. William Fulbright to see what could be done to free Pound. He also wrote Secretary of State Christian Herter, who replied that he would do what he could. MacLeish then approached Milton Eisenhower, president of Johns Hopkins and the brother of the president of the United States. Dr. Eisenhower replied with a stern warning that Pound should expect that the government would press charges against him and bring him to trial if he were released. MacLeish then sent a fuller appeal:

> WIDENER W CAMBRIDGE 38
> January 11 1957

Dear Milton:

I am still hard at work on the Ezra Pound matter about which I wrote you some time ago. After careful consultation with authorities at St. Elizabeths, including Dr. Overholser, I can say with confidence that it is the opinion of the responsible doctors that Pound is not now fit to stand trial and never will be. Under these circumstances the perpetuation of the legal charges against him seems to be irrelevant, not to put a stronger word to it. Robert Frost, T. S. Eliot and Ernest Hemingway are therefore writing the Attorney General suggesting that in view of his eleven years incarceration the nol prossing of the charges against Pound would be in order, not only in the interests of common humanity, but in the interest of the good name of the United States.

I know that you dissent from my view on the latter point. You wrote me, as you may recall, that it makes no difference whatever that Pound is a poet. In terms of logic this may be true but in terms of history and of civilization it is not. As you know better than I, nations are judged in the perspective of history by the way they treat their poets, philosophers, artists and teachers.

The reason for this present letter relates to this fact. I have the very best reason to believe that Pound is shortly to be awarded the Nobel Prize in Literature. I can think of nothing which would make this country look more ridiculous than to hold in an asylum, under criminal indictment, a recipient of the Nobel Prize in Literature. Everything our most virulent critics say about us would be justified by that single dramatic fact. If our action in so holding him could be justified in common sense we could perhaps shrug it off, but since in view of the medical testimony it cannot be justified we would look very silly indeed.

I trouble you with all this, not to try to convert you to my view but because I care deeply, as you do, about the repute of this republic, and because you are in a position to do something about it. I need not add that what I have told you about the Nobel Prize situation should be treated as confidential, except in so far as its repetition in confidence might help to bring about the desired action. By the desired action I refer solely, at this time, to the quashing of the charges, then remitting the whole problem of Pound's future to the medics who ought to dispose of it.

Forgive me for troubling you with all this again.

Affectionately
Archie

A number of influential magazines began to express support for Pound's release. *Figaro* in Paris ran an appeal entitled "The Lunatic at St. Elizabeths." *The New Republic* wrote that it was in favor of seeing "the government give this old man and this eminent poet his freedom—if not as an act of justice, then as an act of largess." In *Esquire* there was a sympathetic study of Pound by journalist Richard Rovere, followed by letters from Pound's friends Giovanni Giovannini and David Horton. The strongest appeal was in an editorial in *The Nation:* "It will be a triumph of democracy if we set Pound free, not because he is a martyr, but because he is a sick and vicious old man—even if he were not the brilliant poet he is, with a luminous side that all but transcends his faults—he has his rights too. In Italy he may yet write a few more beautiful pieces, and in that cracked but crystal mirror of his hold up to us once more the image of a civilization that too often drives its best creators into self-exile and political horror."

In the Senate, Richard L. Neuberger of Oregon asked the Library of Congress to conduct an investigation into the causes and consequences of Pound's imprisonment. In the House of Representatives, Usher L. Burdick of North Dakota, a friend of Rex Lampman's, requested another investigation by the House Judiciary Committee. It was not honored, but more of those in power heard about Pound's situation. Harry Meacham, then president of the Poetry Society of Virginia, wrote to his senator, Harry F. Byrd, and to Van Wyck Brooks, Norman Mailer, and Secretary-General Dag Hammarskjöld of the United Nations, who sympathized with Pound and discussed his case with Henry Cabot Lodge and several officials in the State Department and, as a member of the Swedish Academy, also raised the possibility of awarding Pound the Nobel Prize.

No one was more persistent, however, than MacLeish. Ironically, as assistant secretary of state during the war, he had been one of the most loyal of Roosevelt's supporters. His letters to Pound were being answered by a bellicose warrior still convinced that he was acting on principle: "I have never said the executive should NEVER exceed his legitimate powers. I have said, when he exceeds, if no ONE protests, you will lose All of your liberties." Pound continued to harangue MacLeish, in one letter comparing Senator Herbert Lehman of New York to Beria, head of the Soviet secret police, and berating FDR. MacLeish finally wrote that he could not and would not discuss Roosevelt with Pound because "your information is all second-hand and distorted. You weren't here. You saw nothing with your own eyes. And what you did see—Fascism and Nazism—you didn't understand: you thought Musso belonged in Jefferson's tradition and God knows where you thought Hitler belonged. I think your views of the history of our time are just about as wrong as views can be. But I won't sit by and see you held in confinement because of your views. Which is what is really happening now. I am doing what I am doing partly because I revere you as a poet and partly because I love this Republic and can't be quiet when it violates its own convictions." MacLeish was being characteristically generous. When John Brown spoke at Harpers Ferry, when a man shouts "fire" in a crowded theater (as in Justice Holmes's classic definition of when free speech becomes agitation), when Pound stayed on the radio after Pearl Harbor— these were actions. And while it is true that Pound suffered tremendously at St. Elizabeths, there is little question as to what his fate would have been had he tried to *defend* America on Rome Radio or in Berlin. Despite the tone of most of Pound's letters to him, MacLeish was impressed by one remark that lay as if buried in the avalanche of abuse: "Forgive me for 80% of the violent things I have said about some of your friends." It was as close to an apology as anyone would ever get from Ezra Pound.

As a Democrat, MacLeish realized that he had limited influence with a Republican administration, and so he tried to recruit the assistance of Robert Frost. Frost had never written or tried to visit Pound at St. Elizabeths. Even more than MacLeish, he had deplored Pound's actions during the war, considered them as dangerous nonsense, and thought that Pound deserved punishment, though after twelve years he agreed that the punishment had been sufficient. Pound had helped Frost gain his first recognition in England forty years earlier, and Frost at this time was the poet in America who commanded the largest audience. Eliot wrote a measured letter to Attorney General Herbert Brownell, Jr., which was signed as well by Frost and Hemingway and typed on stationery of the American Academy of Arts and Letters. The letter noted that Pound was one of America's most distinguished authors and that the perpetuation of charges against him after "Nazis tried and convicted of the most heinous crimes have been released" was indefensible and "unworthy of the traditions of the Republic." Brownell replied to Frost that the matter was under review, but in fact the Department of Justice was unwilling to act, probably because Pound had been linked by a three-part piece in the New York *Herald Tribune* to segregationist extremist John Kasper. Pound refused to publicly repudiate Kasper because he respected Kasper as a man of action "who didn't sit around looking at his navel."

In the spring of 1957, Attorney General William Rogers, who had replaced Brownell, wrote MacLeish that he was prepared to discuss Pound's situation. MacLeish realized that Frost's appearance could be essential, but Frost was in England reading his poetry and receiving honorary degrees from Oxford and Cambridge. MacLeish went to England to talk to him, and with Eliot present, the poets met in London on several occasions to prepare a strategy. The meeting was set with Rogers for mid-July. Frost agreed that he would "hate to see Ezra die ignominiously in that wretched place where he is for a crime which if proven couldn't have kept him all these years in prison." Frost agreed that he could speak for Pound's ability "to get himself taken care of out in the world" but reminded MacLeish that "neither you nor I would want to take him into our family or even into our neighborhood."

MacLeish wrote Pound after the Rogers meeting that the way to his release would not be clear until the Kasper "stink had blown over." Hemingway wrote MacLeish that the Kasper affair was an embarrassment and expressed the fear that once released, Pound might praise Kasper on some television talk show. Hemingway had grounds for his fears. In letters he was writing at this time Pound claimed that *Partisan Review* was run by lice, that his own work was being sabotaged by the publishers, that Adam Clayton Powell, Jr., a black minister and congressman "of New York looks like a chew mulatto." (Ironically, Powell's name is listed just under Pound's grandfather's name in the *Congressional Biographies.*) At the meeting Frost had presented Rogers with new letters from Eliot and Hemingway, and Hemingway sent, as well, a check for fifteen hundred dollars to Pound, representing the last part of his Nobel Prize money. MacLeish felt the visit to Rogers had served at least to open the door, even though no commitments had been made. The issue of where Pound would choose to live was raised as a factor and also the question of how he would be supported. Earlier, MacLeish had met Mary de Rachewiltz in Sirmione to learn for himself what sort of accommodation Pound might expect, and he heard that Laughlin was willing to guarantee three hundred dollars a month for Pound's life as an advance against royalties from New Directions, which would be supplemented by Dorothy's income.

The efforts to free Pound continued even though MacLeish noted in a letter that whoever offered Pound "a hand will have his fingers broken." Hemingway advised MacLeish that Pound's "hunting license should be restricted for him not to write on or indulge in politics." Otherwise, Hemingway warned, Pound would be baited by journalists into saying foolish things that might only get him into new trouble. From England there was a petition to Rogers signed by Cocteau, Graham Greene, Igor Stravinsky, and William Saroyan. James Laughlin's brother-in-law was Gabriel Hague, President Eisenhower's economic adviser, and Hague urged Sherman Adams, White House chief of staff, to raise the matter with the president. In January 1958, Under Secretary of State Christian Herter sent a note to Overholser, whom he had known as an undergraduate at Harvard, asking him to visit because "I would very much like to be fully informed in respect to this difficult individual Ezra Pound." Overholser, as the key figure in Pound's containment at St. Elizabeths, was the man with the power to protect him or declare him sane enough to meet the consequences of trial. Pound could not be released without Overholser's assent and cooperation.

Frost had visited Rogers a second time on October 23, 1957, informing the attorney general that Pound intended to return to Italy, where whatever talk he indulged in would have less consequence than in the United States. At the end of February 1958, Frost attended an intimate luncheon at the White House with Sherman Adams and William Rogers and the Pound matter was again discussed. That evening Frost was President Eisenhower's personal guest at an informal supper. A month later at a press conference in New York City, Rogers disclosed that Pound might escape trial and be freed to return to Italy. It would have been difficult twelve years after the end of the war to have won a trial had it been held, especially because the law had changed, with the result that an accused person was not held criminally responsible if he acted while incapacitated by mental disease. In April, Frost was in Rogers's office to determine Rogers's mood with regard to Pound. According to Harry Meacham, the meeting was brief, and Rogers's position was, "Our mood is your mood, Mr. Frost."

Frost had helped with his personal connections, but it had been MacLeish who had instigated and organized the final campaign. MacLeish also arranged for Thurman Arnold of the prestigious firm Arnold, Fortas, & Porter to represent Pound. Fortas had been a student at Wabash College when Pound had taught there, and at Yale he had been one of Julien Cornell's law professors. Arnold filed his motion to dismiss the 1945 indictment along with an affidavit by Dr. Overholser stating that Pound was still insane and incapable of intelligently cooperating with counsel in his own defense, that his condition was permanent and incurable, that there was a strong possibility that Pound's alleged crimes were the result of his insanity. Robert Frost offered an appeal for magnanimity, and there were supporting statements by Eliot, Hemingway, MacLeish, and others. The motion was heard on April 18 by Chief Judge Bolitha Laws, who had committed Pound to St. Elizabeths twelve years earlier. Julien Cornell was present during the brief proceedings and heard Arnold's argument, which was essentially based on his initial strategy that unless the indictment was dismissed Pound might spend the rest of his life as a prisoner for acts that could not be legally proven. The Department of Justice did not oppose the motion to dismiss the indictment, and Justice Laws ordered that Pound be freed.

Pound continued to live at St. Elizabeths for another three weeks, having some dental work completed and slowly packing his books and papers, storing them in Dorothy's damp and poorly ventilated basement flat. He visited Thurman Arnold to thank him for his help—Arnold did not charge a fee for his services—and Representative Burdick, where he was questioned by reporters. Asked about Frost's role, Pound stated laconically, "He ain't been in much of a hurry." Pound was waiting for his passport, which the State Department was slow in issuing. Pound was officially released on May 7. The same day, the BBC in London aired a broadcast that Pound's friend D. G. Bridson had prepared at St. Elizabeths, an attempt by Pound to explain why he went on the radio during the war. The statement was very personal; Pound went back to his harassment by an embassy official in Paris after World War I over the new passport restrictions and to a meeting he had with Senator Wheeler in Washington in 1939 when Wheeler told Pound of Roosevelt's plan to pack the Supreme Court.

Pound moved to his friend James La Driere's Washington apartment. One evening he was heard groaning as he read the proceedings of the National Institute of Arts and Letters, and he suddenly sat down and typed out a letter of resignation, which he took outside and mailed immediately— it was the poet finally breaking with the American artistic community. James Laughlin came to visit and one day accompanied Pound to a recording studio where Pound read his poems for three hours. Harry Meacham drove Pound to Richmond, Jamestown, and Williamsburg, Virginia. In Richmond, Pound was interviewed by James J. Kilpatrick, a local columnist and a friend of Meacham's. During the interview Pound reclined, resting the lower part of his spine and propping his head against the backrest of his chair. His eyes were closed most of the time, his hands restlessly moving, reaching for a pencil or for his glasses or shaping a point in the air. He moved from idea to idea rapidly, and Kilpatrick compared the movement to a "volcanic churning" on the ocean floor. Pound apologized for the discontinuity of his thought, which he admitted could be compared to "an explosion in an art museum, you have to hunt around for the pieces."

Driven by David Horton, the Pounds spent a night in Pound's old house in Wyncote. The house was then owned by Carl Gatter, who had written to Pound at St. Elizabeths and later compiled a sort of oral history of the memories of those still alive in Wyncote who had known the poet as a boy. Late that night Pound walked the neighboring streets alone, pausing at Calvary Presbyterian Church, where he had planted a tree sixty years earlier. From Wyncote they drove northwest to Rutherford, New Jersey, to visit William Carlos Williams, who was ill and tired. Pound, white-haired, wrinkled, and parched dry, looking remote and very sad, was photographed by Richard Avedon.

On June 30 Pound, Dorothy, and Marcella Spann, who was traveling as his secretary, boarded the *Cristoforo Colombo.* His shirt unbuttoned, still as casual as at St. Elizabeths, Pound received his friends who had come to see him off, Michael Reck, Norman Holmes Pearson, the Italian cultural attaché, Robert MacGregor of New Directions, who brought champagne. Ten days later the ship was in the Naples harbor. "All America is an insane asylum!" Pound declared to the assembled Italian reporters, snapping into the Fascist salute as the visible sign of his insubordinate nature, his refusal to submit to forces more powerful than any single man.

THE SILENT YEARS

I shall have, doubtless, a boom after my funeral,
Seeing that long standing increases all things
regardless of quality.
          "Homage to Sextus Propertius"

DONALD HALL: *Your return to Italy has been a disappointment, then?*
POUND: *Undoubtedly, Europe was a shock. The shock of no longer feel-*
ing oneself in the center of something is probably part of it. Then there is
the incomprehension, Europe's incomprehension, of organic America.
There are so many things which I, as an American, cannot say to a
European with any hope of being understood. Somebody said that I am the
last American living the tragedy of Europe.

                                    Paris Review *Interview*

Pound was seventy-two years old, and he had spent the last quarter of his working life in confinement. He had returned to a country that he loved and where he had many old friends. In Genoa, where Pound and his party disembarked, he was greeted by a swarm of reporters, but friends intervened and brought him to a private home. Giorgio Bocca, an Italian journalist who had covered Pound's landing at Genoa, asked in print, "How is it that you who merited fame as a seer did not see?"

Pound, Dorothy, and Marcella Spann went to Verona, where Pound's daughter met them and brought them by taxi to the village of Tirolo. At Brunnenburg, a small, turreted twelfth-century castle on a mountainside with a sweeping view of Merano below, Pound for the first time met his eleven-year-old grandson, Walter, and his eight-year-old granddaughter, Patrizia. He was given a large room in the tall square Roman tower with views of hillside orchards, several other castles, the soaring Alps, and the Adige River in the valley. He had his books and papers, a group of drawings by Gaudier, and in a private garden Gaudier's *Hieratic Head* facing east to catch the first rays of morning sun.

At first Pound felt invigorated and ebullient. He wrote his old friend Brigit Patmore that "there appears to be more chance of liveliness than at any time since 1919." The renewed energy may have been related to the attentions of Marcella Spann, but it also was a response to the task of finishing *The Cantos* with a "Paradiso" section which could make the entire work more coherent. But paradise was not terrestrial, Pound wrote near the end of *The Cantos*, and with the final rush of his creative powers, he was only able to suggest its possibilities in glints and fragments. First, however, there was the "Thrones" section, cantos XCVI to CIX, most of which had been written at St. Elizabeths, a section in which even more than previously Pound invoked a wide range of mythical, divine, and fabulous entities almost as a form of entreaty, a plea to unseen powers to give him the energy and imagination to complete what he had begun forty years earlier. In "Thrones" the emphasis is on arcane magic and illumination, sight, light, vision, images of crystals and gems, and the metamorphosis and epiphany of the gods. Pound later told Donald Hall that the "thrones in Dante's *Paradiso* are for the spirits of the people who had been responsible for good government. The thrones in *The Cantos* are an attempt to move out from egotism and to establish some definition of an order possible or at any rate conceivable on earth." As he was preparing "Thrones" for press, several cantos began to appear in magazines, number XCIX in the *Virginia Quarterly Review*, number C in a special Pound issue of the *Yale Literary Magazine*, and two more in a magazine started by Oswald Mosley in England called *The Europeans*.

William Cookson, a British university student who had started a magazine called *Agenda* with Pound's guidance, Dallam Simpson, David Gordon, and Noel Stock were all houseguests at Brunnenburg, Stock on a Bollingen grant to take inventory of Pound's archives. Pound was helping Mary with her continuing translation of *The Cantos* into Italian and discussing archaeology and Egyptology with his son-in-law. He was doing some carpentry and gardening, overseeing the planting of five hundred white grapevines in the castle vineyard, unsuccessfully attempting to cultivate New England maple seedlings, and planning but never executing the construction of a marble temple on a mountain nearby. At night he often read aloud to his family and guests from *The Cantos* and from the anthology he was preparing with Marcella Spann. For his grandchildren there was Joel Chandler Harris's *Uncle Remus* stories. He attended horse races in Merano, the largest town in the area, and saw an exhibition of his first editions, letters, and typescripts there on his seventy-third birthday, October 30, 1958. At the opening he declared that "every man has the right to have his ideas examined one at a time and not all confused with one another," a remark that must have been prompted by the sustained criticisms of his work and actions which he read during his years at St. Elizabeths.

At Brunnenburg, Pound began to show signs of his former combative-
ness. When Henry Rago, who was editing *Poetry,* wrote from Chicago, requesting a canto, Pound refused, blaming his "slimy predecessors" and
"your hostile gang of supporters" who for forty years had "used their
wealth mostly for evil and degradation of poetic standards." Rago replied
that Pound wrote about civility without understanding it, calling it coward-
ice or weakness when he saw it in others. To his friend Harry Meacham,
Pound was still writing about the "jewsfeldt gestapo," and to Cookson he
maintained that FDR and Churchill were two of the greatest infamies in
recorded history. In *Illustrazione Italiana,* he published a canto and an attack
on American foundations, endowments, and universities which, in his view,
were "places where history and economics are not taught, where imbecilities abound, and the works of John Adams, Van Buren, Alex Del Mar and
Brooks Adams are not included in the curricula." These comments were
transmitted by the news services and noticed by an embassy official in
Rome. Pound may have heard that they were sent to Washington because
he sent Secretary of State Herter a feisty letter:

14 September 1958

Dear Mr. Herter,

I am informed that some subhuman ape in our embassy in
Rome has stated that I have been making derogatory remarks
about the U.S.

I have no means of verifying this statement, but may say in
this connection that a certain Cose-schi has invited me to lecture or
was suggesting that I do so, and that I have declined, as I needed
three months' rest. I have also declined invitations to speak on
Canada Radio, and am declining an invitation to speak on the
British Radio.

I would point out, vide enclosure [reprint of *Illustrazione* in-
troduction] that objection to the state of american universities,
specifically for their neglect of U.S. History, does not constitute an
attack on the U.S. but is rather a defense of what decency there is
left in our country.

If some of the minor officials in your department consider the
study of american history as aid and comfort to Moscow, that again
displays a state of mind that might, or even should, arouse curiosity.

By the beginning of 1959, conditions at Brunnenburg were becoming
difficult for Pound. His health had begun to deteriorate, he was suffering
from constant pain in his back and neck, and it was hard for him to breathe

the Alpine air. He also hated the fierceness of the winter and the sharp blasts of cold air.

The castle was only partially heated, and Pound could never find a spot that was quite warm enough for him. Emotionally, matters were even worse. Pound had become infatuated with Marcella Spann, who ostensibly had accompanied him to Italy to help collect the poems for the *Confucius to Cummings Anthology.* The problem was compounded by tension between Dorothy and Mary, who each had a possessive attitude about Pound. Though they inhabited separate areas of the castle, the jealousy became intolerable. At St. Elizabeths, Dorothy had been his legal guardian and Dorothy had maintained her power of legal guardianship, which meant that in effect Pound had no resources of his own and had to obtain Dorothy's consent for any expenditure. He felt frustrated by this situation and twice wrote to Dr. Overholser at St. Elizabeths asking his help. In the spring of 1959, Pound, Dorothy, and Marcella moved to Rapallo, where Olga Rudge was waiting, and they rented an apartment near the center of town, taking the place on a Sunday only to realize the next day that it was above a boiler factory.

In May, Pound and Dorothy took Marcella on a trip to see a bit of Italy. They went first to Pisa and then to the Disciplinary Training Center, which had been turned into a rose nursery. According to Eva Hesse, Pound's German translator and friend, in Sirmione Pound began to talk irresponsibly about marriage to Marcella. Sirmione had always been a place of enormous romantic possibility for Pound, its flowers and views and the ruins of Catullus's villa sources of inspiration. For Pound, Marcella represented a desperate last chance, not only for romantic love, but for youth, energy, and the making of poetry, which had always been connected for him with some sort of passionate attachment to women. Pound was then taking the notes for the last cantos, which later appeared in their unfinished state as "Drafts and Fragments." In "Canto CXIII," he offered a picture of Marcella:

> The long flank, the firm breast
> and to know beauty and death and despair
> And to think that what has been shall be,
> flowing, ever unstill.

Quite suddenly, the "sun and serenitas" of Lake Garda changed to "pride, jealousy and possessiveness," the "3 pains of hell." When "one's friends hate each other," Pound queries in the notes for "Canto CXV," "how can there be peace in the world?" Asperities such as these had once been diversions, but at this point Pound was exhausted, though still capable of reflecting his condition with a magnificent lyricism:

A blown husk that is finished
            but the light sings eternal
    a pale flare over marshes
        Where the salt hay whispers to tide's change.

Dorothy's position had always been to permit her husband his indulgences
with other women. She recognized that the license was related to Pound's
creative drive. But the talk of divorce shocked her into using her power. At
St. Elizabeths her husband had been so dependent on her that he refused
even to go out on the lawn without her. With Marcella Spann, a woman
forty years younger, he tried to rebel against this dependence, but he no
longer had sufficient strength. Dorothy still had the legal hold over his
royalties, and Pound had been worrying irrationally about the possibility of
poverty ever since being released from St. Elizabeths. By October, with
Dorothy, Olga, and Mary joining forces, Marcella was on her way back to
America, and the Pounds were back in Brunnenburg. This was no solution.
Pound felt himself like a "whale out of water." He wrote Hemingway,
"Old man him tired." To MacLeish he wrote that he was of "no use to
myself or anyone. . . . One thing to have Europe fall on one's head. Another to be set in ruins of same." Laughlin, who had visited him, wrote
Overholser that Pound was "now at the bottom of the pit of melancholy,
and most of his talk was about dying and 'losing his mind.' " By December,
Pound's spirits seemed a bit recovered and, with Mary, he went to Darm-
stadt, Germany, to see a production of his version of the *Women of Trachis*,
of which the British critic Kenneth Tynan wrote, "The tragedy comes across
like thunder."

    In January he was in Rome. Daniel Cory saw him and remembered in
Encounter that Pound was embarrassed by his own nervous state. Pound
complained that on one day he was able to talk like a parrot while on the
next he would find nothing to say. By turns he was alert and energetic,
despondent and apathetic. "It was obvious," Cory explained, "that some
profound emotional ebb tide was leaving him stranded and incapable of any
sustained concentration." Omar Pound wrote to Overholser that his father
now regarded his thirteen years at St. Elizabeths as martyrdom and that his
lifework, *The Cantos,* was purposeless. Pound wrote Eliot, full of despair,
remorse, and anxiety. Eliot's response was sympathetic. He could not understand why Pound was so depressed about his work or his life—he was
one of the immortals of poetry, and at least part of his work would survive.
Knowing how work kept one healthy, Eliot encouraged Pound to try writing a critical commentary on the younger poets. Eliot's reply was a temporary tonic and Pound began rereading Eliot's plays and *After Strange Gods.*

    In Rome, Pound was interviewed for the *Paris Review* by Donald Hall,
a young poet who came recommended by Harry Meacham. Hall, who had
previously interviewed Eliot, noted that Pound's eyes were watery, red, full

of fatigue. Greeting him, Pound remarked to Hall, "You—find me—in fragments." Pound's voice was theatrical, Hall recalled, a grand rolling of *r*'s, his pitch high until the final word. The two men spoke for an hour, and Hall wrote that Pound's fatigue seemed caused by an "abject despair, accidie, meaninglessness, abulia, waste." The actual interview occurred during the following three days, with Pound seldom completing a thought or a sentence. He would get a burst of energy, pace up and down the room, read from a manuscript alternating eyeglasses like a juggler, and then suddenly his face would "sag, his eyes turn glassy like a fish's" and he would be silent. Sometimes, with a Jamesian parenthesis, he spoke about his difficulties in answering a question instead of providing an answer, and occasionally he would get confused by his own qualifications. At one point, Pound seemed ready to collapse:

> Then suddenly it happened, horribly in front of my eyes: again I saw vigor and energy drain out of him, like air from a pricked balloon. The strong body visibly sagged into old age; he disintegrated in front of me, smashed into a thousand unconnected and disorderly pieces. He took off his hat slowly and let it drop, his scarf slid to the floor; his stick, which had rested in his lap, thudded to the carpet. His long body slid boneless down, until he lay prone, eyes closed, as if all the lights in a tall building went out in a few seconds, and the building itself disassembled, returning to the stone and water and sand from which it had come.
>
> For a few minutes he said nothing, only breathing and sighing.

Later, recovered, he begged Hall, "Don't—let me sound—so tired." Worried about coherence and making sense, Hall understood that Pound then "doubted the value of everything he had done in his life." The interview with Hall was an attempt by Pound to explain himself to a larger public. He had spent forty years writing a long poem few could understand, and which he knew he could not really complete. "It is difficult to write a paradiso," he told Hall, "when all the superficial indications are that you ought to write an apocalypse. It is obviously much easier to find inhabitants for an inferno or even a purgatorio."

Pound was giving in to despair and depression. He was obsessed with fears of disease and mental incapacity and believed harmful microbes were invading his body and sapping his strength. Back at Brunnenburg, he was visited by Eveline Bates Doob and her husband, a Yale professor. Pound had always been a terribly impatient person, Dorothy confided, but then he no longer seemed to have even the patience for small talk—he would barely say anything. It was almost as if Hall, a younger poet, had inspired the last continuous flow, even though Hall admitted his interview was put together only by editing the fragments into what seemed a continuous reply to his questions. When Pound did speak, half of what he said was often mumbled, so that it was inaudible. When Mrs. Doob questioned him to draw him into the conversation, Pound simply blinked his eyes and stared directly at her. She felt Pound was "unbearably discontent with himself" because of a "deep, deepening depression." Pound had stopped eating and drinking and had become very thin. Mrs. Doob noticed that he kept putting his hands over each other, glaring down at them, and staring at her. Dorothy wrote Harry Meacham that her husband seemed "oppressed always by some sense of not having done what he should with his life." He was full of regret for what he had done, and told Eveline Bates Doob that there was even "something rotten behind" *The Cantos*.

In the summer of 1960, his weight diminished and his mood still bad, his daughter placed him in a clinic near Merano. Pound refused all visitors except his wife and daughter, but when he heard that Mary Barnard was at Brunnenburg, he asked for her to visit. What she saw shocked her. Pound looked "not like an old man, but a dead man, with a fleshless head such as one might see on a slab in a morgue." He was questioned by a reporter who stood at his bedside and asked him if he knew where he was living. Pound's reply was as if out of an allegorical tale by Nathaniel Hawthorne—"In hell." "Which hell?" the journalist questioned insistently. Putting his hands on his heart, Pound murmured, "Here, here."

By the end of the summer, he began eating again, gained strength, and returned to Brunnenburg. But the melancholia persisted, and with it Pound's absolute refusal to speak. As a young writer he had declared that "a man should not speak until he has something to say." At this stage he felt he had said too much. By the spring of 1961 his health was complicated by a urinary infection, and he began to run a daily fever. He was visited by classics scholar J. P. Sullivan, by H.D.'s daughter, Perdita, by Robert Lowell and Michael Reck. On some of these visits he did not speak at all, on others he said merely a few words. All the visitors, however, had the impression that Pound was able to follow whatever conversation occurred. Dorothy no longer felt able to care for her husband, and he went to Rapallo to be with Olga Rudge for the summer of 1961. The following fall he went to her house in Venice. Work on *The Cantos* had stopped and he was hardly even writing letters. He confided in a note to Harry Meacham, "The plain fact is that my head just doesn't work." There was another temporary revival of spirit and energy and Pound returned to Rome to stay with his old friend Ugo Dadone, a former Fascist military officer whom he had known before the war. He began attending social gatherings, spending time with the literati in Rome, with Ungaretti, Montale, and Pasolini. He was photographed at the head of a neo-Fascist May Day parade in 1962, five hundred men wearing boots and black armbands, carrying swastika flags, shouting anti-Semitic slogans, and fighting with bystanders.

It was to be the last parade for Pound. His energy again began to wane, and he went from clinic to clinic, in Rome, Rapallo, and back again near Brunnenburg. On several occasions in succeeding years he was injected with sheep cells in Swiss clinics to induce vitality. He developed a prostate infection and in the summer of 1962 had a prostatectomy. Living exclusively with Olga Rudge, in Rapallo and in Venice, he seemed physically recovered, climbing the steep hill from Rapallo to Sant Ambrogio, reading detective novels by Agatha Christie, Simenon, and Edgar Wallace, playing chess, and taking long walks in Venice. But the depression was unrelieved. In Venice he told novelist Richard Stern that he had been "Wrong, wrong. I've always been wrong." One day he was disturbed by a journalist who was expecting to be greeted by Olga Rudge. Caught off guard, the journalist asked him how he was. His answer was one sharp word as he slammed the door: "Senile!" He wrote a note to Ronald Duncan confessing that he had treated his children very badly. He heard from Robert Lowell, who tried to cheer him, asking him to remember the "thousands of kindnesses you have shown your friends and how you've been a fountain to them." He was awarded a five-hundred-dollar prize from *Poetry* in 1962 and a five-thousand-dollar award from the Academy of American Poets. But these honors seemed small compensation. Furthermore, many of his closest friends had died: Lewis in 1957 of his brain tumor, Hemingway in 1961 by a self-inflicted shotgun blast, Cummings in 1962, and Williams the following year.

In the spring of 1963, he consented to an interview with Grazia Levi for an Italian magazine. He was then seventy-eight and he had been back in Italy for five years. The interview began with an epigraph quoting Pound as saying, "I know that I know nothing," and a brief preamble by Levi calling Pound a "weary, stricken man" who had "painfully reached a state of silence and complete uncertainty." Levi felt that though Pound was physically restored he was not any longer himself. His eyes seemed glazed; he looked straight at her with "aching steadiness." Levi indicated that she had certain trepidations about coming to see Pound. The reply defined the tone of the interview: "Afraid? I understand. I spoil everything I touch. I have always always blundered." A bit later in the brief interview, Pound admitted, "All my life I believed I knew nothing, yes, I knew nothing. And so words became devoid of meaning."

On January 4, 1965, his friend T. S. Eliot died. A month later Olga Rudge accompanied him to England for a memorial service at Westminster Abbey. Pound composed a brief but touching epitaph which appeared in the *Sewanee Review:*

His was the true Dantescan voice—not honoured enough, and deserving more than I ever gave him. I had hoped to see him in Venice this year for the Dante commemoration at the Giorgio Cini Foundation—instead: Westminster Abbey. But, later, on his own hearth, a flame tended, a presence felt.

Recollections? let some thesis-writer have the satisfaction of "discovering" whether it was 1920 or '21 that I went from Excideuil to meet a rucksacked Eliot. Days of walking—conversation? literary? le papier Fayard was then the burning topic. Who is there now for me to share a joke with?

Am I to write "about" the poet Thomas Stearns Eliot? my friend "the Possum"? Let him rest in peace. I can only repeat, but with the urgency of fifty years ago: READ HIM.

E.P.

In the summer of 1965, Pound was at the Spoleto Festival, where his *Villon* was performed as a ballet, but it disappointed him. At a public reading at the festival, he read poems by Marianne Moore and Robert Lowell, not from the stage but from a private box. Lawrence Ferlinghetti described his voice as "so soft, so thin, so frail, so stubborn still." That fall Pound reached his eightieth year. There was a flurry of articles and CBS television did a program. Noel Stock edited *Perspectives,* a series of tributes by many of the writers who had known Pound, including Marianne Moore and the Scot poet Hugh MacDiarmid. To celebrate, Pound and Olga Rudge went to Paris, where Pound met old friends at the home of Natalie Barney, then eighty-nine, with whom he had corresponded for as long as he could still write letters. He met Samuel Beckett and saw his play *Endgame,* with its crippled blind old man in a trash can; he told James Laughlin that he was that old man. He told Dominique de Roux, who had published the French translation of *The Cantos,* "I did not enter into silence, silence captured me." The remark was picked up by *Time* magazine and thus became a sort of living epitaph for Pound in his remaining years.

Natalie Barney subsidized a trip to Greece for Pound and Olga Rudge the following year. He went to Joyce's grave in Zurich to see the bronze statue of "Jaunty Jim." He returned to Paris for the publication of three of his books, *The ABC of Reading, How to Read,* and *The Spirit of Romance,* and visited the Gaudier room at the Musée de l'Art Moderne.

In the fall of 1967, a few days before his eighty-second birthday, he was visited in Venice by Allen Ginsberg. The two poets had met at Spoleto in 1965: no words had been exchanged but Ginsberg had put his hand on Pound's shoulder. They had met a second time in Rapallo a month earlier and had enjoyed a silent lunch together by the water. In his Buddhist phase, Ginsberg chanted Buddhist mantras and played a harmonium and recordings of the Beatles and Bob Dylan. Pound remained silent until Ginsberg asked him certain specific questions about *The Cantos* as they refer to exact place locations in Venice that Ginsberg could not find. Ginsberg then acknowledged his poetic debt to Pound and Williams, but Pound claimed that his own poems did not make sense. *The Cantos*, he said, were "a mess. Stupidity and ignorance all the way through." Ginsberg continued to praise his work, realizing that Pound's remarks were those of a tired and defeated man and explaining how significant a model *The Cantos* were for the poets of his generation. Pound repeated his own sense of failure. Slowly but emphatically he added, "But the worst mistake I made was that stupid suburban prejudice of anti-Semitism. All along that spoiled everything." It was like a moment of ritual penitence, one priest confessing to another of broken taboos.

A year and a half later, Pound flew to New York with Olga Rudge. He attended the annual meeting of the Academy of American Poets, visited his publisher James Laughlin in Norfolk, Connecticut, and accompanied Laughlin to Hamilton College, where Laughlin was to receive an honorary doctorate. Wearing a cap and gown, Pound was received with a standing ovation. Returning to New York City, he stayed in Laughlin's apartment in the Village and, at the New York Public Library, examined the original manuscript of "The Waste Land," complete with his own emendations and marginal commentary. He dined with Mary Hemingway and visited Marianne Moore and Robert Lowell. He wanted to visit his birthplace in Hailey, Idaho, but somehow the distance seemed too great and the trip was never attempted.

Returning to Europe, he occasionally saw Dorothy during that portion of the year that he spent in Rapallo, but even with her he did not speak. "Too much anxiety loaded onto such a sensitivity" had been her explanation several years earlier. Always discreet and aloof, Dorothy at this time was living with her son in England. In Venice, as usual, there were the visitors—a reporter from *Life*, another from the New York *Times Magazine*. A German television crew did a film for which he would not speak, the film ending with a final focus on Pound's cracked and furrowed face. There was another filmed interview conducted by Pier Paolo Pasolini, a writer and filmmaker who had opposed Italian fascism. The questions were formidable and Pound remained coherent, simple, and dignified in his answers, but there was really nothing new for him to say. The visits continued: Norman Mailer, Anthony Burgess, Cyril Connolly, Hugh MacDiarmid, R. Buckminster Fuller, Isamu Noguchi, and Julian Beck and Judith Malina, who had performed Pound's *Women of Trachis* in New York. Through all these visits Pound maintained his mysterious silence.

Near the end of Pound's life there was one final flare of controversy when a nominating committee of the American Academy of Arts and Sciences moved to give Pound its Emerson-Thoreau Award. The committee, chaired by Leon Edel and including John Cheever, Lillian Hellman, James Laughlin, Yale professor Louis Martz, and Harvard professor Harry Levin, wished to present Pound with the award in recognition of the impact of his work on modern American writing. One member of the nominating committee, however, the historian Lewis Mumford, disagreed, and the recommendation was contested by Harvard sociologist Daniel Bell, who argued that the broadcasts during the war disqualified Pound for a humanistic award:

> We have to distinguish between those who explore hate and those who approve hate. In short, one may appreciate the painful work of a man who has, at great personal cost, spent a season in hell; but it does not follow that one honors a man who advocates a way of life that makes the world hellish.

Pound was no longer able to play chess with friends or to walk on the Zattere, the long promenade across from the Giudecca favored by Venetians where he had formerly gone for lunch. But there is a photograph of him at this time, standing remarkably erect in the street, a thin brittle stick in the wind with a shock of white hair. In the fall of 1972 he was eating less and less and spent more and more time in his bed. Two weeks before his eighty-seventh birthday he read at a small café for an intimate gathering of friends. The material included a sort of postscript to *The Cantos:*

> re USURY
> I was out of focus, taking a symptom for a
> cause.
> The cause is AVARICE.

It all seemed like an apologia, even the final fragment of *The Cantos:*

> I have tried to write Paradise
> Do not move
>   Let the wind speak that is paradise
> Let the Gods forgive what I have made
> Let those I love try to forgive what I have made.

On his eighty-seventh birthday, October 30, 1972, Olga Rudge invited a dozen friends and children and prepared a party with cake and champagne. Pound remained in his bed, feeling too weak to join the others, but the guests came up to his room individually to wish him well and sip a bit of champagne. During the night he began to feel unwell, and Olga had him moved to a hospital. At the hospital she sat talking with him until he dozed off. He died in his sleep, one blue eye open. He was taken to San Giorgio, across the lagoon from San Marco, where his coffin stood amid four giant candles. There was a brief ceremony organized by Olga and attended by a few friends and Pound's daughter and granddaughter. Dorothy was in England, too weak herself to travel, and Omar arrived a few hours after four gondoliers, dressed in black, rowed the body across the wide mouth of the lagoon to the burial island of San Michele.

In Venice everything, even death, is different because of the water. Venetians speak of the *fuochi fatui,* the phosphorescent gas fires over the graves caused by the spontaneous combustion of decomposing bodies, which can be buried only three feet deep because of the water. On November 1, among tall cypress trees, Pound was placed in a grave near those of Diaghilev and Stravinsky. It was the Venetian Day of the Dead, the time when the ferries to San Michele are free and crowded with Venetians going to decorate the graves of their beloved with flowers. It was also the time of the *acqua alta,* the high water that swamps parts of the city each fall, and the *scirocco,* the sultry wind from northern Africa, and the misty fog that bathes everything in a mysterious light. The lagoon was reaching out to reclaim the land. For Venice, it was a mythic moment to die.

NOTES

I have relied heavily in this book on the letters written by and to Ezra Pound which are collected at various universities: the Beinecke Library at Yale, the Humanities Research Center at the University of Texas in Austin, the Van Pelt Library at the University of Pennsylvania, the Lilly Library at the University of Indiana in Bloomington, the Manuscript Division of the Library of Congress, the Berg Collection at the New York Public Library, and smaller collections at Cornell University, the University of New York in Buffalo, and Syracuse University. I have also used the Pound files of the U.S. Army, the Justice Department, and St. Elizabeths Hospital. Useful to me at various points were the earlier biographies: John Edwards's 1952 Ph.D. dissertation at the University of California; Charles Norman's impressionistic but lively *Ezra Pound,* published by Macmillan in 1960; Noel Stock's *The Life of Ezra Pound,* published by Pantheon in 1970; C. David Heymann's *The Last Rower* (Viking, 1976), which emphasizes political aspects and the latter years of Pound's life; and E. Fuller Torrey's *The Roots of Treason,* published by McGraw-Hill in 1984, which takes a psychoanalytical view. A brief though perceptive book is Peter Ackroyd's *Ezra Pound and His World* (Thames & Hudson, 1980). A portion of mostly literary letters are assembled in *Selected Letters of Ezra Pound, 1907–41,* edited by D. D. Paige (New Directions, 1971). Donald Gallup's *Bibliography* (University Press of Virginia, 1983) is essential to establishing the chronology of publications and the development of Pound's career as a poet. Pound has inspired an entire library of learned and critical studies, monographs on stages of his life, and more journalistic accounts. The magazine *Paideuma* has been a center for Pound studies for the past fifteen years. Such sources, especially the thousands of letters—there are, for example, some twelve thousand at the Lilly Collection alone—have been invaluable aids. What follows is a listing of other sources that proved helpful for individual chapters.

AN AMERICAN YOUTH

The sources for Pound's childhood are Pound's own veiled autobiographical account, "Indiscretions," reprinted in *Pavannes and Divagations* (New Directions, 1958); the Carl Gatter Collection at the University of Pennsylvania of memorabilia and statements by some of the people who knew Pound as a child; Nancy Cox McCormack's recollections at the University of New York at Buffalo; Noel Stock's monograph *Ezra Pound's Pennsylvania* (University of Toledo Press, 1976); the Homer Pound scrapbook at the Beinecke Library at Yale; Jerome Kavka's "Psychiatric Case History," in St. Elizabeths Hospital File number 1381, dated January 24, 1956. Two genealogical studies are by James Wilhelm, "The Wadsworths, the Westons and the Farewell of 1911," *Paideuma* 12, no. 2 (1983), and "Ezra Pound's New York, 1887–1909," *Paideuma* 12, no. 1. Pound remembers his grandfather Thaddeus Pound and his father at the Mint in his "Economic History of the United States" and "A Visiting Card" in *Selected Prose* (New Directions, 1973). There is another description of the Mint in the interview Donald Hall did for *The Paris Review* (Summer-Fall, 1962). An important letter on his father's support and on the perpetual disagreement with his mother was written to Richard Harding Davis, dated only 1955 at Yale. H.D. describes Pound's parents in *End to Torment* (New Directions, 1979). A good view of Pound's poetic origins is derived from his "How I Began," which originally appeared in *T. P.'s Weekly* in London in 1913. Important sources for the college years are Charles Norman's interviews with his undergraduate classmates; William Carlos Williams's *Autobiography* (Random House, 1951) and *Selected Letters* (McDowell, Obolensky, 1957), especially a letter to his mother dated March 30, 1904; Frank Lorenz's pamphlet "Ezra Pound at Hamilton College," printed by the Hamilton College Library, and "A Troubador at Hamilton"; and John Brown's piece in the *Hamilton College Literary Magazine* 62, no. 2 (November 1932). Pound's relationship with Hilda Doolittle is treated in Barbara Guest's inspired *Herself Defined* (Doubleday, 1984); and also by Michael King in "Go, Little Book," *Paideuma* 10, no. 2 (1981). Sources for the Wabash incident are Pound's letters to Viola Baxter at Yale; his letters to Mary Moore at the Van Pelt; James E. Rader's "Ship in the Night," *Bachelor* (May 1958); James E. Rader, Viola Wildman, and Fred H. Rhodes's "A Pound of Flesh," *The Wabash Review* 6 (1959); and James J. Wilhelm's "On the Trial of the 'One' Crawfordsville Incident," *Paideuma* 13, no. 1 (1984). Wilhelm's useful articles have been collected in *The American Roots of Ezra Pound* (Garland, 1985).

LONDON

An interesting commentary on Venice is found in Mary de Rachewiltz's remarks in the *Collected Early Poems of Ezra Pound*, edited by Michael King and Louis Martz (New Directions, 1982), pp. 314–16. Pound described his Venetian sojourn in letters to Mary Moore, at the Van Pelt, and to Viola Baxter Jordan, at Yale. Faubion Bowers wrote an account of Katherine Ruth Heyman in *Paideuma* 2, no. 1 (1973). Manning's letters to Pound are at Yale, Pound's replies are at Syracuse, and a group of Manning's letters to Dorothy are at the Mitchell Library, New South Wales, Sydney, Australia. Two excellent essays on Pound's early London years are Donald Davie's "Ezra Among the Edwardians," *Paideuma* 5, no. 1 (1976); and William French and Timothy Materer's "Far Flung Vortices and Ezra's 'Hindoo' Yogi," *Paideuma* 11, no. 1 (1982). Important new sources for this period are the courtship letters of Pound and Dorothy Shakespear, edited by Omar Pound and Walton Litz (New Directions, 1984). Pound describes aspects of his 1910 trip to New York in "Patria Mia," in *Selected Prose* (New Directions, 1973). Some background information came from Jeanne Untermeyer's *Private Collection* (Knopf, 1965); and Justin Kaplan's *Lincoln Steffens* (Simon & Schuster, 1974), especially from Chapter 11, "Winds of Change."

Background information on London, circa 1910, came from various sources: Douglas Goldring's *Odd Man Out* (Chapman & Hall, 1935); Van Wyck Brooks's *Autobiography* (E. P. Dutton, 1965); W. S. Blunt's *Diaries* (Octagon, 1980); Patricia Hutchins's *Ezra Pound's Kensington* (Henry Regnery, 1965); George Dangerfield, *The Strange Death of Liberal England* (Capricorn Books, 1961); J. B. Priestley, *The Edwardians* (Harper & Row, 1970); and Leonard Woolf's *Beginning Again* (Harcourt, Brace & World, 1964). Material on *The New Age* group came from Philip Mairet's *A. R. Orage: A Memoir* (J. M. Dent & Sons, 1936); Paul Selver's *Orage and the New Age Circle* (George Allen & Unwin, 1959); and Beatrice Hasting's *The Old New Age* (Blue Moon Press, London, n.d.). There are two useful pieces on Allen Upward in *Paideuma,* one by Bryant Knox in Volume 3, no. 1 (1984), and a second by A. D. Moody in Volume 4, no. 1 (1975). A basic perspective on Georgian poetry is Edwin Marsh's *A Number of People* (Harper & Brothers, 1939).

The impact of China is best discussed by Hugh Kenner in *The Pound Era* (University of California Press, 1971); and some of my material was drawn from Van Wyck Brooks's *Fenollosa and His Circle* (E. P. Dutton, 1962). Some of the material on Imagism is from John Gould Fletcher's *Life Is My Song* (Farrar and Rinehart, 1937); Harriet Monroe's *A Poet's Life* (Macmillan, 1938); S. Forster Damon's *Amy Lowell* (Houghton, Mifflin, 1935); and Stanley K. Coffman's *Imagism* (University of Oklahoma Press, 1951). My perspective on Ford Madox Ford was influenced by Arthur Mizener's *The Saddest Story* (World, 1971); Richard M. Ludwig's edition of *The Letters of Ford Madox Ford* (Princeton University Press, 1965); Douglas Goldring's *South Lodge* (Constable & Co., 1943); and Violet Hunt's *I Have This to Say* (Boni & Liveright, 1926). A good history of *The Egoist* is Jane Lidderdale and Mary Nicholson's *Dear Miss Weaver* (Viking, 1970). Material on the London art scene was drawn from *The Letters of Roger Fry,* edited by Dennis Smith (Chatto & Windus, 1972); C. R. W. Nevinson's *Paint and Prejudice* (Harcourt, Brace and Co., 1938); and Richard Cork's *Abstract Art in the First Machine Age* (Gordon Fraser, 1976), a very detailed two-volume account of Vorticist origins and directions. Another valuable account of Vorticism is Timothy Materer's *Vortex: Pound, Eliot and Lewis* (Cornell University Press, 1974). Material on Wyndham Lewis comes from Hugh Kenner's monograph, *Wyndham Lewis* (New Directions, 1954); *The Letters of Wyndham Lewis,* edited by W. K. Rose (New Directions, 1965); Jeffrey Meyers's biography, *The Enemy* (Routledge & Kegan Paul, 1980). The best book on John Quinn is B. L. Reid's *The Man from New York* (Oxford University Press, 1968). Other useful sources were Richard Ellman's *James Joyce* (Oxford University Press, 1969); Peter Ackroyd's *T. S. Eliot* (Simon & Schuster, 1984); Ronald Bush, *The Genesis of EP's Cantos* (Princeton University Press, 1976); John Harrison's *The Reactionaries* (Schocken, 1967); Margaret Anderson's *My Thirty Years' War* (Horizon Press, 1969); John Williams's *The Home Fronts* (Constable, 1972); and Pound's letters to Natalie Barney, edited by Richard Sieburth, *Paideuma* 5, no. 2 (1976).

PARIS

Background information was drawn from a number of sources: Hugh Ford's *Published in Paris: American and British Writers, Printers and Publishers in Paris, 1920–39* (Macmillan, 1975); *The Left Bank Revisited: Selections from the Paris Tribune, 1917–34,* edited by Hugh Ford (Pennsylvania State University Press, 1972); William Wiser's *The Crazy Years: Paris in the Twenties* (Atheneum, 1983); and Calvin Tompkins, *Living Well Is the Best Revenge* (Avon, 1971). Material on the art scene came from John Alexander's essay "Parenthetical Paris," in *Pound's Artists: Ezra Pound and the Visual Arts* (Tate Gallery, 1985); *The Dada Painters and Poets,* edited by Robert Motherwell (Willenborn, Schultz, 1951); and Andrew Clearfield's essay, "Pound, Paris and Dada," *Paideuma* 7, no. 1 (1978). Material on Jean Cocteau came from *Jean Cocteau and the French Scene* (Abbeville Press, 1983). An account of the Morand affair is found in Breon Mitchell's introduction to *Fancy Goods and*

Open All Night: Stories by Paul Morand (New Directions, 1984). Two sources for material on Antheil were "Virgil Thomson on George Antheil and Ezra Pound: A Conversation," *Paideuma* 12, no. 2 (1983); and William Hoffa's article, "Ezra Pound and George Antheil," in *American Literature,* March 1972. A number of important first-person accounts are found in Ford Madox Ford's *Thus To Revisit* (E. P. Dutton, 1921); and *It Was the Nightingale* (J. P. Lippincott, 1933); Gertrude Stein's *The Autobiography of Alice B. Toklas* (Harcourt, Brace, 1933); Ernest Hemingway's *A Moveable Feast* (Scribners, 1964) and *Selected Letters,* edited by Carlos Baker (Scribners, 1983); *Pound/ Joyce: The Letters of Ezra Pound to James Joyce,* edited by Forrest Read (New Directions, 1970); Robert McAlmon's *Being Geniuses Together* (Doubleday, 1968); William Carlos Williams's *Autobiography* (New Directions, 1967); William Carlos Williams, *Selected Letters,* edited by John C. Thirlwall (McDowell, Obolensky, 1957); *The Paris Review* interview of E. E. Cummings, vol. 39 (Fall 1966); and *Selected Letters of E. E. Cummings,* edited by Frederick W. Dupee and George Stack (Harcourt, Brace and World, 1969). Glenway Wescott's memory of Pound is in his foreword to Hugh Ford's *Four Lives in Paris* (North Point, 1987).

ITALY

Elizabeth Delehanty's account of Pound in Rapallo appeared in *The New Yorker* in 1940. Several useful articles were Timothy Materer's piece "Doppelgänger: Ezra Pound in His Letters," *Paideuma* 11, no. 2 (1982); Daniel Pearlman's "Fighting the World: The Letters of Ezra Pound to Senator William Borah," *Paideuma* 12, no. 2 (1983); Wendy Stallard Flory's "The Pound Problem," in the *Ezra Pound, William Carlos Williams Conference Papers,* edited by Daniel Hoffman (University of Pennsylvania Press, 1984); and Barry Alpert's "Ezra Pound, John Price and the Exile," *Paideuma* 2, no. 3 (1973). An essential account is Mary de Rachewiltz's *Discretions: Ezra Pound, Father and Teacher* (New Directions, 1971). A recollection of Pound's 1939 trip to America is found in Mary Barnard's *Assault on Mount Helicon* (University of California Press, 1984). Nancy McCormack's recollections are in an unpublished manuscript and are reproduced with the permission of The Poetry/Rare Books Collection, Universities Libraries, State University of New York at Buffalo. Information on Pound during the war is found in the FBI files; an abbreviated version is available in the Van Pelt Library. See also Nichola Zapponi's "Ezra Pound e il fascismo," *Storea Contemporanea* 4, no. 3 (1964); Robert Corrigan's "Ezra Pound and the Italian Ministry of Culture," *Journal of Popular Culture* 5, no. 4 (1971); Tim Redman's "The Repatriation of Pound, 1939–42," *Paideuma*

9, no. 3 (1980); Eleanor and Reynolds Packard's *Balcony Empire* (Oxford University Press, 1942); and Daniel Pearlman's "America's Wandering Jew," *Paideuma* 9, no. 3 (1980). Roman Bilenchi's 1941 account of meeting Pound was translated by David Anderson and appeared in *Paideuma* 8, no. 3 (1979). The radio broadcasts are collected in Leonard Doob's *Ezra Pound Speaking* (Greenwood Press, 1978). An intriguing account of wartime Italy is Iris Origo's *War in Val D'Orica* (Godine, 1984). Information on the Disciplinary Training Center at Pisa comes from Jack La Zebrick's "The Case of Ezra Pound," in the *New Republic,* 1 April 1957; Robert L. Allen's "The Cage," *Esquire* 49 (1955); Michael King's "Ezra Pound at Pisa: An Interview with John Steele," *Texas Quarterly* 4 (1961); "Ez at the D. T. C.: A Correspondence Between Carroll Terrell and John Steele," *Paideuma* 12, no. 2 (1983); and Ben D. Kimpel and T. C. Duncan Eaves, "More on Pound's Prison Experience," *American Literature* 53, no. 3 (1981).

There are also some useful books of criticism: M. L. Rosenthal's *A Primer of Ezra Pound* (Grosset & Dunlap, 1966) is a good beginning, and the standard account is Hugh Kenner's *The Poetry of Ezra Pound* (New Directions, 1974). There are also a number of good theoretical forays into Pound's work, among them Herbert Schneidau's *The Image and the Real* (Louisiana State University Press, 1968); Donald Davie's *Ezra Pound: Poet As Sculptor* (Routledge & Kegan Paul, 1965); Daniel Pearlman's *The Barb of Time* (Oxford University Press, New York, 1969); and, more recently, Michael André Bernstein's *The Tale of the Tribe* (Princeton University Press, 1980). Readers of *The Cantos* may want to avail themselves of J. H. Edwards and W. W. Vasse's *Annotated Index to the Cantos of Ezra Pound* (University of California Press, 1971).

WASHINGTON

A basic source for this period is the Pound dossier at St. Elizabeths, two volumes containing his daily hospital record, psychiatric evaluations, and other relevant letters and documents. There are also twelve thousand items at the Lilly Library in Bloomington, Indiana, mostly letters written to Pound while he was at St. Elizabeths. The essential accounts are Julien Cornell's *The Trial of Ezra Pound* (John Day, 1966); *Charles Olson and Ezra Pound: An Encounter at St. Elizabeths,* edited by Catherine Seelye (Grossman, 1975); Harry M. Meacham's *The Caged Panther* (Twayne, 1967); Michael Reck's *Ezra Pound: A Close-Up* (McGraw-Hill, 1967); Charles Norman's *The Case of Ezra Pound* (Bodley Press, 1948); and Eustace Mullins's *This Difficult Individual* (Fleet Publications, 1961). E. Fuller Torrey's *The Roots of Treason* (McGraw-Hill, 1984) was especially useful in this section. William Carlos Williams's Chapter 51 in his *Autobiography* (New Directions, 1967) is about

Pound at St. Elizabeths. Archibald MacLeish's *Letters* are edited by R. W. Winnick (Houghton Mifflin, 1983) and MacLeish also writes about Pound in *Riders in the Earth* (Houghton Mifflin, 1978). A crucial letter is MacLeish's to Milton Eisenhower, which is at the Library of Congress. There are a number of useful articles: William French's "For 'Gentle Graceful Dorothy' A Tardy Obit, *Paideuma* 12, no. 1 (1983); Richard A. Cassell, "A Visit with Ezra Pound," *Paideuma* 8, no. 1 (1979); David Rattray, "Weekend with Ezra Pound," *The Nation,* 16 November 1957; Sheri Martinelli, "Duties of a Lady Female," *The Floating Bear* 32 (1963); Marcella Spann Booth, "Through the Smoke Hole: Ezra Pound's Last Year at St. Elizabeths," *Paideuma* 3, no. 1 (1974); and "Ecrology: The Class of '57," *Paideuma* 13, no. 1 (1984). Robert S. Bird's series on John Kasper appeared in the New York *Herald Tribune* in February of 1957; and Robert Hillyer's attack on Pound was in *The Saturday Review of Literature,* 11 and 18 June 1949. An important essay is Alfred Kazin's "The Writer As Political Crazy," *Playboy,* June 1973.

LAST YEARS

A key source is Donald Hall's *Remembering Poets: Reminiscences and Opinions* (Harper Colphon, 1979). A useful little book is *Ezra Pound: The Voice of Silence* (Permanent Press, 1983), which originally was a piece by Alan Levy in the New York *Times Magazine,* 9 September 1972. Grazia Levi's interview with Pound was translated by Natalie Harris for *Paideuma* 8, no. 2 (1979). Michael Reck recorded "A Conversation Between Ezra Pound and Allen Ginsberg," *The Evergreen Review* (June 1968). Some other useful accounts are Eveline Bates Doob, "Some Notes on Ezra Pound," *Paideuma* 10, no. 1 (1981); Cyril Connolly, "My Friend, Ezra Pound," *The Times* of London, 5 November 1972; James J. Kilpatrick's "A Conversation with Ezra Pound," *National Review,* 24 May 1958; Desmond O'Grady, "Ezra Pound: A Personal Memoir," *Agenda* 17 (1966); Richard Stern, "A Memory or Two of Mr. Pound," *Paideuma* 1, no. 1 (1972); and S. Singh's recollections of Pound in *Paideuma* 3, no. 2 (1974).

INDEX